Luton Sixth Form College
Library

• 39324

909.82

WITHDRAWN

The Squandered Peace

D0566483

By the same author

Capitalism
Social Democracy
Scenes from Institutional Life
The Political Economy of Education
The History of British Steel

The Squandered Peace

The World: 1945–1975

John Vaizey

HODDER AND STOUGHTON
LONDON SYDNEY AUCKLAND TORONTO

00017647

Luton Sixth Form College
Library

39324

British Library Cataloguing in Publication Data

Vaizey, John
  The squandered peace
  1. History, Modern – 1945–
  I. Title
  909.82'4   D840

  ISBN 0 340 33127 5
  ISBN 0 340 24560 3 Pbk

Copyright © 1983 by John Vaizey. First printed 1983. All rights reserved. No part of this publication may be reproduced or transmitted in any form or by any means, electronic or mechanical, including photocopy, recording, or any information storage and retrieval system, without permission in writing from the publisher. Printed in Great Britain for Hodder and Stoughton Limited, Mill Road, Dunton Green, Sevenoaks, Kent by St Edmundsbury Press, Bury St Edmunds, Suffolk. Photoset by Rowland Phototypesetting Limited, Bury St Edmunds, Suffolk. Hodder and Stoughton Editorial Office: 47 Bedford Square, London WC1B 3DP.

Take them, Love, the book and
me together

Acknowledgments

I should like to thank the Librarians of the House of Lords and Brunel University for much help. I am in the debt of Ion Trewin of Hodder and Stoughton, and Venetia Pollock, for superb editing. I am grateful to Mrs Annemarie Maggs for devoted work. I warmly praise St Thomas' Hospital, the Royal Army Medical Corps and the Army Physical Education Corps.

Contents

Luton Sixth Form College
Library

Introduction

Each day that passes makes a nuclear war more certain, even though everyone knows that it is impossible to 'win'. Each Polaris submarine, the main nuclear attacking forces of Britain and the United States for a decade, carries more explosive power than all the bombs dropped and shells fired in the Second World War. Yet these weapons, obsolete at the time of writing (1982), are now being replaced by more powerful weapons, each side training them on the other's main cities and military bases. One day war will begin. That will be the end of our civilisation. The only alternative seems to be a binding agreement between America and Soviet Russia never to use nuclear force against each other nor to allow such weapons to be used anywhere by anybody else.

Such an agreement, it will be argued, is unlikely. Yet in 1945 agreement *was* reached at Yalta, and the main outlines of that pact have lasted. Lasting agreement is therefore not impossible, because the impossible *has* happened. We have had nearly forty years of relative peace.

But we have not used those years wisely. We have squandered them away. Instead of creating an efficient, lasting, effective peace-keeping force, organising an intelligent system of disarmament or using our new-found technology and prosperity rationally and positively for the good of all, we have spent the intervening years nervously in fear of war. Freedom and liberty have not flourished, tyranny in many guises has grown and blossomed unimpeded.

How and why has this been allowed to happen?

At the end of the Second World War an atavistic and evil tyranny, Nazism, was defeated by the three main powers, two of whom, however imperfectly, represented good liberal values: objectivity, kindness, rationality. These powers have since failed to put forward their ideas with conviction or with success: they have failed to lead. The third power, Soviet Russia, has not only entrenched its position, but has extended its rule to almost the whole of the Balkans and Eastern Europe, whilst its own special brand of Marxism has become one of the most widely received orthodoxies. Ramifications of Marxism flourish further afield in Africa and the Far East. To some the tyranny of Communism is at least as pernicious as Hitler's Nazism. Information filtering through from Soviet spheres of influence is filled with details about pogroms, purges and gulags; recent Soviet behaviour in Czecho-slovakia, Hungary and Poland has displayed a signal lack of enthusiasm for human rights; people in once-prosperous farming areas are starving under Communist agricultural methods, yet as knowledge of these atrocities, inefficiencies and stupidities in-creases, the number of people espousing Marxism rises. How has it come about that as the capitalist world becomes richer and altogether more prosperous and successful, its moral power has seemed to wane, whilst Communism, despite open knowledge of its drawbacks, has gained increasing numbers of followers?

That is one strand I would like to look at in this book. Another is the problem posed by technological advance in the last three decades. Modern science has brought unprecedented prosperity on a scale unparalleled to many hundreds of millions of people throughout the world. Technology has linked diverse peoples together through the use of common artefacts, such as television, transistors, trucks and aircraft, binding all with common sets of ideas, aims and suppositions. These new inventions have lessened the differences between countries, groups and tribes and have brought into prominence many smaller nations so that they now play a much greater part in world affairs. But despite the enor-mous, irrevocable, fundamental and unique changes brought about by science, old patterns of behaviour still persist and con-tinue to thrust themselves forward. Nationalism is still immensely powerful; religion is still a surging strength which has to be reckoned with. Old ideologies of various kinds are still deeply entrenched; terrorists and extremists can still wield startlingly disruptive force.

I am also interested in disentangling a third thread from the untidy knots and twists of the post-war period: that concerned with the drift towards authoritarianism shown by those countries which started off their lives with liberal constitutions, bequeathed to them by those who liberated them from paternalism, colonialism and violence, but which have slowly drifted into one-party rule. What is it that has led such diverse countries as Algeria, Cuba, Pakistan and Indonesia, to name but a few, to prefer benevolent or cruel despotism rather than to seize the opportunities for liberal democracy?

I was fifteen years old when the war ended, so I have lived through the peace. My children have grown up in it. When I came to read about it I found much that I vaguely remembered springing into sharp focus. It is my hope that I have succeeded in communi-cating the excitement of my rediscovery of the recent past.

I wanted to write a history of the public events of my own

lifetime but it was not merely the indulgence of a personal concern. Young people not only have no memory of recent history, but they have little idea of the sequence of events which has led to the present condition of the world. The people whom I recall more vividly than almost any present-day leaders, Truman, Dulles, Khruschev, Macmillan, even de Gaulle, are rarely known to them. This ignorance seems to me to be regrettable because it has not only been a fascinating period to have lived through but also – more deeply – because young people are judging present events on the wrong premises, often indeed on the basis of sheer propaganda. A slur may be referred to as McCarthyism, for instance, but who remembers what Senator McCarthy actually did? How many know that America first backed Ho Chi-minh in Vietnam at the end of the war and then switched allegiance? That Stalin originally helped Chiang Kai-shek and ignored Mao Tse-tung? What of those moments when East–West tension could have been eased but for the chauvinism of the West; those times when nuclear war seemed so near? Yet it is the turns and twists of initial actions which make countries end up in unusual alliances. Every actor in the drama of the present starts off with a clean sheet in the eyes of the young, but many have dubious records that are relevant to their current actions, many whose past behaviour makes the old appear cynical or sceptical about their potential.

As I read and read books and then archives, I realised that my own picture of the world since 1945 was inevitably a partial one, and my memory extremely defective. Lack of information, lack of sustained interest, persistent myths and many other sources of error had crept into my view of the world so that inevitably, even in themes where I might be counted a professional, my views required to be modified or profoundly changed. In the greater part of this book, I am but an intelligent layman.

Nobody is an expert over this large terrain. There are libraries of books, there are warehouses of archives, there are miles of shelved records; nobody can know anything but a tiny part of the whole. Nevertheless I have found it invaluable experience to write a panoramic study on so large a scale. The subject is utterly fascinating and it has been an absorbing task, to try to put it into coherent order.

This is a book to be read. For that reason I have decided not to load it with footnotes. The argument is of interest to scholars, but the critical apparatus is redundant for them. On so big a canvas, there are bound to be errors, and I accept full responsibility for those that remain. I must stress that it is the argument that matters since the book is an attempt to understand what has happened. I have tried to use my critical intelligence on behalf of all of us, to try to answer a very big question – was it inevitable that the peace was squandered? How did it happen?

I would like to share my knowledge of past events with the rising generation, to explain why and how we behaved the way we did when we were young; to find out if we could have avoided frittering away the peace; if we can learn anything useful.

The organisation of this book is simple. There are five main parts; the first covers Yalta to the Korean War, that is 1945 to 1950, the second deals with important events in the 1950s. Part three discusses technological progress and the rise of the Third World and part four looks at mounting instability during the 1960s. Part five recounts increasing diversity in the 1970s. Each section is not an exact decade since there is considerable overlap. Rather more than thirty main episodes have been taken to illuminate the way in which the tensions and problems of the world have been related to one another. They vary from descriptions of broad and general episodes such as the emergence of China, to specific cases, such as the Vietnam War. Inevitably this means going back and forth in time; it is for instance impossible to tell the story of de Gaulle and the Fifth Republic without describing the Algerian War, and that means a jump back in time at the beginning of the chapter and a jump forward at the end of it. Many of the links are indirect. Nevertheless the pattern is clear. There has been a struggle between a group of countries that tend to support liberal ideas, and the Marxist powers. In the process former colonial powers have yielded to a nationalism that has not always been liberal and Marxist thought has triumphed among intellectuals in a way completely unrelated to known conditions in Marxist countries. Divisions in the liberal camp have often led to the rise of anti-liberalism: for example the shortsighted desire of the United States to evict Europeans from the Middle East and the willingness of Europeans to see Americans defeated in Vietnam. The United Nations' ideals and internationalism have been swamped by the rise of the Third World and the growth of nationalism. It is the complexity of the struggle, the shifting alliances and differences in purpose which have led to the squandering of the possibilities of peace.

PART ONE

The Road from Yalta

The 1940s

Chapter 1

The world in 1945: Yalta

In February 1945 three elderly gentlemen sat in chairs to be photographed. Franklin Delano Roosevelt, President of the United States, two months short of death; Winston Churchill, Prime Minister of the United Kingdom, aged seventy and shortly to face electoral defeat; Joseph Stalin, tyrant, and the only man to continue in office in the immediate post-war years. The place was Yalta, in the Crimea, where they met to plan the last stages of the war, especially in the Far East, but above all to divide the spoils of the victory over Germany. The meeting was at first kept secret. Then in a carefully orchestrated press campaign a few days later, its significance was sold to the people of the allied and neutral countries as a plan to bring the world war to an end. Germany was to be divided into occupied zones after its unconditional surrender. And the consequent peace would be permanent, guaranteed by the three united allies.

Yalta was a necessary step in settling the fate of Germany. The Red Army was about to capture Berlin and the allies had reached the Rhine; decisions on the future of liberated Europe and occupied Germany could no longer be delayed. When the 'Big Three' had last met at the Casablanca conference in 1943, it had been agreed to accept from Germany nothing less than unconditional surrender. It had seemed obvious that the permanent division of Germany – its dismemberment – would prove to be the best guarantee of future peace.

From December 1941 to December 1943 Churchill, Roosevelt and Stalin, to their own initial surprise, had been forced into a close alliance, and now they were having to decide (as it seemed to them) the fate of the world. All three were old, tired and busy ruling their countries as well as waging war; thus the time and energy at their disposal for planning the victory were limited. Yalta was hastily summoned and ill prepared. The delegations were meant to be small, less than one hundred people in all, but in the end over one thousand people attended. And the issues could not be settled immediately and irrevocably, because the apparent unity brought about by the war could not be maintained once the defeat of Hitler, the sole object on which they were apparently agreed, was achieved. Each wanted something different from the victory.

It was after all an historical accident that the United Kingdom, the United States and the USSR were allies. Britain had been the first belligerent. Goaded beyond endurance by Hitler's breach of the Munich Agreement of 1938, it had unwisely and impotently guaranteed the frontiers of Poland. Consequently, when Hitler invaded Poland on 1 September 1939, it had declared war on Germany, joined by its fellow Commonwealth members (except Ireland) and by France. Stalin, meanwhile, in August 1939, had signed a non-aggression pact with Hitler. When Churchill was Hitler's bitterest opponent Stalin was Nazi Germany's close ally. Then in 1940, by a series of lightning moves, Germany occupied Denmark and Norway in April, Belgium and Holland in May, France in June. Italy then joined the war on Hitler's side and subsequently Yugoslavia and Greece also fell to Germany. Britain was left alone.

Winston Churchill had been only First Lord of the Admiralty when war broke out but he had rapidly become the acknowledged natural leader of the country and so, after the German invasion of the Low Countries, he had been asked to form a Coalition government. It is often forgotten that he was not uniformly popular during the war even with his own Conservative party and that he was frequently criticised on his conduct of the war in Parliament. His reputation was higher abroad than at home.

Churchill had both been a minister and fought in the First World War and these experiences had led him to realise that it would again be necessary to inveigle the United States into the Second World War if the German–Japanese–Italian axis was to be defeated. The accident of Hitler's support of the Japanese, disastrous though its initial military consequences were, was from Churchill's point of view fortunate, for it eventually brought the United States into the war. Thereafter Churchill's main concern was to preserve, at almost any cost, the Anglo–American alliance, although, perhaps because of his American mother, he was overconscious of the importance of the English-speaking world and exaggerated the value that Roosevelt and his advisers placed upon the 'special relationship'.

Despite his loyalty to the American alliance, however, Churchill had a realistic sense of the possible. He foresaw deep economic and financial problems for Britain after the war, since so much of its reserves and overseas assets had been spent before the end of 1941. He knew that Britain could not withstand the might of any further Russian advance alone so that it was vital that the American army be kept in Europe as long as possible. He feared that the United

States might withdraw their forces all too soon, and was thus prepared to go to almost any lengths to support Roosevelt, to keep the Americans in Europe and to intensify their special relationship, and it was in this context that he agreed to the division of the world at Yalta.

Above all, Churchill remained convinced that 'Uncle Joe' Stalin was still territorially ambitious and would soon resume the world revolutionary path first trodden by Lenin in 1917. To this end Churchill was convinced that a revival of France as a great power was not only inevitable but desirable, if Western Europe was to be preserved from Communist domination. Britain must have an ally on the continent. He also saw that it would eventually be necessary to revive Germany, perhaps without Prussia, in order further to help the balance of power in Europe and as a major trading partner in the future economic order. He was therefore against excessive demands for reparations from Germany as he remembered the economic consequences of the peace of 1918 and the slump that followed.

'. . . I think the end of this war may well prove to be more disappointing than the last,' Churchill cabled to Roosevelt on 8 January 1945, and the course of the Yalta conference confirmed his view. He feared that he might be about to exchange Stalin's domination for Hitler's – a bitter outcome of so terrible a conflict.

Stalin, at Yalta, was the fittest man present; at sixty-six years old, he had been dictator of Russia for sixteen years. Astonished by the German invasion of Russia and aware of how near the defeat had been, his concern for Russia's security and the safety of his regime was obsessional. The Soviet Union had lost over twenty million dead in the war, far more than the other allies combined, but nevertheless she had rallied her retreating and demoralised armed forces and organised a sweeping victory. The magnitude of the Russian military effort and its success remains astonishing even though achieved at enormous cost. By 1944 the Russian army was engaging three quarters of Germany's army in frequent violent battles; indeed without the Russian front it is unlikely that Germany would have been defeated, despite Western air superiority which, by 1944, became supremacy. Admittedly, there was also a war in the Pacific and the Far East, where the American effort was enormous, but even so the Russian army was by far the most effective at waging war in Europe. As a result Stalin had gained a vast, possibly undeserved reputation as a strategist and a war hero and the Soviet Army was considered the overall victor of the war in Europe. To seek to oppose the USSR, to halt its advance, even to cause its troops to withdraw from territory it already occupied, would have entailed a military posture inconceivable either to the British or the Americans.

For the past eleven years Stalin had been a tyrant on a scale equalled only by Hitler and had been personally responsible for sending millions to their deaths and further hundreds of thousands into labour camps in Siberia and the gulag archipelago. An extra-ordinarily complex man, he appeared outwardly jovial, but his own personal style was dark and secretive and his mind turned towards obscurantism. His loathing of foreigners and his anti-Semitism combined with his fanaticism to make him seem almost paranoid.

Stalin feared the resurrection of a united Germany. He wanted the foe to be rent asunder and for them to pay full reparations. He argued consistently and steadily for the division of the world into spheres of influence. For this purpose he was prepared to divide Germany into three zones, and to claim for Russia the whole of the Balkans except Greece; his earlier concessions on Yugoslavia and Hungary were forgotten as the USSR actually came to sweep through them before British or American troops could arrive. But usually where a boundary was drawn Stalin respected it.

The idea of spheres of influence was perhaps the most significant of the implicit arrangements at Yalta because it formed the basis of the post-1945 settlement *de facto*, rather than *de jure*. At Yalta it was assumed that the war would end with a peace treaty, freely and openly negotiated at leisure by all the parties. But though such treaties were eventually concluded with some belligerents, notably Italy and Japan, no general peace settlement ever took place. In particular, there was no German peace treaty. The special settlement of Yalta formed the basis of the peace; and since it was both hasty and *ad hoc* it was open to misunderstanding.

The magnitude of the Red Army's victory over Hitler brought, first, deep sympathy and support in the West – not least in occupied Europe – and, secondly, a genuine possibility that the Russian army might advance far further west than it did. The plan fixed at Teheran had been for the British and the Americans to occupy France, the Low Countries and Italy, and for Germany to be divided roughly at the river Elbe. The British had already landed in Greece and Churchill intended to break out of Italy into the Balkans, above all into Yugoslavia. But while the Yalta conference was still convened, Stalin halted the Russian advance to Berlin and switched the Soviet effort into the Balkans which were rapidly occupied by Soviet troops, including neutral Bulgaria. Far from allaying Churchill's fears of Soviet expansion in Germany, it encouraged him to think that his October 1944 meeting with Stalin in Moscow, where Yugoslavia and Hungary had been put fifty:fifty in the British and Russian spheres of influence, had in fact led to a position where both had fallen irrevocably into Russian hands, and that the rest of Europe might well follow. In return for the Eastern part of Europe remaining in the Soviet sphere of influence, Stalin was prepared to leave the Western half alone. This division of the world between Communism and the Western powers was to bedevil the whole period from 1945 onwards, squandering the peace so dearly bought.

Franklin Delano Roosevelt had been an opponent of the Nazis in principle and, to a far lesser extent, in practice before America was forced into the war. Once in, he vied with Stalin in the totality of his war aims, being an exponent not only of unconditional surrender, but of the dismemberment of Germany into several independent states, as it had been before 1870, and its de-industrialisation, as proposed by Henry Morgenthau, his Secretary of the Treasury, at the second Quebec conference in September 1944. (Morgenthau was advised by Harry Dexter White, a supposed Soviet agent.) The dismemberment of Germany would, in Roosevelt's opinion, create circumstances in Europe that would remove the preconditions of a further war.

His almost unprecedented authority, deriving both from his personality and his political skills, and from the fact that he was the only President to be elected for four successive terms, meant that he and his faithful staff dominated United States policy to an extent unseen since Lincoln.

Roosevelt, superficially a bluff, hearty, outgoing man, at heart perhaps, cold, devious even, possessed of superb political acumen and magnificent oratorical abilities, distrusted the British to a considerable degree, although he never let Churchill suspect this.

American distrust of Churchill had several sources, not least Roosevelt's deep dislike of the British Empire in particular and imperialism in general – he was not going to allow American soldiers to die to save empires. As Eden wrote, 'Roosevelt did not confine his dislike of colonialism to the British Empire alone, for it was a principle with him, not the less cherished for its possible advantages.' There was a suspicion in Churchill's mind – and even more in Eden's and in de Gaulle's – that Roosevelt's anti-colonialism was designed to open up new fields for American business to conquer. Of this suspicion no confirmation is to be found explicitly in American papers except that the future policy of Germany should conform 'to the general economic foreign policy of the United States'. Rather, Americans seemed concerned that they might be asked to pick up the bill at the end of the war for the restoration of a world order which, of its very nature, had caused the war in the first place and might start another.

In his dislike of Communism, and in particular his view that Germany might be entirely occupied by the Soviet Union, Roosevelt did not differ from Churchill. But he held, nevertheless, that the reconstruction of the world economic order on sounder lines than those which had brought about the great depression would lead to a recrudescence of a more moderate, more radical world. The 'economic foreign policy of the United States' was to be precisely this. And, to bolster this view, there was the concept of a new world political order.

Roosevelt had been a junior member of Woodrow Wilson's administration, now he saw himself in a position to achieve successfully the peaceful settlement that Wilson had negotiated at Versailles in 1919, but which had been rejected subsequently by the United States Senate. The conception of the United Nations was to replace the League of Nations. Based upon the victorious allies, it was to owe allegiance to certain international principles which would radically alter the world order. These four freedoms – later embodied as the Atlantic Charter – freedom of speech and expression, freedom of every person to worship in his own way, freedom from want, and freedom from fear – were like the basic freedoms of the United States Constitution. Churchill regarded these as banal platitudes. The only copies of the Atlantic Charter had been both signed by President Roosevelt alone; this was no accident or Freudian slip; it was a revelation of the American belief that there were fundamental human rights that would underlie any stable political order. It was also Roosevelt's conviction that by guaranteeing the peace, through an agreement to invoke force against aggressors, the fears and threats of Russia would be appeased.

In his foreign policy during the war, Roosevelt came to have far too direct and simple a trust in Russian good intentions, as well as a bitter detestation of British and French imperialism. His views on France were coloured by a contempt for its failure to defend itself in 1940 and an unwillingness to trust de Gaulle, whom he disliked intensely. There is no doubt that Roosevelt's influence at Yalta was to hand over Eastern Europe to Communism, by default.

Subsequently it was alleged that the sick Roosevelt had been used by Soviet agents. Undoubtedly Soviet espionage had penetrated the Western governments. Stalin knew about the atom bomb that was shortly to be tested, though he affected otherwise when he was subsequently told at Potsdam. Yet it would be naïve to assume that Anglo–American concessions were simply due to

Marxist sympathies in high places in the State Department and the Foreign Office, though such sympathies – extending even to treason – were prevalent. It was rather that American propaganda about the heroic Russian people had convinced the propagandists themselves that Stalin was a true ally who had changed his spots. This was a profound misconception. Stalin remained deeply paranoid, deeply foreign to American ideas, and deeply Communist.

Each power knew what he wanted but they were not of one mind and never had been. Churchill was forced to defer to, and to some extent admired, Roosevelt, who was uneasy with this admiration; Stalin trusted nobody; Roosevelt probably trusted Stalin more than Churchill. The Soviet Union wanted reparations and did not want France involved, two points which Churchill did not agree with, for a start. Nonetheless decisions were made and Yalta was the key to much that was to happen in the next few decades.

Exactly how Germany was to be overthrown was also discussed at Yalta. The Russians wanted the West to attack in order to divert German divisions from the Eastern front. The Western allies pointed to their air superiority, and in turn asked for Russian efforts to divert German troops from the Rhine. These matters were not settled by military considerations of what would lead to the quickest victory with least allied casualties. The liaison between West and East took place through Moscow, not between operating units. The ultimate positions of troops after victory therefore would be determined not so much by military tactics, the desire for a speedy victory or even good will between allies, as by political decisions taken at Yalta. The one exception was the Balkans where the Soviet Army's sweep forward, stopping only at the Greek border, led to Soviet domination of an area which was to have been divided.

The basic dissension at Yalta was over Germany. There was a measure of agreement on unconditional surrender, total disarmament, and punishment, but it was not complete. In retrospect, failure to question each of these points in depth was a major error. Who was to surrender, and was the surrendering government to be the future German government, *de facto*, as had been the case in Italy? How was dismemberment to be carried out? Roosevelt's idea was to divide Germany into three zones of occupation and subsequently into a number of separate states, whereas Stalin began with the states, on which the zones would be based. (Here were the seeds of the subsequent division of Germany into two republics.) The agreement was for a southern state, centred on Vienna, the elimination of Prussia, and the internationalisation of the Ruhr and the Saar. In the end, the full document of the conference included a protocol which had 'dismemberment' as part of the terms of surrender. The proposal in the main document was for three zones to be co-ordinated by a Control Commission which would supervise the extirpation of German militarism, the punishment of Nazi party members, the eradication of Nazi institutions, and the payment of reparations.

The USSR, devastated as it was, argued most strongly for reparations. All three men were agreed on the need to dismantle Germany's heavy industry in order to eliminate German war-making potential. Stalin then wanted the dismantled plant sent back to Russia, and to make Germany's remaining industries produce goods for the USSR.

Stalin, arguing from a Marxist standpoint, saw that transfers of real productive assets could be of genuine value to the Soviet Union; Churchill, arguing from the precedent of the reparation clauses of 1919 and from some understanding of neo-classical international trade theory, saw that the transfer of liquid assets would entail a counterbalancing monetary payment from the Western banking system to the Germans, if a round of competitive devaluations and inflations was not to be started again. Eventually, as in the case of dismemberment, the Western powers agreed to reparations, not intending (particularly in the case of the United States) to claim reparations for themselves, but to satisfy the Russians. The failure to fulfil the letter of the bargain and the disruption caused to Germany by the Russian attempts to implement the reparations agreement were to be a potent source of trouble.

Further problems were created by the need to accommodate France and Poland; two ancient allies, both knocked out of the war, and each falling within a different zone of influence.

Churchill had welcomed General de Gaulle to London and gave limited recognition to his government as the legitimate successor to the Third Republic. He had resisted Roosevelt's attempts to exclude de Gaulle from North Africa in 1943. After Anglo–American differences, and with lack of enthusiasm, de Gaulle was now installed in Paris at the head of a provisional government of France, still distrusted and disliked by the Americans who continued to see Vichy as the legitimate heir to the Third Republic. The British wished to give the French an occupation zone in Germany and to make France part of the Control Commission. This was part of Churchill's design to make France once more a great power who could help the British to counterbalance Russian might.

France did not loom large in Roosevelt's thought. To Roosevelt ancient European cultures – German, Spanish, Italian, French – counted little more than as ethnic votes in particular states of his vast, almost homogenised country; their present condition, as nations which had caused war after war, and which were now in consequence completely prostrate, seemed fitting retribution. It led him to postulate a binary model of the world, the Union of Soviet Socialist Republics on the one hand, and the United States of America on the other, with China more aloof, but perhaps crucial again in Asia, now that Japan was on the verge of defeat. Both the USSR and the USA were federations of ethnic diversity, organised round an idea, rather than ancient and continuous national societies. This was the brave new world.

In such a perspective, de Gaulle seemed tiresome, his grandeur preposterous and a possible source of renewed major conflict. France might wish to extend its frontiers to the Rhine, and Stalin suspected that other countries, such as Belgium and Holland, might then wish to share in the spoils. It would be simpler to ignore French claims. But at the same time Roosevelt hoped that American troops would only have to stay in Europe for two more years at most. Who would then keep Germany disunited and powerless? The French clearly had an interest in policing Germany for a long time, perhaps for ever. For this reason, therefore, despite considerable misgivings, Roosevelt decided after all to support Churchill's position, that France should have a zone of occupation in Germany, and that it should share in the Allied Control Commission (or Council as it was originally called).

Stalin, determined to limit the occupation to the three victorious powers, debated with skill that the admission of France would entail other occupiers – Belgium, Holland, Poland. But as soon as Roosevelt switched his own view and suggested that America would not long keep troops in Europe, Stalin accepted France as an occupier. It was one more way of preventing a German revival. But he still opposed the idea of France as a member of the Control Council, which Stalin wished to preserve entirely as an American–British–Russian body. Churchill and Eden argued powerfully that a French zone of occupied Germany entailed French membership of the Control Council. After prolonged argument, Churchill's case for putting France on the Control Commission was accepted after a private agreement between Roosevelt and Stalin; the result appeared to strengthen Britain's position that in policing Germany it was France and Britain that would limit Russian influence, even if the Americans quit, as they had in 1919, Russia's agreement to French participation also appeared to be connected with America yielding on reparations – suggested as a total of $20 billion, over ten years – both in payments and in the direct removal of industrial and other assets from Germany to those who had 'borne the burden of the war and organised the victory' – that is, chiefly to Russia. The negotiations at Yalta were, therefore, to some degree an attempt by Stalin and Molotov to seek Roosevelt's support for reparations, and of concessions by them to this end.

Poland had been the cause of Britain entering the war. Britain felt it had a moral case to argue and, for once, Roosevelt supported Churchill. As well as a legitimate Polish government in London there was a puppet Polish government in Moscow, sent to Poland with Stalin's occupying troops. (It was called the Lublin government after the town where it was first installed.) Stalin had three major aims. He wanted to settle Poland's frontiers. He wanted access to Germany. He wanted a loyal ally. After achieving a Soviet frontier to the west of the 1939 position, and compensating Poland by giving it large parts of Prussia, Stalin demanded guaranteed ease of passage for his troops through Poland to Germany, and a Polish government that would be loyal. By this he meant a government of Communists and fellow-travellers, established by the Russians. The occupation of the Baltic republics by the Russians, the shift westwards of the Polish frontier with Germany, and the establishment of guaranteed friendly governments in Poland and other states on the Soviet frontier, created a barrier of buffer states through which any revivified capitalist Germany, allied with Britain and the United States, would have to advance before it reached Russia. For Stalin, then, the Eastern question was one of Russian security, rather than of spreading Communism.

How different was Churchill's position? To restore a free and democratic Poland had always been a principal British war aim. The legitimate pre-war Polish government had spent the war in London, they had been tiresome but he supported them and recognised that their troops had fought bravely. On the other hand Churchill understood Russia's desire for security and accepted the need for the easy passage of Soviet troops to its zone in Germany. He also acknowledged how aggravating the Poles had always been to the Russians. But it was clear to him that the Communist-supported Lublin government represented scarcely anybody in Poland at all and was neither free nor democratically elected. Roosevelt, with a large Polish–American community, and a commitment to Wilsonian principles of national self-determination, was adamant for some sort of independent government; he accepted neither the London nor the Lublin factions as representative of the Polish people – a view in which he was most probably correct. He wanted free elections, a point Stalin was not prepared to concede. Neither Roosevelt nor Churchill, however, thought the issue of Poland was important enough to divide the Western allies from Russia, though they did not wish Poland to become just a Russian subject-state.

At the time of Yalta the allies were not prepared to acknowledge, least of all to themselves, that the Soviet Union already dominated Poland. Meanwhile the USSR regarded France as an Anglo–American subject state, or pawn, in the West; and it expected Poland to be acknowledged as exactly analogous – as a joint ally in controlling Germany, and as a Russian buffer state, just as France was (in their eyes) the British buffer state. The fact that France was a democracy unlike Poland was neither here nor there.

After some prevarication, the Western allies accepted the Curzon line as the appropriate Polish eastern frontier, and repudiated both the London and the Lublin governments for they hoped that by so doing, they would force the Russians to allow new free elections. But this diplomatic game was lost. Once the London government had been repudiated, the Russians gave even greater support to their puppet Lublin government, which was actually in Poland. All that the West could do was to reiterate again and again that what they really wanted was a free, independent and representative government.

Stalin then seemed to accept. He offered two new suggestions, both morally dubious. First, Poland should receive substantial parts of Prussia – to the Oder–Neisse river. This violated the Versailles Treaty provisions about nationality, but as it was at the expense of the Germans it was difficult to argue against it.

Secondly, Stalin (after accusing the London Poles, with some justification, of organising resistance against the Red Army) offered to bring the London and Lublin Poles together. This would have led – had the two sides ever agreed, and it was already known they would not – to a right-wing–Communist coalition government installed by the allies, quite blatantly unrepresentative of the people inside Poland and, more important, almost certainly unworkable.

Stalin then suggested that a slightly enlarged Polish provisional government of National Unity should oversee free elections with a secret ballot, in which democratic parties could put forward candidates. The elections were to be supervised by an allied commission consisting of Molotov, the Soviet Foreign Minister, Clark Kerr, the British Ambassador in Moscow and a strong Soviet supporter, and Averell Harriman, the American Ambassador in Moscow. There were to be no impartial observers except the ambassadors in

Warsaw who, naturally, would be limited by the terms of their accreditation to the government holding the elections. In fact, this meant that the United States accepted the Soviet position in Poland, whereas Churchill sought to adopt a stronger line both about the provisional government and about the supervision of elections. As a result Roosevelt's successors were left in a most difficult position, since the USSR could argue cogently (and did so) that they were abiding by the Yalta agreement when the whole of Eastern Europe had Communist governments imposed by Russian political and military force with American acquiescence.

In the give and take of Yalta Roosevelt took a slack line about elections, because he thought the United Nations of greater importance. For him it represented what the League of Nations had not been, something that the United States would support, and which could grow into a form of world government, abiding by principles similar to those on which the United States was itself based. If the United Nations could guarantee peace and stability, the causes of totalitarianism – fear of attack, or resentment at injustice, such as Germany had felt about the Versailles Treaty of 1919, would fade away. Therefore the problems over Poland's elections would eventually be solved by the growing sense of security that the USSR would feel. The United Nations could eventually enforce human and democratic rights throughout *all* countries. That, at least, was the optimistic interpretation of Roosevelt's attitude. More prosaically, the American proposals for the United Nations involved equal rights for all states, Great Power supremacy in enforcement, and the liberation of colonial nations. This was to be in the form of an organisation with a General Assembly, a Security Council where the US, USSR and UK would have a veto (as well as executive power), and a Trusteeship Council to supervise the liberation of colonial peoples. The dismantling of the British, French and Dutch empires was to be followed by American economic imperialism – John Foster Dulles told Harold Macmillan in 1942 that the British would have 'to invite the co-operation of the United States in the development of your colonies after the war'.

Despite the obvious anti-British Empire vision of the United States, the actual structure of the proposed new UN body envisaged a permanent Western numerical dominance over the USSR. It followed, therefore, that Stalin could not regard the United Nations either as impartial or even as a guarantor of the rights and defence of his country. That could only be achieved by Russia's own military strength, by its defence in depth through a system of client states, and by a bilateral bargain with the United States. For that reason, therefore, he was prepared to propitiate Roosevelt, regarding him as a guarantor of Soviet rights. Churchill, too, regarded the United Nations with deep suspicion, since it seemed as though the trusteeship system, to be applied to conquered enemy colonies, might be applied to the British Empire.

The Yalta conference did however settle the list of those nations to be invited to the San Francisco conference to establish the United Nations. But implicitly, acceptance of spheres of influence, and adoption of the Great Power veto in the Security Council, meant that the United Nations could not be an independent force in post-war affairs.

Although the position in the Far East was also discussed at Yalta, Chiang Kai-shek, the official Chinese leader, was not present; nor was his main opponent, the Communist Mao Tse-tung. As events turned out, China was to be one of the central areas of dispute between Russia and America within two years. The attention of those at Yalta, however, was concentrated on Japan and its defeat, not upon the future of China, at that time in the American sphere of influence. Stalin too had supported Chiang Kai-shek in the 1940s, not Mao. Now it was decided to give America free access to Japan, China and the Far East and to return to Russia those territories it had lost in 1905. Roosevelt specifically assured Stalin that Britain and France should have no further interest in Asia and suggested that Russia should assume Britain's place in shipping in the Pacific. As a result of America's primacy in the war against Japan, Britain had little influence in the Far East, though of course Britain continued to hold India; and Roosevelt's ambition to exclude Britain from China and Burma, and France from Indochina, had as a direct aim the involvement of Russia in the war against Japan to counterbalance Britain. Roosevelt hoped to develop the Far East as an exclusively American sphere of economic and political interest. These consequences of Roosevelt's agreement with Stalin were far-reaching, leading to the eventual loss of China and Indochina to the Communists. Roosevelt thought that the rehabilitation of China would be accomplished by a putative coalition between Chiang Kai-shek and the Communists, but he withdrew some of America's support from Chiang Kai-shek prematurely, which created a vacuum that the Communists rapidly filled.

Roosevelt's policy in the Far East, which offered unilateral advantages to the Russians at the expense of his allies, Britain, France and Nationalist China; his abandonment of free elections in Poland; his agreement that Yugoslavia should be given to a Communist government under Tito, with only minimal non-

Communist participation – all this can be interpreted in several ways. Roosevelt wanted to defeat Germany and Japan. He wanted to end British and French colonialism. He wished to open the Far East and Europe to American investment, trade and to some degree to American political control. And he wanted to believe that Stalin's intentions were for the best.

Like Churchill, he accepted that Russia was once more a great power whose interests had to be accommodated. In his view accommodation of those interests would be followed by trust and reconciliation.

It may be that the USSR sought security for itself and nothing else. Stalin certainly took the view that given half a chance the capitalists, having defeated the axis, would turn on Russia. The Munich agreement of 1938 and the attack by the Germans in June 1941 presented massive confirmation of the quasi-Marxist thesis that capitalists, in one form or another, would seek to destroy the embodied working class as represented by the USSR. Stalin had, however, repudiated Trotsky and the thesis of permanent world revolution. Under the impact of the Second World War – known in Russia as the Great Patriotic War – it was certainly true that the Soviet Union had embraced some aspects of Russian nationalism; and it was undoubtedly also the case that many Western commentators took the view that Stalin had been metamorphosed into a traditional Czar.

Nor must it be forgotten that in the State Department and in the Foreign Office there were people who, while no longer maybe belonging to the Communist party, had had a thorough Marxist indoctrination at one point in their lives. People who detested the Nazis, and whose hatred, far from diminishing as defeat became certain, actually grew with the revelations about concentration camps; people who were passionately anti-imperialist and who had a profound sympathy for the sufferings of the Russian people, whom they admired. These people felt that Russia was at worst merely asserting herself and at best was a 'good thing'.

This was not, however, the only view. To many it seemed that Russian nationalism had been added to totalitarian Stalinist Communism; that millions had died in the Lenin–Stalin purges and remained in prison during the war; that the Polish officers shot at Katyn (and the many subsequently shot and imprisoned after their repatriation in 1945 and 1946), all proved beyond a doubt that Stalinist Russia was at least as great a threat to the world as Hitler. But to hold such views in 1945 often appeared at odds with moderate, let alone progressive, opinion.

It is not necessary therefore to posit the opinion that Roosevelt

was a tool of Alger Hiss in his determination to achieve a settlement with Russia at least as favourable to Stalin as Munich had
been to Hitler. Indeed, it is sometimes argued that Yalta represented a realistic settlement of the post-war world into spheres of
influence, and that it was Truman's inexperience, subsequently
aided by Bevin's bellicosity, that led to a repudiation of Yalta, at
least by the time of Potsdam five months later, and so led the
USSR to take up a defensive, isolationist, Cold War posture
which was in turn interpreted by the West as a confirmation of the
view that the primary objective of Soviet policy was expansion.

The final plenary session of Yalta was held on Sunday 11
February 1945, and an agreement was signed by Churchill, Roosevelt and Stalin: the only time in the twentieth century when all the
major powers came to a joint view of the future, based upon an
agreed diagnosis of the present balance of world forces. The
agreement lasted for three months. By May 1945, after Roosevelt's
death on 12 April 1945, his successor, President Truman, was
already arguing that the Yalta agreement meant a freely elected
democratic government in Poland – which it had not; in June,
Truman was repudiating the agreement on reparations from Germany, by arguing that they should come only from the zone
occupied by each respective power, thus denying Russia access to
the Ruhr; on 5 June 1945, dismemberment of Germany was
repudiated, and (with the atom bomb on hand) the Russians were
not needed in the Far East.

Was Yalta a sell-out to the Russians? Or was it an attempt to
reach a high-level settlement based on realism which America
repudiated after Roosevelt's death?

To see the beginning of an answer to that, it is necessary to go to
Potsdam.

Chapter 2

Potsdam

After Yalta the war in Europe exploded into its last three months. British and American troops under Eisenhower and Montgomery crossed the Rhine in March to capture Cologne. By April they were well into the heart of Germany, having captured the Ruhr, the main industrial base of the Third Reich. This victory led to the liberation of Holland, which had suffered terribly in its last few months of German occupation. Only Denmark and Norway remained under the Nazis until almost the end of the war.

The Russians continued to press forward on the eastern front, meanwhile consolidating their hold in their occupied territories. In March, a Communist-dominated government was imposed on King Michael of Romania, and another on King Simeon of Bulgaria, while in Poland the Communist regime was reinforced rather than broadened as had been agreed at Yalta. Churchill was furious, but he could get no support in his protests from Roosevelt, who was in bad health. Without Hitler's knowledge some Germans began to try to negotiate a separate peace with the Western powers, but their overtures were repulsed. The Russians became aware that something was going on and their suspicions became the subject of the last exchanges between Roosevelt, Stalin and Churchill before Roosevelt died suddenly.

'In this melancholy void one President could not act and the other could not know,' was Churchill's comment on the period of feebleness before the death of Roosevelt and the weeks in which Truman, his successor, took over. Roosevelt's twelve years in the unique office of the Presidency left nobody with remotely comparable experience to succeed. In Churchill's view the collapse of Germany and its allies left Russia supreme on the European Continent. It was 'a mortal danger to the free world'; the accords reached at Yalta were almost valueless and therefore British and American troops should drive as far east as possible – and specifically reach Berlin and Prague before the Russians. Thus on the basis of the final meeting place of the armies, they should seek an ultimate settlement between East and West, before the British and American armies were demobilised. In Churchill's subsequent opinion, the failure of American leadership caused by Roosevelt's death left Russia in a far stronger position than it need have been.

But this is to accept a far more benevolent interpretation of Roosevelt's attitude towards Soviet policies than Yalta had in fact revealed.

The weakness of the British in 1945 was not transient. It was permanent. Paradoxically the degree to which Britain had mobilised, with millions of men and women in the forces, the greater part of its production devoted to munitions, and its foreign reserves handed over to the Americans to pay for weapons and raw materials, had substantially reduced its potential for action independent of the Americans. Churchill had even handed over the British scientists and technologists who developed the atom bomb; and the British armed forces were subordinated to the American generals Eisenhower and Marshall. Had the British mobilised less intensely and retained freedom of manoeuvre, especially diplomatically, deals might have been struck with the Germans no longer loyal to Hitler, and with the Russians, which might have saved Czechoslovakia, Hungary and Yugoslavia for a European settlement.

Since the bulk of Hitler's army had been massed against the Russians, it followed that the Western armies had an opportunity to advance against lighter opposition. Understandably, the Germans preferred to surrender people and towns to the Western allies rather than to the Russians; equally understandably, that was especially hard for the Russians to appreciate at its face value. This added to Soviet suspicions of British intentions. The Soviet Union also knew from their agents in the British Foreign Office that Churchill wanted a peace settlement that did not divide Europe into zones of influence. This made them doubly suspicious of allied intentions, though they did not understand the degree to which the British forces were subordinate to the Americans.

The struggle for a non-Communist Poland was doomed to failure because it was on the frontier the Russians were determined to defend against any future attack. In any case, throughout April and May Stalin's attitude to the non-Communist Poles hardened; many were liquidated. This caused serious concern to Churchill and, in turn, as he became aware of what was going on, to Truman. As spring came to Europe the war continued to be fiercely fought to the end. Huge armies advanced across Germany, but German resistance continued. In these conditions, the most organised and efficient administrative units were bound to be the military formations of the victorious powers. In France and Belgium, and to a lesser extent in Holland, the civil administration remained intact and, until the leaders in exile returned from London, the local governments were able to cope with urgent problems. In Northern

Italy and the rest of the Balkans fighting continued: civil war raged in Greece, and in Yugoslavia Tito was bent on the destruction not only of those who, like the Croatian troops, had supported the Germans, but all the non-Communist guerrillas as well.

This disruption caused by the war can hardly be exaggerated. It presented difficulties which required urgent *ad hoc* solutions and often these solutions became part of an enduring structure which subsequent hindsight sought to see as part of a predetermined plan for a final settlement of Europe. Bombing, and the retreating Germans, had destroyed bridges and railways and blocked roads. Except where there had been fighting, farms and small workshops in the countryside functioned normally, but often without men of military age and without supplies from the towns. At least the peasants had enough to eat. The towns had frequently been severely damaged or even destroyed. For every city, such as Paris or Rome, which was undamaged, there was a Le Havre, a Caen, a Cologne, a Hamburg, where the destruction was massive, with millions squatting in makeshift shelters in the ruins. Above all, the interruption of supplies meant that large numbers of people in the towns were hungry. This hunger was the more shocking because until early 1945 the Germans in particular, but Europeans in general, had been well fed. Suddenly liberation meant near-starvation.

In addition social disruption was caused by the purges of pro-Nazi elements, and the emergence of partisan fighters, often Communists, who sought to rule whole localities, which meant that the restoration of ordinary processes of civil life was made particularly difficult. Hundreds of thousands of people, many with responsible jobs, were shot or imprisoned. The German population fled from Prussia as the Russians advanced, while the prisoners of war and foreign workers in Germany and other occupied territories formed a floating, rootless mass which had to be fed and housed and, eventually, resettled by the allies. The liberation of the concentration camps revealed the remnants of the Jewish population, six million of whom had been murdered, and other sad victims of Nazi terror.

The Soviet commissars extracted most of the Russian survivors, many of whom were immediately executed, while the great majority of them were sent to the gulag. The Western powers, seeking to restore order, felt obliged to relieve the distress of those whom they had liberated. *Ad hoc* military administrations had, therefore, to be established in Germany and Austria, while elsewhere the existing local authorities were recognised, almost willy-nilly, in order to cope with the immense tasks that imposed themselves. An enormous reshuffle of people took place – men making their way home from the various armies in which they had fought, men and women returning from forced labour and seeking to reunite their families, refugees trying to get back to their own towns and villages, refugees fleeing from the Red Army, children and adolescents who had lost their parents – all this in a continent accustomed to centralised administration, which had largely broken down, and with local governments of varying degrees of effectiveness and acceptability attempting to preserve some elements of order. This turmoil continued for months and, indeed, worsened during the winter of 1945–6 as problems of housing, heat, light and water and food shortage became more desperate for people already weakened by hunger, shock and loss.

In April 1945, however, the crowning military achievement was the surrounding of Berlin by the Russians, and the first contact, on the banks of the river Elbe, between units of the American and Red armies. Over a million German soldiers were taken prisoner by the allies in April, and a further three million more in May. The Americans entered Czechoslovakia but the Russians captured Prague. It was, to some degree, a race to see how much land would fall into either camp, with the Russians well to the west of Berlin and Eisenhower deliberately halting the British and American advance in accordance with what had been agreed at Yalta. At the end of April, after heavy fighting, the allied armies occupied Northern Italy and on 2 May the enemy surrendered. With Hitler's death, probably by suicide, on 30 April 1945, the way was clear for an unconditional surrender of the German armed forces, which was agreed on 7 May and took place on 8 May.

The position in Europe was clear. The Continent was divided between the Russians and the Western allies. There was a *de facto* division which had to be brought into line with the hastily drawn boundaries of the occupation zones of Germany and Austria agreed at Yalta. In practice this meant the withdrawal of British and American troops from Czechoslovakia, and from the middle of Germany and the Baltic coast, while the Russians had to offer zones in Berlin itself to the Americans, British and eventually to the French.

The war against Japan continued.

The need to settle Europe was, however, important. For that reason it was agreed, on Churchill's initiative, that Truman, Stalin and he should meet. On 12 May, in a message to Truman, Churchill referred to 'an iron curtain' which the Russians had pulled down on their front. Behind it, what was going on could not be known, though fleeing refugees told horrifying tales, many of which were not believed but which were in fact an understatement of conditions in the Soviet empire. The gulags had never been dismantled after the terrible persecutions of the 1930s; now they were refilled with returning soldiers, such as Aleksandr Solzhenitsyn, suspected of disloyalty to Stalin, with new camps added for millions of Germans, Austrians and other troops captured by the Red Army.

Truman sailed to Europe for a meeting of the three leaders at Potsdam near Berlin, which began on 15 July, ten days after the British general election, whose results had yet to be declared as the votes from the far-flung troops would not all be in until 25 July. Churchill was accompanied therefore by Attlee, the leader of the Labour party, in case he should win the election. Stalin flew in to Berlin from Moscow.

Harry S. Truman was a modest man. Though he was actually quite tall – six inches taller than Stalin according to his diary – and was to prove effective and pugnacious, he seemed at first to epitomise the Little Man, Mr Average American. Born in 1884 in Independence, Missouri, he had served in the First World War, and then entered local politics. He later became an influential and effective Senator. Chosen to be Vice-President in the 1944 campaign to reassure the South, he had never been part of the President's inner circle. Nobody thought he counted. Vice-President for little more than three months before becoming President, he was only distantly aware of the extent of the current complex international problems. His first act, keeping Roosevelt's Cabinet, which was in fact sensible, gave the impression of a man overwhelmed by events, overshadowed by far better-known American statesmen and generals, who would have to act on his behalf.

This was not so. Truman was a man of shrewd and determined judgment, full of vitality, and deeply suspicious of many of Roosevelt's team. Inevitably, when events were moving so fast, it took time for Truman to become familiar with the circumstances. But indeed he learned quickly.

Truman had not met either Churchill or Stalin until he arrived at the conference which took place in requisitioned houses in Potsdam, a rich Berlin suburb, where the lake was full of corpses of wounded German soldiers whom the Russians had drowned. As the photographers clicked away at Potsdam, however, the brute realities of the violence of the immediate past seemed to lift. The European civil war which had raged since 1914 seemed suspended. It had overthrown European civilisation, leaving a revolutionary tyranny in Russia and most of Europe and Asia ravaged by death and destruction. A sick and exhausted world hoped that the declarations of the United Nations were to become the new, more rational, realities, and that peace, prosperity and justice would prevail.

But this was not to be. Judged by the high hopes of the optimists, the peace lamentably failed. Oppression spread. Military might grew and grew. Yet it must be said that the decisions arrived at by the Big Three at Potsdam, arrived at perhaps by default, almost unconsciously, led to a world settlement that endured, perhaps as a caricature of itself, longer than any other settlement since the Treaty of Vienna in 1815.

Certainly, few major nations had ever been apparently so cruelly crushed as Germany and Italy. No resistance survived. The three victorious nations had therefore eliminated their European enemies in an almost unprecedented manner. The victors then set about reshaping their enemies' political structures and dismembering their armed services in a way that had not been seen since Napoleon's treatment of the states he had occupied. In short, had the wartime alliance endured it could have been seen as a combination literally without precedent in the history of the world because there was nowhere to be found a state, or group of states, with any significant power independent of the three major allies.

In China, the armies of the Kuomintang and Communist groups were ill-equipped and already fighting each other. India had the fourth largest effective army in the world, but it was in the main officered by Britons. France had a token force in the occupation of Germany; Spain's army was old-fashioned and relatively small. Only Canada and Australia could rank as discernible powers in comparison with the victorious three. But the way the war had been fought hid the latent power of several states. Had China been governed by an effective coalition of Chiang Kai-shek and Mao Tse-tung it would have taken a seat at Potsdam. Had France been liberated a year earlier it could have had a powerful army. More speculatively still, had the British accepted Nehru as Prime Minister of an independent India, then India could have emerged a decade earlier as a major country. Since by 1950 these three states loomed large on the international scene, it is clear how temporary was the dominance of the Big Three.

The purpose of the Potsdam meeting was not only to settle post-war Europe but also to prepare to end the war with Japan. Stalin and his delegation were eager to enter the Japanese war in order to make the territorial gains in the Far East that had been offered to them at Yalta and also to get a share of the occupation of Japan. Stalin was still prepared to support Chiang Kai-shek against the Communist Mao Tse-tung. Almost immediately after the end of the war in Europe he began moving troops in very large numbers to the Far East, to prepare for the invasion of Manchuria and the subsequent occupation of Korea and parts of Japan. The Japanese government was already prepared to accept defeat, but the military would not agree to the American terms of unconditional surrender, involving (as it appeared) the abdication of the Emperor, who was ritually and religiously the embodiment of Japanese nationhood. As the Soviet Union in July 1945 was still officially neutral in the Japanese war with the allies, the Japanese government sought to use Soviet good offices to achieve a negotiated peace. Stalin had the opportunity in these circumstances to do a private deal. The Americans intercepted the messages from Tokyo to the Japanese Ambassador in Moscow and were keen to accelerate their own victory over Japan, so as not to have to share influence in the Far East with Russia (or even with Britain). Seeds for further dissension between Russia and America were also sown at this time for it was agreed at Potsdam that American troops should occupy the southern half of Korea up to the thirty-eighth parallel and that Russian troops should occupy the north.

During the Potsdam conference the results of the test of the first atom bomb became known to President Truman and the decision was taken to drop two bombs on Japan. Truman agreed with Churchill that this would substantially shorten the war against Japan, saving American and British casualties, and the lives of many others including the Japanese troops who would otherwise fight to the end. The main American objectives, however, were less acceptable. The ending of the war, because of vast American superiority, was certain to happen; but if it happened with less than complete surrender to the American commander, MacArthur, the other allies, especially Russia, would muscle in. The explosion of the atom bomb would also help to contain Stalin's ruthless ambition. The atom bomb test was therefore kept secret from Stalin who, however, knew of it from the Soviet spy, Klaus Fuchs, even before Truman and Churchill.

The Potsdam conference opened in a sombre mood and almost immediately a series of major disagreements occurred. Molotov wanted reparations at a level of $10 billion for the USSR and another $10 billion for the other allies. The Americans resisted this figure on two grounds; first, that the Soviet Union already occupied parts of Germany holding half its wealth and, second, that America would have to support Germany while it was producing commodities for reparations. This dispute led to a scaling down of Soviet demands and, step by step, as will be seen, to the creation of a West German state. The Soviet Union suspected that the incorporation of Germany in a Western bloc as an armed ally lay behind the American opposition to Soviet demands.

The second disagreement was about Poland. Truman decided that on this issue the USSR had already done down America. He was partly wrong and partly right about that. He assumed that the Yalta agreement was meant to lead to free elections in the Western sense. The Soviet Union assumed on the other hand that Yalta put Poland securely into the Soviet sphere of influence, which in their view entailed a Polish government sympathetic to – indeed controlled by – Russia. Free elections would almost certainly lead to the opposite of this. Therefore free elections could not take place. Inevitably Poland was a source of profound irritation throughout the conference.

And Germany, too, could not be dismembered (as had been half agreed at Yalta) if it was to survive as an economic entity. The Russians were not concerned with its survival as any kind of entity, and were therefore eager to secure control of the zone which their troops were already occupying.

The early meetings of the conference and of the Foreign Ministers broke into recriminations about these issues; about the oppression in Soviet-occupied Europe, and about British support for the reactionary government of Greece which was fighting a civil war against a Communist armed rising. Through it all the unspoken knowledge of the atom bomb, and of Russia's military superiority in Europe, dominated the tone of the discussions; Russia dominated Europe but America could possibly dominate the world.

The conference adjourned with nothing settled while Churchill, Eden and Attlee flew back to Britain for the results of their general election. The Labour party won and Attlee became Prime Minister. He returned with Bevin, the new Foreign Secretary, and the conference was further thrown into confusion as Stalin now distrusted the new leadership of both the British and the Americans, a fact which further exacerbated the underlying differences between the two sides. Moreover, the British and the Americans were divided among themselves, and the disappearance of Churchill and Roosevelt meant that personal contact based on past meetings could no longer bridge gulfs that existed from differing concepts of interests. For example, the British were eager to restore French influence in Syria; to the Americans this was imperialism, and it threatened America's oil interests. Similarly in Iran, a major oil producer, where all three powers had troops, Truman urged British withdrawal, rightly convinced that Iran would fall into the

American sphere of influence and add to America's control of world oil. In 1945 America controlled 57 per cent of the world's oil supplies, Britain 27 per cent, and the Russians 11 per cent. This was a major basis of post-war dissension, in which once more the Russians and the British had reason to feel that the US was attempting to limit their influence.

The US, however, was engaged in a more subtle diplomatic game at Potsdam. With the dropping of the atom bomb, it was hoped to exclude the Soviet Union from the end of the Japanese war. At the same time, Truman and his advisers decided that a peace conference to end the war with Germany was undesirable since it would involve so many nations and diminish American authority in the West. Truman preferred to deal directly with Stalin, ditching both Britain and France as partners in the post-war settlement. But he accompanied this line with a demand to the Russians that the governments of the Eastern European countries should be 'reorganised' so that they were 'democratic'. This Stalin equally bluntly refused to accept.

But Potsdam did see agreement on the division of Germany (and implicitly of Europe as a whole), and on a basis for the allocation of reparations to Russia. Though lip service was paid to a common four-power control of Germany, the realities were accepted to be different. The meeting drew to a close and the former allies flew home to cope with the peace and to finish the war with Japan. Each participant began his own task of post-war reconstruction but not as a team. Potsdam had revealed the flaws of Yalta and the deep underlying distrust of ally for ally.

On 6 and 9 August 1945 the American air force dropped atom bombs on Hiroshima and Nagasaki, and the Japanese surrender was accepted on 14 August. A few days before the surrender the Soviet Union declared war on Japan. But already the Cold War, as it was to be called, had begun between Russia and its allies. The Foreign Ministers met as scheduled in London in September. The United States and the United Kingdom continued to refuse to recognise the Soviet puppet governments in Eastern Europe; the Soviet Union purported to fear a reunited Germany and attacked the government of Greece. No agreement was possible even on the procedure of the meeting, and the Foreign Ministers broke up without conferring. The post-war world had begun.

The immediate repercussions of Yalta and Potsdam, culminating in the Korean War of 1950, form the subject matter of the next ten chapters. These years between 1945 and 1950 see Europe's initial post-war struggles to rehabilitate through various forms of Social

Democracy, a political form also emulated by the newly independent India and by Japan. Marxism succeeds triumphantly in China
and intensifies throughout the whole Soviet sphere of influence.
However, before embarking on these events, I must devote a few
brief pages to explain why Roosevelt's new world organisation
failed to enforce peace and justice amongst all nations.

Chapter 3

The United Nations

Improbable as it may seem, one of the hopes for peace had been the creation of an international organisation which would not only arbitrate in disputes between states but would also evolve into some sort of supra-national sovereignty. But these hopes were rapidly dashed by the bitter division that swiftly developed between the Soviet Union and the other powers.

The League of Nations, created by the Versailles Treaty, effectively collapsed in 1939, though it was not formally wound up until 1945 when its assets were transferred to the United Nations. This new organisation grew directly out of the wartime alliance, having its origins in the British and American desire to replace the League with an effective international body to preserve world peace. In its short life the League had been weakened by America's refusal in 1920 to take part, falling to a body blow when the Soviet Union was expelled in December 1939 after the invasion of Finland. A prime aim of British policy, therefore, was to create a world organisation to which the United States could belong and, after 1941, an organisation that could include the USSR.

By 1944 Roosevelt had become the leading proponent of the new world organisation. As well as the participation of all the major powers, he attached great importance to the participation of the small nations of the world. The organisation, in other words, was to become an agent of decolonisation. In a sense it was modelled on the United States Senate where every state, big or small, has two Senators. In the eyes of liberal idealists – especially those who had supported the League between the wars – the new world body was to become embryonically at least a federal or world government, perhaps with a monopoly of arms and forces, which would adjudicate in international disputes and perhaps enforce its adjudications. It was not at this time seen as an active agent of social and economic development though this came later, with the emergence of the specialised agencies (including one survivor from the League of Nations, the International Labour Office, in Geneva). The United Nations in its conception was a purely political, inter-governmental peace-making body.

The original proposals had been worked out in September and October 1944 at the Dumbarton Oaks conference despite a crisis on the issue of membership and of voting. The conference had been saved by Roosevelt, who announced that these matters would be decided at a summit conference – which turned out to be Yalta. The crucial issue – whether parties to a dispute could vote on it, even if they were permanent members of the Security Council – was clearly of critical importance to the Russians since they would almost certainly be in a minority in the organisation. As a compromise it was agreed that for minor disputes, where a peaceful settlement was envisaged, parties should abstain, but for serious disputes the permanent members of the Security Council could use their veto. This represented a major shift from the original American position, and in effect gave the Russians the power to block. This was important to them for political and legal reasons. They wanted to say that what they were doing was legal; despite the width and depth of Soviet terror Stalin gave great weight to what was 'legal' and what was not. And, some of their use of state power in international affairs was purportedly in support of legal obligations laid upon the Soviet Union by international agreements. Thus their behaviour in Poland and elsewhere was not, according to them, naked aggression; it fulfilled a treaty obligation. Even more significant, however, was the possibility that the United Nations might eventually control armed forces of its own.

The idea of an international army was quickly scotched; the organisation had the power, nevertheless, to call upon member states to use force to support its decisions in cases of a breach of the peace. Thus, the United Nations inherited some of the powers of the wartime alliance, as well as becoming a potential focus for a new alliance against any nation formally labelled as an aggressor.

Not that that elaborate theory necessarily worked in practice. The fear of a veto was the exact contrary to the idea of the weight of the wartime alliance; it was to be used when the alliance had broken down and unanimity no longer ruled; the small nations could justifiably think that the veto might be used to prevent action being taken to protect them, in which case what was the point of joining the United Nations? Similarly, trusteeship of colonial territories applied only to ex-enemy countries and not to colonies of the victorious powers, thus protecting British interests.

At Yalta the main outlines of the new organisation were agreed. It was to be called the United Nations, the phrase now generally assigned to the allies that were fighting the axis powers. Its original members were to be the allied belligerents, with some neutral countries possibly allowed to join later, followed eventually by the successor states to the defeated axis states.

The main body of the new organisation, the General Assembly, was to be representative of all member states, including members of the British Commonwealth. In the eyes of the Russians and to some extent the Americans this gave multiple membership to the British, since it was not accepted that Australia, Canada, New Zealand and South Africa were independent of the United Kingdom and in the case of India self-evidently that was not the case. The Russians therefore wanted representation of the constituent republics of the USSR, even though, constitutionally, they had no autonomous foreign policy. Ultimately they settled for two additional seats, for Byelorussia and the Ukraine.

The next problem was the executive body of the organisation, responsible for enforcing its decisions. Partly this was to be elected from the membership. But representatives of, say, Guatemala or Greece would not carry much clout. The preservation of peace depended upon the continuation of the alliance between the great powers. This alliance had to be cemented into the organisation. The permanent members of the Security Council, therefore, were to be Britain, America and Russia, but the British insisted on including the French, and the Americans on adding the Chinese. This left the Russians permanently outvoted, which meant that unless they were to be exposed to the risk of always being victims, either a unanimity rule was necessary, or a veto, on certain resolutions.

The first meeting of the United Nations – to agree its Constitution – was solemnly inaugurated by the new American President, Truman, at San Francisco in April 1945. Ironically the senior permanent official delegate for the United States was Alger Hiss, later revealed to be a Soviet intelligence agent. With insignificant changes the charter represented the agreement reached in Yalta. To ensure America's enthusiastic support, so conspicuously lacking for the League of Nations, New York was chosen as the seat of the organisation, though until its headquarters were built the Assembly was peripatetic. Its first Secretary General was the Norwegian Foreign Minister, Trygve Lie. Subordinate organisations were established – the International Labour Office, the World Health Organisation, the United Nations Educational, Scientific and Cultural Organisation, the International Bank for Reconstruction and Development, the International Monetary Fund, the United Nations Relief and Rehabilitation Agency. As well as finding well-paid jobs for seemingly numberless Scandinavians and, subsequently, Indians, these bodies rapidly became essential diplomatic meeting places. Despite the apparent ineffectiveness of the UN itself in creating a peace based on disarmament, it was a forum where debate could take place; and the absence of such a forum had been important in the series of misunderstandings that had led up to the lack of resistance to German aggression in 1939. In 1956, for example, the United Nations was instrumental in achieving the Suez cease-fire, and it brought diplomatic and other pressures to bear at many places which were potentially sources of major disruption. The emergence of the Third World, too, made the United Nations an important source of multilateral aid. Although its major role was frequently superseded by regional pacts, these had been clearly foreseen when the organisation was established. These, however, tended to be drawn up defensively, on an ideological basis, rather than on the more straightforward continental basis. The old League of Nations headquarters in Geneva, for example, became the seat of the United Nations Economic Commission for Europe, under the leadership of the Swedish economist and statesman, Gunnar Myrdal, but the widespread assumption that this would be the major seat of the reconstruction of Europe after the war proved incorrect. Power passed, in 1948, to the Organisation for European Economic Co-operation in Paris, the agency for the Marshall Plan, and to Comecon, the Soviet economic organisation, whilst Latin America was dominated by the Organisation of American States.

The United Nations did not, as had been hoped, become either a world parliament gradually accruing power to itself by broadening from precedent down to precedent, nor did it become the supreme assembly above a series of subordinate regional assemblies. It was too hopelessly divided into rival camps. Its sessions ended in impasse. Rather, the co-ordinating power in world affairs passed predominantly to Washington and Moscow, with the beginnings of a Third World non-committed consciousness after India became independent and Tito broke with Stalin.

Early sessions of the United Nations were marked by the outbreak of the Cold War, and the continuous use of the Soviet veto by Molotov, who also became especially obdurate at meetings of the allied Foreign Ministers. Meanwhile the new organisation and its agencies began to do a considerable amount of detailed and specialised work, in such diverse activities as malaria control, setting up a meteorological system, in the enforcement of anti-slavery protocols, and the preservation of cultural monuments, but its central objective – asserting positive values of peace and freedom – could not be achieved as a result of the continuous sense of isolation and paranoia felt by the Russians, who in early 1950 staged a boycott following the UN's refusal to replace the Chinese Nationalist representatives by Communist counterparts after their victory in the civil war. But the boycott rebounded on the Russians. When North Korea invaded South Korea in June 1950, the United States proposed a peace-keeping resolution to the Security Council, which, with the Russians' absence, was passed. Officially, therefore, the allied troops in Korea were United Nations troops, but it was, in effect, a United States presence. Thus when the Russians returned to the Security Council in August 1950, it was too late to recall the troops, which remained in Korea under UN auspices under the Uniting for Peace resolution of the General Assembly.

The United Nations had a skyscraper glowing above New York. It had wordy and worthy Secretaries General. Its staff was lavishly paid, and spied upon each other and their host countries with enthusiasm on behalf of the KGB, the CIA and MI5, but it was a colossal though well-intentioned failure judged by its ideals. Perhaps it would have been better never to have invented it. But having invented it, nobody had the heart to kill it and it provided a valuable diplomatic forum.

The United Nations succeeded in a few cases in policing territories where small powers were in conflict – Kashmir, Cyprus and the Sinai Desert – and which were potentially sources of major confrontation. Whenever a major country like the United States or the Soviet Union was directly involved in a dispute the concept of an international peace-keeping agency went out of the window and direct negotiation came in by the door. The reason for this was simple. The Anglo–American ideal of a 'neutral' international arbiter was unacceptable to the Marxist Soviet Union, where nothing could be 'neutral' or above the struggle. In such circumstances the concept of 'neutrality' was itself defined as serving Western interests. And, to be fair, that was what it often was; though as Western interests involved the preservation of the rights of small peoples they were not necessarily self-serving.

The mechanism which had been envisaged for maintaining peace proved to be exceptionally weak. Once again the struggle of the great powers – the principal cause of the two world wars – was to remain the prime mover of the course of world history. The chief hope for which the Western nations had said they had fought the war, the establishment of an organisation such as the United Nations to enforce peace and justice, proved by 1947 to be unachievable. Instead peace was to be maintained by a balance of power. And that balance of power depended in the first instance upon the restoration of Western Europe.

Chapter 4

Economic reconstruction

The direct economic consequences of the war were loss of economically active population, destruction of capital assets and loss of output. Trade was also disrupted as were international monetary arrangements, banking and credit. Some economists thought that it would be necessary to impose strict controls in each country with a multiplicity of rules, regulations and plans; others felt that the world economy would soon reassert itself, if left to its own devices. All were to be startled by the speed with which most countries recovered although rates of growth were not uniform.

The USSR had lost over 10 per cent of its population between 1940 and 1944 or over twenty million dead, on top of the severe losses suffered before the war during the collectivisation of agriculture and the Stalin purges when it has been suggested that out of a population of 180 million in the 1930s over five million may have died. In Germany over four million died, including many killed by bombing, in Japan between one and a half and two million, but the combined figure for France, the United Kingdom and the United States was less than one and a half million. All told, some thirty million or more people died in the war or died indirectly because of the war, even more if the victims of the Bengal famine are included.

The destruction of capital assets was greater, though difficult to measure. If all the worn-out equipment that was destroyed was replaced, then a country was sooner or later better off than it had been because the new equipment incorporated technological progress. And while it is true that the enormous amount of material made for the war effort was wasted, in terms of satisfying ordinary peacetime human wants, the technological development which came about because of the war effort partly offset this loss.

The effects of the war on output were capricious. At the end of the war, German national output was about three quarters of what it was just before the war. Greece was producing about a third of what it had done in 1938 while in the UK output was higher than before the war. In France and Holland output was just over half and in the USSR it was about two thirds of what it had been in 1939. In Denmark output was three quarters of the pre-war levels while in the neutral countries output was maintained: in Switzerland at just under pre-war levels and in Sweden just above. Across the Atlantic it was different. The United States was one and a half times richer than before the war, and the same was the case with Canada, Mexico and Australia.

These figures show how the weight of production shifted from Europe to North America, and also how the Americans became increasingly better off compared to the Russians who had a standard of living only about a fifth or less of the American throughout the 1930s and 1940s.

The economic consequences of the war on the Soviet Union and Japan, where a huge war effort had been made and fighting and bombing had destroyed much of the capital equipment, including housing, factories, railways and shipping, were great. The Soviet Union's loss of equipment in the occupied zones was only partially made up by new industrial development in Siberia, whereas Germany's capital assets accumulated rapidly in the war, and these were only in part destroyed. Some of those countries where fighting had taken place and which had been occupied by the enemy, namely the Netherlands, Italy, Greece, and above all Yugoslavia, suffered collapse of industrial output and their agricultural output dropped to near-starvation levels. In France the decline of industry was however accompanied by a prosperous and undamaged agriculture. The United Kingdom was not invaded by the enemy, but industrial output was increased and diverted from consumption by households to the war effort. The efficiency and relative incorruptibility of the British civil service enabled a more complete mobilisation of resources than elsewhere; indeed the United Kingdom was too efficient: the harm done to the economy by the scale of the diversion of people and plant to war production was considerable. In terms of the contribution to the allied war effort, in material rather than men, the British effort was dwarfed by that of the United States. But its effort cost the United Kingdom dear during and after the war, without profoundly influencing the war's outcome. Was the price perhaps too high?

In the United States, Canada, Australia and South Africa the increase of output was such that living standards rose. The unimaginable riches of these countries in the eyes of those who had suffered in the war were transmitted on film and in books and created an image of an eldorado beyond the seas. But in Europe, too, neutral countries such as Switzerland and Sweden at first recorded small falls in per capita output, largely through lack of raw materials and the high number of people kept in the armed forces, and then an immediate upsurge of output as materials again became available and men returned to work. Their gleaming lights and prosperity seemed like oases in the darkness of post-war Europe. And then, lastly, in Mexico, and many Latin American and African nations, output rose dramatically in response to the war needs of the belligerents. Indeed the war actually accelerated economic development in those continents.

International monetary arrangements and trade had been badly disrupted by the fighting. Britain had been banker to half the world and it temporarily shelved this role; the government sold the greater part of British overseas assets to finance the war effort. It was deeply in debt to countries as diverse as India and the United States. The banker was bankrupt. The Continental countries, except Germany, had largely held on to their assets, but their import needs were so vast that there was little possibility of their being financed except by borrowing from the Americans, whose ability to lend did not match the demands for loans, and whose banking system was not ready to rise to the opportunity.

The virtual collapse of international trade over wide areas of the world was prolonged into the immediate post-war period. In some areas bilateral barter developed, indeed barter was the basic foreign trade doctrine of the Stalinist states, which raised the question, was it possible to restore an acceptable international monetary mechanism or would barter in future be the basic medium of international trade, jettisoning the lessons of a century and a half since Adam Smith had advanced the theory of free trade in *The Wealth of Nations*? After all, it was argued, a century of free trade had culminated in the slump; laissez-faire theory, therefore, was probably wrong.

Credit did not flourish easily in the tangled chaos of war's aftermath; consequently the link between producers and market was broken. Economic activity was further handicapped by the virtual collapse of the transport system, both by sea, railway and road. Some of the worst-affected areas were under Soviet control, especially Poland and Yugoslavia, but perhaps Germany itself offered the example of the most severe economic disruption, with some of its cities largely in ruins, and its economy dominated by four occupying powers, two of which – Russia and France – were more concerned with reparations for their own sufferings than with any attempt to get Germany functioning again. In Western Europe even Britain, which had not been occupied, was seriously short of raw materials and lacked the foreign exchange to buy what were available. The Continental countries such as France and the Netherlands which had been occupied by the Germans were in even worse plight.

At Yalta it had been anticipated that the German economy

would provide both equipment, from its dismantled factories, and goods and services from those that remained, to help the stricken victors. It was not appreciated how disorganised Germany was. Only the Russians, using five million German prisoners, and systematically looting their occupation zone, were able to make any substantial net contribution to their economy from reparations; the British and Americans found themselves losers for they had to pay out in money and kind to avert widespread hunger and suffering amongst the German population. The United Nations Relief and Rehabilitation Agency was able to feed, house and repatriate millions of refugees and displaced people but only in the short term. The first winter was the worst, but by the summer of 1946 urban starvation had been frustrated and many peasants had acquired jewellery, watches and gold coins to put under their mattresses. Roads and bridges were repaired and railway lines were soon mended so that town and country could exchange food and goods. The market economy began to restore itself. In Germany and Hungary, where roaring inflation destroyed the currency, alternative means of financing transactions occurred, cigarettes being the most popular.

In general this was a period of endless official controls, controls on the movement of people, of goods, the allocation of supplies and rationing. In some countries, notably Britain, the regulations were mostly observed. In others, such as France, they were ignored. People could only feed their families and get the necessities of life by ignoring the regulations – which under the German occupation had been said to be a patriotic duty. The controls did not make it impossible for business to function as the black market became the way in which the affairs of ordinary life were conducted – and not only ordinary life but big business too. But the black market had enormously high costs precisely because it was illegal and barter is a most inefficient way to conduct economic life. Above all, agricultural workers will not respond to government orders to hand over their crops, nor will they sell them for rapidly deteriorating paper money. So a country such as Belgium which scrapped most of these controls experienced the most rapid rise in living standards and a rise in output as normal trade and entrepreneurial relationships were established, whilst Eastern Europe, where the regulations were part of the new Socialist order, experienced a prolonged economic decline. In 1946 by contrast food was abundant in Brussels because the farmers were selling it.

It was assumed, almost unanimously by European economists and politicians of the time, that the economic and social problems facing Europe were almost insuperable, and that to overcome them the mobilisation of an entire society was necessary, arranged around a plan which gave high priority to investment and low priority to consumption. Power would be exercised by the state in the interests of all; private interests were necessarily antagonistic to the common purpose and had to be subordinated to it. The Labour government in Britain, elected in 1945, not merely retained but intensified the wartime controls which had been so patiently, perhaps even willingly, borne. Within a couple of years bread was rationed; the weekly ration of eggs, butter, margarine and meat was reduced; indeed the state of supplies in the peace seemed worse than in the war. This was accentuated in 1946 when food was sent to Germany. The strains of the peacetime economy were increased by the acute shortage of foreign exchange in a country that imported over half its food and raw materials. The response of the British government was to intensify controls still further, and to take into state ownership the 'basic' industries of energy and transport.

American economic thinking however was averse to controls. Their economists thought at first that the ordinary processes of the market place would soon assert themselves and world economic order would return. Meanwhile it was a matter of traditional American virtues – of investment and hard work, of rebuilding factories and houses and getting businesses back on their feet. Above all, many American businessmen looked with disfavour at 'Socialist experiments'. They were prepared to extend pump-priming aid and emergency food for the near starving, but they were not willing to finance Socialism.

This left not only a choice to be made between an international market economy and a Socialist planned world, but also between two versions of the market economy, the American and the British, the orthodox and the Keynesian. The Americans argued for orthodoxy.

The pre-war economy – by which was usually meant the world in 1938 (though of course Russia and America did not go to war until 1941, and China and Japan had been at war long before 1938) – was presented as a golden era to which it would be desirable to return. In fact, of course, it was far from being so. The First World War of 1914–18 had disrupted the international monetary mechanism, based on the international division of labour in a world with relatively free movement of labour and capital, and with monetary stability guaranteed by the gold standard. An attempt had been made to re-establish the gold standard after that war, and the prosperity of the late 1920s seemed to show that prosperity indeed could be built upon such a basis. But the

Western economy suffered a substantial slump beginning in 1929, so that by 1933 output of industrialised goods was only about two thirds of what it had been in the main manufacturing countries four years earlier. Simultaneously there was a collapse of prices in the agricultural and extractive (mineral) sectors. The Brazilians burnt coffee, the Americans burnt wheat, and everywhere people went hungry. There were probably forty million unemployed in industry in the Western economies in 1933. By 1938 the world economy had to some extent recovered, though output was still far from capacity.

The new international monetary system created towards the end of the 1945 war could not cope with the problems of the peace. In setting it up the assumption was made that the post-war economy would still be dealing with the consequences of the collapse of the world monetary system in the slump of the early 1930s. This collapse had been accompanied by the movement of the major currencies away from the gold standard. This abandonment of gold was a delayed and indirect result of the swing of the centre of world trade from London to other centres as a consequence of the First World War, and it was also part and parcel of the great slump when first the pound and then the dollar were forced off the gold standard as exports collapsed, and the gold standard rules required the monetary authorities to take ever more savage deflationary action.

The recovery of world trade in the later 1930s had been accompanied by the erection of large tariff barriers and other restrictions on trade by all countries, including those hitherto dedicated to free trade, such as the United Kingdom. The recovery of economies from the slump was accompanied by what was called autarchy. When the outbreak of war brought most trade which was not bilateral to an end, the United Kingdom rapidly ran out of reserves. Its war effort, in foreign exchange terms, was then largely financed by the invention of a device called Lend-Lease, by which the United States lent war material and other resources to the United Kingdom and subsequently to the USSR, in return for access to British and other overseas military and naval bases. The loans were in fact gifts.

Towards the end of the war the United Kingdom government and the United States government jointly sought to re-establish the international monetary system. The conference was called at Bretton Woods, New Hampshire, where the Americans were led by Harry Dexter White and the British by John Maynard Keynes, later Lord Keynes. The problem was clear. The gold standard, which automatically settled all international monetary balances, was dead. In its place two new standards had been established, the pound sterling and the dollar, based on the two major international currencies, in which other countries settled their international debts. For a true international system the two currencies had to be linked. But the dollar was strong and the pound was weak, because the war had strengthened America and weakened Britain. Nor was the situation helped by the American establishment regarding the sterling area as an imperialist device. At the same time, too, Keynes was opposed to the deflationary tendencies of the gold standard, whilst American bankers were deeply suspicious of anything that smacked of monetary irresponsibility.

At Bretton Woods Keynes expressed the view that an international clearing bank should be established with a new world currency, possibly called Bancor, which would operate as a reserve currency for all other currencies. This credit base would expand regularly year by year so that the world would never again run the risk of a slump. The contrary view, argued by Harry Dexter White, was that the international mechanism should be based on the diminution of barriers to trade, and that the international reserve should be created by the deposit of member states of a proportion of their own reserves, which could be lent at substantial rates of interest to countries which fell into chronic balance of payments deficits. There would be no compulsion upon creditor countries to expand their level of activity, and so their trade, in order to diminish the rate at which deficits accumulated. Keynes saw clearly that in the world as it was at the end of the Second World War, the United States had an overwhelming power to export, while most European countries, and countries elsewhere affected by the war, had a tremendous potential demand for imports. The possibility therefore arose that the whole world would become chronically indebted to the United States. Under the rules of orthodox, Harry Dexter White, economics, the United States would in such circumstances be obliged to undertake a massive expansion of its home demand in order to absorb the imports of the other countries as soon as production could be started again. Keynes thought this an impossibility. He foresaw tremendous economic difficulties in consequence – unnecessary unemployment, hardship, perhaps even starvation – as the Europeans sought desperately to export goods they needed themselves, and the Americans refused to buy European goods because they were themselves producing enough already. It was for this reason that he favoured extensive credit lines to Europe.

In the event, the United States view was dominant, and the International Monetary Fund (IMF) was created along the lines that Harry Dexter White proposed. Alongside it was founded a small vestigial international bank, the World Bank, which would raise money on Wall Street and in other financial centres and lend it at the going rate of interest to developing countries. Keynes argued that as a result the world would be chronically short of foreign exchange, namely dollars, for a long period. While the war lasted, Lend-Lease covered the deficits of the major importers. But when the European war ended, President Truman abruptly ended Lend-Lease, thus leaving the United Kingdom, in particular, in grave danger of being unable to pay for its imports. Since the original United Kingdom reserves had been largely expended in the first two years of the war to buy food and raw materials, since substantial balances in sterling had been built up in London by Commonwealth and colonial governments, and since Britain had bought their products during the war to finance the war effort without having exports to send in return, the United Kingdom was in danger of a major default.

The new Labour government therefore sent Keynes to Washington to negotiate a substantial dollar loan from the United States together with a smaller one from the government of Canada. This loan agreement was finally accepted by the United States Congress. The terms were onerous, one currency could only be exchanged for another under strict control. The loan required almost immediate convertibility of sterling, into other currencies without government restrictions, as a condition for its acceptance. The loan arrived in 1946, at the same time as Germany and other European countries were presenting the United States and the United Kingdom governments enormous problems of financing their imports. Once the pound was declared convertible, the entire dollar loan disappeared in exchange speculations. The United Kingdom was therefore forced immediately to suspend convertibility, but by this time the Marshall Aid negotiations for a European mutual aid programme underwritten by the United States and Canada were under way. Had these occurred a year earlier, the loan need never have been lost. And had the Bretton Woods system been different, there need never have been a Marshall Plan.

The speed with which countries recovered drew attention to the fundamental fact that a crucial element in modern economic growth is technological knowledge. Provided there can be a sufficient adjustment in the way in which countries are managed and governed, then output can recover dramatically. Germany and Japan, which suffered severe capital and population losses, had by 1950 restored their pre-war output levels. This was even true of the

Soviet Union despite its social and economic structure which was unsuited to high levels of economic growth.

It followed, logically, that output was a function of existing capital, which could be adapted with ingenuity, and the labour force. Once demand was restored, and that demand could express itself through the market, the activities of entrepreneurs, farmers and managers ensured that output levels would in general reach as high a level as they could, which was in many cases above the 1938 levels.

Post-war economic experience therefore showed that when the most elementary transport and market mechanisms were re-established – bailey bridges and local food markets, and above all a reasonably sound currency – the economy demonstrated astonishing recuperative powers. The great capacity of mankind for improvisation and adaptability, in the face of extraordinary devastation and shortages, enabled output to be restored in agriculture and in some parts of industry with a speed which invalidated the pessimistic estimates of the experts. It was argued by economists in Britain, for example, that the shortage of animal fats was permanent, so the world would have to live on margarine made from monkey (ground) nuts. Consequently expensive programmes were set up to grow nuts in Africa. Those few nuts that were eventually grown were thrown on a market groaning with butter.

By 1948 much of the more devastated areas of the world had achieved or exceeded their 1938 levels of output, even if the restoration of damaged houses and buildings took far longer. Furthermore, the recovery was not only rapid and complete, but the pre-war conditions of widespread depression and unemployment were overcome and astonishing technological advances began to be made, in consumer goods such as cars, radio and television sets and domestic appliances, in pharmaceuticals, and in producers' goods. Within a very few years Europe was bound on a course that was to take it to unparalleled heights of prosperity.

What remained to be explained was the fact that though the recovery was widespread its consequences were not a uniform rate of growth after the immediate post-war period. As will be seen, some countries exploded into high rates of growth, whilst others lagged behind. The initial effort of the restoration of the normal working of markets was rapidly to restore the world to the state it had been in 1939. Those that grew fastest were those that adopted non-Marxist policies. But the belief was widespread, in 1945 and later, that only Marxist planning could save the world from the failures of capitalism which, it was argued, had created the collapse of 1931 from which the war had itself emerged.

Chapter 5

The Soviet Union revives terror

Marxist planning demands that societies be completely controlled from the centre, a system which seems only capable of being sustained by terror. As all checks and balances, all institutions and independent power bases are removed, it is difficult later on ever to liberalise such societies in any way: to relax the iron grip of a rigid authoritarian regime is like taking the spine out of a vertebrate animal and expecting it to walk upright.

In order to understand Stalin's behaviour within the Soviet Union, towards the satellite states and towards the West, and to comprehend later problems faced by his successors, it is essential to recognise certain facets of Communism clearly, in particular its tyrannical nature, its deep fear of democracy, capitalism and Fascism, and above all to comprehend the inherent problems created by extreme central control.

Marxism, as developed by Marx and Engels, is a product of the Western European enlightenment. Like Darwinism and natural science, liberalism and the Western social sciences, Marxism is part of the intellectual search to understand the world by logical processes, itself the outcome of the enlightenment. As in other physical and social sciences, it had practical outcomes as well as intellectual understanding as its aim. Its practitioners – like many scientists – wished to understand the world in order to change it.

Intellectually, however, it is to be distinguished from those physical and social sciences characteristic of Western civilisation since the Renaissance by two special qualities. It is based upon Hegel's idea of alternation – of swings between opposites – rather than upon the idea that nature is a continuum (the adage that nature does not make jumps is basic to scientific ideas), and it is also apocalyptic. In this sense Marxism draws attention to polarising issues in society, rather than to what people and groups have in common. Its theme is revolution and not reform. That its history in power has been one of oppression is no accident since the aim set for a Marxist society is achieved by the dictatorship of the proletariat which in turn is exercised by the Communist party, the conscious and organised instrument of the working class.

The key elements of Marxism were its belief in an immanent historical process, the dialectic, whereby history revealed an inner purpose. This was the emergence of a classless society from a history of class struggle, which had itself developed from a materialist base; history was ultimately determined by the technological conditions of production. All other social relations were a superstructure erected on this economic base. Each class had a historical purpose; once that purpose was fulfilled, the class was destroyed by its successor. Thus the capitalists had a function, which was to create capital. This they did by accumulating the surplus value created by the working class. The capitalist system was so designed that it could lead to mass production, but not to sufficient consumption. The function of the working class was to overthrow the capitalists and adapt the processes of mass production to mass consumption.

At each stage of the historical process a struggle took place between the controlling class and its oppressed successor-to-be. These struggles – the English Civil War, the French Revolution – formed the stuff of political history. What was contingent had to be separated from what was essential; and the essential was not the passion and personalities of political strife, but the structure of class relationships. It was inevitable that the capitalist class would decline, and decline with a struggle, and that the working class should succeed. But there would be many eddies on the way.

The working class, Marx argued, would organise itself in trade unions and political groups which would overthrow the capitalists. Lenin argued that in the process of defending their power the capitalists would form monopolies which would dominate nation states, and from these nation states create empires. Imperialism was the process by which the capitalists found ever-cheaper labour, more markets for their produce, and raw materials. The struggle of the imperialists, of which the First World War was characteristic, took the form of struggles between empires.

Lenin further argued that the working class would succeed to power by the process of the dictatorship of the proletariat. This would be by means of the conscious and organised section of the workers, organised by the Communist party (the Bolshevik section). It was on this basis that power was seized in Petrograd in October 1917 and the Soviet Union was born.

The Soviet Union was organised on a centralised basis, with all power in the hands of the Communist party which was in turn dominated by the Politburo and its General Secretary. According to George Leggett's The Cheka (1981) Lenin ordered in 1918 'apply mass terror immediately'. Fourteen million people died between 1917 and 1922 in the Civil War and the Terror. After Stalin's assumption of power, the land was collectivised and all industrial production was nationalised; the entire state in all its aspects – economic, social, political – was tightly controlled by the Communist party. From 1930 onwards Stalin turned this system into a personal despotism, deliberately creating a famine in the Ukraine, culminating in the great purges and show trials in which many thousands died, and millions were sent to forced labour in the camps of the gulag. As the Polish philosopher Kolakowski argues, 'The object of a totalitarian system is to destroy all forms of communal life that were not imposed by the state and closely controlled by it, so that individuals are isolated from one another and become mere instruments in the hands of the state.' Stalin's great purge, probably without parallel in the history of the Western world and unequalled until the Marxist conquest of China ten years later, weakened the Soviet Union in the early years of the war but, once the war was over, ensured that Stalin had virtually no opposition at home. At any one time, Solzhenitsyn suggests, perhaps ten million or more people were in the gulag, desperately oppressed.

Leninism was a cruel philosophy and its implementation was bloodthirsty. The suffering involved in the Civil War, the turmoil that followed it, the elimination of the bourgeoisie, Stalin's murder of the Kulaks (the land-owning peasants) – these events were so horrific that they defy description. The numbers of people murdered and imprisoned were so great that they seemed then – and seem now – unbelievable. The population of the Soviet Union was around one hundred and eighty million in the 1930s. Over five million peasants were driven off the land in that dreadful decade, and many, many died, of starvation and worse.

Wholesale removal of all opposition made the population of the Soviet Union extremely docile and Stalin saw to it that they remained quiescent. Much information has now come out of the Soviet Union as to the number he had killed, imprisoned and deported to Siberia, which was not known in the 1940s. The numbers are so great they are difficult at first to take in but the following details are drawn from standard sources, from Khruschev's denunciation of Stalin in 1956, from Khruschev's own memoirs, from Count Nikolai Tolstoy, from the writings of Solzhenitsyn, Akhmatova, Natalia Ginsberg and others.

It is now clear that virtually the whole of Siberia from the Urals to Vladivostok was a series of slave camps, and so was northern European Russia. (That is roughly equivalent to the whole of Canada.) In 1941 perhaps a quarter of the Soviet labour force were slaves, men separated from their women, women from their children, and the children also working as slaves, dropping dead in the Siberian cold, tortured, starved.

In 1936 there were one million political prisoners. In 1937 and 1938 seven million prisoners were added in the Great Purge. By 1940, eleven to fifteen million people were in the gulag, according to NKVD estimates confirmed by Khruschev in 1956. Some estimates by prisoners suggest eighteen to twenty-five million, but these are probably too high *because they do not make enough allowances for death*. By 1953, when Stalin died, twelve million people had died in the gulag, of whom three million had died in the Kolyma gold fields. In Kolyma, there were never fewer than 500,000 slaves, of whom one fifth died annually; in 1950, when it looked as though the American army fighting in Korea might invade Siberia, Stalin ordered plans to be made ready for one million slaves at Kolyma to be murdered.

Many hundreds of thousands of Russians, Poles and people from the Baltic states had fled from Russia from 1917 onwards, settling all over Europe. During the Second World War about seven or eight million people were brought from Poland and Russia into Western Europe by the Germans as prisoners of war and forced labour or, in a few cases, as volunteers to fight against the Soviet Union and its allies. At Yalta it was agreed that all these nationals should be repatriated. In the case of the Soviet Union this was not as simple as it seemed. Many nationals had left the USSR as refugees or emigrants in 1941. Others came from Poland and the Baltic States and did not therefore believe themselves to be Soviet citizens. Furthermore the Soviet authorities regarded all their prisoners of war as traitors.

Thus the seven million original prisoners in the gulag by 1938 were strengthened by one to one and a half million Poles arrested when the USSR invaded Poland in 1939 – that is out of a population of twelve million. In Latvia, two per cent of the population was arrested as the Soviet army arrived in 1940. Five and a quarter million Soviet prisoners – many of whom had fled before 1921 – were sent to the gulag after being released from Western and Central Europe; two and a quarter million were forcibly repatriated by the British and Americans in 1945 and 1946. These people were assembled for interrogation by the Soviet secret police, and although some returned voluntarily, they met the same fate as those liberated by the Soviet troops; some were even shot within the hearing of British and American troops on the zonal borders. Many prisoners refused to be repatriated. It was widely assumed at first that these were all people who had collaborated with the Nazis, as the Russians asserted. The American authorities soon realised, however, that the people were victims – often pre-war émigrés, or Poles, or people who had suffered bitterly under Stalin. The Americans therefore slowed up the repatriation of the 'displaced persons' to whom the Soviet authorities laid claim. The British Foreign Office, however, adhered to the letter of the Yalta agreement and well into 1946 insisted on sending convoys of people to the Soviet zones of Germany and Austria, despite mutinies, suicides, desperate appeals and clear evidence. According to Count Nikolai Tolstoy more than two million people were murdered or sent to the gulag. The names of the British officials who insisted on this policy are known. Anthony Eden, Foreign Secretary until the 1945 election, believed in not offending the Soviet Union at any cost to individuals, lest the wartime alliance be broken.

To summarise the wartime losses is difficult, but it is known that the Germans killed four and a half million Soviet troops; the NKVD killed three million of their own troops. Of the twenty-two and a half million Soviet civilians who died, four million were killed by the Germans, seven million were killed in the gulag, and four million minority groups (Volga Germans, Karelians, Ukrainians) were deported, most of whom died. How the remaining seven and a half million people died is anybody's guess.

That roughly was the price of Stalinism.

At the end of the war Stalin sealed off the Soviet Union from the rest of the world, not even allowing contacts with Eastern Europe, except by a very few party officials, many of whom were subsequently purged. Eastern Europe was in turn isolated from the West. This double *cordon sanitaire* screened a major development of terror within the Soviet Union, which was not subjected to any criticism within the Eastern bloc nor reported abroad as most of the potential critics had been eliminated and the rest were silenced.

Before going on to deal with life in the Soviet Union under Stalin, I would like briefly to discuss some problems which his behaviour posed. Knowing what we do now about Stalin's tyranny, it is difficult for us to understand how so many people at the time thought that he was 'a good thing', how others saw him as less evil than Hitler and how many intelligent people in the Western democracies were immensely impressed with both him and his ideas.

Abroad, Stalin had enormous numbers of supporters, 'a remarkable triumph of doctrinaire ideology over commonsense and the critical instinct', as Kolakowski indulgently observes. 'Hypocrisy and self-delusion had become the permanent climate of the intellectual Left.' In reality, 'By the end of the 1930s Marxism had

taken on a clearly defined form as the doctrine of the Soviet party
and state. Its official name was Marxism–Leninism, which . . .
meant nothing more or less than Stalin's personal ideology.'

What was the source then of the delusion that Stalinism was
good? It was the power of *a priori* reasoning. In a Socialist society,
it was said, there was no exploitation and all work was for the
common weal. There was no unemployment – a powerful point
after the depression of the 1930s – no starvation and no one went
without a roof over their head: it was a working man's paradise.
Conditions might at first be meagre but they were fairly shared.
Moreover under Socialism there would be no more wars, for wars
were fomented by capitalists who made money creating armaments, by conquering foreign markets and sources of raw materials
for profit. The war just ended had been against Fascism and
Fascism was the ultimate evil. This war had been won by the Red
Army: Socialism had triumphed.

Fascism was a word which accumulated many meanings. Originally it came from the emblems of Mussolini's party in Italy – the
fasces – and represented the authority of the state. Later the
concept was extended to include the Nazi party in Germany and
Franco's Nationalists in Spain. When Japan joined in the war, it
too, was described as a Fascist power. Eventually it was debased to
mean any authoritarian or right-wing party. But there was a
common link: that the state or party concerned had earned the
enmity of the Communists and their allies. The Communists
advanced the theory that Fascism represented the culmination of
monopoly capitalism and that the objective function of the Fascist
parties was to protect the interests of the big capitalists and
landowners. They pursued a strong nationalist policy, it was
argued, to secure the support of the army and the police, and to
bemuse the working class. The state's power was used to abolish
the autonomous institutions of the workers, especially trade unions and Socialist parties. This enabled the employers to use cheap
labour without opposition. And the power of the state could be
used for aggressive foreign policy, to conquer colonies, to attack
Socialist countries such as the USSR, and to attack each other.
According to Communist ideology the outbreak of the Second
World War was caused by the proliferation of Fascist parties, as
monopoly capitalists tried to put the clock back. The Fascists had
then begun to conquer other countries, as Italy conquered
Ethiopia in 1936, and to wage civil war to suppress left-wing
movements, as in Spain in 1936–9. Then the capitalist civil war had
turned into an attack on the Socialist sixth of the world.

Intelligent people had seen with their own eyes the emergence of authoritarian regimes in Spain, Italy and Germany, the sheer wickedness of which had seemed to dwarf the 'problems' of the USSR. They had moreover seen Socialism conquer these Fascist regimes and had seen Socialists fight alongside Americans and British. Co-operation was possible with the USSR and now a better, more equal, more prosperous world was about to be ushered in with a shift towards Socialism. Russia offered the proof that Socialism could be made to work, for Stalin had not only overpowered the Nazis but he had succeeded in raising Soviet industrial output to its pre-war levels by 1949, followed by a fifty per cent rise by 1953, even if slave-type labour had been involved. Many Western intellectuals hoped that once the USSR was freed of her enemies and had overcome the difficulties of achieving social and economic reform, then universal peace would soften Stalin into becoming constructive and less oppressive.

To some intellectuals therefore the Soviet Union, however imperfect, was identified with their concept of Socialism. To others, evidently the majority in Western Europe, the idea of Socialism was more that of Social Democracy in which constitutional government, a diversity of political parties, personal freedom and a welfare state were combined with economic prosperity achieved by state planning. To both, the idealised version of Soviet society understandably exercised great fascination. The Soviet Union had unquestionably played the major part in the defeat of Germany. And, according to the propaganda, Russia was striving for prosperity and equality in its own society within a world order of peace and freedom. Stalin, at worst, was breaking eggs to make an omelette: Whatever cruelty he might practise now, Communism offered hope.

The concentrated propaganda of the USSR deceived many people as to the true nature of its society, subsequently admitted by Khruschev in his denunciation of Stalin at the Twentieth Congress of the Soviet Communist party in 1956 and in his memoirs. Moreover there was a predisposition in the left wing in allied countries in favour of the Soviet Union because of its heroic war effort, and because of its claims to represent true Socialism. There were plenty of Communists, some open and some concealed, in non-Communist countries; in France and Italy they were the main opposition parties, and they had provided a focus (after 1941) for the resistance elsewhere. The attractions of Communism were that it claimed the loyalty of the working class. In Germany and France its claims antedated the Soviet revolution. Marxism as a doctrine was subtle and sophisticated. Fascism was seen as the 'real' enemy. And the 'excesses' in the Soviet Union could be explained away, if they were admitted at all, as the consequences of enthusiasm rather than ill intent.

Even so, it was widely known in the West that oppression in Eastern Europe was growing – though it had some redeeming features: non-controversial culture flourished, for example, and basic education was developed. But the degree to which Marxism was freely adopted as an ideology in the West, especially in France and Italy, was notable. Stalinism may have been regarded as an aberration, but many distinguished people – Joliot-Curie, Bernal, Eluard, Aragon, Sartre – were its ardent supporters. And, though after Stalin's death the more outrageous aspects of his regime were modified, Communism became a potent factor in non-European countries despite the known oppression in the Soviet Union.

In the immediate post-war period Stalin consolidated his power, to a considerable degree that of an arbitrary tyrant, but ruling through a tried and trusted band of supporters – Molotov, Voroshilov, Kaganovitch, Mikoyan, Andreev, Zhdanov, Malenkov, Beria and Bulganin – all linked by a common ideological training and united for absolutism. Beria, as head of the secret police, was the most feared of Stalin's group in Russia itself, whilst Molotov spoke for Stalin in foreign affairs.

Molotov's face on newsreels and his apparent implacable hostility to the West soon made him the best-known Russian abroad. He came to embody the quality of denial – his repeated *nyet* at the United Nations especially – of humane and liberal values that the war had ostensibly been fought for.

Immediately after the end of the war the marshals and generals who had been popular heroes were quietly removed from office and their names disappeared from the press and the radio. Meanwhile Stalin set about reconstructing the Communist party, which had been allowed to increase its membership and so dilute and diminish in authority and ideological purity during the war. As new recruits were brought in, so older, less reliable people were removed.

The armed forces were maintained at high strength, but the officer class was purged, as were soldiers who had served in occupied Germany and Austria and were possibly contaminated by bourgeois envy as a result. Zhukov, the marshal who had captured Berlin, was exiled to the provinces. Stalin thus cemented his hold on the military machine, preventing it from exploiting the power and prestige it had gained in the war.

While Molotov was implacable abroad, soon after the war a major purge, known as the Leningrad affair, signalled the revival of the Terror; this purge led to promotion for Malenkov, while

Khruschev, who was firmly based on the Ukraine, also rose in importance. As they were to be Stalin's successors, it was in this period that they cemented their hold on the party organisation. But like any tyrant, Stalin was frequently capricious in the way that he moved people about, demoting some and promoting others, while, frequently, execution followed a spectacular disgrace.

Andrei Zhdanov conducted a purge of all intellectuals and officials, which reached the scale of the great pre-war purge, and until his death in the summer of 1948 he managed to eliminate almost all possible opposition to Stalin's authority.

In the first year after the war, Stalin concentrated on eliminating opposition within the enlarged Soviet Union. Yet he was also beginning systematically to purge the occupied countries of Eastern Europe, where private enterprise existed and non-Communist parties survived in the governments.

In the states that had fallen under Soviet rule, Stalin imposed regimes that were ideologically identical to his own, and linked to it through the successor to the Comintern (Communist International). The Marxist–Leninist doctrine was revised, indeed turned upside down, so that revolution could be imposed from above, and economic transformation would follow the political changes. This was a logical corollary of Stalin's convenient doctrine that Socialism could be built in one country; and the doctrine, extended to the People's Democracies, was promulgated as the exact opposite of what Trotsky, the apostle of permanent international revolution, had stood for. Stalin's doctrines were enthusiastically endorsed by the Nineteenth Congress of the Communist party of the Soviet Union, in 1952; and Trotsky was persistently defined as the enemy. Curiously enough, Stalin's doctrines were compatible with the co-existence in the world of different social systems. If he were left free to do as he wished in the East, then the West was also free to do as it thought fit in its own sphere. Paradoxically this ultimately converted the Communist party into a co-operative rather than a disruptive force in Western Europe, a fact but dimly seen at the time.

Stalin's *Economic Problems of Socialism* became a basic text, in which he sought to rival Marx and Lenin as an original Socialist thinker of great stature. What then was Stalinism? It was partly personal terror, but it was far more – a culmination of the doctrine of Socialism in one country, or rather one empire, and the essence of a totalitarianism never seen on such a scale before.

Immediately after the war Stalin decided not to accept or request Western aid for the reconstruction of his country, but to insist upon reparations in enormous quantities from Germany and its other defeated allies, and at the same time to impose a forcible holding down of the Soviet standard of living while industry was completely reconstructed.

On 9 February 1946 Stalin announced the first post-war Five-Year Plan as part of a fifteen-year prospective, which was to raise the output of steel to sixty million tons a year, of coal to five hundred million tons, and of oil to sixty million tons. Heavy industry was the priority, with the total reconstruction of steel, largely based upon plant brought from Germany and other occupied countries. He was surprisingly successful, for by 1950 output was over 40 per cent above 1940 levels.

He was not able to be so ebullient about his agricultural plans for yield on the farms continued to remain low. There was a shortage of labour, especially of able-bodied men; most of the crops grown were forcibly removed by the state to feed those in the towns, leaving the peasants starving; nor was there any incentive for the farm labourers to work hard since there was no market economy and they received little recompense for their efforts. It was very like the situation in France and Germany immediately after the war when official price controls operated; the system worked on quotas and targets which were frequently set too high. Even if, for example, the people in the towns wanted more eggs and indeed the peasants' hens could lay them, the peasants were not allowed to sell more than their quota nor to obtain more money for them so there was no incentive to produce more. Moreover if the peasant had produced more and gained extra money, he would have been denounced as a kulak and punished severely. With no interplay between supply and demand, output dwindled. Khruschev, who was in charge of agriculture at this time, now put together larger and larger farming units and then herded the villagers into bigger and bigger 'agro towns' which they loathed. The farmers had always hated collectivisation and now Khruschev had increased the size of the units still further, making them even more unwieldy. Collectivised farming was a political principle; even when it did not seem effective, it could not be changed because it was a matter of basic Soviet dogma. Large-scale farming methods can of course be efficient, as in Canada, but they must be backed by equally large investment in roads, combines, pesticides, fertiliser, silos and machinery. The Soviet Union preferred to invest in heavy industry. This lack of capital spending in farming, coupled with general inefficiency from badly run impersonal state bodies, lack of open-market economy, added to the obsession with political dogma to make Soviet agriculture a disaster. By the end of 1946, farming had virtually collapsed and the peasants were struggling to feed themselves. This agricultural disaster scenario was to be met with again and again under Communism, both in the Soviet Union and in the satellite countries.

Towards the end of the 1940s the rift between America and the Soviet Union increased, culminating in the Cold War. Much of Stalin's behaviour sprang from a genuine fear of Western aggression for he was a paranoid Communist who thought that the class struggle was the reality of history, and that his Soviet Union embodied the values of the workers which the capitalists wished to destroy. He considered democracy a sham, a facade behind which capitalists oppressed workers and encouraged Fascism.

Stalin reasoned that the German capitalists had taken over Germany in 1933 and, supported by other capitalist states, had all along decided to attack the USSR. Repulsed in 1946, the Nazi baton had now been handed on to the Americans and the British who, in turn, were bound to attack the Soviet Union. So he wanted to create a strong workers' movement in the West, to defeat the recrudescence of Fascism. He wanted to establish defence in depth for the Socialist heartland by creating a series of client states across Eastern Europe. He had to eradicate counter-revolution at home by keeping revolutionary terror at fever pitch. And, he hoped, perhaps cynically, to try to establish some sort of *modus vivendi* with Western states, in the hope that they might attack each other before they attacked Russia. All these strands of policy had been adopted in the 1930s and could be seen in the twists and turns of his behaviour – in 1938 supporting the Popular Front and an anti-Nazi alliance, and in 1939 signing the Nazi–Soviet pact – which was based on the Marxist analysis of a Socialist society in a capitalist world.

Stalin did genuinely fear the West: the West's fear of Stalin was equally real. The Cold War was seen by each side to be the result of the other's intransigence. Stalin had lost more than the other allies in the war, and he feared the resurrection of a united Germany. He had wanted reparations from the whole of Germany, not just his zone, and he felt that his original demands had been scaled down. He thought that Poland had been securely put in the Soviet bloc at Yalta; since he needed a loyal government there, sympathetic to him, he could not understand why the allies wished to interfere. The Americans now had the atom bomb and as far as he could see they were becoming increasingly belligerent, interfering and awkward. Nor had they kept to the spirit of Potsdam and Yalta as he remembered it. The West was alarmed by Stalin's hard line in the satellite states, by his refusal to hold democratic elections and by his twisting and turning over Poland. They saw too his huge standing army: that force that had overpowered Nazi Germany. Molotov said *nyet* at every suggestion in the UN and the iron curtain had come down like a shutter from Stettin in the Baltic to Trieste in the Adriatic.

Some historians thought that the Cold War struggle was ideological, others saw it as a matter of power politics: both sides negotiating hard for their own interests: six of one, half a dozen of the other. But this view discounts the genuine idealism of Britain, America and the liberated countries for a new world order based upon the acceptance of universal libertarian principles in which prosperity could be created by the use of science and technology, inside a system of universal government in which war and violence were unthinkable. The West was preoccupied with reconstruction, it genuinely wanted to disarm as soon as possible.

But as Stalinist oppression was shamelessly revealed throughout Eastern Europe, culminating in the Czech coup of 1948, and as Molotov blocked all attempts at four-power agreement on Germany, and the Greek civil war was fought with Soviet help for the Communists, it seemed that Russia was poised to strike at the West.

The Americans took so much and then responded with the Truman Doctrine, promulgated on 12 March 1947, in which President Truman took over from Britain the protection of Greece and Turkey and announced a general defence of the Western world from Soviet attack. One immediate result was the sudden end of the Foreign Ministers' conference which had begun in Moscow only two days before. It dispersed immediately, and Stalin intensified the purge throughout Eastern Europe. The Polish, Hungarian, German, Romanian, Yugoslav and Czech opposition was eliminated, culminating in a series of show trials in which even former faithful members of the Communist party were put on trial and executed. In September 1947 the Cominform was founded under the leadership of Zhdanov and Malenkov, who organised the Soviet sphere; meanwhile the French and Italian Communist parties were formally denounced for having served in coalition governments in their countries at the end of the war: they must withdraw from any participation in government from now on.

By this time, Stalin was apparently convinced that the West was likely to attack Russia. He explained the need to defend Socialism by reconstructing Eastern Europe on Russian lines, and by seeking a conflict within Western countries between the capitalists and the workers. All Western diplomacy was directed (in his eyes) at undermining Socialism in the USSR. The idea of co-operation in reconstruction seemed a Trojan horse whereby capitalism would infiltrate the Socialist world.

Stalin rejected the American offer of participation in the Marshall Plan for the reconstruction of Europe and insisted that his dependent countries should take no part. The demobilisation of the Soviet army from eleven and a half million to less than three million men was reversed, with a peacetime level fixed at five and a half million. This in turn slowed up Soviet efforts for economic recovery. Stalin organised a massive supply of goods and services to Russia from the occupied countries by the creation of Soviet-dominated 'joint stock companies', in which Hungary, Romania and Bulgaria exchanged shoddy Russian goods and worthless credits for food and raw materials, while reparations in kind from Hungary, from former German territories now included in Poland and Czechoslovakia, and from East Germany were substantial.

The collapse of the standard of living in Eastern Europe was dramatic, even for those countries which had been severely occupied by the Germans, and at the same time the purge reached new heights. The most persistent opposition was in Czechoslovakia, where Edouard Beneš was President and Jan Masaryk was the Foreign Minister. The Czech Communist party evicted the bourgeois members of the government, and Masaryk was almost certainly murdered. The process by which the Eastern empire was consolidated was one which revealed Stalinism as naked terror in a form as pure as that of the Great Purge of 1937.

To sum up: under Stalin, the centripetal nature of Communism was intensified into tyrannical despotism. At the time the extreme barbarity of his rule was not appreciated and many in the West swallowed Soviet propaganda, believing Communism to be a lesser evil than Fascism or Nazism, even an ultimate form for potential good. Others judged Soviet behaviour by what they saw: the arms build-up, the tough line on the satellite countries, and they were afraid. On his side Stalin feared a revival of Germany, he distrusted Western interference to his sphere of influence and he felt that the allies had not been consistent since Yalta and Potsdam over Poland, Berlin, German reparations or dismemberment. Truman's slow shift away from Roosevelt's pro-Stalin views fed Stalin's paranoia.

Chapter 6

The generous victor: America under Truman

The conditions of Russia and America at the end of the Second World War could hardly have shown a greater contrast. The war had revitalised an American society drained by the slump in the 1930s, bringing prosperity, excitement and recovery. With peace, the GIs came back and went to college, married and had large families – the baby boom was symbolic of the recovery of optimism. America went headlong into prosperity; automobile production soared, television spread quickly across the country, new houses, new refrigerators, dishwashers, new fashions based on new materials (of which nylon stockings were the exemplar), new music like that of *Oklahoma*, or songs sung by Frank Sinatra, new movies, all created an American culture which swept the world. It was this prosperity, this 'get up and go' which impressed young foreigners, which created a zest for emulation in West Germany and a profound distaste among the French intellectuals. Yet from these early roots of emulation, envy and spite sprang the later ambivalence about America. In the 1930s it had been fashionable to admire American modernism; in the 1950s to be pro-American was a sign of cultural helotism. The world wanted American abundance and material success, but claimed that it did not want to be Americanised.

At home President Truman faced considerable opposition. Left-wing opinion wanted a high-spending domestic economy like the New Deal to create prosperity because they feared that the end of the war would mean a slump. Businessmen wanted the federal government off their backs for they knew good times were just around the corner if only they had a free-market economy. The liberals wished to keep America involved in international affairs and many of these people preferred the Soviet Union to imperialist Britain. Others wished America to be preoccupied with America and to eschew complex foreign involvements. The Republicans, led by Senator Vandenberg, were anti-Soviet and indeed Truman himself was slowly shifting away from Roosevelt's pro-Stalin views as he watched what was happening in Eastern Europe. But it would be a mistake to think that the United States' shift from a pro-Soviet

Union stance to an anti one, was either monolithic or sudden.

America had been the European left-wing ideal for over a hundred years, after 1776, since it combined political equality with economic prosperity for the Europeans who settled there. But the growth of great capitalist empires had darkened this picture, and created a demonology of Rockefeller and Vanderbilt, which culminated, in the slump of 1929–33, in a reinterpretation of America as the capitalist heartland, as the very focal point of capitalist aggression and suppression.

In America itself, however, politics were not polarised on a class basis as they were widely in Europe, and the myth of America as the classless society full of opportunity continued to be accepted and was not replaced by a Marxist or quasi-Marxist analysis of America's economic, social and political problems. Roosevelt was a classic liberal, and it was he who emerged in 1933 as the popular (and populist) hero. Despite the problems of unemployment, poverty and the position of the blacks and other marginal groups like the Hispanics, there was no great move to Socialist ideas. The 1920s did see, however, the emergence of the Jewish community as the intellectual leaders of America. Anti-Semitism became a central question, and the persecution of the European Jews gave American Jews a profound concern with European affairs not shared by most other ethnic groups. The explanation of anti-Semitism, the interpretation of the harshness of American society, led some intellectuals to one or other of two creeds founded by great Jewish thinkers – Marxism and Freudianism. Many intellectuals flirted with Marxism in the 1930s, and there was a powerful intellectual (but not political) commitment to Trotskyism in particular, rather than to Stalinism. But some people – from different ethnic backgrounds – became orthodox Communists, especially as the true nature of Hitler's Germany became apparent. The majority of American intellectuals, however, became Freudian, and trod the path that led to the couch rather than to Moscow. The call was for the fuller realisation of the self rather than the reform of society.

In America, therefore, there was little naïve pro-Socialist opinion within which Stalin's apologists could sustain consistently pro-Soviet arguments, once the wartime alliance had lost its *raison d'être* with the defeat of Hitler.

In November 1945 Truman's Secretary of State James Byrnes, Molotov and Ernest Bevin met in Moscow where they agreed to recognise the Hungarian Communist government as a prologue to an international peace conference of twenty-one nations which would settle the Eastern European question. Byrnes also agreed to an eleven-nation Far Eastern Commission to supervise General MacArthur's occupation of Japan. By Christmas however Truman and Bevin were convinced that Russia had no intention of allowing non-Communist governments to be elected by free democratic elections in Eastern Europe and they were also concerned that Soviet influence was spreading wider and wider. They feared that Stalin might move against Germany, Italy or France.

But Stalin felt that Eastern Europe was in his special sphere of influence so he interpreted the British and American call for free elections in all countries formerly occupied by Germany as interference, a blatant attempt to restore capitalism, and to destroy the Soviet Union.

On 6 March 1946 President Truman chaired a meeting at Fulton, Missouri, where Winston Churchill made a speech calling for Anglo–American co-operation in maintaining peace and freedom, and referred to the iron curtain that Stalin had drawn across Europe. Churchill and Truman were if anything understating their fears. They were, however, accused of beginning a Cold War.

In March 1946 Truman gave Stalin an ultimatum which resulted in Soviet withdrawal from northern Iran and stopped Soviet claims for control of the Dardanelles. Truman was accused of using his monopoly of the atom bomb for Cold-War purposes. In fact, Truman from the first insisted that atomic energy should be under civilian, not military, control and in June 1946 his Ambassador, Bernard Baruch, presented a plan for international control to the UN, which the Russians rejected because it removed the veto from the UN system.

Truman's policy was not universally approved in America. The Rooseveltians were staggered by the speed with which the Russians were being denounced. Indeed, the President was immediately confronted by Henry Wallace, a member of his Cabinet as Secretary of Commerce, and the man designated by Eleanor Roosevelt as F.D.R.'s political heir. Wallace argued that the Russians were negotiating from weakness, not from strength, and that they should be given substantial economic aid. He made a speech along those lines, attacking Byrnes' foreign policy, at Madison Square Garden in New York City in September 1946. This made him a focus for left-wing and liberal support, including the majority of New Dealers, and most prominently Eleanor Roosevelt herself. The consequent split in the Democratic party was a major factor in the party's big defeat in the 1946 Congressional elections. 'The tougher we get, the tougher the Russians will get,' Wallace said, and he urged that Eastern Europe be left as a Russian sphere of influence. Truman had cleared the speech before it had been delivered, probably carelessly, and he paid the price. If America's allies, not to speak of the Republican leader, Senator Vandenberg, as well as the rest of Truman's Cabinet, were dismayed, the Social Democrats in Europe, seeing the steady liquidation of their colleagues in the Soviet zones, were appalled. It appeared that Truman was unaware of his own foreign policy and had no mind of his own.

With the United Nations conference still in session in Paris this was especially distressing. Wallace was therefore dismissed. Truman, Byrnes and Vandenberg were united in a hard-line, anti-Soviet policy and not prepared to propitiate Wallace, Mrs Roosevelt and the New Dealers. As a result the liberals broke away from Truman who, in their view, was the originator of the Cold War. At the same time, domestically, Truman moved to free the economy by abolishing most of the wartime price controls. The result was a further split in the Democratic party, a number of people holding the view that the only way to prevent a post-war slump was to keep the economy tightly controlled. After these splits the Democrats suffered a severe defeat in the November election. As Truman had no electoral mandate, except as Roosevelt's Vice-President, there were demands for Truman's resignation in favour of a Republican Secretary of State, who would be appointed by Truman after consultation with the Republican Congressional leadership. Truman while offering a tough face abroad was incredibly weak at home, with the Republicans electorally strong and his own party split.

Wallace formed the Progessive Citizens of America, as the basis of a third party to run against Truman in the 1948 Presidential election. But it was infiltrated strongly by fellow-travellers, a name given to pro-Communist liberals. At the same time many New Dealers, led by Chester Bowles, a publisher, later Governor of Connecticut and Ambassador to India, formed Americans for Democratic Action, with the aim of shifting the Democratic party to the left, to keep it true to the New Deal, and to moderate the incipient Cold War. Although this programme was presented as President Roosevelt's legacy, it is always a danger to speculate what dead men might have said, and nowhere more than when circumstances have deeply changed.

Despite these liberal moves, a basic tide of anti-Communism was rising in America, and rising fast, as Molotov's hysterically anti-American performance at international meetings continued and as the evidence of Soviet repression and infiltration accumulated. In March 1947 President Truman imposed loyalty tests in the civil service, to expose Communists. A major Canadian spy case

had revealed, by the defection of Gouzenko, a counsellor at the
Soviet embassy in Ottawa, a network of Soviet spies in Canada
extending through the United States and Great Britain, and as the
Hiss, Rosenberg, Blunt, Maclean and Burgess cases were gradually to show the Canadian report was, if anything, an understatement. Nevertheless the attempt to unmask spies was presented by
the left as profoundly illiberal.

In September 1947 Congress passed the National Security Act,
which created two new and powerful organisations, a Combined
Chiefs of Staff, and the Central Intelligence Agency (CIA), which
took over the functions of the wartime Office of Strategic Services.
The Secretary of the Navy, James Forrestal, who was made the first
Secretary of Defense, had a deeply depressed view of the American position in the world and he, too, was regarded, like Marshall,
as a 'hawk' in the Cabinet. His depression became so severe that he
committed suicide by jumping from a window, leading to the
opinion that much anti-Communism was in fact paranoid in origin.

Even so, the United States made the decision to defend its
sphere of influence.

Though post-war demobilisation was swift there were still many
American divisions in Germany and Japan, in Italy and Korea;
American bombers were still based in Europe and Asia, and the
United States (above all) had its atomic forces. This made it
potentially very powerful, perhaps dominant; yet the disarray of
the United States armed forces was such as to leave Western
Europe apparently open to a major assault from the large, standing
Soviet army.

One of Truman's most important tasks was to create adequate
permanent post-war armed forces capable of defending the United
States and its allies. The separate arms of the services lobbied the
Congress in their own interests, although a unified system would
(in Truman's opinion) have led to a more efficient and economical
system. Permanent conscription, the draft, was to be maintained
indefinitely.

In early 1947 General George C. Marshall was appointed Secretary of State. His immense experience, culminating in his period as
Chief of Staff, made him the most powerful member of the
administration. Born in 1880 in Uniontown, Pennsylvania, he had
a brilliant career in the First World War, and in 1939 he became
Chief of the United States Army General Staff, which made him
very much senior to Eisenhower, who was a Colonel. He organised
the entire United States military war effort as Chairman of the
Joint Chiefs of Staff in Washington throughout the war, and on the
military side he was Roosevelt's right-hand man. After the end of

the war he went to China, seeking to mediate between Chiang Kai-shek and the Communists, but rapidly became aware that the Chiang Kai-shek forces were hopelessly demoralised and its government corrupt. Merely for reporting this fact he was labelled pro-Communist, yet he returned to the United States to become Secretary of State in succession to James Byrnes in January 1947.

In March 1947 the British, having supported the government of Greece militarily, and exercised a defensive role in the eastern Mediterranean, told Truman that they were unable, financially, to bear this burden any longer. Although about to withdraw from India, they were embroiled in Palestine, where American opinion was deeply pro-Jewish, and British policy basically pro-Arab.

Britain, which had played the major role in defending Southeast Asia, India, the Middle East and Western Europe, now found the responsibility beyond its resources, militarily, politically and above all financially. In consequence the United States was faced with the question of whether it could take over or at least reinforce the British task in the eastern Mediterranean.

The Greek and Turkish regimes were reactionary, and the British were unpopular in America, partly because they were regarded by Rooseveltians as colonialists but mainly because of Bevin's Palestine policy. An agonised choice was necessary. To stop Communism, it seemed, unpopular regimes had to be supported and unpopular policies adopted. The Greek and Turkish programmes of military and economic aid were announced by Truman on 12 March 1947, as a contribution to defence against Communist attempts to subvert the national independence of Greece and Turkey, and as part of a programme to defend the Middle East and Western Europe's free institutions.

This Truman Doctrine represented the end of the Roosevelt era, which culminated at Yalta, of attempting to collaborate with the Soviet Union. From 12 March 1947 onwards the emphasis was on containing the Soviet threat of expansion. It also represented the end of an attempt to use the United Nations as a forum for settling international differences, especially between the US and the USSR. This was the shift, within two years of Roosevelt's death, that shattered the American internationalists.

Here was the beginning of American involvement in a world-wide defensive alliance, even if it involved a paradox that was to haunt the post-war world. The regimes that formed part of the 'free world' were defined as such by their hostility to the Soviet Union and the Soviet Union's hostility to them. Yet, often, they were anything but liberal, as in Turkey and Greece where the regimes were electorally popular but too reactionary to suit Americans.

Nor could the governments throughout the Soviet sphere of influence have gained office in anything resembling a free election. But from world-wide propaganda it seemed that the Americans could only hold their own sphere by supporting reactionary governments, of which the military regimes in Latin America were to become the archetype.

The necessity for the Truman Doctrine emphasised the extent to which European countries – including France, Italy and Britain – had yet to recover and were still exposed to severe shortages, and hence to subversion and external threat. The fact that the British could not afford to support Greece and Turkey even though they had been allocated them at Yalta was one of the symptoms of the general malaise that led to the Marshall Plan. For although Truman was under attack by Wallace and Mrs Roosevelt for being fanatically anti-Communist, the Marshall Plan, which saved Western Europe, and Point Four, which saved India, pointed in exactly the opposite direction, since aid was offered to all countries whatever their regimes.

On 5 June 1947 Marshall made a speech at the Harvard Commencement calling for a co-operative effort to rebuild the shattered European economy, including the Soviet Union. He said that American 'assistance must not be a piecemeal basis as various crises would develop . . . [it] should provide a cure not a palliative . . .' It would require 'some agreement among the countries of Europe as to the requirements of the situation and the part those countries themselves will take . . . The initiative, I think, must come from Europe.'

This speech was seized on by Ernest Bevin and became the basis of the Marshall Plan for the reconstruction of Europe. Molotov came from Moscow to the summit meeting in Paris with the British and the French, and plainly regarded the plan as a plot. He doubted whether the United States would give enough money, or whether Congress would vote the credits. He also doubted whether the proposed plan was technically feasible. He left Paris on 3 July 1947, denouncing the Marshall Plan as a form of American imperialism disguising German revanchism. Shortly afterwards the Soviet Union announced that it would not participate on the grounds that it wanted bilateral aid from the US to each European state, and no discussion of investment decisions by states with each other or with the US.

An invitation to a conference in Paris was then extended by the United States to all European nations. Ultimately sixteen nations, including three neutrals (Portugal, Sweden and Ireland), and ex-enemies Austria and Italy, met from 12 July to 22 September

1947, to form the Committee for European Economic Co-operation. The Marshall Plan therefore became the nucleus of a Western alliance, based on the Organisation for European Economic Co-operation (OEEC), which reconstructed the Western European economy. Substantial United States aid was disbursed by the Organisation, on the basis of agreed plans between the agency and the recipient countries, and of the development of co-operation and mutual assistance. The United Kingdom, for example, granted as much aid to its European allies as it received from the United States.

The original idea advanced by the United States State Department was for short-term aid to eliminate critical European shortages of food, seed, coal and steel and a longer-term policy for European recovery. The scheme included the revival of the Ruhr's coal and steel production, a particularly critical issue. The hard winter of 1946–7 had revealed coal shortages all over Europe.

When Marshall made his Harvard speech, it was against a background of American preoccupation with the settlement of Germany. The Americans were giving substantial aid to the Germans while reparations were being paid to the French. The European response to Marshall's speech was, however, determined by the British wish for the creation of a multilateral lending agency – a version of the Keynes plan for the IMF which Harry Dexter White had torpedoed at Bretton Woods – and French long-term strategic planning as developed by Jean Monnet's Commissariat au Plan.

Under the guidance of Sir Oliver Franks and Robert Marjolin it was agreed at the Paris conference to increase production, to stabilise currencies and to enlarge co-operation. Free movement of goods and people was envisaged; a multilateral trading system with a settling of balances at the centre; a pooling of resources in steel and electricity; and specific targets for agriculture, coal, steel and electricity. The four-year programme was estimated first at $22 billion, but reduced to $17 billion all told.

The necessary legislation establishing the Economic Co-operation Administration (ECA) in Washington passed through Congress in the winter of 1947–8 with little opposition, but in the meantime, the plan began to operate from the Château de la Muette in Paris, with the creation of the Organisation for European Economic Co-operation. The European Payments Union formed a central bank for the participating countries and when a country fell severely into deficit, as Germany did in 1950, it recommended action to redress the deficit. The OEEC set up specialist teams which had expert knowledge and the authority that knowledge backed by money brings. The mechanism was simple. Money was placed in the OEEC by the American ECA, through its administrator Paul Hoffman, and a local account was established from which funds were disbursed on agreed projects. In turn, the local countries made their currencies available through EPU, for the acquisition of goods and services by other European countries.

The original OEEC target was the restoration of 1938 output levels. Austria, whose industrial production was at 75 in the second quarter of 1948 reached 99 a year later; Belgium increased from 114 to 119; Denmark stayed at 132; France increased from 115 to 129; Bizonia – the British and American zones of Germany – from 43 to 73; Greece from 71 to 90; Ireland from 138 to 144; Italy from 98 to 108; Netherlands from 110 to 121; Norway from 133 to 138; Sweden from 143 to 146; and UK from 128 to 137.5. Freight traffic on the railways in Europe rose by a third, and electricity output by two thirds. The bulk of American aid was raw materials and semi-finished products ($1.3 billion), and food, feed and fertiliser ($1.7 billion). The supply of machine tools for industrial re-equipment was small ($0.4 billion), though often crucial to particular industries.

The real problem was the shortage of dollars to buy food and raw materials. By 1948 the United Kingdom had covered its dollar imports by dollar exports, but every other country had a substantial deficit – amounting to $5.6 billion. This severe problem waned in 1948–9; and the achievement of high industrial and agricultural output was followed by a substantial growth of investment to modernise and re-equip Europe's economy. Thus by 1949 the OEEC programme moved on to efficiency and productivity in individual sectors, and the diminution of trade barriers and other obstacles to competition.

This, then, led to the economic recovery of Western Europe. It began one of the most spectacular economic and social advances of all time. Yet the Soviet threat – largely through troop movements in a still disorganised Europe – remained, intensified and became more sharply focused. These threats were first discerned from Soviet attitudes to the Foreign Ministers' meetings which followed Potsdam; by the proceedings at the United Nations, which turned into a series of confrontations; and by the Soviet blockade of Berlin in 1948 which led to the Berlin airlift of essential supplies to Berlin by the Royal Air Force and the United States Air Force.

The Russians' aim was to secure $10 billion in reparations from Germany and four-power control of the Ruhr. Denied both of these, they retreated to a defensive position in the Eastern zone, where the frenzied dismantling programme was continued, leaving East Germany dependent upon Western food and other supplies. So paramount were these Soviet objectives that they rejected a Western proposal for a treaty to forbid German rearmament for up to forty years. They even regarded the first Paris discussions as an attempt to take Germany away from them.

These Paris discussions also marked the decline in the potential influence of the United Nations, which was to have been a forum for all international diplomacy, with the national interests of member states subordinate to it. The United States rapidly lost confidence in it. UNRRA, largely financed by the US, was not controlled by America, yet financed Yugoslavia and Czechoslovakia even though Yugoslavia conducted an active anti-Western policy, supporting the Communist rebels in Greece, trying to annex Trieste and shooting down an American plane which violated its airspace. Following the March 1947 decision to give American aid to Greece and Turkey to replace British support, a United States foreign aid programme was developed, under American control, thereby superseding UNRRA. When this was combined with the aid to German Bizonia, the American funds for the Marshall Plan were available to be channelled into a new international agency, unlike the United Nations, substantially influenced by the Americans, acceptable to its members, and not containing a group of nations actively hostile to the US,

Mrs Roosevelt and others were especially shattered by this shift in world affairs. The shift was to a policy based upon a direct apprehension of America's interests rather than of a generalised idealism. Though how far those interests were the same as the interests of the West as a whole – and even more of a durable and lasting peace – was open to question, and was to cause the great difficulties of the 1950s.

At the same time, domestically, Truman moved to restore his liberal credentials, by cautiously beginning moves towards desegregation of the armed forces and other federal establishments, by preparing some civil rights legislation for blacks, and by vetoing the Taft–Hartley Act which the Eightieth Congress, elected in 1946, passed to regulate trade unions. Although his veto was overridden, it enabled Truman to claim to be a supporter of organised labour. So, too, did his opposition to the end of rent controls and to tax cuts, all legislation passed by Congress.

Meanwhile, throughout 1948, Henry Wallace rallied support across America for his opposition to Truman, and especially for his opposition to the Cold War. The Soviet Union, he held, was a peace-loving power being opposed by fanatical anti-Communists.

In June 1948 he proposed a summit meeting between Stalin and Truman to settle outstanding differences. This was at the height of a Soviet peace offensive, organised through student groups and other front bodies, which sought to label Truman as the war-monger and to present the Soviet Union as a peaceful power, concerned only with reconstruction, beleaguered by capitalist opponents. As the European economy recovered, this propaganda drew widespread support in France and Italy, where the left was largely Communist-controlled. In February 1948, however, the Russians staged a Communist coup in Czechoslovakia and Jan Masaryk, the Social Democrat leader, either committed suicide or was murdered by being pushed out of a window in his office. As a result the Wallace campaign looked even more Communist-inspired than was probably justified. Truman's position was also helped by his immediate recognition of Israel when the state was declared in May 1948, which helped to rally Jewish support.

Consequently, Truman approached the 1948 elections with his principal left-wing critic, Wallace, standing on a third-party ticket. This was important because it prevented any serious fight for the Democratic nomination, but the Republicans were almost universally expected to win. Indeed, Truman was so sure himself that he was a weak candidate that he even approached General Eisenhower, the leader of the allied armies in Europe, to ask whether he would be the Democratic candidate. In June, however, Truman crossed America from Washington to the West Coast on a 'campaign train', with an open rear platform, at which he spoke informally to crowds of people, and developed a folksy line of patter, attacking the 'do-nothing' Republican Eightieth Congress, and the Communists, with equal force. The Republicans played into his hands by choosing as their candidate Thomas E. Dewey, the Governor of New York, who was a singularly colourless machine politician, which enabled Truman to cast himself as the folksy little guy. Truman was nominated at the Democratic convention, and from July to November he ran a hectic campaign, based on an active foreign policy and a liberal programme domestically. He then recalled Congress in special session to emphasise the degree to which, according to him, it had failed the nation. In two weeks the Congress rejected all his bills, which he named 'the Fair Deal', as a successor to Roosevelt's New Deal.

The election in November 1948 seemed such a foregone conclusion that the *Chicago Tribune* printed headlines announcing Dewey's victory. In fact Truman won, and a Democratic Congress was elected at the same time, as well as a series of important governors. This victory cemented an alliance between Truman and younger liberal Democrats – Adlai Stevenson, Chester Bowles, Hubert Humphrey and Eugene McCarthy for example. The Wallace Progressive party did extremely badly at the polls. The Democrats had now won the Presidency five terms running and their hold on Washington became so secure that it was even to survive the later Eisenhower years in many important respects.

The Fair Deal was based upon Keynesian economic doctrine as interpreted by Seymour Harris, a Harvard economics professor, and directed by Leon Keyserling, Truman's appointment as Chairman of the Council of Economic Advisers. This doctrine emphasised the possibility of economic growth without inflation. Before the war, Keynesian economists such as Alvin Hansen stated that America had reached stagnation, since all demands had been fulfilled. Henceforth, however, Keynesians argued for steady and rapid economic growth. The President's re-election was followed by a slight slump in 1949, which pessimists interpreted as the beginning of the recurrence of the inter-war slump. It was the occasion for the beginning of Keynesian deficit budget policies which had been promoted by Harris and Keyserling. These restored growth in the economy, further bolstered by the substantial rearmament associated with the Korean War.

On a basis of burgeoning prosperity Truman not only gained Congressional support for the continuation and expansion of the Marshall Plan but also for a massive programme of aid for the developing countries, notably India and Pakistan. All this was part of his anti-Communist strategy, but it also went much further as part of a humanitarian programme for the relief of poverty, as well as part of an economic strategy for world economic growth – what was later to be denounced as dollar imperialism.

In the three years of Truman's presidency there had been a slide from Roosevelt's idealistic, even pro-Soviet public attitudes, to a position where even the principal architect of an anti-Soviet coalition could be labelled a Red. The reasons for this rapid shift of attitudes were not far to seek. Roosevelt's policies (sold by wartime propaganda) were based upon a complete misapprehension of the nature of Soviet policies and the theory and practice that lay behind them. When the reality emerged, then, of course, there was a search for scapegoats whilst, elsewhere, the reality was simply denied.

Chapter 7

Losing by winning: Great Britain

Great Britain seemed to emerge as an unqualified victor in 1945 but the nature of that victory proved illusory, yielded few spoils and brought heavy burdens.

Continental Europe, as it revived, became a main focus of British foreign policy and interest. Yet at the same time the British were not prepared to commit themselves to Europe: they relied for their position in world affairs upon their special relationship with the United States, a sentiment which was not reciprocated as the Americans deeply disliked the British imperial claims. Gradually what was Empire became the Commonwealth, a link between nations, once colonies and now independent, at first owing allegiance to the Crown (which is why Eire left in 1948), but then merely acknowledging the Crown as Head of the Commonwealth. This loose alliance handicapped the British substantially – it claimed their loyalty and prevented a cool assessment of self-interest; it caused them to direct their trade to markets which were linked by protection and by the use of sterling, and the sterling area based on debts built up by Britain during the war became a substitute for a rational external economic policy. As a result of the triple commitment to Europe, to America and to the Commonwealth, Britain had a foreign and defence policy that greatly exceeded its means. It was all very well to hold India with a few thousand men, paid for by the Indian taxpayer, as was largely the case before 1939, but it was quite different to have hundreds of thousands of men and their expensive equipment committed to almost every corner of the globe as was the case after 1945.

All this over-commitment exacerbated Britain's chronic economic problems. For the first decade after the war Britain became relatively poorer and weaker. Many causes can be adduced but chief amongst them must rank British foreign policy. From a strictly economic point of view the disposition of many British overseas assets, and the incurring of substantial debts, was aided by the wartime device of Lend-Lease with the United States.

The illusion of the special relationship between the two countries – at least in the economic field – was not dissipated as it should have been by the abrupt ending of Lend-Lease, and the absolute refusal of the United States to adopt the Keynes plan for the international economic post-war settlement. The acute balance of payments crisis that these decisions imposed on the United Kingdom became chronic; and although alleviated by the dollar loan of 1946, the conditions (the convertibility of the sterling equivalent of the dollar loan into other currencies) ensured that this was soon all lost. Even from the Marshall Plan the British gained relatively little, although the restoration of international trade helped, and it is arguable that but for the plan, the British would have been forced into a totally different, reduced, yet ultimately more powerful international role. As it was, they staggered on, assuming responsibilities without the power to rise to them, occupying the Ruhr zone and to some degree assisting in the reconstruction of West Germany; maintaining (relatively) the largest Western armaments during the years from 1945 onwards, including nuclear weapons; policing the Middle East, culminating in the Suez fiasco of 1956; and, as a result of the delusions of grandeur that this role entailed, declining to join the early Franco–German discussions that led to the Common Market, and so finding itself excluded on several occasions when they sought to join, and then joining on disadvantageous terms.

Initially the war was fought far too strenuously by the British both materially and economically. Moreover by achieving victory through central planning, domestic reconciliation and harmony, the illusion was created that bureaucracy and state control worked well for Britain. As a result the state machine was encouraged to grow after the war, bureaucracy increased, government interference proliferated and the welfare state blossomed. But it was those countries which freed their economies from central control fastest which recovered first.

As well as being on the winning side in the war, Britain had the further illusion that it was she, principally, who had won it: a fantasy not shared by Russia or America. Britain was always taking on heavy responsibilities and shouldering burdens which she imagined her status required of her but which were ultimately detrimental to her slender means.

Clement Attlee with his colleagues Ernest Bevin, Herbert Morrison, Hugh Dalton and Sir Stafford Cripps had won the 1945 election by arguing that only by continuing the system of managed economy which had won the war could Britain cope with the massive problems of post-war reconstruction. Coal, railways, energy and steel were to be nationalised; there was to be a free and universal health service, sickness benefit and old age pensions for all.

This was a Social Democratic prospectus. It rested upon the

thesis that some sort of Socialism had been achieved by the civil service control of the economy and large parts of society during the war, that the problem of production had been largely solved and that the question in future lay in the realm of the equitable distribution of a large national income. It was assumed, too, that dissolution of Western empires would accompany a three-power concordat which would ensure the peace of the world. This set of amiable delusions was only slowly to be shattered, though events, little heeded, showed their falsity.

The new Prime Minister, Clement Attlee, was a man of quiet mien who had held office twice before the war and had served in the Coalition government for five years; at sixty-two therefore he was a tough, experienced politician with a clear mandate. Among his Socialist colleagues, he was close to Ernest Bevin, whom he made Foreign Secretary. Ernest Bevin was a self-made man of formidable intelligence who had left school at eleven and then slowly worked his way up the trade union ladder until he became General Secretary of the Transport and General Workers' Union. A man of outstanding ability and personality he accompanied Attlee to Potsdam and quickly realised that his first concern must be the successful prosecution of the war in the Pacific, and the settlement (if it were possible) of the outstanding questions in Europe, of which the most serious were the future of Poland and the four-power occupation of Germany. Bevin and Attlee were strongly anti-Communist, though in the euphoria of the wartime alliance Bevin had formed the opinion that Stalin – though still an aggressive and cruel despot – might have changed from what he had once been, to a patriotic and more moderate statesman in his international policy. Left could speak to the left, he asserted, not because they were brothers under the skin, but because Labour, lacking any imperialist ambitions, could speak directly for the international community, especially through the United Nations.

Within weeks, however, Bevin had first-hand experience of the strong, almost paranoid line that Stalin intended to adopt in the post-war world, especially in Eastern Europe. It revived Bevin's memories of Communist tactics in British trade unions before 1941. Poland and the control of Germany were issues on which the Russians were especially unresponsive to arguments of liberty or allied unity. In the autumn of 1945 the Foreign Ministers of Britain, America and Russia met in London, as had been agreed at Potsdam, but for nearly two months the Soviet representative stalled on every issue, initially on the right of France and China to attend the meeting, and then on the Polish elections, eventually building up an atmosphere of hostility that pushed Bevin into the position of a leader of the anti-Communist world, and identified him as almost the first 'cold warrior'.

The British left wing had been relatively uninfluenced by Marx. Its philosophical ideals were rooted in Protestant Christian teachings, and its support was drawn largely from trade unions, on whom the influence of intellectuals was slight. During the 1930s a few university graduates became Marxists, but the ideology was never widespread. The Communist party was always small, and even at its largest, during the war, had only some fifty thousand members. Britain shared with America a predilection for pragmatic politics, not rooted in ideas.

Under the influence of Bevin the Labour party was staunchly anti-Communist, though among the MPs elected in 1945 there was a substantial number of open Communist sympathisers, secret members, and sentimental optimists. When the government came into head-on collision with the Soviet Union therefore, first over Poland and then over the Greek civil war, a substantial and voluble body of public opinion was built up to present Bevin as an anti-Communist ogre. To this was added the passionate feeling of Jews and Zionists that Bevin's Palestine policy was outrageous. Bevin therefore was represented to many as a mindlessly reactionary tool of the Foreign Office, blindly anti-Communist and anti-Semitic. There was a small element of truth in all these charges, though the reaction to Communism was based upon bitter experience at home and abroad, and the hostility to Zionism (to which the Labour party was strongly committed) was bred by the fervent Zionist opposition to his Palestine policy. The Foreign Office was certainly anti-Zionist, as it had a long history of pro-Arab policies, partly for reasons of straight anti-Jewish prejudice, partly from the wish to safeguard the route to India and the Far East, partly to protect British oil interests, and partly out of sentimental allegiance to the romantic Bedouin. Under the influence of its officials, however, the Foreign Office had no strong anti-Communist line and indeed it was more anti-American than anti-Russian. Bevin could not be said, therefore, to have slavishly followed an official line. To the middle of the road and right-wing parts of the electorate, Bevin represented the continuity of Britain's stalwart wartime policy of sticking up for democracy against totalitarianism.

These foreign policy issues dominated much of the political scene for a number of separate but connected reasons. In the first place, Britain had large forces overseas, especially in the Far East, the Middle East and Germany. Inescapably, therefore, they were in action in Greece and Palestine; they policed Germany, Egypt,

Indonesia and India; they were available for rapid action over wide parts of a disorganised and violent world. Secondly the question of the size of the defence budget was closely related to the future of international policies to which Britain, especially, had idealistically subscribed, including the United Nations. If defence expenditure could be cut then there was a prospect of more rapid growth of the social services. Thirdly, Britain's economy had to be reconstructed; its foreign trade position was disastrously bad; and the economic future depended in large part therefore upon the taking of international measures, including those to do with exchange rates, credit and trade barriers. In particular, it was calculated that exports had to increase by between one third and two thirds over the 1937 level if the same level of imports was to be guaranteed. As North America was the only prosperous part of the world, this led to a dollar-export drive.

The central post-war problem, as Ernest Bevin agreed with James Byrnes, was Germany. Its occupation laid a heavy burden upon the British government, as the British zone included some of the most heavily damaged areas, including Hamburg, Cologne and the Ruhr, and the de-industrialisation and reparations policy, agreed at Yalta and Potsdam, contended with the need to feed and maintain the German population, including several millions of German refugees from the Russian zone and others who had been prisoners of the Germans or had fled from the Russians. The Russians insisted on the return of all Soviet citizens, and the Foreign Office, with great zeal, complied. Some two million, including even elderly couples who had fled the 1917 revolution, were repatriated from the British zone and the majority were either shot or sent to the gulag. The work of repatriation and resettlement, together with the attempt to prevent widespread starvation and epidemics in Germany, coincided with relief efforts for the many countries in Europe which had suffered under enemy occupation, notably Holland, France, Greece and Yugoslavia.

The demand for troops, ships and aircraft which arose from the range of British foreign policy interests meant that for a time British military forces were bigger than those of the United States. And as the United States forbade their allies access to atomic secrets, the decision was taken in 1947 for Britain to have its own atomic weapons.

Through the latter half of 1945 and 1946 demobilisation of British troops went ahead, slowly but surely, under a scheme which combined allowances for age and length of service; many wartime soldiers were not released until 1947, as a result of a policy of 'fairness' above all else. This was an illustration of the way in which the zeal to be fair exceeded common sense and the release of as many men as soon as possible. There was, too, a belief that if the men were let on to the labour market too quickly they would be unemployed. In the meantime conscription of eighteen-year-olds, for a period of two years' service, was maintained.

A double consequence followed. While defence expenditure remained a substantial proportion of the gross national product and of the government's budget, the economy was acutely short of labour. The fear had been that the inter-war unemployment levels would recur (and indeed the desire to prevent this was one of the main causes of the slowness of the demobilisation scheme), but full employment, it was eventually realised, had returned to stay, including unprecedentedly high levels of women and the elderly.

The government's preoccupation with foreign affairs, clearing up the consequences of the war and accommodating their policies to the post-war realities of Soviet policy, was accompanied by a series of decisions about the future of the Empire. Self-government and virtual independence for all colonial territories and India had been a bi-partisan objective for some stage in the future. But at the 1945 election, it was specifically a Labour party commitment. The immediate matter at issue was India, which, it was hoped, would become an independent member of the Commonwealth as soon as possible. (For further details on this, see Chapter 11.) Lord Louis Mountbatten was sent out as Viceroy with express instructions to arrange British withdrawal from India no later than the summer of 1947. Mountbatten's price for going to India was an earldom, with reversion of the title to his elder daughter, and the promise that his naval career would not be interrupted. The price paid by the people of India was several million dead as the process of withdrawal was accomplished, but the British people were relieved of their main imperial responsibility. The government was left, however, with Palestine, where a similar decision to withdraw (in May 1948) was taken, and with other interests in the Middle East and (especially) Africa.

The policy for Africa was one of gradualism. It was held that educational and economic development could take place only slowly, and that independence (for the great majority of territories) would therefore be at least two generations away. A Colonial Development Corporation was established, and a series of marketing boards for tropical products, such as cocoa, while the need to increase British supplies of food led to the development of a groundnut scheme in Tanganyika and chicken-farming in Sierra Leone, both of which ended in disaster.

The retreat from empire was achieved with little loss of life by

the British and almost no discernible political and social consequences for Britain itself, such as affected France over Indochina
and Algeria. The switch from an almost universal conviction in
1939 that Empire was an essential part of Britain's national identity, to a view of Empire as an expensive irrelevance, was staggering.
But two costly legacies remained: the idea of the Commonwealth,
whose influence was supposed to be great, and which for over
twenty years formed a substitute for a foreign and overseas trade
policy, and a diplomatic infrastructure far too great for a small
island nation.

Foreign affairs, therefore, which had seemed peripheral to the
election campaign in 1945 (except in so far as there was a determination to keep the peace), became central to the life of the
government. Meanwhile on the domestic front policies were also
constrained by the problems of the British economy, with which
the government was continually concerned.

The early Labour Cabinet gave an impression, not wholly
undeserved, of a high degree of competence. Attlee grew in
reputation as the government proceeded, and his position was
assured by the distinction of his colleagues; Bevin had been a great
trade union leader, Herbert Morrison had run the London County
Council for years, Hugh Dalton was a well-born intellectual, and
Sir Stafford Cripps was a high-minded, austere, bloodless lawyer
of great rectitude.

It was a Cabinet of talent and experience. The outsider was
Aneurin Bevan, whose task was the creation of the National
Health Service and the development of the housing programme.
The first he fulfilled triumphantly; the second was a failure. Bevan
became a controversial and major figure in the government and it
was his resignation which helped precipitate its downfall.

From the beginning the government was, however, dogged by
economic troubles. British economic policy was dominated by the
need to increase exports in order to finance essential imports.
These were severely limited by world shortages, including mer-
chant ships, but above all by lack of foreign exchange – a condition
shared by every European nation except Switzerland and Sweden.

The result was severe import controls – with, for example, no
petrol for private motoring and virtually no imported timber for
housing – together with a tremendous effort to restore exports,
first to a level one third, then to two thirds above the pre-war
volume, which was achieved by 1950. But in order to tide over the
economy, consumption had to be severely limited, yet investment
was increased in order to make up for wartime destruction and
dilapidations, and the need to overcome the pre-war and wartime

lags in investment which had left much of British industry old-fashioned, especially as the United States made big technological advances in the war. Ultimately much of the recovery was achieved, but the process was lengthy and painful.

Immediately after the war, the shortages which rationing was designed to alleviate grew worse as Britain no longer had privileged access through Lend-Lease to American supplies. Consequently, in the first two and a half years of the Labour government, rations grew smaller and the atmosphere was summed up as one of 'austerity' – which, by the winter of 1947, had lasted for eight years. People grew weary of frugality. Restraints, moral and legal, against the black market became less enforceable, particularly as illegal supplies and purchases developed on a substantial scale. By 1948 considerable numbers of production controls were reduced, but the full weight of consumer rationing continued until the early 1950s.

Whether the recovery would have occurred more rapidly and more effectively in the absence of controls, as the West German experience was to suggest, is a matter for debate. It is clear, however, that between 1945 and 1947 external support for the pound was required to cover the deficit between exports and imports, and only the United States and Canadian governments seemed in a position to help.

The ordinary economic consequence of a demand on limited resources was assumed to be a steady rise in prices. The high cost of imports was partly to blame, a situation exacerbated when the pound was devalued in 1949. Prices in fact remained remarkably steady under the Attlee government, partly through substantial subsidies, especially on foodstuffs, partly through price control (which necessitated rationing), and partly through the manipulation of an out-of-date price index, which involved price-fixing of articles no longer in common consumption, such as tallow candles and calico underwear. In this way index-linked wages were kept down. Nevertheless, the fact that prices were artificially low at the same time as demand for goods and services was growing throughout the economy meant a chronic imbalance of supply and demand.

Though the nation's budget initially fell as wartime needs were cut back, the maintenance of substantial defence forces, food and housing subsidies, and rapidly increasing sums for what became known as the welfare state, led to public expenditure and taxation levels which were high by ordinary peacetime standards. In an attempt to keep down the cost of servicing the huge public debt incurred in the war, and in order to stimulate investment, a policy of low interest rates was maintained by Hugh Dalton; indeed, it was an attempt to force the rate down from 3 per cent to 2½ per cent which led to sustained discussion on the inflationary consequence of the low interest rates and, eventually, to the abandonment of the cheap money policy. Both low interest rates, to finance substantial public borrowing, for example, for the conversion of private shares to public stock for the nationalisation programme, and high public expenditure seemed, according to the generally accepted economic arguments of the time, inflationary. Yet, by past standards, economic growth was high – whether measured by output, productivity or exports – and inflation, by future standards, was low.

Initially, criticism of the government was muted. The legislative programme of the government was received with enthusiasm, since nationalisation of the coal mines, and the National Health Service, were popular. The Conservative opposition, moreover, was disorganised by its defeat and Churchill was concentrating on his war memoirs. Yet the appointment of Lord Woolton, the popular wartime Minister of Food, as Chairman of the Conservative party, and the development of a moderate and coherent policy for the future by R. A. Butler, based on an acceptance of his opponents' more popular doctrines, led to a revitalisation of the Conservatism. From early 1947, indeed, the end of the Attlee government could be dimly discerned, for that winter was remarkably severe, and the nation, which had newly nationalised the coal mines, ran out of fuel. All the controls in the world, all the new spirit of Socialism, could not mine enough coal nor, having mined it, transport it on its state-run railways. Controls and nationalisation became a byword for inefficiency and low standards of work and output.

Though the summer of 1947 was brilliantly sunny and hot, the rigours of the winter were followed by an apparent financial calamity in the late summer when the convertibility provisions of the US dollar loan led to a run on the pound. Early in 1948, the growing danger (as it seemed) of a new war took the radiance off the Labour government's promises. Increasingly as the government seemed battle-shocked and weary, the Conservatives developed a sustained criticism of the controls which were exercised by the government. Far from stimulating economic growth, it was argued, the controls hindered it. Yet the evidence shows that substantial levels of growth were obtained.

The Labour government's version of Socialism was in practice coloured by the wartime experience of economic controls exercised by the civil service, which they maintained and developed.

But these controls became increasingly arbitrary, pointless and bureaucratic (that is, serving the interests and the careers of civil servants), and the reverse of the daring, creative reconstruction of the economy by strategically placed investment that was allegedly needed, and actually occurred in France and Germany. The civil service may have been incorrupt but it was incompetent for its new job, and no new bodies such as the French Commissariat au Plan were created to carry out a long-term strategic plan for restructuring the economy.

As the Labour party drew much of its support from the North of England, Scotland and Wales, which had suffered most from unemployment before the war, the priority was not for a new economic structure, but the avoidance of unemployment. And Britain's belatedly recognised economic genuis, Lord Keynes, had apparently discovered how to cure it. As he died in 1946, nobody knew whether or not his ideas were what were being implemented, but being dead he was canonised. A Cambridge don of great brilliance, a gifted polemicist, Keynes had been a powerful figure in the Treasury in both world wars, and a trenchant critic of the official economic policy between the wars. His important new theory of employment had been published in 1936, and some of its ideas lay behind the full mobilisation of the economy during the war, a mobilisation achieved without inflation.

The government should, he believed, spend its way out of a depression, by unbalancing its budget and planning a programme of public works and other socially useful expenditure. The Labour party (and perhaps, more important, the civil service) adopted his theories, grafted them on to the wartime apparatus of controls, and prepared for the inevitable post-war slump. Day-by-day niggling control of the economy, budgets calculated to take out or put in a little demand superseded any idea of a long-term strategic economic plan. It was disastrous.

Socialist economic planning, therefore, was a simple re-run of the war; Socialism meant nationalisation of the 'basic' industries, long demanded by the trade unions with the Labour party, as an essential 'tool' of economic control. The tool soon broke.

The model chosen for nationalisation was that of a public corporation, London Transport, which had been set up before the war by Herbert Morrison. The corporation was entirely owned by the state and the board was responsible to a minister, but not directly to Parliament. Copying such a model led to irresponsible bureaucracy. All the 'basic' industries named in the Labour party manifesto Let Us Face the Future (written by Michael Young) were nationalised – the Bank of England first, in 1946, followed by coal in 1947, electricity, gas and transport, and aviation, and eventually in 1949 iron and steel. Nationalisation was initially popular with the mineworkers, but it soon attracted widespread and growing criticism for its bad service to consumers and the fact that the 'management' was usually identical with what had been there before, and treated the workers no differently. The nationalised industries, especially coal and the railways, were for the most part old and inefficient. The service they gave varied from bad to appalling. The boards were criticised by workers and the public alike for their remoteness from criticism and lack of response to reasonable requests. As a result, by 1950, when the election came, one of Labour's major policies was almost totally discredited. Nor was the original purpose, the planning of public investment in these industries to help economic growth, ever fulfilled.

Labour's assumption, that once the principle of production for use rather than production for profit had been adopted, the economic problem would be solved, was false. The economy recovered fairly well, though not as fast as the recovery elsewhere, and since British Socialism was fairly mild, Britain never remotely suffered the full economic horrors of Russia and Eastern Europe. But Labour's planned prosperity was never able to pay for Labour's social programme.

Initially the welfare state was a great popular success because it was genuinely bi-partisan. The Education Act of 1944 had been introduced by a Conservative minister in the Coalition government and the Family Allowance Act of 1945 by Churchill's caretaker government. These were followed by Labour's National Insurance Act and the National Health Service Act, both of which came into operation on 5 July 1948. But Labour's flat low-rate national insurance scheme was not graded by size of contribution nor previous income, in contrast to European schemes where the social security benefits were larger, so the British scheme grew progressively less lavish as inflation diminished the value of the benefits. And the glorious beginning of the National Health Service was clouded in the first year when expenditure was over three times the original estimate. This was incorrectly thought to be due to excessive demands by many patients for free spectacles, false teeth and medicines. Endless queues for treatment were not popular either.

Labour's housing programme was notably unsuccessful. Much of the country's housing was elderly and unfit; much had been damaged or destroyed in the war; Labour's policy was to provide new rented accommodation through local authorities – council housing – which slowed up the rate of building and created artificially large waiting lists. Timber and bricks were scarce and the building industry was inefficient and plagued by red tape which was further exacerbated by controls on town planning on environmental grounds. The government declined to nationalise land, imposing instead a cumbersome system of controls and levies, through the Town and Country Planning Act of 1947. This led to widespread inefficiency and corruption and to some of the dullest housing estates in the world.

By late 1948 the welfare state was flourishing and popular. The economy was reviving. But the movement towards Socialism ran out of steam; the Socialist idea of planning was overtaken by civil service day-by-day control of the economy, and a series of moribund and autonomous state industries. The Socialist idea of creating an equal society was replaced by one of a decent minimum adequate structure of social services freely available to all. There was little of William Morris's ideal of Merry England, or Marx's revolution about Mr Attlee (later Earl Attlee) and the future that he and his colleagues created.

Britain recovered after a war effort that had been relatively larger than in any other country except Russia, and from a position in the world which had been declining since before the First World War. The Americans had pre-empted much of its foreign policy role; but it was still left with a large world responsibility in Europe, the Middle East, the Far East and Africa. It wanted both to retreat from Empire and yet to continue to protect those empire markets. Until late 1947 it had the only effective military force in Europe capable of resisting the Russians. Consequently its international commitments were enormous, while its economic base was weak through its international trade and payments position and its industrial structure. Thus, paradoxically, it proved more difficult for Britain to recover from the war because of its large wartime and post-war geopolitical commitments, than for two countries, France and Italy, which had been occupied and fought over, and even Germany which had been apparently shattered. Britain's adoption of a mixture of economic and social policies, labelled Social Democracy, at first seemed a moderate way ahead from capitalism but it was rapidly overtaken by the social market economies of the defeated nations.

Chapter 8

Strength through defeat:
France and Italy

Two defeated nations, France and Italy, faced the problem of
reconstruction with completely different attitudes from the British. Though the Americans had dominated the last stages of the
war in the West, the British were European top dogs, although
somewhat patronising, perhaps, to the joint liberators of two old
European civilisations whose political structures had let them
down, whereas the British political structure not only triumphantly
survived but had (so the British said) won the war as a result of the
way it had enabled the nation to unite during solitary opposition
to the Germans and Italians. The British kept their institutions and
created the welfare state, the two Continental nations underwent
what seemed to be major constitutional changes and, ironically,
recovered more quickly from the war.

France had been a centralised nation-state for centuries. Subject since 1789 to frequent constitutional changes – three republics, two monarchies and two empires – essential continuity lay in
its persistent culture and its machinery of government. It had been
Churchill's view in 1940 that, however severe the defeat, France
would remain by its cultural heritage and its geographical position
a key European, indeed a world power. The speed with which
France recovered its position in Europe seemed to show he was
right.

The magnitude and suddenness of the French collapse in May
and June 1940 recalled the collapse of the Inca empire before the
Conquistadors. Perhaps the Germans were a new Aryan super-
race; more likely, and the view gained almost universal acceptance, the Third Republic was utterly corrupt. French society was
rotten to the core, missing the political generation of a million men
killed between 1914 and 1918, and ruled by a class of get-rich-quick
capitalists and quasi-Fascists who positively welcomed the Germans in order to eliminate once and for all the left-wing parties,
especially the 'Blum clique' of Socialists and Jews, who had formed
the Left Coalition government of 1936.

The liberation of France was completed almost as quickly as
the German occupation four years before. The Anglo–American

armies landed in Normandy on 6 June 1944, Paris was liberated at the end of August, and by late September virtually the whole country was free of German troops. Contrary to such contemporary popular impression, the French were not seriously short of food, except in the big towns. Nor had France suffered as much damage as other European countries except in limited areas where the battles had been fought: large parts of Caen, L'Orient, Le Havre and Dieppe were destroyed, but Paris, Marseilles, Lyons, and the coal and steel areas were virtually untouched. Paradoxically, the material position of the French declined after the liberation, as the normal economic processes were disrupted by the invasion, and the division between the big cities on the one hand and the countryside and small towns on the other was accentuated.

The psychosis of defeat was serious in France at first. The army had been routed in 1815, 1870, 1914 and now 1940, the government had changed sides from an alliance with Britain against Hitler to an alliance with Hitler against Britain; Pétain had become the legitimate government and now in 1946 he was on trial for treason. To come to terms with all the switches in allegiance and the ups and downs of fortunes required time. Though the administrative machine remained intact, with the ousting of the Germans, there were few political leaders remaining who had not capitulated in 1940; just a few heroes from the concentration camps, and a new generation of obscure *résistants*. Many, many officials and people from all classes had been loyal to the now suspect Vichy regime, while many others had actively worked for the Germans. Two million people had demonstrated in favour of Marshal Pétain when he visited Paris in May 1944. At the same time over one million men and some women were prisoners in Germany. The nation was therefore bitterly divided. Overnight the myth had grown up that the French resistance had beaten the Germans and were the legitimate heirs to the state of France.

Charles de Gaulle had other ideas. He had left France for England in June 1940, making himself head of a provisional French government that still retained control of some parts of the African French empire and, after 1943, Algeria. He returned to France in the wake of the allied armies, and with some reluctant support of Churchill and despite the dislike and opposition of the Americans, he made himself master of France. A lone wolf with a messianic vision of his part in French recovery, de Gaulle had two major aims, to re-establish the French position internationally and to give France a new stable constitution.

First he re-equipped the French army with American and captured equipment and rejoined the war, sending the Leclerc Division racing through a collapsing Germany to Austria. He then saw that France received the occupation zones in those countries which had been so reluctantly agreed at Yalta. Next he set about trying to alter the Constitution of the Third Republic in order to replace it with a presidential system.

Elections held in the summer of 1945 created a Constituent Assembly roughly divided between four groups, the Communists, the Socialists, the Radicals and a new Christian Democratic party the MRP (Mouvement Républicain Populaire), the forerunner of those moderately progressive Roman Catholic parties which would come to dominate Western European politics. De Gaulle governed through a coalition Cabinet representative of all French opinion, except the collaborationists – a large exception indeed.

Not that de Gaulle was wholly successful. Inflation was raging; the rationing system broke down and the black market was all-powerful. When the economics minister, Pierre Mendès-France, proposed a monetary reform which, two years later, was to solve far worse economic problems in Germany, de Gaulle failed to support him and he resigned. The government became increasingly unpopular and while de Gaulle won a referendum which jettisoned the Third Republic, the newly-elected Constituent Assembly proposed a constitution with a figurehead President, and a Prime Minister dependent on a majority of the National Assembly which would be disastrous in de Gaulle's opinion. In January 1946, after an apparent show of disloyalty by Socialist and Communist deputies, de Gaulle resigned. He wanted to demonstrate to the French the instability of their parliamentary system, to show them how much they needed a powerful presidency. De Gaulle was suspected, wholly incorrectly but perhaps understandably, of Bonapartist inclinations – a general who wished to be a strong patriotic President.

What, then, was the cause of de Gaulle's dissatisfaction? Partly it was vanity: a conviction that he alone could guide France – a proposition that required no empirical testing since it was axiomatic. He also attached great importance to the prestige and significance of the head of state, who, he believed, ought properly to embody the qualities of his mystical concept of France. Above all, however, his strategic concept of France's security was entirely different from that of other leaders of the Fourth Republic. Moreover he profoundly distrusted the Anglo–Saxons and the Germans. He wanted France to be independent, and allied, if allied at all, to nations such as Russia and China which were distant, not near neighbours. The working out of this counter-

European, counter-Atlantic vision was to play a most important part in France's evolution in the 1960s.

But before de Gaulle resigned, his government had brought about major reforms. Women were given the vote, the welfare state, dating from before the war and enhanced by Vichy, was lavishly extended, basic industries and banks were nationalised, the land was redistributed to the peasants and, most profound of all, a Commissariat of Planning was established under Jean Monnet, a brilliant businessman who came to be considered the creator of the idea of a united Europe. All this led, eventually, to unprecedented prosperity. But it did not have immediate outcomes.

These reforms were achieved partly through a group of politicians who formed de Gaulle's first government, a Cabinet of unknowns such as Mendès-France, and partly through a new generation of highly able civil servants who took the top jobs, especially in Monnet's Commissariat au Plan. Consequently French society was rejuvenated. It was the consensus of the politically articulate that France should move to a Socialist society with a centralised planning of investment. This move was made easier by the élite character of the education system, culminating in the *grandes écoles* (a new one, the École Nationale d'Administration, was founded in 1945), which produced young and able men with a common background in the top jobs in politics, diplomacy, the civil service, banking and industry, able to mix across the board from private to public sector with ease.

The right wing, the nationalists, and the top echelons of business and politics were for the most part hopelessly compromised by their behaviour before and during the war. Their views on the future of France were discreetly hidden. New political parties and new newspapers were founded, all paying lip service to the new ideals of radical reconstruction of French society. Intellectuals such as Jean-Paul Sartre, a Marxist, and Albert Camus, a Socialist, set a predominantly left-wing tone to French intellectual life, previously a dialogue between Catholic reactionaries and ardent anti-clerical Radicals and Marxists. The new Christian party, the MRP, channelled many French Catholics, hitherto reactionary and anti-republican, into a movement of moderate social reform; accepting the republic was a major political achievement and cultural shift. The fact that the right was silent did not mean it did not exist; it wisely refused at this time to show its head above the parapet.

The Communist party in France was the main working-class party. Its strength lay in its control of the larger part of the trade union movement, and in the allegiance of a substantial number of intellectuals. The Socialist movement in France, split between Communists and SFIO – a Socialist party owing allegiance to the defunct Second International – had become Marxist before the Russian revolution. Marxism was a respectable philosophy, attractive to the French reared in metaphysical traditions largely alien to the pragmatic, utilitarian Anglo–Saxons of Britain and America. The Communist party owed allegiance to Moscow, but remained to a degree independent, and rooted in the internal problems of French political life. The Communist party, therefore, though powerful in one sense, was weak in another, occupying a solid but detached position in France. De Gaulle had Communist ministers in his government; after his resignation, the Communists were in permanent and respectable opposition.

When de Gaulle's Bonapartism failed in 1946, the new and old politicians adopted, after two referenda, a parliamentary constitution for the Fourth Republic, under a figurehead president, the Socialist Vincent Auriol. Although a new government was formed, which despite its shifting membership endured until 1958, the apparent chronic instability of French politics returned: there were frequent changes of Prime Minister and shifting sets of coalition parties. This instability, far more apparent than real, remained the source of de Gaulle's constant hostility to the regime.

Accepting that a significant proportion of the electorate supported the Communists, who were in permanent opposition, the other parties were broadly linked in liberal republican beliefs, with a strong Roman Catholic element uneasily tied to the Radical anti-clericals. The civil service, always powerful in France, continued to govern almost regardless of personalities or parties.

France was thus embarked on its own version of the post-war European capitalist revolution but, by 1947, it had yet to solve its problems of governance, nor had it overcome immediate and serious economic difficulties. The Marshall Plan was a specific help, but the modernisation of French industry depended to a considerable degree upon the need to co-ordinate with Germany in the alignment of investment and market policies, especially German coal to help produce French steel, and a wider market for French industry.

Apart from two hopeless colonial wars, in Indochina and Algeria, which developed in the early 1950s, French foreign policy was conducted with remarkable success and skill. Economically, as well as joining the Marshall Plan, France played a major part first in the creation of the Iron and Steel Community and then in the Common Market; it joined all the world organisations, including the United Nations and the International Monetary Fund; by a series of treaties it was integrated into European defence arrangements, culminating in the North Atlantic Treaty. Had it not been for Indochina, Algeria and the Suez expedition – admittedly big exceptions – it would be difficult to see a move made by France under the Fourth Republic which did not substantially add to its military and economic strength.

The Italian declaration of war on Britain and France in 1940 had brought the terrible retribution of the allied invasion. Though the oldest centre of European culture, Italy had been a unified state only since 1870. The post-war possibility that the centralised state might collapse was a real one. The fissiparous characteristics of the Italian political system were likely to reappear. Not only had Mussolini's Fascism put an end to fifty years of parliamentary rule, but a quarter of a century of day-by-day constitutional political experience had been lost, and authoritarian habits had been acquired by officials and businessmen. The division between the industrial North and the impoverished South, between Church and Communist, all made for a pessimistic outlook for Italy as a democracy.

Mussolini and his mistress were executed after being caught on the shores of Lake Como. A consultative assembly was called under the presidency of Count Carlo Sforza by Crown Prince Umberto, who acted as Regent, with the pre-Fascist politician Ivanoe Bonomi as Prime Minister.

The Roman Catholic Church set about creating a middle of the road Christian Democratic Party which was sufficiently independent of the Vatican to seem not too closely under clerical control. Its appeal, like that of the MRP in France and the Christian Democrats in Germany, was to the middle class, because of its pragmatic and liberal approach to the economy, rather than to zealous Catholics. Not that zeal was lacking, however. As evidence of Catholic persecution by the Soviets and their new East European puppet regimes mounted so Pius XII issued stronger and stronger condemnations of Communism. In 1948 voting Communist became defined as a sin.

Devastation was enormous, not only in the towns, but in the countryside. The disruption of the economy was almost complete. The major transport network was not working. While hundreds of thousands of Italian soldiers were prisoners in Britain, Canada and the United States, many foreign refugees and displaced persons were in Italy. The administration, in the process of being purged of Fascists, was barely functioning. The allied armies and the defeated German army were still in Italy. There was galloping inflation, severe unemployment and acute hardship and hunger, especially among the poor whose homes had been destroyed by war. Italy lacked food, raw materials, energy and transport.

The referendum on the monarchy in June 1946 determined that the country should be a republic. A new constitution was then drawn up and adopted. The government was initially a coalition of six parties; and in the 1946 election the Christian Democrats (207) gained most support, followed by the Socialists (115) and the Communists (104). The leader of the Christian Democrats, Alcide de Gasperi, became Prime Minister, Pietro Nenni, the Socialist leader, Foreign Minister, and Palmiro Togliatti, the Communist, was Minister of Justice. Saragat, the Social Democrat, was also in the government. These four men dominated Italian politics.

The coalition did not last long because the left fragmented between Marxists who followed Moscow, were hard-line Stalinists and so refused to compromise, and the Social Democrats who received some support from the British Labour party and probably some American funding. De Gasperi finally led a Christian Democratic coalition and put Italy firmly in the Western camp.

Italy was required to pay reparations to Russia, Yugoslavia, Ethiopia, Greece and Albania but as the Cold War developed, the British and the Americans were determined to stop Italy from becoming Communist. Yalta had put Italy, with Greece, in the British sphere of interest and therefore it was unlikely that the Soviet Union would attempt to intervene directly; on the other hand there was the example of Greece to show that a Communist-led guerrilla movement could gain apparently wide support – and the Italian elections showed substantial support for the Communists, especially in the Northern cities. When the British handed their responsibilities in Greece and Turkey to the Americans, the latter also assumed responsibility for Italy. With a substantial population of Italian extraction, the United States had an especial interest in Italy, and the Catholic vote was particularly important in American elections.

American support was vital for the recovery of Italy. In August 1947 the economy virtually collapsed and emergency credit restrictions were imposed. Italy was a major beneficiary of the Marshall Plan which began to operate that year. Its defence was also ensured as the Truman Doctrine enlarged in scope until in 1949 NATO was founded and Italy joined as a member, a bare two years after the peace treaty.

American aid was used to excellent purpose. Italian manufacturing industry in the North was at the point of take-off. A group of brilliant entrepreneurs, outstanding designers, and a flood of willing and cheap labour from the South were allied to a strong tradition of craftsmanship which stretched back to the earliest times. Olivetti, Fiat and many other names became famous in the light-engineering field. This swift and overwhelming industrial renaissance was aided by a phenomenal export boom, by an abundance of bank finance, and by a semi-state corporation – IRI – which gave active support to the modernisation process. Trade unions were weak, wages low and exports excellent. The result was expanding economic growth up to the 1960s, which was further stimulated by progressive removal of Fascist and wartime controls although a central state holding company was still maintained for the development of the South, the Cassa per il Mezzogiorno. Unfortunately the initial result of high investment in the North was a flood of migration from Calabria and Apulia which made the South even more backward and desolate. Some consolation was however provided by the break-up of the great estates and the creation of a new peasant property-owning class but the deep rift between North and South still remained.

The war forced France and Italy to rethink their political systems and to make fundamental reappraisals of their economies. This gave them zest for growth and an impetus for change whilst Britain had but tinkered gingerly with her war-weary and jaded old set-up. Both British and French bureaucrats kept their countries stable in a time of upheaval but the French appeared to be more adaptable and flexible than their stodgier British counterparts when prosperity increased. Italy had to pay reparations but she had no colonial dependencies to drain her energies. In both France and Italy there were small nuclei of Communists whose leaders were nationally recognised and who were to increase their power base despite encouraging economic growth.

   The most startling post-war revival however came from the most destroyed and divided nation of all, Germany.

Chapter 9

The emergence of West Germany

There were seven million German prisoners of war in the Soviet Union, two and a half million of whom died. In Germany itself three million houses and flats were destroyed. The authorities also had to cope, as a result of war injuries, with a million severely handicapped people, as well as eight million refugees who poured in from the German communities in Eastern Europe and from the Eastern zone of Germany into the Western zone. Every major city had been heavily attacked from the air, and these cities were the places in which the refugees largely settled. From the tremendous prosperity of the Hitler years, when the Germans thrived upon the loot of a whole continent, there was a sudden and dramatic decline in the urban standard of living. In the Western zones, too, nearly one million Germans were subjected to the de-Nazification process and forbidden further public employment.

By November 1945, except in the French zone, local German officials were dealing with strictly local matters, whilst an army of carpetbaggers from Britain and America arrived to supervise the occupation in the two major Western zones. Nothing like it had been seen since the reconstruction in the South after the American Civil War. In the Eastern zone the Communist party was in almost complete control under the supervision of Soviet officials.

Reparations in cash and in kind were demanded by the Russians and the French. Nobody wanted a German revival and it was almost universally assumed that occupation would be followed by dismemberment. Twenty-five million tons of coal from the Ruhr were wanted immediately to restart Western European – especially French – industrial production.

The American financier Henry Morgenthau and others had argued during the war that since German military strength rested partly, perhaps mainly, on its heavy industry, then the German economy should be pastoralised. At the end of the war, therefore, all the allies began removing heavy machinery and equipment from Germany. But the allies also wanted reparations in kind – coal, chemicals and consumer goods. Without equipment and factories, how were the Germans to make and supply them? The American commanders and officials, especially General Lucius B. Clay, were shocked by the appalling human distress and poverty that they saw all around them and they were determined to take steps to alleviate this. It was clear to the Americans that before reparations of output could begin, pump-priming financial assistance would have to be made to German firms and the people would have to be fed, housed and organised. Moreover if Germany was over-exploited, morale would suffer, resistance might occur and military problems increase. Diminish, de-Nazify and demilitarise by all means, thought the Americans, but be logical and thoughtful about possible outcomes. As a result the Morgenthau doctrine was not followed and the Americans found themselves in the curious position of pouring aid into all the zones of Germany whilst the French and the Russians took out as much as they could as fast as possible.

The Russians engineered a great inflation which spread throughout Germany, by printing money to pay for whatever they did not requisition; the German coal mines in the Ruhr were under British control but the miners needed food; the American zone based on Bavaria alone had enough food, but had no fuel. The lack of trade between the zones exacerbated shortages. Above all, the size of reparations was still unsettled. After Yalta it had been decided that over half the reparations should go to the USSR but the Americans put this figure at 55 per cent of $14 billion whereas the Russians thought the total should be $20 billion.

The only agreed allied aim was to keep German living standards no higher than the European average and to extract any surplus as reparations. This meant controlling the level of German industrial output, or what was known as the level-of-industry plan. The Allied Control Commission decided that the German living standard should be three quarters of the 1938 average; that is, about the level prevailing in 1932.

This problem proved insuperable. The Allied Control Commission adopted its plan in March 1946, but its extreme provisions were astonishingly unrealistic. The outcome was complicated not only by the difficulty of settling individual industrial targets, but by the lack of data about population, about actual output, the fact that Germany was in chaos and was not an economic unit, that it had no settled frontiers or political status, and that it required Germany to export competitively in a world where trade was severely disrupted and the allies themselves wished also to export to save their own economies. Even if the plan could have been enforced, it would have entailed substantial burdens on Britain and the United States for many years. Steel production, for example, was to be limited to 5.8 million tons, which meant that Britain would have had to supply nearly two million tons of her own steel to Germany so that

Germany could make goods with which to meet its reparations obligations. The British acceptance of the plan was based on conditions that made the plan unworkable: that German exports would pay for German imports and that Germany would be treated as a unit. The French agreed with the British, adding the further condition that German food imports must be minimised and its coal exports maximised. The Americans regarded the plan as one for the period of reparations and not a permanent limitation, which left the Russians as the plan's main supporter, and even that degree of support was provisional.

This failure therefore to agree over Germany's future made it look as if its economic collapse was inevitable: but German economic stability was central to the reconstruction of Europe; seventy million people could not be left in limbo, for the most part hungry, with many homeless and unemployed, if only because virtually the whole of European reconstruction was posited upon German reparations. There was no central German government, as all powers feared a new Germany and the French specifically did not want a Russian-dominated all-German government on their frontiers. The Soviet Union just as adamantly supported the Potsdam policy of economic unity but argued practically that for the first year at least Germany had to be administered on a zonal basis. The French opposition to any central government was regarded by the Russians as a manifestation of British and American policy (which it was not); and this led to growing mutual distrust. The absence of central government, and the suspension of reparations from the American zone on 3 May 1946, made a breakdown of attempts at agreed four-power control inevitable. Reparations were at the heart of the matter.

The Russians wanted to unify Germany on the basis of the Potsdam accords and levels-of-industry plan, to demilitarise Germany, to extract reparations, and to create a country that was either friendly to them or at most neutral. But this attitude in fact entailed a continuation of the economic collapse of Germany which was of no great concern to the Russians so long as they could remove the heavy machinery and employ German prisoners of war as labourers, and as long as Germany remained under allied control and no longer posed a military threat. The USSR removed railway lines as well as machine tools and established over two hundred jointly-owned stock companies in their zone to produce goods which were sent to Russia.

The British took some equipment from the Ruhr, including the Hermann Goering steelworks which ended up years later in a Manchester suburb while the Germans had a superb new steelworks supplied to them by the Americans. The British then quickly set about rehabilitating their zone, by reconstructing education, the trade unions and local government along Socialist lines. They wished to see a German Social Democratic republic with the former armaments empires of Krupp and Thyssen in democratic public ownership. The trade unions were reorganised into sixteen major unions; in education, teachers were given responsibilities rather than having slavishly to follow authority (and Nazi teachers were replaced); and a free press and a radio and television system were set up, based upon British models. The zone was divided up into a series of *Länder* which were to form units for local elections, laying the foundation for a genuinely democratic German constitution.

The Americans occupying the largely rural and Catholic south, principally Bavaria, took scientific and technical knowledge as their reparations. They were bitterly opposed to any form of Socialism, and strongly supported steps towards a restoration of liberal, constitutional and above all federal democracy, such as had to some degree existed in the Weimar Republic. Thus the rise of a new Germany from the ashes of the Third Reich was largely an invention of the Americans and above all of General Lucius B. Clay, the head of the American occupation forces.

The Americans were faced with a different and opposite set of problems from the British and the Russians. With the Russians now seen in America as a growing threat to the West, it was felt essential to keep an American presence in Europe as a deterrent against future aggression. It was also necessary to build up Britain and France so that they could help to defend Europe against the Russians. Above all it was necessary to settle the long-term nature of the American presence in Germany. It was obvious that a lengthy American occupation was entailed by the Russian threat, and by the Russian determination to remain as occupiers of East Germany. It was also obvious, however, that to remain in Germany entailed American support for the German economy. It is hardly too much to say that from mid-1945 onwards American policy towards Europe was almost entirely preoccupied by the German problem.

If the American troops were to remain in Germany, a judicial basis had to be found. If the German economy was to be restored, it meant that the policy previously agreed with the Russians could not be upheld, since it was inherently contradictory, and was likely to become a permanent drain on American finance. American aid had to concentrate on reconstruction; and if German reparations were essential to French recovery, then American aid to France would have to be a substitute for reparations from Germany.

The French, non-participants at Potsdam, and kept out of the September 1945 Foreign Ministers' conference in London by Molotov until almost the end, shared the Russian view that the reason for occupying their zone was to milk it dry. But they opposed Russian demands on the Ruhr because they put the independence of the Rhineland as a French-controlled buffer state as their next strategic objective. Thus they became powerful opponents of the Russians not, as the Americans were, out of regard for the suffering of the Germans but because they had a well-thought-out political objective, which was a divided Germany.

France had been given an occupation zone along the Rhine at Churchill's insistence. France was also potentially left wing, even a Communist country, and it became important to Truman and to Bevin to strengthen its central political parties and its economy, for they shared Churchill's view that European peace required a strong France. Under de Gaulle, however, France became Europe's 'awkward squad'. Not having been represented at Yalta and Potsdam, it did not feel bound by the agreements reached there. Georges Bidault, de Gaulle's Foreign Minister, demanded the cession of the Saar to France, and an independent French-controlled Rhineland, including the Ruhr. Bidault argued that the failure of the 1919 Treaty of Versailles to prevent a second German invasion of France pointed to the need for a more drastic solution this time; and that the dismemberment of Germany had already been agreed at Potsdam. If much of Prussia and the Silesian coal fields had been ceded to Poland and Russia, then why not the Saar to France? The French used their veto in the Allied Control Authority in Berlin to prevent the function of any central German authority until their Saar and Rhine demands were accepted.

Thus technically it was the French who first stopped the effective development of the Allied Control Authority. But the Russians also wanted complete control of their zone, and perhaps more. The Russian behaviour in Poland gave solid grounds for thinking that they were determined not to compromise their complete control of that country, whatever had been agreed at Yalta. The London Poles, and the non-Communists, were rapidly squeezed out of any posts of authority in Poland. It seemed, too, that the Russians wished to extend their influence across Germany to the French and Belgian frontiers. The Foreign Ministers' conference in London in the autumn of 1945 proved a harbinger of things to come in that Molotov blocked any joint agreement; his manner was as disagreeable as his matter; and while there might be grounds for supposing that the West was ganging up on him, this could not entirely account for so complete a rejection of all compassion and agreement.

His performance led Bevin to the conclusion that it was necessary for the Western allies to unite against Molotov. Even so, a complete division of Germany between the East and the West was not yet by any means inevitable.

By early 1946 the German Communist party under Walter Ulbricht was bidding to take over all Germany and it used the French claims on the Saar and the Ruhr as a means of presenting itself as the party of German nationalism which was also acceptable to the Russians. George F. Kennan, the American Ambassador in Moscow, who, as Mr X, in a famous article in *Foreign Affairs*, became identified with the origins of the Cold War, laid especial emphasis, in a telegram on 24 February 1946, and another on 10 March 1946, upon the Soviet attempt to control all Germany, and then to bring France within its sphere of influence. He therefore advocated the division of Germany, isolating the Soviet zone, so that a Western buffer zone could be created which would be immune to Soviet penetration and 'integrated into an internationally organised Western Europe'.

The influence of this diagnosis was profound. According to revisionist historians it presented a serious departure from the reality of American–Russian dealings in Germany; it substituted *a priori* reasoning about Russian intentions for the clear evidence that Russia was abiding by the letter and the spirit of the Potsdam agreement. The Potsdam agreement, however, was inherently favourable to the Russians, based as it was upon Yalta and the victory of the Soviet army on the Eastern front. Furthermore it was unenforceable and unworkable unless the German standard of living was to collapse totally and probably permanently.

On 3 May 1946 America suspended reparations deliveries from her zone to the others. The French accepted as a *quid pro quo* the isolation of the Saar, with a view to its independence or its incorporation into France. Surprisingly the Russians did not react with hostility to the suspension of reparations, although they did refuse to accept the American position, that all-German economic unity was necessary to restore the German economy before reparations could be resumed. The Americans gradually interpreted this Russian attitude as a Russian demand that they economically support the Soviet zone, while it was stripped for reparations for Russia; but while this was the logic of what was happening, it was clear that the Russians genuinely did not see it like that. It became axiomatic to the West that the Russians had decided not to unify Germany on a four-power basis, because they wanted to strip Germany and leave the problem of supporting the German population to the Americans. The antithesis of this view was that the German economy had to be restored and that this could only be safely done in a context of European unity.

At the Paris conference of Foreign Ministers on 10–11 July 1946, however, there was near-agreement on a proposal by Bevin that the surplus in trade of any zone not required by any other zone would be available for reparations. This would have led to a preliminary stage of *de facto* unity, since in the end all intra-German trade would balance and reparations could be resumed. But Molotov finally said that the Bevin plan was not acceptable because it did not put reparations first; Bevin thereupon pointed out that Britain could not afford to continue to pay dollars to buy food for Germany, so the British zone would now be organised unilaterally on a Socialist basis, with the coal mines nationalised, as in Labour Britain. Byrnes then offered to join the American zone to all the others except the Saar, for economic purposes, in order to avoid the Socialist Bevin solution. The Russians would not agree to this unless all zones had all-German political organs – a government, a Parliament – which the French would not accept. The British, however, accepted the American plan, and an Anglo–American Bizone was created in which Ruhr coal and steel complemented Bavarian foodstuffs. This Bizone, as it was called, was the beginning of the division of Germany, and the origin of the Marshall Plan; but it began pragmatically as a solution to the problem of food imports and coal production in the British zone.

The Western political aims – to begin to restore democratic and constitutional government in Germany and to restore the West German economy – were gradually achieved, first of all by *Länder* elections in January 1946 in the American zone (Bremen, Bavaria, Baden-Württemberg and Hesse), and in April 1946 in the British zone (Schleswig-Holstein, Lower Saxony, Hamburg and North-Rhine Westphalia). The American *Länder* had drawn up constitutions by the end of 1946, and James Byrnes, the American Secretary of State, affirmed the American commitment to a free democratic Germany.

James Byrnes announced in Stuttgart that while America agreed to Germany's new eastern borders, and that the Saar should go to France, it did not favour further dismemberment; and he added insult to injury by saying that the level of industry plan was impracticable. In just over a year American pragmatism had engineered a complete reversal of their German policy. He also gave assurances that American forces would stay in Germany as long as other occupying forces. This gave a guarantee that Europe would not be abandoned to the Russians. This speech was anti-Russian but it was more immediately anti-French, in that it opposed their demands for dismemberment and reparations, removing any hope of substantial German help for the French economy; and it left the economic problems of the Bizone jointly in British, American and German hands – since by this time the *Länder* had Minister–Presidents with whom economic and other civilian matters were discussed and who assumed responsibility for exercising authority.

Behind the four-power manoeuvring, German politics were restored. Three major parties were established, the Communists, the Socialists and the Christian Democrats. It was a slow procedure for the great mass of Germans were disoriented. The Nazis had ranged from maniacs and bureaucrats such as Speer, who were to be put on trial at Nuremberg, through authoritarian Prussians, straightforward civil servants, and big businessmen such as the Krupps, to the great mass of ordinary Germans who just wanted to get on with their own lives and not only saw nothing wrong with Nazism but had also experienced the great benefits it had brought. Germans after all are patriotic and for nearly nine years Hitler had won on a Napoleonic scale. Until Stalingrad, remarkably few of their highly skilled and successful troops were killed. The opposition to Hitler consisted, after Russia was invaded in June 1941, of disorganised groups working underground or from abroad. Among the Communists Walter Ulbricht, a future Prime Minister of East Germany, was in Moscow. Among the Social Democrats, most of whom were abroad, Willy Brandt, a future West German President, was in Norway. Of the religious groups, surviving Jews had mainly chosen Britain, while the Lutherans had for the most part either conformed with the Nazis or kept quiet, although Pastor Niemöller emerged as an anti-Nazi. As the Catholics had yielded to Hitler except for a few priests, the Church establishment was forced into a rapid about-turn after the defeat. So, too, was royalty (a large class) and the aristocracy, who had served the German Reich, though a few such as von Stauffenberg had opposed Hitler. There seemed to be few untainted with the Nazi brush from whom to choose new officials.

The first post-war political party formed in Germany was the Communist KPD, under the control of Walter Ulbricht. The KPD then amalgamated with the eastern Social Democratic Party, the SPD, to form the Socialist Unity Party, the SED, under Otto Grotewohl, a vain careerist who sought to seek support from the electorate on the basis of a unified Germany, though clearly under

Soviet domination. Thus the Russians had a possible German Communist-dominated government available for them to run a united allied-occupied Germany.

The first political party to be formed in the Western zone was the largely British-inspired Socialist Democratic SPD, led by Kurt Schumacher, which attracted refugees who had spent the war out of Germany. In his first political speech, before the war was over, Schumacher had strongly attacked Hitlerism, and called for the restoration of the Weimar Republic. Now he was supported by the British and in a few months came to expect to be made the head of a government which would counterbalance the SPD government formed by Otto Grotewohl in the East. His refusal to join the merger of the East German SPD and KPD meant that he had to rely upon weak local Western-zone support as the traditional Socialist areas of Saxony and Thuringia were in the Eastern zone.

Initially the elections were for local government, and Berlin's were critical. In spite of the loss of the traditional East Berlin working-class Socialists to the Soviet zone, Schumacher won the Berlin election on 20 October 1946 by an absolute majority. Schumacher had hoped to form a government which enjoyed the support of the newly-founded Christian Democratic Party led by Konrad Adenauer, the mayor of Cologne, but Adenauer refused.

Konrad Adenauer had been Mayor of Cologne from 1917 to 1933. Strongly opposed to Nazism he had then retired to the Eifel mountains until reinstated as mayor again by the Americans in March 1945. There he would have been happy to remain as he was already sixty-nine, had not a British brigadier dismissed him on 6 October 1945 on the ground that he was secretly helping ex-Nazis back into office. Now anti-British and deprived of a local political career, he entered the national scene and soon became the first chairman of the CDU.

Adenauer wanted a traditional Conservative party which was not tied to a particular religious sect, whereas the Catholics wished to have a party which was committed to some form of Christian Socialism, including central economic planning, the nationalisation of heavy industry and major reforms in the way in which industry was managed through joint workers' and managerial councils. This was not acceptable to Adenauer, nor did it seem to the Vatican compatible with the 1931 Papal Bull *Quatrogesima Anno* which had said that 'Christian Socialism is a contradiction in itself. It is impossible to be simultaneously a good Catholic and a real Socialist.'

The CDU's first meeting in February 1946 at Neheim-Hüsten had already managed to avoid a commitment to central planning and to the nationalisation of industry, and as the British influence in Germany declined and the American influence grew, so the CDU found itself advocating a social market economy which appealed to the more conservative elements in Germany and which also appealed to the Americans. Their platform condemned traditional capitalism, committed the party to social justice, and to joint worker–management councils to control industry while leaving the ownership in private hands. Adenauer and his colleagues made great play of the fact that the Nazis had called themselves the National Socialist party. The word Socialism was anathema, so was central control. The economy had been tightly controlled under the Nazis and even more so under the allies, therefore it was quite clear that to the majority of Germans the concept of a benevolent bureaucratic state was no longer attractive.

Schumacher, having regarded himself as the British candidate for the leadership of a democratic restored Germany, with a constitution similar to that of the Weimar Republic, found himself condemned to permanent opposition, while his former Socialist allies in the East threw in their lot with the Communists. Meanwhile, the hitherto obscure Adenauer, seventy years old in the 1946 elections, rapidly established himself as the leader of post-war West Germany.

One of the first problems confronting the new *Länder* governments was collaborating with the allies over coal production. Jean Monnet decided he wished to raise French industrial production by 150 per cent by 1950 and to do this he needed cheap German coal. The French took the German coal and so the ever-generous Americans were expected to supply fuel to Germany's other traditional markets, to stop their industries collapsing. The British found that they were paying large sums for imports to Germany, and for other occupation forces in their zone, but delivering coal at laughably low prices from the Ruhr, to France.

It was like a game of pass the parcel. France had negotiated a loan from America to pay for imports; the British wanted the French to pay proper world prices for Ruhr coal from the American loan; with the proceeds the British deficit to America could be reduced since it was caused in substantial part by the heavy costs they were incurring in Germany. A settlement of the coal question, then, involved indirectly an American subsidy to Germany which could pay reparations (in coal) to France and (in dollars) for imports from Britain.

For that to happen, however, coal had to cease to be treated as reparations – underpriced, virtually loot – so that Germany could earn enough to pay for its imports. The Monnet plan offered a promise of self-sufficiency for France. It therefore needed an international mechanism into which American support could go because the Monnet plan carried the virtual certainty that the aid would be self-limiting. On 11 July 1947 the Joint Chiefs of Staff, still responsible for the occupation of the American zone of Germany, stated that 'In cases where the restoration of normal international commercial relations between Germany and the rest of Europe would involve an increase of US dollar expenditures . . . funds for German expenditure shall be increased, or the German economy compensated through provision by the US of sufficient relief monies to the country or countries so benefited to enable them to pay Germany.'

It was this 'financing' of international trade which was the central mechanism of the Marshall Plan; the American dollars became the pump-priming which allowed the other exchanges to go ahead. Truman had sent ex-President Herbert Hoover on a mission to Germany to find out the true position. He reported to Truman that the German economy should be rebuilt; that reparations should stop; that the Ruhr and the Rhineland were essential to the recovery of Germany; and that the Bizone at least should be made self-sufficient. German recovery was indeed essential for the re-covery of the rest of Europe. This programme accorded strongly with the views already reached by leading members of Truman's administration. It therefore virtually assured bipartisan support in Congress for the reversal of the Potsdam agreements on the German economy. General Marshall, who succeeded Byrnes as Secretary of State, was strongly persuaded of the value of the Hoover policy. At the Moscow Conference of Foreign Ministers in March and April 1947 Marshall and Ernest Bevin agreed that Russia desperately needed reparations in the form of current production from Germany, but that this required a self-supporting German economy. On this basis, Bevin urged the restoration of the economy of the Bizone, especially of coal and steel production from the Ruhr. But Bevin wanted the economy to be Socialised. This presented insuperable difficulties to the Americans since Hoover and the Republicans regarded such proposals with horror.

By April 1947 it was clear that the Soviet Union was operating its occupation zone independently. The rest of Germany was bank-rupt and its imports were being financed by the British and the Americans. The British themselves had substantial balance of payments problems which made it impossible for them to contri-bute much longer to financing Germany. The Americans feared that Communism would spread in France, Benelux and Denmark as a result of those countries' own economic problems. The rehabilitation of West Germany was essential; but its coal and steel exports to other Continental nations had to be replaced while reconstruction took place. The Monnet plan based on pump-priming for industrial reconstruction offered a model of what would be done in countries other than France, if imports of raw materials could be found to enable production to pick up. The original concept of an enlarged Monnet plan for Europe was of a 'coal for Europe' programme, partly of coal exports to Europe from America, but mainly of coal-mining machinery and food for the miners in the Ruhr.

The use of such aid could also be a means of requiring the British to drop their plans to Socialise German coal and steel industries. This Socialisation was partly ideological in origin but also based upon the view that Krupp and the other German capitalists had been the forces behind Hitler's rise to power, and that war profits (as well as the suppression of the German workers) had been among their primary motivations. In this they had the strong support of the German Social Democrats who in Bizonia were proving more adept at gaining crucial economic posts than the American-supported Christian Democrats. The Americans used their military rights to prevent any Socialisation measures, ordering General Lucius B. Clay to veto any such proposals.

Instead of concentrating on long-term measures concerned with ownership of the means of production, the Americans turned to immediate proposals to raise coal output, by offering $600 million of food to raise miners' rations to 4000 calories a day, and other inducements to obtain more miners and equipment for the mines. The British accepted these proposals and were prepared to defer their Socialisation proposals because the *Länder* elections gave the German Social Democrats, the SPD, majorities in all the British *Länder*, except North Rhine-Westphalia. Here the Christian Democrats, the CDU, had a small plurality, which meant that they would have to govern with SPD consent and where the Minister–President was anti-capitalist, and spoke of new 'communal', or co-operative, enterprises.

Marshall's main concern was to increase German coal production. Bevin was also obsessed by coal – he had said that his foreign policy would be transformed if British miners could produce 200 million tons of coal a year – and although he thought the German mines should be vested in the *Länder* governments (specifically North Rhine-Westphalia) he shared the American view that coal output came before ideology. On the other hand he had to think of the political repercussions in the Labour party and the SPD of delaying Socialisation. Above all, he held that coal production was

good / bad

not purely a technical problem, as the American experts seemed to argue, but depended upon a general reconstruction of the German and, indeed, the European economy. In this view he was strongly influenced by Jean Monnet and Robert Marjolin who were developing French plans for a France–German programme of reconstruction, and by Sir Oliver Franks, who had grasped the central concept of a multilateral European agency to co-ordinate plans for European reconstruction.

Meanwhile a number of German politicians were emerging amid the conditions now experienced by the *Länder* governments – Kurt Schumacher, the Social Democratic leader, was, perhaps, initially the most impressive, while Konrad Adenauer showed the greatest degree of doggedness and skill in manipulating the Americans. The *Länder* governments collaborated with the occupying powers in seeing that the machinery of government worked. In early 1948 the conference of Minister–Presidents of the *Länder* agreed with the British, French, United States and Benelux governments to choose a Parliamentary Council of sixty-five men and women from the *Länder* (nine, including the French zone of Rhineland Pfalz), to draw up a federal constitution to unite them.

The Russians, who from 1945 onwards printed Marks to finance their occupation – thereby causing an advanced inflation – refused to accept the decision by the Western allies to reform the currency in their zones. Confrontation was in the air. Reputations were being forged. The national career of Konrad Adenauer effectively began after the breakdown on 19 March 1948 of the last opportunities to form a national German government with the unilateral decision on currency reform. The Western powers undertook currency reform in their zones, when the old Reichsmark currency was called in and new Deutsche Mark currencies were issued in the ratio of twelve to one. The Western allies also agreed to unify their zones.

The Christian Democratic Union's importance in this particular context was the way in which it attracted conservative voters into the mainstream of German politics, while at the same time attracting a number of more progressive individuals who had become disillusioned with Socialism as a result of the Nazi experience. Its emphasis was on pragmatism, and Adenauer also played a crucial role in making the Christian Democratic Union an ecumenical party which included Protestants and agnostics and did not pay any particular attention to the teachings of the Vatican except when it suited, and in those circumstances appeared to pay no heed at all to the Vatican's instructions on day-to-day politics. Adenauer also ensured that the CDU had a large number of Protestants in prominent positions and that the trade unions should be well represented. In particular, he remained a close ally of the DGB, the Deutsche Gewerkschaftsbund, the equivalent of the British TUC, which was not tied to the SPD as the British TUC was to the Labour party.

The nature of German Christian Democracy was different from either French or Italian, not just through being non-denominational, but also because in Germany, beginning as it did with *Länder* elections and only gradually moving to federal elections, the CDU was more powerful in its local and regional branches than it was as a national party. Different parts of the country might have different emphases in their local policies, but at federal level the party was tightly organised and rapidly grew in importance.

Within three years of its unconditional surrender, Germany was divided into four occupation zones and effectively two successor states. Both East and West Germany were beginning to be absorbed into their respective sets of alliances, and the change in Germany's post-war reputation was remarkable: from being considered a race of veritable ogres, it swung – in the case of West Germany – to being thought a model of constitutional democracy, most-favoured ally of the United States.

Initially, with Hitler's death, the hostility to Germany was profound. Its division, persisting and made virtually permanent, was a necessity if either the Russians or the other Europeans were to trust Germany again. As the division hardened so the Americans became more and more involved with West Germany's reconstruction. And it was through this involvement that they became drawn into the task of reconstructing the Western European economy and building up a durable Western defence alliance.

In this process the Germans, especially Adenauer, played a critically important part. Had the division of Germany never occurred, had it been possible to create a genuinely neutral and disarmed Germany, then neither the Marshall Plan nor NATO would have taken the forms they did.

The *Wirtschaftswunder*, which began to transform West Germany two years after the currency reform, made Germany a model of economic growth. The economic reform and the apparent political stability in West Germany immediately led to the beginning of an economic revival, and a period in which output increased, but above all in which goods and services became freely available and the black market disappeared. At first unemployment rose steeply but inflation stopped and output rose.

Social problems were acute. The flood of refugees from the East continued. Yet at the same time the need to rebuild the cities, and to regenerate ordinary political life, was vital. In view of the history of the Weimar Republic, which had collapsed under the need to provide reparations and to govern a country which was faced with severe economic problems in the face of a major military defeat, the outlook for a democratic government seemed poor. The creation, therefore, of what was to become the Federal Republic was a risky enterprise, opposed outside Germany not only by Communists but by many other Europeans of all parties who had suffered from German invasions and attacks, and also by those inside Germany who wished to see a unified Germany, come what may.

The economic reform which went ahead in the Western zone represented the final breakdown of the idea of coherent four-power control of Germany. But Berlin was still governed by the four powers, even though it was in the middle of the Soviet zone. The routes which British, French and American troops used to gain access to Berlin took them through the Soviet zone which was in the process of becoming East Germany, the German Democratic Republic. The Russians claimed, not without reason, that if the Western allies were prepared to go ahead unilaterally with currency reform in their zones, effectively separating them from the Soviet zone, the position of the Western enclaves in Berlin became both anomalous and insupportable. They therefore turned back allied vehicles at the zonal boundary, cutting off the allies in Berlin from their supply base.

This was interpreted as one stop short of an act of war.

From the beginning of the Soviet blockade of Berlin on 24 June 1948, an allied airlift of military and civilian supplies, including coal and food, was inaugurated. Thus the year 1948 marked the effective beginning of the economic restoration of West Germany in conditions where unity between the East and West was clearly impossible and where the threat of a Soviet invasion seemed a distinct possibility.

The airlift, which lasted until the Russians climbed down a year later, marked a shift of attitudes in the West. Allied public opinion rallied to the 'good Germans' in the new Federal Republic who became potential heroes of the resistance to Russian aggression, whilst the Berliners were actually besieged by a hostile Soviet army. The West Germans themselves realised how vulnerable they were to Soviet invasion and how important it was to cement their alliance with the West.

The German Parliamentary Council representing the nine *Länder* of the three Western occupying powers met in August

1948, with twenty-seven Christian Democrats, twenty-seven Social Democrats and eleven other members. It devised a Basic Law, accepted by all the *Länder* except Bavaria (which accepted it at the second time of asking), and approved by the allies in May 1949, that provided for a federal constitution, in which basic rights were entrenched. The government was parliamentary, elected by proportional representation, with a President whose office was mainly ceremonial – the last President, Hindenburg, having used his powers to help the Nazis.

In the first elections held in 1949 Adenauer, who had been Chairman of the Parliamentary Council, led the Christian Democrats, opposed by Kurt Schumacher for the Social Democrats, who were confidently expected to win. The result was close but unexpected: the Christian Democrats winning 7,360,000 votes, and the Social Democrats just under seven million votes, to give the CDU 139 seats against the SPD's 131. The Free Democrats, who at that time were appealing chiefly to refugees, had fifty-two seats, and other smaller parties held the balance, so that a coalition was inescapable.

In order to govern, the Christian Democrats had to form a coalition, but here again there was a surprise. Most people thought that Schumacher, the experienced and charismatic anti-Nazi Socialist leader, strongly supported by the British, would lead a coalition relying chiefly upon the CDU and the SPD. Although this would entail the withdrawal of Adenauer from political office – since he was antipathetic to Schumacher, strongly anti-Socialist and had fought the campaign on the creation of a social market economy, at that time an untried experiment – in the distressed conditions of the time rationing and state control of the economy seemed essential. It was also thought that at the age of seventy-three Adenauer was unfitted to assume the office of Chancellor. At a meeting of CDU deputies, however, Adenauer put himself forward as a candidate for the Chancellorship, while suggesting Professor Theodor Heuss of the FDP as the first President of the Federal Republic.

After much manoeuvring, Adenauer emerged as the head, or Chancellor, of a coalition government and Schumacher as leader of the opposition. The wily old fox had once more outwitted everybody. Adenauer's policy was based upon the scaling down of the monopolistic ownership of industry, towards a mixture of private and public control with the workers having representation, and the freeing of the German economy. He also wished to forge a peace treaty with the Western allies, leaving the question of relationship with the East to a later date, although he did state that he was opposed to the Oder–Neisse line as the permanent frontier of Germany, a view which caused severe anxiety in Western Europe as well as of course in the East. Adenauer was convinced that German sovereignty should be restored and that the Federal German Republic would be the proper representative of all the German people. His foreign policy was based on a deep-rooted hostility to the Soviet Union and the conviction – reflecting his Rhineland origins – that an alliance with the French was Germany's best possible security.

Adenauer's original government rested upon an inchoate and unstable parliamentary majority, completely unused to normal procedures of free democratic government. The equally inchoate and difficult problems which faced the SPD under Kurt Schumacher meant that Parliament itself in the early days seemed hardly a promising place in which to develop coherent democratic policies for the reconstruction. Nevertheless, Adenauer soon established a benevolent despotism both in Parliament and over his own Cabinet, where his only equal was Ludwig Erhard, who was made Minister of Economics. The outlook was unpromising: 'the antics of German parliamentarians brought home to me the demoralising effects of a long occupation', as Sir Ivone Kirkpatrick, the British High Commissioner, said.

The new federal state was faced by three major internal problems, not least the continuing Berlin airlift, the Soviet threat, and the organisation of its defence by the British and Americans.

In foreign affairs Adenauer first attempted to achieve reconciliation with France. The European coal and steel community was designed as a Franco–German cartel similar to that which had operated between the wars. Adenauer, who was deeply suspicious of the British, partly out of dislike but partly through their open support for the SPD, relied closely upon American support. This link was helped by the American High Commissioner, John McCloy, being a distant relative of Adenauer's wife: they became staunch allies.

The agreement by McCloy on 15 December 1949 that Marshall Aid for Germany would no longer be paid through the occupation authorities but would be put directly at the disposal of the federal government, was the most important development of Adenauer's early years in office. By March 1950 Germany had representatives at the Council of Europe, was a member of the European Payments Union, and had Consuls-General in Washington, Paris and London.

On 9 May 1950 Adenauer began discussions with the French Foreign Minister, Schuman, on the European Coal and Steel

Community. The talks about the future of the Schuman Plan, within which there would be free trade in iron and steel and joint agreements on production levels and prices, included France, the Federal Republic, Italy, and Belgium, Holland and Luxemburg. This meant that Germany had now fully reappeared in Europe as an autonomous nation with the respect and support of its neighbours. However Schumacher and the SPD objected to the Schuman Plan on the ground that it was in fact a form of prolonged French occupation, similar to that of the Ruhr in 1923. But Adenauer's decision to accept the French invitation for discussions led to the allies abolishing all forms of occupation controls on 15 May 1950. Adenauer made two concessions: to give the Saar autonomy, so that it could decide whether or not to remain part of Germany, and to agree to participate in the defence of Western Europe. The Saar issue was one which continued to affect the future of the Federal Republic. The French desire was to incorporate the Saar into France or alternatively to keep it as an autonomous or Europeanised zone between Germany and France.

Adenauer had managed to get powerful British and American armies stationed in Germany to defend the country as allies against Soviet aggression, and not mainly as armies of occupation. He had begun to cement an alliance with France which represented a repudiation of the *entente cordiale* between Britain and France, a cornerstone of European policy for half a century. He began the process of replacing Britain as America's most loyal European ally, and he rallied the German people behind democracy and against the Soviet Union. In so doing he abandoned his Eastern fellow-Germans to the Soviet Union. A neutral Germany, its neutrality guaranteed by East and West, would have been a possibility on several occasions, but it proved repeatedly unacceptable to the Western powers, for what seemed at the time good reasons. This possibility – discussed in the last chapter – forms the basis of the accusation that the Cold War was invented by the West.

In its place a powerful West German state was created based on the social market economy. The achievements were astonishing – rebuilding the factories and the cities, settling the refugees, of whom there were eight million, with many more arriving daily from the East. The Federal Law of Restitution was passed, under which the victims of Nazism were compensated, and goods worth three and a half billion Marks shipped to Israel as an act of atonement. The introduction of *Mitbestimmung* or co-partnership for the workers in heavy industries meant that German trade unions were involved in membership of the supervisory and managerial boards of the largest companies in heavy industry.

By the early 1950s the German economic miracle was well on its way and, with the creation of the nucleus of the Common Market, Germany was virtually restored to its pre-1939 position, despite being divided into two parts. It had been largely an American creation, and the American presence in Europe was in the main due to the need to save Germany. In the process Germany became once more an important nation, the most powerful in Western Europe, a fact which the Soviet Union deplored.

Chapter 10

Stalin builds Socialism in Central Europe

Stalin deeply resented the Western allies' refusal to make Austria and East and West Germany into one neutral buffer zone. He also greatly disliked the ceaseless barrage of Western interference in Central Europe where the West was always demanding that he have free elections, democratic votes, fair play and freedom of speech. The Red Army had swept across Latvia, Lithuania, Estonia, Poland, Hungary, Bulgaria, Romania and Czechoslovakia into East Germany as conqueror: won by the sword, these lands were part of Soviet Russia's own domain: Stalin had had this notion ratified, as he saw it, at Yalta and at Potsdam by the allies and he was careful to abide meticulously by the unwritten rules which he thought applied. Stalin saw these areas as part of his autocratic centralised Communist empire. The Soviet Union controlled all foreign and defence policies for these countries and so their internal domestic policies must reflect this. Moreover any search by them for any variation in their Communism was fraught with danger for it might contaminate the heartland itself. In the satellite buffer zone Soviet rule was utterly inflexible, completely authoritarian and totally centralised under Moscow.

Stalin did not see countries beyond his immediate satellite states in quite the same light for he differentiated clearly between those areas which he had been allowed to think of as coming within his sphere of influence at Yalta and those which did not. For example, when the Red Army reached the Greek borders, it adhered strictly to the Yalta agreement and stopped, for Greece had been assigned to the British sphere of influence. Despite the presence of a strong Greek Communist party (EAM) crying out for help, with its powerful army (ELAS) enmeshed in civil war and badly needing assistance, Stalin kept his word and stopped troops and tanks on the border. It did not stop him supplying guns and money to the Communist guerrillas in Greece, but to him that was an entirely different matter. His attitude towards Yugoslavia was different again.

To demonstrate variations in Soviet behaviour in Central Europe in this chapter, I have chosen to deal with Czechoslovakia, Greece, Poland and Yugoslavia.

Czechslovakia had established a government-in-exile in London during the Nazi occupation under President Beneš and his Foreign Minister Masaryk. After their experience at Munich, the Czechs no longer trusted the British or the Americans, so in 1943 Beneš signed a treaty with the Soviet Union agreeing that the moment the Red Army liberated the country, soviet councils would be set up and a government of national unity formed under Klement Gottwald. The Red Army therefore arrived as *the* anti-Nazi liberation force.

Gottwald's new government at first consisted of Communists, Socialists, Social Democrats and the People's Catholic and Slovak parties but Communists were in control of all key ministries. Industries were nationalised and placed under workers' control led by Communist trade unionists, land reform was introduced and all traitors and collaborators were punished. Beneš had a clear understanding of Soviet intentions with respect to territory but he did not appreciate the full extent of Stalin's intentions to impose a copy of the Soviet regime throughout.

The National Assembly elected on 26 May 1946 gave the Communists and their allies rather more than half the seats. Communists terrorised the countryside and arrested many non-Communists who were put in prison camps no different from those opened by the Nazis. To back up its moves Czechoslovakia gained a panoply of security services: a reorganised police force, an armed reserve called the Workers' Militia, revolutionary guards and a military security service, the OBZ. Thus a system of terror was imposed on the country. Meanwhile the Russians were removing property from Czechoslovakia on the ground that it had previously been German-owned, while the Western allies were supplying relief through UNRRA.

In July 1947 Czechoslovakia proposed to go to Paris to discuss the Marshall Plan, whereupon Gottwald and Masaryk were summoned to Moscow and ordered by Stalin not to participate in the Marshall Plan talks, since the Soviet Union, Poland and Yugoslavia were boycotting them and he would regard participation as an act of hostility against the Soviet Union. Meanwhile the Soviet Union concluded agreements with Czechoslovakia on trade, which were drawn up in such a way that the Czechs were required to supply manufactured goods to the Soviet Union in return for raw materials. But the raw materials were of such poor quality as to be unusable, so the Czechs were reduced to importing materials from elsewhere in order to manufacture and export, below cost, to Russia. This was one of the ways by which the Russians exploited satellite states. The economic system was made even more difficult by the particularly hot summer of 1947 with a drought which led to a disastrous harvest. As many farmers were in grave difficulty for money, the Communists proposed that there should be a capital levy to compensate them for their losses. This capital levy would have fallen most severely upon small businessmen, shopkeepers and medium-sized farms. The non-Communists in the cabinet opposed the levy, and this brought Masaryk into severe conflict with them, since he sought to pacify the Communists by accepting this.

The students agitated for greater freedom of thought and speech. Mounting evidence of Communist control of the state led to a growing feeling of revulsion among the students and other groups, and it became clear that in the 1948 elections the Communists might lose seats, had the elections been free. The Minister of Information then delivered a speech which was later published under the title 'We Mobilise', which threatened that 'he who takes a stand against the Communists is guilty of high treason'. When the students demonstrated they were suppressed by force. The winter of 1947–8 was particularly hard and unrest became widespread.

When the election campaign began in February 1948, President Beneš welcomed the new British Ambassador to Czechoslovakia in a statement in which he said 'as you in your country, we value above all else personal freedom, social progress and justice, a peaceful and happy life free from fear and hatred. Our laws are and will remain in this spirit and in this spirit we pray that our democratic institutions may develop.

'Our great President-Liberator, T. G. Masaryk, of whom you spoke, taught us all these ideals and to his teachings, which make up the tradition of our whole history, we shall remain faithful.'

This was as clear a statement repudiating the Communists as any man in his position dared to make. It seemed to show that the election, if freely conducted, would probably end Communist control of Czechoslovakia. Despite two and a half years of open terror the opposition was not yet broken.

The Communists decided, therefore, to use the security police to undertake a putsch, and when the opinion polls established that they were losing significant proportions of their vote, they organised the trade unions and instructed the shock troops of workers' militias to rise. The signal for this was given on 14 February 1948 in the Communist newspaper *Rudě Právo*. The Communists said that the non-Communist ministers were attempting to form a national government from which the Communists were to be excluded. Gottwald, the Prime Minister, refused to allow the cabinet to discuss this question, and the National Socialist party, the Catholic

People's party and the Slovak Democratic party thereupon withdrew and complained to President Beneš. On 19 February Zorin,
the Russian Deputy Foreign Minister, arrived in Prague and made
final arrangements for the coup. Many of the non-Communist
ministers resigned and on Friday 20 February 1948 the Communist
party issued a statement calling for the people to rise in support of
the government. On 21 February all broadcasting was taken over
and air flights were forbidden. Meanwhile mass meetings were
held throughout Czechoslovakia, and on 22 February the troops
moved to occupy major cities, including Prague.

Beneš refused to form a purely Communist government, but at
this point the ever-hesitant Social Democratic ministers, the
majority of whom were, in fact, Communist stooges, decided not
to resign, thus allowing the Communists to maintain the government in being with a non-Communist party, the Social Democrats,
as their allies. On 25 February students rioted against the government and a number were shot; the same day Gottwald formed a
new government, with eleven Communists, three 'Social Democrats' for show, six representatives of minor parties and three
independents, including Jan Masaryk.

Masaryk had always tried to bring the Soviet Union and the
West together in an attempt to develop a neutral Czechoslovakia,
though his own personal inclinations were passionately pro-
American and British. As the provisional government was progressively taken over by the Communists his despair became more
profound, especially as it became clear that the Western nations
had no intention of guaranteeing Czechoslovak independence.

The Communist party took over completely on 26 February 1948
and began to create an orthodox police state. A Stalinist purge
began. Teachers and university professors in particular were dismissed from their posts, some members of Parliament were
arrested. The Western powers protested, but Gottwald taunted
them: 'We do not have to heed lectures on democracy by those on
whose conscience lies Munich, those who bargained for our existence with Hitler's Germany.' Beneš swore in the new government
but declined to talk to Gottwald. The purge intensified and on 10
March 1948 it was announced that Jan Masaryk had committed
suicide by throwing himself out of his window. It now seems likely
that he was shot behind the right ear and then thrown out of the
window.

His murder was the symbolic act that showed the West that
reconciliation with Stalinism was not possible in practice.

The tragedy of Czechoslovakia proved that even where the
Western powers deliberately abstained from all attempts at inter-

vention, where the non-Communists enthusiastically supported the Communists and the Russians, the creation of a Soviet republic was conducted with great violence. The Russians had come as liberators but their presence was lethal.

Greece's battle to rid itself of the Communists began with British aid and ended with American involvement. In March 1947 Attlee told the United States that Britain could no longer afford substantial help to the Greeks. President Truman reacted with $300 million aid through the auspices of the Truman Doctrine. The aid was slow to come; a government offensive in the summer of 1947 petered out, and towards the end of the year the Communists once more overtly controlled the northern mountains, which they had nominally ceded at the cease-fire. In December American military advisers effectively took control of the planning of the Greek army's counter-insurgency, and American military equipment began to arrive in large quantities. Soon serious efforts were made to clear the mountainous areas and to suppress the Communists active in politics.

Events outside Greece also helped. In mid-1948 Tito quarrelled with Stalin. As a result Communist supplies from Yugoslavia stopped when the Greek Communists sided with Stalin. But perhaps more important, the long-run hope of the Greek Communists that they could form a government linked to those of the neighbouring Communist states now became implausible. Nevertheless, by the end of 1948, despite the Communist defeats, continued and vigorous Communist attacks continued, and towns were captured and held for weeks at a time. The Greek people, after eight years of guerrilla war, were exceedingly weary; and the government, never popular, reached new depths of unpopularity. But when in June 1949 the Greek northern frontier was actually closed, the supplies for the Greek Communists from other Communist states were insufficient for them to hold out against the vigorous attacks of the Greek army using modern American equipment, including trucks, tanks and aircraft in considerable numbers. Albania, which had become the main Communist base, closed its frontiers in August 1949 and on 16 October the Communist Democratic Army announced a cease-fire.

As American economic and military aid flowed in, so constitutional democratic government was gradually restored and, after a referendum, George II was confirmed as the monarch; he died a few months later and was succeeded by his brother Paul. Under its new government, Greece joined the Marshall Plan and began reconstruction.

Luton Sixth Form College
Library

Poland's first post-war government consisted of some Communists and some London-exiled Poles but the sovietisation proceeded quickly. Those who opposed the Communists were immediately arrested by the security police. Some Poles returned from the Soviet Union, others were expelled from the territory which had been given to Russia at Yalta. Meanwhile the territory allocated to Poland from Germany was stripped of equipment by the Russians and then, under the agreements signed with Russia, twelve million tons of coal were to be supplied by Poland to Russia at a nominal price. The Peasant party was reorganised with a Communist membership, the former members of the Peasant party being expelled. Anyone who sought to join the Peasant party or a group other than the Communist party was immediately arrested; non-Communist leaders were murdered after being tortured. The German concentration camps were reopened to accommodate the large numbers of political prisoners. All those non-Communists who had been in the resistance were arrested as well as some Communists. As the Red Army swept westwards, German nationals either fled from the occupied territories and their own homelands or were expelled over the Oder–Neisse border. Meanwhile Poles in the areas annexed by the Soviet Union were subjected to a reign of terror and, in what then became Poland, a vast trekking of the population took place. The home army, the Polish resistance, was liquidated, with its members hounded down in the forests or placed in the former German concentration camps. Yet somehow the country survived the first post-war winter of 1945.

Russian plans for Poland gave priority to heavy industry and the resettlement of the population in the former German areas. But like other East European countries now under Russian domination, Poland was ordered in July 1947 to have no part in the Paris conference which discussed the setting up of the Marshall Plan. Meanwhile the education system was revived under Communist direction, and although Poles were free to read and write in their native language, the matter of the syllabus was completely dictated by the Soviet Union. The authorities engaged in a severe campaign against the Church, culminating in the arrest of Cardinal Wyszynski, accused of spying for the Americans. The Church became the centre of resistance to the Communist state, even though the Cardinal was not allowed to travel and the Church's control of education was completely taken away. The Church became known as the Church of Silence: first in disappointment, then in pride.

During the war two powerful resistance groups developed in Yugoslavia, the Serbian royalist Chetniks, led by Mihailovič, and a stronger southern Communist Partisan group led by Josip Brož, who was also known as Tito. He controlled large tracts of remote mountainside and dealt heavy blows against the Germans in the towns, while the Chetniks were more cautious, refraining from actions which might bring fierce reprisals on local people. By late 1943 19,000 partisans were holding down a German led army of 117,000; by mid–1944 the partisans had swelled to 350,000. Tito, who had been trained in Russia before the war, therefore became the only genuine communist resistance hero in Eastern Europe.

Because Tito was so successful, he was eventually recognised by the British and sent arms and assistance, although there was in fact a Yugoslav government-in-exile in London under King Peter which the British also recognised. However the British hoped that after the war, the King would accept a coalition which would include Tito.

Tito had been only a junior party functionary but the splendour of his military campaigns and his political skills brought him to prominence. He therefore owed little to Stalin, but much to the British, even though he was at the time an orthodox Stalinist. By the end of the war power was in Tito's hands, and within nine months the Communists were in complete control. Yugoslavia thus became the only country which had voluntarily accepted Communism without Soviet occupation and whose leader was a national hero of genuine stature. Communist membership was drawn from all sections of Yugoslavia and represented all national and ethnic groups, it had defeated the Germans with little outside assistance, other than arms from the British, and it was quite clear therefore that the regime had a legitimacy denied to others in Eastern Europe.

Yugoslavia had suffered enormously in the war from death, starvation and devastation, but true to his Stalinist principles Tito immediately began with a purge of non-Communist political elements: many were executed, many thousands more were sent to prison. The Yugoslav equivalent of the KGB, the UDBA, was at least as ruthless as any of its Eastern European opposite numbers. Moreover, though Yugoslavia had been strongly supported by the British and the Americans, it immediately began an anti-Western campaign, occupying Trieste before the New Zealanders to whom it had been assigned. Only after threats of war by Ernest Bevin did the Yugoslavs withdraw, though they still occupied the country-side around the city.

The army continued to put down the remnants of Mihailovič's Chetniks with considerable cruelty. Mihailovič himself was cap-

tured on 14 March, tried and executed on 17 July 1946. The trial of
the Archbishop of Zagreb, Stepinac, followed, on grounds of
pro-Fascist activity during the war, and had far-reaching implications. The Communist lawyers were able to prove that the Roman
Catholic hierarchy had collaborated with the Fascists, both Italian
and Croatian. The Archbishop was sent to prison for sixteen years
and his priests were purged. They were also able to suggest that
Mihailovič had been keener to destroy Tito's partisans than to fight
the Germans.

Arguing, with some justice, that the pre-war regime had been a
dictatorship and pro-Nazi, Tito was at first regarded abroad as a
relatively desirable, indigenous and benevolent Communist, compared with the puppet regimes installed by the Russians in other
Eastern European and Balkan countries. Nevertheless, in 1946
and 1947, in a series of show trials held throughout Yugoslavia,
Radicals, Democrats, Socialists, Croatians and Slovenians were
charged with conspiring with British intelligence to overthrow the
Yugoslav government. The persecution of these groups continued
until well into the 1950s. This suggested both that there was
extensive opposition to Tito, and also that there was no significant
difference between Tito's oppressive Communism and the
straightforward tyranny in overtly Stalinist countries such as
Czechoslovakia and Poland.

The Churches were regarded with suspicion: the Roman Catholic Church, as an outright enemy, was persecuted and its bishops
and priests imprisoned, but the Serbian Orthodox Church became
a puppet of the regime, like the Orthodox Church in Russia, and
the Muslim religion was also put under secular control. More
positively, however, the Communists made a major effort to settle
the nationality question.

On 31 January 1946 the constituent assembly adopted the new
Constitution of what was called the Federal People's Republic of
Yugoslavia, which created six People's Republics. Serbia was
made an autonomous province.

By 1947 Tito was riding high. A peace treaty gave Yugoslavia all
of Istria except Trieste and substantial reparations from Italy,
Hungary and Bulgaria. With the Eastern European Communist
parties plus those of Italy and France, Tito played a leading part in
establishing the Cominform alliance in September 1947.

Not surprisingly, the Western allies were disillusioned by Tito's
activities, particularly as he was also reinforcing the Greek Communist rebels and offering them a refuge. It also looked as though
the newly independent Albania, which had been occupied by the
Italians since 1939, and which had a Communist dictator, Enver

Hoxha, might become a constituent republic of Federal Yugoslavia. Thus Tito seemed to be another Stalin.

Despite its federal nature, Yugoslavia was largely a charade with the Communist party itself not only highly centralised, but almost inevitably dominated by Montenegrins and Serbs, since the Croatians had been a source of support for the Nazis. Possibly only a centralised government could have restored a country which had lost 11 per cent of its population, in which about a fifth of the remaining population were homeless, and where a third of industry, about half the livestock, 80 per cent of agricultural equipment, and most of the railway system had been destroyed. Starvation was only avoided by UNRRA aid. Volunteer and forced labour slowly restored factories, railways and roads, so that by the end of 1946 about four fifths of industry and nine tenths of the railways were working again; within a year Yugoslavia was actually producing as much as it had before the war in industry and more in food. Although industry and banking were nationalised, much of it was foreign-owned, largely by the Germans, therefore nationalisation did not outrage the people as much as it did in other countries. Agriculture was not collectivised, but the spread of electricity and the forced industrialism were signs that the regime was adopting the Russian principle of Socialism.

In 1948 Stalin denounced Tito and ordered the federation of Bulgaria and Yugoslavia, the implication being that Tito's wider ambitions were not supported and, possibly, that Dimitrov, the Bulgarian leader, might supersede him. The Yugoslavs refused to accept this federation, with the result that they and the Bulgarians were summoned to the Kremlin to be denounced by Stalin personally for their policies in particular their independent foreign attitudes. Tito's deputy, Kardelj, who went on his behalf, signed a formal agreement promising prior consultation on foreign policy before he left Moscow. Stalin attempted to replace Tito as dictator of Yugoslavia, and on 4 May 1948 the Soviet Communist party accused the Yugoslavs of indulging in boundless self-praise, denigrating the other Communist parties and decrying the role of the Red Army in liberating Yugoslavia. Tito was thereupon denounced by Romania and Albania, and the Yugoslav–Soviet trade agreement was suspended. Tito went to his Central Committee for its first full session since before the war, and received a unanimous vote of support.

The Cominform – minus Tito – met in Bucharest, condemned the Yugoslav Communists, and voiced charges that they were leftist, adventurist, demagogic and impractical. In the face of this emergency the Yugoslav Party Congress met in Belgrade in June.

Stalinists were rounded up; the Chief of Staff of the army, Jovano-vic, was killed by border guards while trying to escape to Romania; others defected or were locked up. On 31 July Tito became the acknowledged leader of an independent Yugoslav Communist party, the only genuinely autonomous party in Eastern Europe, having achieved its position with little Soviet support.

As the leader of a strong state with a powerful army, Tito was the main proponent of a Balkan federation, to include Bulgaria and Albania, and possibly Greece and Romania, which would, to a degree, be independent of the Soviet Union. He was also carrying on an aggressive policy to annex parts of Greece, Italy and Austria which Stalin had at Yalta and Potsdam agreed should be allocated wholly or partly to the West. Tito had unwittingly, therefore, taken Moscow's aggressively anti-Western line too literally and exceeded the bounds that Stalin had secretly set.

When the denunciation of Tito and his group came in March 1948, the Yugoslavs denied the charges. In May 1949 the Yugo-slavs refused to attend the Bucharest meeting of the Cominform and were expelled. Both Stalin and Tito had overestimated their own power – Stalin assumed that Tito would be overthrown, and Tito assumed he could act independently of Stalin in formulating Cominform policy.

In 1949 the Soviet Union identified Yugoslavia as its chief enemy, with Tito as the successor to Trotsky. In the purge that followed throughout Eastern Europe a Titoist, Xoxe, was ex-ecuted in Tirana on 11 June 1949, Laszlo Rajk and his colleagues were hanged in Budapest after a show trial in September 1949, Kostow was tried and executed in Bulgaria, and Gomulka in Poland was charged with being a Titoist. A growing number of Soviet agents penetrated Yugoslavia, and in November 1949 the Cominform called on Yugoslav Communists to overthrow the 'Tito clique of Fascism', Tito himself was described as the leader of a political gang consisting of reactionary, nationalist, clerical and Fascist elements and running a brutal Gestapo-style terrorist regime.

Tito's views on economic and political policy at that time varied little from Stalin's; his Communist party had behaved exactly like those of the rest of Eastern Europe in the suppression of freedom and the persecution of the majority of the population. His differ-ence was that he wanted to be independent of Stalin. This was his heresy.

Isolation not only deprived Yugoslavia of economic and military assistance but it also resulted in Soviet-inspired internal disrup-tion. So Tito needed Western links in order to survive. Yet until the middle of 1949, Tito and others hoped against hope for a reconciliation with the Soviet Union, but by that stage they discovered that Stalin's organisation of a blockade and boycott of Yugoslavia by the Eastern European bloc was a final decision by the Soviet Union that Tito could not be received back into favour.

The 1948 harvest was especially bad, and the winter of 1948–9 was therefore extremely tough. The party intensified its fundamentally Stalinist Five-Year Plan, which of course made matters worse by giving priority to heavy industry and by a decision to progress with the collectivisation of agriculture, which immediately led to severe peasant resistance. The collapse of the harvest in 1949 and a severe drought in 1950 resulted in the grain output falling by over a half; thus the total agriculture output slumped to three quarters of the pre-war level and town-dwellers were on the edge of starvation.

Faced with economic collapse, and external disruption from the Soviet Union and its satellites, Yugoslavia took the initiative and opened negotiations with the West. The first result was an American loan of $20 million in September 1949, which helped to avert famine the following winter, and an American Military Assistance Advisory Group, which was sent to Yugoslavia to support the Yugoslav army.

On 29 November 1950 Truman asked Congress to support a Yugoslav Emergency Relief Act, on the ground that the continued independence of Yugoslavia was of great importance to the security of the United States. Thus the Yugoslav Communist regime became the first Communist regime since just after the end of the war to receive United States aid in substantial amounts. Yugoslavia did not go so far as to join NATO, but just before Stalin's death in March 1953 it signed a treaty of friendship and cooperation with Greece and Turkey.

Once the United States had supported Yugoslavia, Britain and France followed with almost $600 million between 1950 and 1955. In addition, Yugoslavia was given substantial technical and managerial help in order to develop its own economic and social infrastructure.

This led to the so-called Yugoslav Road to Socialism, which became known as Titoism, a term of opprobrium in the Soviet Union but one which became increasingly acceptable in the West. Titoism was a pragmatic ideology dependent more upon Tito's own views than the genuine intellectual conversion of a large group of people. It began with the rereading of Marx's *Das Kapital* by Djilas and the realisation that whatever Lenin and Stalin had said, Marx himself was opposed to bureaucracy, and

that the principle of social self-management could be drawn from
large parts of Marx's work. This led to the idea that the factories
should be owned by the workers; the workers' groups be loosely
associated with each other; the state, to which they should pay
taxes only for essentials like military and other needs, would have a
minimal role. Self-management became a dominant theme of the
revolution, and to this was added the concept developed during the
war of a Federal Yugoslavia with power devolved to the autonomous republics. But as Stalinism was gradually abandoned, a
Marxian Socialism based upon free associations linked together in
a loosely-organised federal republic became the norm, together
with autonomous local government services. Increasingly, too, a
theoretical attack was mounted upon the autocracy of the Soviet
Union and its imperialist ambitions, and it was described by
Western Marxists inspired by Trotsky as state-capitalism, which
was worse than ordinary capitalism.

The intellectual development of Socialism in Yugoslavia depended more upon self-help and self-development, and a shift
from bureaucratisation: in agriculture kolkhozes and state farms
were supplanted by producer co-operatives with technical and
marketing assistance provided centrally, as in the West. Such
co-operatives had been known in pre-war Yugoslavia; they origin-
ated in Sir Horace Plunkett's experiments before 1914 in Ireland.
In 1952 the private ownership of agricultural land was finally
conceded. Elected workers' councils were set up in some enterprises in 1949, and these became a common model in 1950.
Gradually this federal bureaucracy was dismantled and the posts
went to the constituent republics.

As the fight with the Cominform developed, so the process of
market Socialism and Socialist democracy became a central feature of Tito's Yugoslavia. The Law on the Planned Management of
the economy abandoned the Soviet system and replaced it with a
series of indicative plans, setting targets but not compelling their
acceptance. They were based upon the calculation of the minimum
levels of utilisation of capacity in the industrial sector of the
Republic; the total volume of investment was distributed through
two sets of funds – a general investment fund and republican
investment funds – and a fund was used to pay the wage bill. Thus
the basic tools of planning remained with the government, giving it
underlying control of the economy: and all else was left to the
autonomy of the enterprises operating within the market system.

By 1951 the economy was booming, and started to develop like
other economies bordering the Mediterranean. By 1954 free price
competition in consumer goods and free market arrangements for

agricultural produce replaced the State Control Commission.

By the end of the 1940s Stalin had come to ruthlessly dominate Romania, Bulgaria, the Baltic States, East Germany, Poland and Czechoslovakia, but Yugoslavia broke free from his control and Greece never entered it, despite the efforts of the local Communists, because Stalin ultimately abided by the Yalta agreement and so Greece received first British and then American aid.

Czechoslovakia was the test case. It was assumed by the Western allies that a democratic republic like that of the inter-war years would be restored, while Stalin imposed a Soviet-style dictatorship with the active support of a fairly substantial minority of Czechs. Perhaps the allies were self-deluding to expect that any non-Soviet regime could persist in Stalin's conquered lands; on the other hand, had it been possible to neutralise a defeated Germany, and achieve a Continent-wide settlement, then perhaps Stalin would have permitted more liberal regimes in some of the Eastern European countries. Austria and Finland were permitted free regimes provided they were neutral internationally. Until the Soviet archives are opened this possibility of 'Finlandisation' will remain speculation, but the balance of probability is against it for Eastern Europe as a whole. Leninism had been a system of tyranny from the beginning. Stalin's own rule had been monolithically tyrannical, through collectivisation, the Great Purge and the war-time purges. It was his usual way of operating. Only fear of further war restrained him from overthrowing Tito in 1948. His chronic suspicion of all those who were not his abject servants, his capricious destruction even of those who were his most willing tools, make it highly improbable that any solution short of what was achieved in Eastern Europe in the three years after 1948 was possible. There were small, very small, differences in the Soviet treatment of ex-enemy countries like Germany, on the one hand, and Czechoslovakia on the other hand; but the conclusion seems inescapable that Stalinism was a totalitarian doctrine, permitting little variation in the treatment of different countries. Stalin respected treaties, almost superstitiously, and therefore did not actively support subversion in countries not allocated to him at Yalta or Potsdam, though even in that case the insurrection of Greece, the blockade of Berlin, and the invasion of South Korea in 1950 suggest that he was ready to seize any opportunity. The argument that the Cold War was not inevitable, and was not caused by Stalinism, ignores the nature of Stalin's tyranny, the full horrors of which are even now not fully known. But, as the last chapter discusses, a 'neutral' continent was perhaps a possibility.

Chapter 11

Dismembering Indian and Asian empires

Stalin's expansion of Soviet influence and his annexation of the satellite states after the war could be considered imperialist: it was in marked contrast to the voluntary and involuntary withdrawals of Britain, France, Belgium and Holland from their empires. The Dutch, so liberal in Europe, were old-style colonialists abroad. The big archipelago of the Dutch East Indies was highly profitable to Dutch businessmen, traders and planters. The Belgians were even more open in their view of the Congo. It had been a personal possession of the King of the Belgians and it was run on a straightforward exploitative basis. No rhetoric about self-advancement here. The Belgians were frank about their pragmatic aims. In the new post-war liberal world the Dutch and the Belgian colonies were anachronistic to say the least and their withdrawals were not accomplished without difficulty. The French also faced problems for the essence of French culture and political institutions made it a necessary truth that the summit of human ambition was achieved by becoming a full member of French society. Indeed there is much to be said for this view. Far from seeing an independent future for its colonies, therefore, France concentrated on converting its subjects into French people, and incorporating the overseas territories into France itself. This led to direct conflict with indigenous nationalism, especially when that nationalism was buttressed, as in Algeria and Syria, by a strong Arab and Muslim sensibility. Britain had always talked about giving her overseas possessions independence one day, but had consistently procrastinated over dates.

This chapter compares and contrasts the ways in which India, Pakistan, Indonesia, Malaya and Vietnam gained their independence. Algeria is discussed in Chapter 18, the Congo in Chapter 22.

The critical epicentre for the post-war history of imperialism was India. It had been the greatest European prize: a vast subcontinent with the potential of immense wealth; a legendary history; the jewel in the British crown. It was to become a future powerful force for peaceful coexistence but it has since had a centripetal tendency towards mild despotism which one may be able to detect in its birth pangs as a nation. The handing over of power without a bitter armed conflict between the British and the Indians was the model against which other transfers in Vietnam, Indonesia and Algeria were to be seen as failures; likewise the contrast between the two powerful and apparently stable states that inherited the Indian Empire and the weak and ill-prepared client states elsewhere.

India presented a challenge to the idea of independence within the Commonwealth. A sub-continent of coloured peoples, it owed no racial allegiance to Britain. For years it had been offered internal self-government, but no agreement had been reached on how this might be achieved. Progress towards independence was complicated by the position of the princes, who had direct links with the British crown; by the Muslims, especially in Sind, the Punjab and East Bengal, who did not wish to be subordinate to the Hindu majority; by Churchill who remained opposed to Indian independence; and the power and authority of Gandhi in the Congress movement, a man with a personality and a philosophy which made him a singularly difficult, indeed often incomprehensible, opponent of the Raj.

Gandhi had been called to the English Bar, had been a leader of an Asian community in South Africa and eventually became the spiritual and religious leader for Indian independence who used non-co-operation and non-violence as a weapon against the British. Although a Hindu, Gandhi's political vision was of a united India with a multiplicity of diverse faiths. As his political figurehead, Gandhi used Jawaharlal Nehru, a Kashmiri Brahmin. Nehru had been educated in England. After his return to India, he had spent almost nine years in prison for illegal and subversive acts although he was not anti-British, merely *for* an independent India, governing through Congress.

However when the war ended, Congress was not self-evidently, as it had been from 1937 to 1939, non-sectarian. To most British officials it seemed disloyally anti-British and by its reaction to Jinnah's call for Muslim self-rule, sectarian. Congress, therefore, did not seem in 1945 the inevitable and natural successor to the Indian Raj.

Jinnah was a Muslim who was neither fluent in Urdu nor particularly religious. A bachelor who had settled in London, he, almost alone, created the concept of Pakistan. He was not however responsible for the movement of Muslim nationalism which, throughout the 1930s, was developing in Egypt, in the Arab countries, in Malaysia and Indonesia, and which would in the 1940s and 1950s catch fire. But Jinnah exploited it. It was his ruthless will which more than anything created the idea of a Muslim state based on Sind and Punjab in the west, and Bengal in the east, with possible extra provinces in Kashmir and Hyderabad.

By 1945, therefore, India was in considerable disarray. The British had more forces there than ever before, and independence, which had long been promised, seemed no nearer.

When the Labour party won the British general election of 1945, the new Attlee government, although committed to independence for India as rapidly as possible, had no clear policy as to how this could be achieved. Preoccupied with economic problems at home and the Soviet threat in Europe, it had to pull its own armed forces out of India in order to speed up demobilisation and save money.

Labour's own links were with Gandhi and Nehru, both Socialist and anti-colonialist heroes. They seemed the rightful heirs to the Raj. But all the evidence showed that the withdrawal of British forces would be followed by violence and even anarchy – because of the absolute refusal of the Muslim League to accept second place to the Congress party in a united India.

Thus Wavell, the Viceroy at the end of the war, had to try to reconcile three men: Gandhi, Jinnah and Nehru. Wavell was a sensitive soldier, not especially successful as a military leader, and distrustful of all politicians, having been bruised at their hands. It proved an impossible task for him. The Indian government had a strong army and probably the best high-level civil service in the world. The state could function whoever was in office. But to whom could power be handed over? Jinnah disliked Gandhi and detested Nehru, a feeling that was mutual. Jinnah's stated aim was Pakistan, as a sovereign state with complete control of its foreign affairs and defence. Yet it seemed from time to time that he was prepared to compromise.

Immediately after the Japanese war was over, in September 1945, Wavell announced not only that a constitution-making body would convene, but that central and provincial elections would also be held. In these the League gained control of the Muslim-majority provinces, with Congress victorious elsewhere. Congress and League then failed to agree on fundamental rules as to how the Constituent Assembly was to meet and what it was to do. It was soon clear that Congress was determined to resign from government if League members stayed, whilst League members would not attend the Constituent Assembly under Congress's rules.

Here was a sad position. The British were keen to hand over power. But the Congress could receive it only if they accepted Pakistan; and to accept Pakistan meant not only a rejection of the concept of a secular, united India which had been the most prized achievement of the Raj, but also a virtual certainty of communal violence as people moved to areas where a majority of their own faith were in control. The threat of violence was gigantic when literally thousands of villages and towns throughout India had mixed populations. Had the Muslims all lived together in one contiguous area a peaceful partition might have been possible; even after Pakistan was created from the predominantly Muslim provinces; however, over fifty million Muslims continued to live in India.

The problem of ending an Empire legally and peacefully was tremendous. The princes, for example, owed loyalty to the King–Emperor. The Cabinet mission made it clear that this relationship could not survive independence, yet sovereignty could not be transferred without the consent of the princes to the successor. Interminable procedural wrangles exasperated the Attlee government which at home was faced with a severe economic and financial crisis in the bleak winter of 1946–7. They had to get the British army out of India and cut through the argy-bargy. On 20 February 1947 it was announced, in what was effectively an ultimatum, that power would be transferred to Indian hands on 30 June 1948 either to a central government 'or in some areas to the existing Provincial Governments' or in other unspecified ways. Wavell, who was partly blamed by the government for the failure to reach agreement, was hastily replaced by Lord Mountbatten, an admiral and a cousin of the King, who had commanded the allied forces in Southeast Asia towards the end of the war.

The Mountbattens went to India and quickly gained the confidence of Gandhi and Nehru – indeed Lady Louis was a close friend of Nehru – but they alienated Jinnah. On Mountbatten's advice the handing over was to be done as rapidly as possible ten months *in* advance of the set date. The outcome was not just the rapid setting up of an Indian government and the even more hasty creation of Pakistan, but considerable communal bloodshed.

His initial gambit was to try for a unified federal India, by threatening Jinnah with a truncated Pakistan. This failed. He then tried a union based on two sovereign states. By 20 April 1947 Nehru had accepted Pakistan, with reluctance and dislike, but was adamant that no area that did not wish to join Pakistan would be required to do so. This was a belated realisation that the Congress demand for an all-India federation was unrealistic; and it was this demand which had prevented agreement the previous year. By the time Nehru made his concession, Jinnah was convinced that a sovereign Pakistan could be achieved and he had no further reason to compromise. Congress was concerned, as always, that this concession should not lead to the fragmentation of India into innumerable petty states, which was why they insisted that Pakistan should in effect secede from the state that would succeed the British Raj.

From Britain Mountbatten called out Sir Cyril Radcliffe, a distinguished lawyer, to draw the boundary line, which he did with great speed, in an atmosphere of mounting communal tension. Arrangements had hastily to be made for all-India services such as the army and the civil service to be transferred to Pakistan, a state that did not yet exist and had no capital or Parliament, merely a leader, Jinnah. The interim suggestion was for two dominions within the Commonwealth and the same Governor-General, a job that Congress believed should go to Mountbatten, but Jinnah had another idea and became Governor-General of Pakistan himself.

After it was clear that 30 June was too early a date for the transfer of power, 15 August 1947 was chosen as the final date – subsequently changed to 14 August by the astrologers. The transfer of power to India was straightforward. That to Pakistan involved much improvisation as a new government machine had hastily to be created in Karachi. Meanwhile Muslim troops, officers and civil servants had to make the agonising choice between loyalty to Delhi or loyalty to the new state. Moreover the boundary report was not published until just after independence day, in order to reduce to a minimum the possibility of a major civil war.

But communal rioting had already begun and millions of people were fleeing from their homes all over India but especially in the divided provinces of Bengal and Punjab. Lahore, in many respects one of the cultural centres of India, was given to Pakistan, the border with India being drawn a few miles to the east, though its population included hundreds of thousands of Hindus and Sikhs. Rioting, which began in 1945 in Calcutta with its large Muslim minority, grew all through 1946 and well into 1947. Both Lahore and Calcutta were therefore potential centres of civil war. Jinnah and Nehru pleaded with their countrymen for peace. Gandhi went to Calcutta to fast for four days and probably by this means averted a massacre there. In August 1947 the exodus of Sikhs and Hindus from the Punjab into India, and of Muslims from Calcutta into East Pakistan, took on the character of one of the great migrations of history, and the violence was such, especially in the Punjab, that many people, probably over a quarter of a million, died.

Nevertheless it was considered miraculous that most of the sub-continent survived without massacres, and that the transition from the Raj to the two successor governments was effective. For

Pakistan this was a particularly remarkable achievement, as the two parts of the country were separated by a thousand miles of India, and new capitals with all the apparatus of government had to be created in a matter of weeks at Dacca in the east and Karachi in the west.

Mountbatten always held that the transfer of power would have been impossible had it not been done quickly and that the bloodshed would have been greater had the handover taken place over a longer time. The Indians were so pleased with Mountbatten's role in the handover that he became the first Governor-General of independent India and stayed for nearly a year before returning to his naval career, eventually becoming Chief of the Naval Staff, and head of the Defence Staff.

Nehru's first task as Prime Minister of India was to fill all the government posts being vacated by the British and by those Muslims who chose Pakistan. Next he established a Constitutional Assembly to frame a constitution for India. In doing this, he refused to recognise the independence of Hyderabad, with a Muslim ruler but a Hindu electorate, although he accepted Kashmir into India despite its Muslim majority.

It was only after these necessary preliminaries – more prolonged in Pakistan's case as Jinnah was starting from scratch – that Nehru could turn to the essential task of economic and social change. But even then his energies were directed by two other purposes – to defend India against Pakistan, and to play a part on the world stage.

Nehru rapidly became the neutralist leader of the uncommitted nations in the Cold War, but he was full of contradictions. Although his sympathies as a Socialist and a parliamentarian were with the West, his desire for the decolonisation of the rest of Asia and Africa made him the West's opponent. Although he depended upon Britain and America for aid, politically his weight was usually behind the USSR.

As though the fates had struck, within a year Gandhi was murdered by a Hindu fanatic and a little later Jinnah died of a long-standing illness. Mountbatten left India, to be murdered in 1979 by Irish fanatics. India became a republic, like Pakistan, but both remained within the Commonwealth.

Jinnah had to create a completely new central administrative machine in Karachi from Muslim members of the Indian civil service and also to set up a subordinate administration in Bengal, separated by thousands of miles of India. All the paraphernalia of state from a governor-general and a national anthem to a diplomatic service had to be invented in a few weeks. There was a massive refugee problem and widespread violence and rioting.

Karachi, a small port in the poor province of Sind, was a wholly unsuitable capital, lacking everything from a sewage system to telephones. The new government began to operate in temporary offices, shacks and tents. Jinnah, as Governor-General, ran the country as much as he could through direct contact with the British officials he appointed as governors of the provinces. The real government was at provincial level. Jinnah arrogated to himself emergency powers under the Government of India Act, 1935, and attempted to rule as a dictator. The central administration of the new state worked in West Pakistan, but in East Pakistan there were virtually no experienced officials, businessmen or professional people, almost all of whom had been Hindus based in Calcutta. The division of Bengal left no effective provincial government based on Dacca. The new officials sent from West Pakistan spoke Urdu and not Bengali, and East Pakistan, with the majority of Pakistan's population, soon began to feel like the poor relation, which it was.

It was widely accepted by impartial experts in India and Britain that Pakistan could not survive for long, particularly as the Hindu commercial and professional classes fled, leaving the new country short not only of administrators but of leadership in every other field. Lahore, once an intellectual and cultural capital of India, had been reduced by the flight of the Hindus, and the massacres, to a dim provinciality.

The violent civil strife in the Punjab profoundly affected opinion in both India and Pakistan and the border was sealed after the millions of refugees had passed and hundreds of thousands of people had been massacred. The division of the Punjab left the headwaters of the Indus river system in India, which by using its waters for its own irrigation schemes threatened to deny water to the West Punjab, now in Pakistan – the land of the five rivers, as it is known. The resulting dispute was solved by a division of the waters. This solution was to some extent vitiated by the growing salinity of the soil, due in turn to over-exploitation of the water resources. The unified control of the river systems was necessary to fight salinity which destroyed the fertility of the soil. But the first major border dispute was over Jammu and Kashmir which had been substantially incorporated into India by the accession of the Maharajah, despite its Muslim majority, and where a truce line was drawn, after bitter fighting, on 1 January 1949.

Pakistan's infant government suffered a major blow from the death in 1948 of Jinnah, who suffered from tuberculosis and knew that he could not long survive. His successor, Liaqat Ali Khan, was assassinated in 1951; and there followed a series of weak and corrupt federal and provincial administrations.

The British and the Indians had cause for self-congratulation over the handover of power. For the British it seemed as though the long years of tutelage were justified. They proved to the world by the speed of the handover that they were not besotted imperialists and the Labour government demonstrated the sincerity of its anti-colonial protestations. The Indians showed to themselves, and had little hesitation in telling the world, that they could run India better than the British. A new dawn was here; now that the imperialists had departed economic and social development along the path of Indian Socialism would take off. Caste, untouchableness, the Princes, all were things of the past. The modern Fabian age of which they had talked and dreamed in the British universities had arrived. Gandhi was revered, but the future lay with the Five-Year Plan, not the spinning wheel and the ashram. Even Pakistan, a theocratic anomaly, showed that for Indians the ultimate tolerance was possible; they could tolerate intolerance and bigotry. Mountbatten returned to the Royal Navy covered in even more glory, and counted the many lives lost in partition a sad, but necessary price for a stable political settlement in the subcontinent. Britain's imperial adventure had been glorious whilst it had lasted – Clive, Warren Hastings, Macaulay, Wellington, Disraeli and the Empress Victoria, Curzon, Linlithgow, Wavell and Mountbatten – a brilliant roll call which had ended most satisfactorily with a democratic Socialist self-government; not a bad culmination and one of which the Attlee government was proud.

To the rest of the world, though, it looked rather as though the British had scuttled before they were pushed. The power of nationalism seemed less strong than the weakness of Britain. And the Americans were only too willing to rush aid into India and Pakistan. Independence had come in August 1947; on Inauguration Day in January 1948 President Truman announced Point Four, a programme of aid to the poorer countries of which India and Pakistan were virtually the only non-Latin American exemplars. India had perhaps moved from the British Empire (though it remained in the Commonwealth) to the American. And Nehru was rapidly calling in the Soviet Union to redress the balance of the New World.

Compared to the British in India, Dutch behaviour seemed spectacularly reactionary to outside observers. They had given their native peoples few political rights and little expectation of eventual freedom and independence so that when the Japanese invaded, resistance was slender. Many Indonesians collaborated with the Japanese in order to achieve some limited social and economic improvement: the Japanese were, after all, fellow Asians. (It is not to be denied that some Indians also sided with the Japanese but for the most part, even those who had previously been imprisoned by the Raj, stayed loyal.) Among the group of native intellectuals educated by the Dutch in Holland was a natural political leader, Sukarno.

When the atom bombs were dropped and Japan collapsed, Sukarno declared a Republic of Indonesia on 17 August 1945. Faced with insurrection abroad and chaos at home, the Dutch asked the Japanese to remain in control until British troops could arrive from India and denounced Sukarno as a collaborator.

Britain's Labour government were embarrassed for they were committed to colonial independence, not to holding the fort against genuine local patriots. Moreover they were already under attack for supporting the Greek monarchy against the Communists. The British authorities arrived on 15 September 1945 to find Sukarno's Indonesian Republic the *de facto* government of the two largest islands, Sumatra and Java. By normal international practice the Foreign Office would have recognised Sukarno. By grotesque irony the defeated Japanese army which had surrendered unconditionally now began, on Dutch instructions, to disarm the Indonesian guerrillas who were peacefully policing the country on behalf of what seemed to be a legitimate government. Sukarno appealed to the United States for assistance. The Americans, half-recognising the Sukarno regime, advocated mediation between Sukarno and the Dutch.

Meanwhile the Dutch, who had been imprisoned and maltreated by the Japanese, were themselves persecuted and harassed by the Indonesians, who had themselves once been collaborators of the Japanese. To the Dutch, the Japanese and the Indonesians were both cruel, savage enemies; to the Indonesians however the Japanese had seemed to some degree liberators; the idea of an economic system for the Pacific run by Asians for Asians seemed a welcome replacement for Dutch colonialism.

Attlee, the British Prime Minister, called Dutch government representatives to see him in order to insist that negotiations between them and the Indonesian Republic should begin. He was unwilling to continue to use British troops to repress the rising, especially as the British troops were conscripts, who had for the most part voted Labour, and were anxious to go home. The Acting Governor-General of the Indies, H. J. van Mook, agreed to form a Dutch–Indonesian cabinet with a view to developing the internal self-government and ultimately granting independence between 1960 and 1965. International agitation grew.

The Dutch and the Indonesians negotiated throughout 1946 with a great deal of mutual distrust, but on 15 November 1946 the Linggadjati Agreement was signed, giving the Republic *de facto* authority over Sumatra, Java and Madura. It was agreed that the Dutch and other allied troops would gradually withdraw from the islands where the Indonesians were already in control, so that on 1 January 1949 a United States of Indonesia would be created while two additional quasi-independent states under Dutch protection would be created in the rest of the islands, to include Bali and Dutch Borneo, though over 90 per cent of the population would in fact live in the new Republic itself.

Meanwhile the Dutch continued to send troops to Indonesia and by July 1947 there were 110,000 Dutch soldiers trying to destroy Sukarno's army and to control the central government of the new Republic, which was actively negotiating with a substantial number of countries for recognising its independence. These international contacts proved of crucial importance. On 30 July 1947 Australia and India brought the matter before the Security Council, and a resolution for a cease-fire was adopted, which was accepted by the Dutch as they had by that time effectively destroyed the Indonesian guerrilla army.

A United Nations mission was sent to Indonesia in late 1947 to examine the situation. Enormous pressure was put on the Dutch, who had just joined the Marshall Plan and were busily reconstructing their economy. The prevarications and double dealing had to be brought to a stop and the American version of anti-colonialism adopted. Eventually a further agreement between Holland and the embryonic Indonesian Republic was signed on the United States naval vessel, the USS *Renville*, on 17 January 1948. A greater symbol of the American role in decolonisation could scarcely be imagined. But the *Renville* agreement was not all loss because it gave the Dutch control of the main export-producing parts of Indonesia – sugar, rubber, coffee, tea, as well as the oil fields in Sumatra. This considerably weakened the position of the Indonesian government; it also excluded American oil companies from a profitable new area of exploitation.

The weakened Republic might have been built up into a proper government by an orderly transfer of power, but its efficiency was zero and its authority negligible. It was now threatened by an internal Communist revolt in September 1948 which was ineffectively repressed by Sukarno, lacking as he did power, legitimacy or authority. The Dutch continued to assault the remnants of the

Republic in the name of re-establishing order. Under the pressure of world events, however, the Dutch restored the Republican government on 6 July 1949 and continued negotiations with it, finally creating an independent Republic of Indonesia which was loosely allied with the Netherlands in a treaty of friendship. Independence was declared on 17 August 1950.

The Dutch had failed to establish themselves as beneficent post-war administrators; they had failed to create institutions to accept the transfer of power and they had procrastinated in granting genuine independence. But it was true that Sukarno had, in their eyes, been a collaborator with the enemy, he had created anarchy, crops were ungathered and prosperity inhibited under his in-efficient and corrupt regime. Would the British have managed so well in India if it had first been totally occupied by the Japanese and had consisted of a group of far-flung islands?

Perhaps Indonesia and India make poor comparisons. A better answer to these questions can be found it we look at what happened in Malaya, which had a mixed population of Indians, Chinese, Malayans and British and was conquered by the Japanese. The Japanese capitulated however so suddenly after the descent of the atom bomb that the Communists, whose underground movement was strong in the towns, were unsure whether to prepare for a guerrilla struggle, as in China, or openly to declare a Communist government in the main cities. The British (with Indian troops) took advantage of the hesitation and by November 1945 were fully in control of the peninsula. The Malayans wanted independence, not domination by either Chinese or Communists. But the only organised political party was the Communist one so the British decided to delay immediate independence until internal self-government in the various states was stronger.

The Communists retreated to the jungle where they continued to support insurrection and violence, hoping for Soviet military and moral help. But Communist strategy was not genuinely popular, its support coming only from a small part of the Chinese community and not from the Malays and Indians. Above all the British had a plan for the political evolution of the country which was widely accepted, especially by the native Malay rulers, and there was available a competent army and police force of British and local men drawn partly from the communities who feared Chinese dominance, and partly from Chinese anti-Communists. The British had always governed Malaya indirectly, through the native rulers; only Singapore was a Crown Colony.

As a result of native opposition to the 1948 Communist insurrection, the Mao strategy of establishing 'liberated areas' from which the guerrillas could operate was an almost complete failure. Indeed the insurrection might have been completely crushed by August but for the slowness in implementing the British defence strategy of eradicating the Communist jungle strongholds, following the death of the British High Commissioner, Sir Edward Gant, on 2 July 1948, and a delay in appointing his successor, Sir Henry Gurney.

The insurrection consisted almost wholly of sporadic terrorism, financed by a Chinese secret society, the Miu Yuen, drawing money from the Chinese in Penang and Singapore. This terrorism was sufficiently powerful, however, to demoralise large sections of the Malayan peasantry. The Communists were able to recruit continually from young intellectual and working-class Chinese, proud of Mao's achievements in China, and their campaign was helped by the difficult jungle terrain.

General Briggs, the British director of operations, appointed in 1950, decided to police the towns and populated areas, and to use troops to clear the countryside systematically from north to south. The Communists received their chief support from former Chinese workers dismissed by the planters, so it was decided to remove these workers' grievances by giving them equal citizenship rights and land. By February 1952 over four hundred thousand squatters had been resettled in 'New Villages' – deemed as concentration camps by the world radical movement to whom the existence of the Soviet gulag was to come as a surprise. In the meantime, however, terrorism reached a new peak, including the assassination of the High Commissioner, Gurney. This led to further delays in implementing the anti-terrorist policy. Despite the small numbers of insurgents, jungle fighting illustrated what was to become a common post-war phenomenon, the problems for a regular army of eliminating guerrillas from a difficult terrain where they had local support.

In February 1951 Sir Gerald Templer was made both High Commissioner and Director of Operations, and the Briggs plan of systematic clearing from north to south was followed with renewed vigour. The operation was based on the political agreement that there would soon be an independent multi-racial Malaysia including a quasi-independent Singapore, powerful incentives to the classes who hoped to gain from self-government.

The Malayans, perfectly content with their political status, provided it was followed by independence, regarded the Chinese and Indians in their midst as interlopers, brought in by the British. They feared being swamped by outsiders but in September 1952, after much negotiation and British pressure, the Chinese and Indians were given full citizenship as a preparation for Malaysian and Singaporean independence. The British started a substantial drive towards self-rule in the villages, homes of the local police force. As a result the flow of intelligence increased, which strengthened the army and correspondingly weakened the insurgents, many of whom joined the government forces. The professional success of the well-led and well-trained British forces in waging jungle warfare made it easier for the local people to stand up to the terror imposed by the insurgents on villages they occupied.

As a result of their political and military failure the insurgents were not supported financially or with war materials either by the Russians or the Chinese who only backed winners. When Templer left Malaya in 1954, the real emergency was over. In 1955, Malaya and Singapore had general elections, in preparation for independence, governments were formed in Malaya with Tunku Abdul Rahman (a Malayan), and in Singapore with a Labour government under David Marshall. By the end of 1957 most of the Communists had surrendered, and by July 1960 the emergency was officially ended.

In Malaya, as in India, Britain had prepared the people for eventual independence, and organised internal self-government on a solid foundation, encouraged indigenous institutions and groomed local leaders for power; the Dutch had not. Malayan experience showed that if the local people were already anti-Communist at heart, were given independence as a close objective, were strengthened morally, mentally and physically by the allies, then they could withstand Communism. If all these objectives were carried out, the local people had a chance of standing on their own feet after the allies had gone and were less likely to fall for enlightened despotism or dictatorship. But the seeds of success had to be planted before independence.

Militant Communism did not gain a stronghold in either India or Malaya but it was successful in French colonial possessions. Indochina was a complex of societies lodged between China in the north and Thailand in the west: Cochin China, a French colony in the southwest; Cambodia, a French-protected kingdom next to Thailand; Annam and Laos, also French-protected kingdoms; and Tongking, a French protectorate round the Red River delta – much of the land being jungle or mountain, with the French power concentrated in the main towns of Saigon, Hanoi and Haiphong. The French had held the territory from the 1860s, as an administrative unit of Indochina, with varying degrees of local autonomy. But the degree of French cultural assimilation by the middle and upper classes was substantial. Meanwhile the small Nationalist movement had been infiltrated by the Communists. They were led by Ho Chi-minh, a French-educated man with aliases who had been connected with many European left-wing and radical movements including the Irish Nationalists.

When France fell in 1940, the French government in Indochina continued loyal to Vichy but its power was steadily eroded. The Japanese encroached from the north and Ho Chi-minh founded the Viet Minh, as a Communist party fighting for independence in May 1941, and appointed General Giap as head of his forces. Giap had been trained in China by Mao's troops, so the main guerrilla movement in Vietnam was both anti-French and anti-Japanese, controlled by Communists trained in China and devoted to national liberation. Meanwhile de Gaulle's Free French forces, having established contact with Chiang Kai-shek in Chungking, began to set up their own resistance to the Japanese in Indochina. Thus were created the classical conditions for a many-sided civil war.

As guerrilla activity increased, the official Vichy French were unable to cope, and in March 1945 the Japanese occupied all Indochina, interning the Vichy French officials and soldiers. Some six thousand French troops, however, made a fighting retreat into Nationalist China and promised their allegiance to de Gaulle, who was by this time already in power in Paris. The Viet Minh seized this opportunity to become the major guerrilla force. So successful were they in taking over the countryside that soon they began to receive substantial aid from the American OSS (the predecessor of the CIA), which was organising counter-Japanese activities behind the lines. Had the Far Eastern war lasted, it was clear that Ho Chi-minh would have been to Indochina what Tito was to Yugoslavia – a Communist, but also head of an effective Nationalist movement recognised by the allies, and therefore entitled to lead the country eventually to independence with American backing.

Instead, the process was telescoped by the sudden end of the war on 15 August 1945. Following the American anti-colonialist line the local American forces promptly recognised Ho Chi-minh as the indigenous leader. Within a week the Viet Minh occupied much of northern Indochina, and the following month the Democratic Republic of Vietnam was formed by Ho Chi-minh and General Giap. It had however been agreed at Potsdam that Indochina should be divided along the sixteenth parallel, the South going to the French and the North to Nationalist China. The French, who were not at Potsdam were, not unnaturally, enraged by what they considered as a high-handed decision.

As the Nationalist Chinese advanced south to replace the surrendering Japanese, they preferred looting to organising. Japanese arms and equipment were bartered by Chiang Kai-shek's troops for food. These arms soon fell into the hands of General Giap whom the Chinese were perfectly happy to leave in control as long as they kept up the flow of food and loot. The situation in northern Indochina could therefore, with some degree of understatement, be described as somewhat confused.

Meanwhile British and Indian troops landed in Saigon in September 1945, to disarm the Japanese and release allied prisoners in that part which had been handed back to France at Potsdam. Here local rulers might be either French satraps, Japanese commanders or Communists presiding over powerful local liberation movements. The British began by dealing pragmatically with whoever seemed to be running individual areas. But when the first Gaullist French arrived to take over, a major insurrection broke out led by the Communists and supported by many varieties of local Nationalists; the British disarmed the French to stop the fighting, which led to a further outburst of French paranoia.

The Gaullists were convinced that the Americans were supporting Ho Chi-minh in the North and that the British were determined to annex the South. General Leclerc was then sent out from France with fresh troops to reoccupy the towns south of the sixteenth parallel. Ho Chi-minh was by now fairly strongly entrenched in the North under the nominal protection of the Nationalist Chinese who were the legitimate occupying force by right of the Potsdam declaration, which the French did not recognise. After desultory negotiations Leclerc and Ho Chi-minh agreed to recognise Ho Chi-minh's Republic of Vietnam as a French protectorate but the French government repudiated this.

Once more the juridical basis of Indochina was unclear. The British had gone. The French, Chinese and Indochinese commanders on the spot reorganised Vietnam themselves. The allies, whilst recognising a country divided between a Chinese and a French occupation zone, were silent about the legitimate indigenous authority. The French wanted their rich colony back. They controlled the towns and the Viet Minh were forced to retreat to their rural strongholds – though these areas held about two thirds of the Vietnamese population. Politically, the French made imaginative steps towards self-government on their own terms. They created puppet governments of Cambodia, Laos and Cochin China which were admitted to the French Union, and eventually a Vietnamese government was formed under Bao Dai. All were to police themselves under the French umbrella. The French were generous with educational and agricultural provision, too, but they still had to keep an army of 100,000 men (of whom over half were

French) to control and protect the parts of the country where their authority ran from the Viet Minh. The position was stabilised, but hardly stable.

By 1946 Ho Chi-minh controlled Hanoi and the countryside. He was aware that he would have to wage a war of liberation if he wanted to have a Republic of Vietnam. The French controlled Saigon and other Southern towns, Laos and Cambodia, and were waiting for reinforcements with which to reconquer the North. The Chinese were in the further North – for once with enough women and food – waiting to retreat to China after the opium poppy harvest.

The uneasy cease-fire broke down and the full-scale war began. It was to last for seventeen years, half against the French and half against the Americans, and to end in a complete victory for the Viet Minh.

The Viet Minh was an experienced guerrilla army, receiving American aid at first, with Japanese, American and captured French weapons and, in Giap, had a general of genius. The French had highly trained troops and experienced officers. Initially, through 1947, 1948 and 1949, the French seemed to be victorious, in the sense that they won many individual battles. However despite these victories, French troops and their families were gradually withdrawn from more and more places on instructions from Paris, as the war was both expensive and unpopular at home. The Americans now reversed their early pro Ho Chi-minh policy and by late 1949 decided to support the French and sent in substantial military aid. In a series of spectacular defeats, the French had lost the whole of the area of Indochina next to China by the end of 1950. The French had either to win or to get out: their policy of ruling through local puppets was clearly failing in the face of a genuine Nationalist movement supported by Russia and China.

The stalemate was broken by the gradual strengthening inside Indochina of the Viet Minh on Maoist principles of self-improvement, and externally by the victory of the Communists in China. As soon as the People's Republic was declared the Viet Minh government was recognised by China, Russia and the rest of the Communist governments in January 1950. Officially, therefore, the Republic of Vietnam became a liberationist government fighting a colonialist invader. Aid flowed to the Viet Minh across the Chinese border, and the French and Americans genuinely feared a Chinese Communist invasion like that in Korea. Giap began his offensive on classic Maoist lines, first clearing the French from their small garrison posts in territory otherwise held by the Viet Minh, and then occupying the main roads and the small towns.

In December 1950 the prestigious French General de Lattre de Tassigny was appointed Commander in Chief and High Commissioner in Indochina, with complete autonomy of action. He cancelled the withdrawal of French forces and their families. *J'y suis, j'y reste*, so often a disastrous aphorism for French generals, became his motto. At first he was successful but towards the end of 1951 the Viet Minh regrouped and he suffered a major defeat at Hoa Binh. He then became seriously ill and had to return to France, where he died on 11 January 1952. At a critical moment the French had no effective leadership and morale plummeted. General Salan, de Lattre's successor, courageous and professional though he was, and later notorious in Algeria, inherited a retreat which almost became a rout. Inch by inch the French were pushed back. The French government in July 1953 declared Vietnam, Laos and Cambodia independent but under French protection. At this compromise there was great pressure in France for the army to be withdrawn. Salan was replaced by General Navarre who decided to take and hold Dien Bien Phu, a key town where many routes from China met, with twelve heavily armed French battalions. This was the crucial battle of the war. After fifty-five days of terrible fighting Dien Bien Phu fell to the Viet Minh on 8 May 1954 with 7000 French casualties and 11,000 prisoners. The French had lost the war in just under nine years. They began to evacuate North Vietnam, the Americans and the British declining to intervene on their behalf.

A conference of France, Britain, the United States, China, the USSR and North and South Vietnam was called in Geneva to arrange a cease-fire. The cease-fire began on 23 July 1954, and eventually Vietnam was partitioned along the seventeenth parallel, into four independent states, North and South Vietnam, Laos and Cambodia, with a guarantee of neutrality. The French were allowed two bases in Laos, but otherwise their troops were to be evacuated. The Viet Minh occupied all North Vietnam and evacuated South Vietnam. In October Ho Chi-minh re-entered Hanoi and Ngo Dinh-diem became Prime Minister of South Vietnam.

In Indochina as a whole Ho Chi-minh could be said to represent a large part – perhaps the majority – of the local people, and a successful decolonisation of Vietnam would have required his recognition, perhaps as an Asian Tito. But French resistance to him and their unwillingness to leave Indochina until they were militarily defeated meant that he became a Communist and anti-imperialist hero, dependent on the Russians, while South Vietnam became increasingly dependent upon America for its defence and for its economic support.

The French had tried to convert their Southeast Asian colonial peoples to French ways but the arrival of the Japanese conquerors gave the indigenous peoples an insight into the weakness of European power and made them realise that native aspirations for nationalism were feasible. After India and Pakistan became independent, the forces of liberation massed at the United Nations, supported by America and then fuelled by Soviet diplomacy and Marxist propaganda. In that context the Dutch and French defence of their empires increasingly took on the character of rearguard action, a Canute-like attempt to bid the tide to recede. Independence and Socialism were ideas whose time had come.

The Dutch did not see it like that for their own country had been savagely occupied, its dykes burst and polders flooded, its towns bombed and shelled, its people humiliated, hungry, deported and murdered. The wealth of the Dutch East Indies seemed to them essential for the restoration of Holland itself.

The French did not want to liberate their Indochinese possessions either. With crass self-defeating ineptitude they failed to achieve peace or prosperity in their areas post-war, they alienated the local people and did not recognise the looming power of Chinese communism.

The British had cause for self-congratulation – a national vice – over Malaysia and India but if they had not liberated their Asian possessions, would the tide of empire have receded in the Dutch and French areas? India, a liberal democracy, was to set the fashion for neutrality as it became a major power in the neutralist alignment of Third World states. India adopted economic planning somewhat along the Soviet model, and a form of Socialism, nebulous as to detail, though clearly anti private enterprise in its orientation and especially hostile to multinational corporations. India and Pakistan, with other newly-independent countries, became major recipients of substantial aid from the United States. Much of this aid was spent either on corrupt schemes to help the wealthier officials and businessmen or on prestigious, but economically dubious projects. Nevertheless the push given to economic growth by independence enabled India, Pakistan and, to a lesser extent, Indonesia to participate in the world boom – of which Malaysia and Singapore were principal beneficiaries. But the deep-dyed hostility of the newly-independent nations to their main benefactor, the United States, was an important psychological factor. It led, via anti-colonialism, to the bolstering of Soviet strength and Marxist principles, as will be seen in future chapters.

Chapter 12

Two giants stir: China and Japan

The Chinese Communist party was formed in Shanghai in 1921; its origins were quite independent of the Russian Revolution; it was only indirectly Marxist in the sense that none of the founders had ever taken part in any Marxist organisation in Europe, nor did any of them read or speak German so none had read the Marxist classics. The party's first task was to organise the proletariat in Shanghai, China's only large industrial city.

The new Communist party seemed insignificant to the Moscow International. China was in chaos, agricultural production falling, and the country beset by warring armies. Thus in 1923 the Soviet Union agreed to support Dr Sun Yat-sen, a Western-educated scholar, against the warlords who then dominated different provinces of China. The Nationalist party led by Dr Sun was then gradually permeated with newly organised Communists. Meanwhile Mao Tse-tung was employed by the Communist party to organise covert revolution in the countryside of his native province, Funan.

Mao was born to a poor family in 1893 and went to the local village school and then to teacher-training school in nearby Chang Sha. By the time he graduated at twenty-five, he was already a revolutionary spirit. Moving to Peking University as a library assistant, he met a number of celebrated scholars who were the founders of the Marxist Study Group which Mao joined.

In 1925, after Dr Sun's death, Chiang Kai-shek, the most prominent young warlord, was made commander in chief of Dr Sun's Kuomintang forces with a Russian general as his chief of staff. Chiang Kai-shek had been born in 1887 and trained in a cadet school, in a Japanese military school and in the Red Army of the Soviet Union. He had then been appointed principal of the Wham-Po military academy where he had Chou En-lai as a commissar and Lin Piao as a student.

The Kuomintang revolutionary party was at this time allied to the Chinese Communist party and now, with the support of the Communists, Chiang led an expedition up the Yangtse against other warlords. He emerged as a dominant figure.

But then Chiang reversed his political alliance. He became a firm anti-Communist and in 1927 he expelled the Russians from China.

The Communist party in Shanghai was suppressed. Among those who survived the purge were Chou En-lai and Lin Piao who organised a revolutionary rising against Chiang on 1 August 1927 at Nan-Chang, which marked the real emergence of the Communist leadership. Chiang now consolidated his power by marrying a relation of Dr Sun as his third wife and so acquired two powerful supporters in his brothers-in-law, H. H. K'Ung and T. V. Soong; with their support he then waged a civil war throughout China against rival warlords and the Communists. In the midst of this chaotic disintegration of China, the Japanese invaded Manchuria in the autumn of 1931. Having earlier established Korea as a subordinate country, Manchuria, with its mineral and industrial wealth, seemed to them ripe for the picking, and China obviously needed pacifying. The League of Nations sent a Commission of Enquiry and censured the Japanese aggression, but this merely hardened Japanese attitudes.

Chiang was now facing the Japanese, other warlords and the Communists. A Communist Republic was set up in Kiang-Si, with Mao as the much-challenged leader. It collapsed in 1933, and the Communists thereupon began a prolonged rural guerrilla war against Chiang with the aphorism which Mao used later, 'the people are the sea – we are the fish', as an accurate description of the nature of the campaign.

Faced with Chiang's determined efforts to put down their rebellion, the Communists trekked on the Long March from the south of China through the extreme west to Yenan in the north. The 7000 miles took from early 1934 to late 1935. Mao was now the unquestioned leader of the Communist party and as a result of the Long March, a hero. Meanwhile Chiang continued to fight not only the rival warlords but the Communists. Although the Japanese were left to consolidate their hold on Manchuria, which they declared independent under their protection, Chiang gradually became the dictator of much of the rest of China.

Internally strife between Chiang, the Communists and the Japanese might have continued indefinitely but for a significant event in 1936. Chiang was seized by the officers and men of the anti-Japanese Manchurian army who declared that he would be murdered unless he ended the Chinese civil war and united the country against the Japanese. In consequence, Chiang and his powerful in-laws, the Soong family, made an agreement with the Communists represented by Chou En-lai, to establish a common front against the Japanese. But as the war progressed, the Japanese, with their vastly superior army, overran China, except for the small parts around Chungking, where Chiang was in power, and Yenan, where the Communists had their stronghold. By 1938 all the main cities of China, including Shanghai, were in Japanese hands. Meanwhile the Communists in the north became the under-cover government for all the rural areas of the provinces of Hopei, Shansi, Shantung and Honan.

During the time that Mao was holding on in Yenan he developed his own Marxist doctrine and ensured that the members of the Communist party were thoroughly trained and completely loyal to his views: that revolution would start among the peasant masses and need not wait for a proletarian revolution. This was deeply heretical to the rest of the Communist movement.

Throughout the 1930s and early 1940s Stalin ordered the Com-munists to support Chiang, partly because he thought Chiang would win and partly because Mao was a deviationist. After the Japanese invasion of China, according to Soviet doctrine the principal enemy of both the Kuomintang and of the Communists was officially Japan. From 1941 onwards all Soviet aid to the Chinese Communists was channelled through the Kuo mintang led by Chiang.

As soon as the United States entered the war in December 1941 as a result of the Japanese attack on Pearl Harbor, aid on a large scale was given to Chiang, who promptly used much of it to help fight the Communists in Yenan rather than the Japanese. Des-pite his doing this, Chiang was built up by allied propaganda as a strong ally of the Americans, the British and the Russians. The official Nationalist government in Chungking was the government recognised by the world community. It was Chiang, as head of that government, who on the American initiative took part in several of the major conferences of world leaders, with Roosevelt, Stalin and Churchill. The Communists, who actually controlled the larger area of China in the north, made no claim to be the legitimate government of China. Indeed, as most of China was occupied by the Japanese the question of which government was to control China after the war was somewhat academic.

In early 1945 Japan was the major Asian power: China was largely occupied, Japanese troops stood on the borders of India, the whole of what was to be Indonesia and Southeast Asia was occupied. Only in the Melanesian islands were the Japanese slowly being pushed out, at great cost in American lives. Then two atom bombs were dropped: the next day Japan ceased politically and militarily to exist.

When Japan surrendered on 15 August 1945 about six million Japanese soldiers were abroad, throughout Southeast Asia, in-cluding Burma, Malaya, Indochina, Indonesia and the Philippines, and in China, Korea and the Pacific islands. With only a small part of the territory conquered in December 1941 and early 1942 regained by the allies, the war to recover the rest was expected to be severe. A massive invasion force was being prepared to land in Malaya, and another to land in Japan itself. As agreed at Potsdam, the Russians shifted troops from the German theatre, and finally declared war on the Japanese for the last week. Despite Japan's overwhelming victories, it was on the point of collapse. Over half the houses in its cities had been destroyed, the urban economy was in ruins and the agricultural sector was badly affected by the shortage of labour.

Although they had nothing to do with the collapse of Japan the Russians immediately began to collect their booty in Manchuria and the islands to the north of Japan, whilst the Kuomintang became officially responsible for administering China and Formosa, having to cope in the process with millions of Japanese prisoners who were more highly trained and better armed than the Chinese. The Kuomintang, supported by the Americans, signed a treaty of friendship in August 1945 with the USSR, which effectively gave Outer Mongolia to the USSR and established Russian bases in Manchuria. The Communists remained in control of the whole of the area north of the Yangtse, except for cities which their forces surrounded.

On 2 September 1945 General Douglas MacArthur accepted the Japanese surrender on board USS *Missouri* at Yokohama. His appointment as Supreme Commander Allied Powers was perhaps the most powerful post to be held by anybody since the times of the Viceroys of India before representative government. With his background, MacArthur behaved as an exemplary Viceroy might have done.

MacArthur, who was born in 1880 at Little Rock, Arkansas, the son of an American lieutenant general, graduated from West Point. He had been head of the allied forces in the southwest Pacific which eventually liberated the Philippines and he then became Supreme Commander of the Allied Powers in Japan. With long experience of the Far East and virtually total power, many hours away from Washington, he was accustomed to acting independently. He established a personal system of rule for the next five years, relatively unaffected either by his superiors in Washington or by the small allied advisory body that sat in Tokyo.

Under MacArthur's direction, the complete surrender of the Japanese was organised, and then the reconstruction of Japanese society on Western lines. Among his first acts was the confirmation of the Emperor Hirohito in power, whom he refused to have tried

as a war criminal. Through Hirohito, who had ordered the unconditional surrender, MacArthur largely exercised his power, and the
structure of government was entirely at MacArthur's disposal. The
American and British army of occupation was small – only just
over one hundred thousand men – and the formidable Japanese
capacity for organisation was turned by MacArthur to peaceful
purposes.

MacArthur was not, however, responsible for sorting out the
anarchic conditions in China created by the Japanese defeat. The
United States sent General George Marshall to attempt to form a
coalition government between the Kuomintang and the Communists. At a People's Consultative Conference held in Chungking in
late 1945, attended briefly by Mao Tse-tung and for a short period
longer by Chou En-lai, it was clear that there was no possibility of
compromise with Chiang, who insisted that the Communists
should disband their armies, form a political party and fight
elections, which had not been held in China for many years. The
Communists, for their part, offered to join the existing government as equals and to merge their armed forces with Chiang's.
Since their own political and military forces were so highly disciplined, this would have meant the absorption of Chiang into the
Communist system. By the end of the conference the only people
who believed that a compromise was possible were the Americans
who, under wartime agreements, were still supplying Chiang's
armies with supplies, which led the Communists to the understand-
able view that the United States was backing Chiang against them.

Stalin clearly put the interests of Soviet–Chinese official relations before the interests of Chinese Communism, of which he was
deeply suspicious. Almost alone of all the Communist parties in
the world the Chinese paid only nominal attention to Stalinist
orders. Mao, its leader, set himself up as a virtually autonomous
theorist. The Chinese Communists had not been supported by the
Russians before or during the war, and it was clear, therefore, that
Stalin regarded the Chinese Communists not only as heretics, but
as potential losers in the struggle against the Kuomintang. It had
also been part of the understanding with Roosevelt that China was
in the American sphere of influence.

The Soviet Union, who already occupied North Korea, now
invaded Manchuria which, in so far as it was under Chinese control
at all, was in the Communist sphere. The Soviet Union then
retreated, leaving the province looted and desolate, and officially
handed it over to Chiang Kai-shek; one of the earliest post-war
signs that Stalin would not support Mao Tse-tung.

To reach Manchuria and its cities Chiang's troops were either sent by sea from Shanghai to Manchuria or airlifted over Communist areas by the Americans. The Chinese Communists retaliated by attacking and conquering Harbin, and then systematically attacked city after city. Meanwhile in Nationalist China a rampant inflation developed which, with the ineffectiveness of the government and its arbitrary and capricious corruption, led to a mounting demoralisation of the Chinese Nationalist army and administration. In the Communist-controlled areas the long years of intense discipline under Mao paid off, as the People's Liberation Army, as the Chinese Red Army was now called, fought most effectively. They virtually controlled the countryside and could raid the towns at will in what became classic Maoist tactics.

In early 1946, in view of growing Communist power, Chiang Kai-shek determined to renew the civil war, waging it to the full with American and Soviet support, although it was later presented as part of a world-wide anti-Communist struggle. But during 1947 Chiang made a number of major military errors. He sent one army to conquer Yenan, but this was no longer central to Mao's strategy as his forces controlled so much of North China; he attempted to open up the railway system from Peking to Tientsin, but this failed. Meanwhile the People's Liberation Army acquired vast stores of Japanese equipment which had been abandoned in rural areas. Mao regrouped and led his troops against the Kuomintang forces which crumbled before them despite substantial American help. By the summer of 1948 it was clear that Chiang would almost certainly lose the civil war, though it was by no means certain that the Communists would win. Perpetual civil strife seemed the most likely outcome.

The People's Liberation Army now advanced south from Manchuria. Tientsin was taken and Peking. Meanwhile Chiang's main army was defeated in the south at the battle of Huai-Hai which led to a total victory by the People's Liberation Army, with two thirds of the nationalists' forces surrendering and the remainder, some two hundred thousand men, killed. The Nationalists were outmanoeuvred and surrounded, and despite their superiority of heavy artillery and air power, the total collapse of Chiang's army meant that Nationalist resistance was coming to an end.

The Communists offered Chiang the opportunity of integrating the remains of his army into the People's Liberation Army and joining the Communists in a coalition. Chiang however fled to Formosa. In April 1949 when continuing talks between Nationalists and Communists broke down, the Yangtse was crossed and Nanking fell. By early autumn all the south was in Communist hands and on 1 October 1949 the People's Republic of China was proclaimed with Peking declared the capital.

The victory was due to the disciplined fervour of the Communist armies and to the extent to which the Nationalists had crumbled through internal disputes and corruption. With the Americans continuing to recognise Chiang in Formosa as the legitimate Chinese government, the new Communist regime was not admitted to the United Nations.

It is interesting to note that Mao's forces are the only known example of a small local partisan force being able to overthrow a large army without foreign aid. In Yugoslavia and elsewhere the partisans received tanks, guns and aid from outside. In Mao's case the opposition was getting Soviet and American help, yet he triumphed.

During this period MacArthur, now in his fifth year in Japan, virtually as Viceroy, became famous for his authoritarian personal attitudes, and though these were dedicated to the construction of liberal and constitutional societies both in the Philippines and in Japan, he was much criticised. MacArthur rejected outright the plan for dismantling the Japanese economy, put forward by Henry Morgenthau, Roosevelt's old Secretary of the Treasury. Instead MacArthur rigorously pegged the currency both internally and externally and so restored business confidence. Within the context of a liberal economic doctrine, there were severe controls on food, fuel and imported goods.

Japan's first three years of peace, from 1945 to 1948, were marked by low levels of output and high levels of imports from the United States. But by 1948 the level of imports began to diminish and by 1950 Japan had regained the level of output which had been reached in the later 1930s, before the huge war effort. This reconstruction was one of the most remarkable successes of the post-war period, and the condition of Japan may be contrasted strikingly with those areas of Europe which were occupied by the Soviet Union. With singularly few troops MacArthur installed a liberal government, which was chosen from a newly-elected constituent assembly.

In three areas of life MacArthur undertook revolutionary change by Napoleonic means. He persuaded the Japanese Cabinet to adopt a constitutional monarchy, with equality between men and women, and a charter of human rights, and held the first parliamentary elections in 1946, which led to a succession of stable liberal governments, similar in philosophy to those which ruled post-war Germany and Italy. The Japanese supported democracy as firmly as they had previously backed their old militarist regime.

MacArthur transformed Hirohito from a god into a constitutional monarch with limited powers, but as Hirohito retained his previous aura, his transformation paradoxically carried with it the authority to destroy his own authority. The sweeping nature of the transformation was indicated by the rapidity with which American norms became accepted in Japan, and by the speed with which Japan adopted a new non-militarist stance.

MacArthur also integrated Japan into the Western economic system. In striking contrast to three other Asian powers, China, waging a civil war until 1949 and then undergoing a traumatic change to Communism; Russian Asia, exploited as a colony; and India, which grew only slowly, Japan became within twenty years the third-largest economy in the world. But this transformation could not have been achieved without MacArthur's radical redistribution of the land to the peasants, and break up of industrial monopolies.

When the Korean War broke out in June 1950, MacArthur became Supreme Commander of the UN forces with Japan as their principal base. Inevitably the Japanese then became responsible for their own security and, partly as a reward, a peace treaty with the United States was signed in 1951.

The quiet restoration of Japan was, however, overshadowed by events in China. Chiang retreated to Formosa and the Communists became the first *de facto* government of the whole of China for over a century. They were swiftly recognised by India and the European powers but the Americans refused diplomatic recognition, treating them as in a state of almost undeclared war. Stalin was none too pleased by Mao's spectacular triumph against his own ally Chiang, though Russia now became Mao's principal supporter. A treaty between China and the Soviet Union was signed in Moscow in February 1950 after Mao had been kept waiting there for a humiliating two months. Its purposes were anti-Japanese, to confirm the Russian position in Manchuria (though China's sovereignty was recognised), and to cede Outer Mongolia to the Russian sphere. This experience of disdainful treatment, and of Russia's territorial ambitions, disillusioned Mao with the Soviet Union.

Neither China, India nor Japan had counted for much internationally up to 1945; now, in the space of five years, Japan had soared from total defeat to amazing economic recovery, China had irrupted as an independent Communist force and India had emerged as a Social Democracy. Within the next five years India was to become a major presence in international affairs and China to become more important in Asia than she had been for two centuries. Yet in the 1950s, sandwiched between Russia and America, Japan looked like becoming an American colony and China a Soviet satellite. A decade later both these propositions were seen to be wide of the mark.

Japan did not become a military partner of the United States, but it was wholly integrated into the American economic and value system; China was never wholly in the Soviet camp but embraced Marxism with fervour; India sought to play her own game but, despite Gandhi, accepted a Western-style Socialist orthodoxy.

The three great Asian powers had however only re-emerged from defeat and obscurity into the limelight, to be dragged into the power struggle between the Soviet Union and the United States which had begun in Europe. It was in Asia that the shooting war actually broke out.

Chapter 13

The Korean War

Korea, the large peninsula that juts out from Manchuria towards Japan, was formerly part of the Chinese empire, and had a brief period of independence before being annexed in 1910 by Japan, who had occupied it during the Japanese–Russian war. At the Cairo meeting of Churchill, Roosevelt and Chiang Kai-shek in 1943, it was agreed that after Japan's defeat Korea would be independent once again, and this decision was reaffirmed at Yalta by Churchill, Stalin and Roosevelt. At Potsdam, as part of the planning for the Japanese war, the American defence staff arranged for Soviet troops to occupy the Northern half of Korea, to the thirty-eighth parallel, and American troops the Southern half. Russian troops completed their occupation between 12 and 28 August 1945, but the Americans did not arrive in the South until 8 September. Within this four-week period the Russians installed in their section a Communist government under Kim Il-sung, who had been a Korean refugee in Russia, and Korean detachments of the Chinese Red Army were invited into the North.

The proposed joint commission of the Soviet and American occupying forces met briefly but never functioned, so Korea-wide elections were not held. Thus the country was *de facto* divided between Kim Il-sung's regime in the North, supported by the Soviet Union, and an American-occupied zone in the South where a republican government was elected under United States supervision, with Syngman Rhee as President. By early 1949, Russian and American troops had withdrawn from Korea; and the divided country was left with two opposed regimes: one elected, but authoritarian, and the other unelected and imposed; both with growing armies, trained by Americans and Russians respectively, though that of North Korea was by far the more powerful.

The first direct post-war confrontation between Communists and the Americans began in Korea. It seemed for a while as though the fire of atomic weapons would be felt throughout Asia; both MacArthur and Truman (separately) considered their use; the crisis threatened to become uncontrollable.

At the very moment in early 1950 when Dean Acheson, Truman's Secretary of State, inadvertently announced that South Korea was beyond America's defence perimeter, Mao Tse-tung discussed with Stalin the settlement of Far Eastern affairs, and agreed that South Korea should be invaded by the North. On 25 June 1950 the invasion duly began; within two months the whole of Korea, except for a small area around the main southern part of Chusan, was occupied by Northern forces. Though the South had expected an attack, it was relatively unprepared for the North's superiority in numbers and equipment.

The American response was twofold. First it moved a motion in the United Nations Security Council condemning the Northern aggression and arranging for the UN to send a force to defend Korea. This was only marginally legal as the Soviet Union was at this point boycotting the Security Council because the Communist victory in the Chinese civil war had not been recognised by a change in the Chinese representation at the United Nations. The Soviet Union was therefore unable to veto the UN resolution as it would undoubtedly have done had it been present. South Korea was not a member of the UN, its application for membership, like North Korea's, having been vetoed on several occasions. The UN was therefore not responding to a request from a member state as required by the charter, though a 'threat to peace' undoubtedly existed. The second American response was for President Truman to order General MacArthur, the Commander-in-Chief in Japan, to intervene to support the South Koreans. MacArthur was then appointed Commander-in-Chief of the United Nations force, which consisted of the South Korean army, with a substantial American contingent (reaching nearly four hundred thousand men by 1951), a large force from the British Commonwealth (principally from the United Kingdom), and smaller groups from Turkey, Thailand, Belgium and twelve other countries.

As well as defending the area around Chusan, which the North Koreans had been unable to take because their advance had considerably exceeded their supply lines, MacArthur's forces landed in an amphibious exercise at Inchon, a port on the western coast, rapidly proceeding to occupy the capital, Seoul, and to advance across the peninsula. At this point, September 1950, the Communist army began to retreat, a retreat that soon became a rout. The Inchon landing was perhaps the most brilliantly executed military operation undertaken in the years after the Second World War. Breathtakingly risky, it turned a successful Communist invasion into a massive defeat in three months.

With the Korean War the world came nearer to total conflict than at any time since Potsdam. Stalin was at his most expansionist and was building up to the apogee of his domestic terror. Would he now decide to break through in Germany, in Korea or in China? The exact relationship between Mao and Stalin was still unclear to the West, it was assumed that China was part of a fairly homogeneous Soviet bloc, responsive to Stalin's will.

Western European leaders were convinced that Korea was the most likely target for the next Soviet advance. The United States and the United Kingdom, in particular, responded by a massive rearmament programme. As a result of stockpiling, a substantial rise in raw material prices threatened the recovery of the Western European economies, which had been doing so well in the Marshall Plan, although there was a revival of the American economy from its first post-war depression.

Communist aggression and terror had been feared since the original Soviet occupation of Poland in 1945; and it seemed to be increasing. Communist expansion into China itself most frightened the Americans. MacArthur, supported by influential Republicans, discussed the use of Chiang Kai-shek's Nationalist Chinese forces in Korea. However it was feared that this might bring Mao's Red Army into North Korea in great numbers and possibly lure in Soviet troops as well. Such a confrontation might lead to defeat of the UN forces and a general rout involving the loss of Japan and Vietnam.

Would a third world war start because of the American and British response to the Korean affair? By mid 1950 the Americans had about seventy or eighty nuclear bombs and a force of long-distance bombers able to deliver them. The Russians, late into the game but helped by an efficient espionage service, had exploded their first test bomb in August 1949. They had five nuclear bases, each with about three bombs, but few long-range planes. The Americans were planning to use their bombs if necessary and, as will be seen, by the late autumn of 1950 MacArthur proposed to drop a string of them in Manchuria. It seemed highly likely therefore that a nuclear war might break out and since the Russians could not reach America, they might easily decide to hold Western Europe to ransom by threatening to explode their bombs there. Thus a world war in which atom bombs were used could have broken out as a result of tactical decisions taken by MacArthur in Korea.

The Communist propaganda machine was as efficient as ever. As well as suggesting that the South had invaded the North, it accused the South Koreans and Americans of torture and, eventually, of using germ warfare against the North by dropping bombs full of insects infested with viruses. Many Western intellectuals accepted Soviet propaganda about American behaviour at its face value, believing that torture was normal American policy, and that the war had been started to give profits to American arms makers. The truth was rather different. The Syngman Rhee regime may have been brutal, but its brutality was amateur in comparison with that used by the North. Advancing Communist troops had murdered many thousands of South Koreans and brainwashed allied prisoners. At the end of the war in 1953, not only did many thousands of North Korean and Chinese prisoners of war refuse repatriation, but there were three million refugees from the North in South Korea. In 1950 Mao's government openly admitted to the elimination of two million Nationalists in China itself; by the mid 1950s it is estimated that twenty million Chinese had been murdered. The population of the Soviet gulags at this time varied between six and ten million. In all probability, therefore, a reign of terror stretched from Berlin across Russia and China to Korea.

MacArthur was a most distinguished general, he had governed Japan for five years, presiding over its remarkable transformation into an industrial constitutional democracy. But he had not been back to the United States for many years; instead he had used his consummate political skills to build for himself a powerful though isolated position. He represented the long American tradition that the Pacific was naturally an American ocean, while Europe was a dangerous distraction; he held that the loss of China was a disaster due largely to treasonable pro-Communists in Washington. Not surprisingly, he detested Democrats such as President Truman.

The President, therefore, was obliged to go to Wake Island in the middle of the Pacific to consult with his tiresome pro-consul. Not only that: the possibility of the use of atomic weapons brought the British Prime Minister, Attlee, hurrying to Washington to ask that such an act should only follow mutual agreement. At Wake Island, MacArthur said he would pursue the enemy north of the thirty-eighth parallel, in order to restore the unity of Korea and to allow democratic elections to take place, according to the decisions taken at Cairo and Yalta, and in pursuance of a United Nations resolution. But would such an advance to the Yalu River, the Chinese frontier with Korea, bring about Chinese and Soviet intervention? According to MacArthur's intelligence this would not happen.

He therefore authorised the invasion of North Korea in early October 1950, and by the end of the month almost all the country was occupied, including the Northern capital of Pyongyang. On 27 October, however, a South Korean battalion, which had reached the Yalu River the day before, was ambushed and virtually wiped out by Chinese troops. Now it was the turn of the United Nations' army, greatly over-extended and far from its supply lines, to begin a headlong retreat. China had been drawn directly into the war. The Soviet Union also began to supply MIG fighters on a large scale to the North Koreans. The fears of those who had spoken of a world war seemed about to be confirmed. By mid-November about a third of a million Chinese troops were south of the Yalu River. By 24 November, MacArthur planned a new offensive, on the mistaken assumption that only a few Chinese volunteers were in Korea, but the UN armies were demoralised, and continued to retreat despite their superiority in numbers and equipment. By 4 January 1951 the UN had lost Seoul and Inchon; and it was only by late January 1951 that General Matthew Ridgway, the new commander of the United Nations forces in the field, was able to establish a line across South Korea.

MacArthur's brilliant record was marred by what seemed an extraordinary defeat and a gross misjudgment as to Chinese and Russian intentions that could have led to a world war between the major powers. He continued to press Washington for the right to advance back to the Yalu, and to bomb Chinese bases in Manchuria. It was at this point that he proposed the use of atom bombs in China, and a barrier of radioactive cobalt along the Chinese border, to prevent further supplies of men and materials from China to North Korea. This was extraordinarily suggestive of what was to happen nearly twenty years later in Vietnam, with the difference that, in Korea, Truman and Marshall forbade it. MacArthur continued to press, increasingly openly, for an all-out war and the use of maximum fire power, including atomic weapons, to achieve victory. On 11 April 1951 he was relieved of his overall command by President Truman. This dismissal not only bitterly rankled with MacArthur, but it also added to the decline in confidence in Truman's administration, for MacArthur had been a hero and it seemed to many people impertinent for Truman to dismiss him.

MacArthur's dismissal had many political repercussions inside America, playing an important part in the eventual election of Eisenhower. MacArthur toyed with running for the Presidency, but was upstaged by Eisenhower who took the Republican nomination, the only one available to MacArthur. Eisenhower might possibly have become a Democratic nominee, in which case, had MacArthur stood as the Republican candidate, a unique electoral battle would have taken place between two generals. MacArthur retired from the army and became a businessman, finally dying in 1964 during Johnson's Presidency.

The seesaw nature of the Korean War continued, pivoting about the thirty-eighth parallel. The allies had superior troops and weapons but were unwilling to risk a general all-out war, so a bloody stalemate developed along a line eventually adopted at the armistice, roughly the thirty-eighth parallel where it all began. On 10 July 1951 cease-fire talks opened, and despite sporadic fighting, peace slowly returned to Korea. An armistice was signed at Panmunjom on 27 July 1953, possibly brought about at long last by Stalin's death earlier in March and by Eisenhower's threatened preparations for a nuclear assault from Okinawa.

Korea had been devastated from end to end, like no other country except Germany; over one hundred thousand UN troops had been killed, and about two hundred and fifty thousand Communists. The military wounded numbered over a million and so did the civilian dead and wounded.

Korean hostilities posed a number of pertinent questions: if the Chinese were fully engaged in the future, would their sheer numbers be unstoppable except by atomic weapons? They had but been glimpsed in the field but their pressure had been hard to deflect. Was MacArthur as unwise as he seemed in wanting a victory by the use, if need be, of atomic weapons? Would the USSR have retaliated in kind? Were the United States correct in thinking that a purely American army in Korea would have led to instant confrontation with both Soviet and Chinese forces? Had the use of UN troops cooled the temperature? If the US abided by Potsdam boundaries and spheres of influence, would the Russians? Had it been MacArthur's drive across the thirty-eighth parallel which exacerbated events?

The worst confrontation in seven years had been dangerously hotted up by an American general: it had ended in stalemate thanks to a President's statesmanship. Politicians looked at those areas of the world where East and West were closely juxtaposed and wondered which would flare up next, who would intrigue and aggravate whom and who would exert calm: no one took any positive action.

The Korean War occurred in the atomic age. It made the NATO planners realise that a conventional army was still essential to withstand a conventional attack. It led to the US quadrupling their military expenditure and strengthening their armies in Germany. Moreover it raised in acute form the question of German rearmament. Korea also meant that America had committed troops to Asia for a long time to come, and led to a harder line against the Soviet Union and to the development of the hydrogen bomb. From then on the nuclear arms race became a feature of the world political scene.

Yalta to Korea

Roosevelt has often been rightly blamed for what happened to the world after his death. His plans for the post-war world seem to have been based on a dislike of the British Empire in particular and imperialism in general, and an uncritical view of Stalin's Russia. Imperialism, he reasoned, had been the ultimate cause of the two world wars, while Stalin's reactions to aggression were natural; his fears could be calmed. This was a fundamentally incorrect forecast of the future. Stalin *was* paranoid; British imperialism was already well past its peak. Consequently, as far as British imperialism was concerned, Roosevelt was pushing at an open door, whilst he was letting Stalin put his foot firmly into Europe and Asia.

Stalin was a belt and braces man. He wanted to take every precaution against renewed invasion, but by seeking complete control of his sphere of influence, he effectively stopped the neutralisation of Germany. Instead he ended up with a divided Germany and American forces stationed there permanently.

The actual cause of the failure of the agreed German policy was the dispute over reparations. This dispute arose from an intellectual fault. Few seemed to have grasped that plant dismantling made impossible the payment of reparations from current German output, and furthermore, that to get the output, substantial inputs of food and raw materials were necessary. Consequently the immediate post-war German economy looked like a Charlie Chaplin movie, with the British and the Americans sending food and raw materials in through Bremen and Hamburg, while the Russians grabbed what they could as fast as they could. All attempts to explain this problem, once Bevin had grasped it, failed to convince either side of the good faith of the other. As Truman swung strongly from Roosevelt's position at Yalta, he failed to grasp either the Soviet need for goods or their preoccupation with their own security.

Bevin had indeed grasped both facts. But the British were themselves overwhelmed by the need to restructure their economy, to cope with the crisis in India, and by the dispersal of their still-powerful and numerous armed forces. Consequently they were not only unable to play the role of honest broker between the two great powers, requiring as it did strength which was beyond them, but they were soon both economically and militarily dependent on America. The American loan, the American involvement in Greece and Turkey, and the Marshall Plan all provided the basis for a more prosperous country with a much diminished role.

Britain in fact emerged as an exemplar of a new form of Social

Democracy, and it was rapidly overtaken by some of its defeated allies like France, Belgium and Holland, and by its defeated enemies, Germany, Italy and Japan. They all combined constitutional parliamentary democracies with powerful private enterprise companies creating a surge of prosperity, together with a structure of social services based on that prosperity. This type of state – which India emulated – became the norm for the Western world in the 1950s. But its success was by no means guaranteed in the two dark years after the end of the war. To many people a more full-blooded Socialism seemed the solution.

That was indeed the solution adopted in Eastern Europe and in China, and it was the favourite doctrine of the intelligentsia in Western Europe. This solution notably failed to deliver the goods.

While Stalin lived Communism seemed indivisible. But by 1948 Tito had shown that another version was possible and in 1949 Mao led China into yet a different version. But by then, so strong had the image of Stalin's Communism become that it was difficult for any but the most discerning observer to see any shades that differentiated one form of Marxism from another. They all shared terror as a means of achieving a totalitarian form of society. And Stalin was seen as the force that lay behind the whole Communist world. In fact he was seeking to overthrow Tito, and he had preferred Chiang Kai-shek to Mao. Whether, by one means or another, the rest of the Communist empire could have been prised from Stalin's grip, is impossible to say. The fact is that in the Soviet Union itself Stalin systematically eliminated rivals and opponents and potential rivals and opponents, and that as soon as Soviet troops moved into Eastern Europe the same process began.

In striking contrast, the older colonial empires of the British, the Dutch and the French crumbled away. As Western Europe recovered from the war, so it relaxed its grip on Asia, partly from lack of power, but also from a genuine desire to withdraw from direct rule. The Dutch and the French were reluctant to give up their empires, the British eager to do so, but the fact was that whatever the motive, heroic efforts were not made to retain control.

At the time of the Korean War, the world had learned some startling lessons. Stalin was a tyrant, but one who seemed willing to respect arbitrary lines drawn on maps at Yalta and Potsdam. Even so, the West saw Stalin chiefly as an actual and potential aggressor, rather than as the master of an unprecedented system of slave camps throughout what came to be known as the gulag. The full realisation of what totalitarianism implied took a long time to achieve. Meanwhile, the Monnet plan for the revival of France was extended to Germany and, through the Marshall Plan, to the West as a whole. Few people in 1950 could have seen the extent of the two decades of prosperity that were about to begin. The meteoric rise of Germany and Japan was even less imaginable.

Though Korea was a war between the United Nations and the Soviet Union, the full extent of the failure of the international peace-keeping machinery devised at the end of the world war was as yet not grasped. The United States reacted in Korea with hostility, aggressively, even threatening to use atom bombs, but still within the framework of the United Nations. It remained for John Foster Dulles to erect the system of alliances that were to be the substitute machinery.

The Communist threat to the West was seen as either aggression or subversion. The subtle and corrosive effects of Marxism had yet to be seen.

PART TWO

Peace and Prosperity

The 1950s

Chapter 14

Alliances

The 1950s saw the birth of new and stronger sets of alliances built up around the Soviet Union and the United States, which were different in kind from those which had gone before. During the war Hitler and Stalin had been allies, then Roosevelt, Stalin and Churchill had come together, but these wartime alliances had been more apparent than real; when they broke down, they did not entail any collapse in complex inter-disciplinary military joint command. Post-war Anglo–American co-operation was also limited: it was not formalised and military strategy did not become a joint allied activity. Between 1945 and 1948, there was little co-ordination of military policy between Britain and the United States, still less with other Western nations. There was certainly no ganging up against the Soviet Union.

Even with the creation of the Organisation for European Economic Co-operation under the Marshall Plan, Britain and America went their own ways, diplomatically and economically. The British authorised the building of their own atom bomb and concentrated on jet aircraft, whilst the Americans specialised in the development of missiles: there was little standardisation throughout the whole range of military technology and hardware. Nor would it have been true to suggest that there was a Western armed camp dominated by the Americans for there was no co-ordinating central control. The idea of an East–West division between two camps is thus manifestly false, although the Soviet Union did have a central control dominated by Stalin.

But when in 1948 the Russians closed the road and railway links from the Western zones of Germany, running through their zone of Berlin, the allies saw this as a tangible threat and took action accordingly. The Russians blockaded Berlin because ostensibly the creation of a federal German state in the Western occupation zones, according to the Soviet Union, breached the Potsdam agreements for the four-power occupation of Germany and so rendered the presence of the three Western allies in Berlin inappropriate.

The allies' first move was to counter the blockade by airlifting essential goods, including coal, into Berlin. Fortunately the airlift was a success; there were no American troops prepared to open the way to Berlin through the Soviet zone had it been necessary to use force. But the blockade of Berlin exposed the weaknesses of the Western allies. After it had been lifted they decided to reconstitute the wartime Western alliance on a more permanent basis. In March 1948 Britain, France and the Benelux countries formed themselves into a mutual aid organisation, then Louis St Laurent, the Canadian External Affairs Minister, proposed that it should be extended to include Canada and the United States and in July 1948 negotiations began in Washington to create the North Atlantic Treaty Organisation.

The reasons behind this were the growing ruthlessness of Communism, the numerically inferior Western armies, doubts about the effectiveness of the atom bomb as a deterrent and the need for time whilst Britain and France recuperated. It was also a manoeuvre to encourage the United States to maintain a presence in Europe now that the Russians were on the Elbe.

The Soviet threat to Western Europe had been implicit at the end of the war, but increased in force as Poland and Czechoslovakia were ruthlessly intimidated into accepting Stalinist regimes and it reached its peak with the Soviet blockade of Berlin. The Soviets had 140 divisions, 25 of them in Central Europe, whereas the Americans had only 2½ divisions in Germany and hoped to counterbalance this difference with the atom bomb. But the Berlin blockade suggested that the atom bomb might not be sufficient as a deterrent. It was known that the USSR was developing a bomb of its own and that captured German technologists, responsible for the V1 and V2 rockets, were working on a new missile delivery system. The Russians could reach the Pyrenees in a fortnight if they so wished. What was needed was an alliance which would keep American troops in Europe and the American air force hovering nearby with atom bombs aboard so that the Russians felt that the slightest move westwards would involve the United States immediately and provoke nuclear retaliation.

But the new strategic plans drawn up went further than mere suggestions for alliances between the armed forces of sovereign states. Dean Acheson allocated separate responsibilities for different aspects of defence to different allies: the British and French armies in Germany, the Royal Navy and the US Navy in the North Atlantic. No sovereign state in the alliance would be able to go it alone because its forces would be deliberately and consciously 'unbalanced' and only made sense as part of a complex whole. NATO was a supra-national strategic force. In this division of responsibilities, the United States was to protect the sea lanes and to be responsible for strategic bombing, including atomic warfare, while the Europeans were to provide most of the land forces, an assumption that was to lead to the concept of a European army. The European army was to be a mixed force, that is, troops and officers from different states were to be intermingled, as English, Scots, Welsh and Irish are in the British army and navy.

Western governments were initially extremely nervous of accepting a major integrated force permanently stationed in Western Europe. To American politicians it looked like handing over American troops indefinitely to supra-national control, and to this was added the specific left-wing anti-American fear of permanent American occupation of Europe. This anti-American chauvinism was especially strong in France and the attack on American imperialism was also assiduously peddled by the Soviet Union and the Western European Communist parties and their undercover supporters.

However, despite such apprehensions, the joint planning proceeded quickly, mainly on the assumption that a third world war would be like the Second World War, only worse, with America's power to use the atom bomb as the main new weapon. It was implicitly accepted that this new weapon would change the issue from one of fear of direct Russian invasion, to fear of Communist internal dislocation. But the presence of the American atom bomb was probably not critical to Stalin's strategic thinking. He saw that Russia, devastated as it was, could only undertake an invasion of Western Europe if it could accept a major and lengthy war as a consequence. The threat of a Soviet invasion was therefore remote, and could only occur if Stalin saw his power in Russia and Eastern Europe beginning to crumble.

Meanwhile, as a direct consequence of the military moves in the West, the Russians organised their zone into a military alliance. This was a defence against a possible American attack and against internal subversion, a rising by the subject peoples against their tyrannical governments, called CMEA or Comecon (Council for Mutual Economic Assistance), in 1949, principally as a propaganda exercise, but a year after Stalin's death in March 1953 it was decided to integrate the individual economic plans of the Eastern bloc (except for Yugoslavia – then an inactive member). It was drawn up as a mutual aid pact. Nevertheless the practice continued of undercharging exports from member states to Russia, and overcharging for Russian goods. Economic policy was identical since it was based on Stalinist theories. There was common agreement on forced industrialisation as a basis for Socialism. But the common programme was not based on international specialisation, with different countries producing what they were best at producing. Rather, it rested on the parallel development of each economy, and 'extended reproduction' – that is heavy goods, like iron and steel, being made even in backward rural countries like Bulgaria. Some joint projects were undertaken, however, in oil and petroleum, natural gas and electric power. There were, too, bilateral projects – Czechoslovakia developing Polish coal mines for example – but these did not alter the general idea of each country going it alone. Only in 1961 was CMEA given additional impetus as evidence was gathered of the success of the Common Market in the West.

In the West the Marshall Plan provided a clearing mechanism for mutual aid and for harmonising economic policies. From the end of the war, however, the Continental European states had sought to organise their own economic recovery and military defence. The mechanism was principally French, using a supra-national idea, which the West Germans accepted with alacrity as a means of returning to the international community.

Adenauer reconstructed the economy of Germany with a social market policy devised by Erhard, his Minister of Economics. Initially, the currency reform brought about widespread unemployment and European Socialists predicted that the slump would cause a revival of Nazism. But within two years prosperity set in. Erhard said later that he could only have achieved what he did while the Americans occupied Germany. In his second government Adenauer brought into the administration Franz Joseph Strauss, the future head of the Christian Social Union of Bavaria, which at that time was a branch of the CDU, the Christian Democratic Party of West Germany. Erhard and Strauss became the main architects of German economic recovery which was based on a sound currency, with an integrity guaranteed by the independence of the German Federal Bank and by a balanced budget as required by the new Constitution. The state rebuilt roads, railways and other essential parts of the infrastructure, but priority was given to loans to individuals and housing associations to reconstruct houses and flats, and to private industry for investment in new businesses. These were largely governed by supervisory boards made up partly of managers and partly of workers. The German trade unions behaved with great responsibility (which was particularly galling to observers in Britain twenty years later), having been reorganised into sixteen major industry-wide unions on the recommendation of the British trade union advisers who were sent to Germany after the end of the war. Agriculture remained prosperous, and food shortages soon disappeared.

Externally, Adenauer's policy was built upon a strong alliance with France and close defensive arrangements with the United States through NATO. To cement the relationship with France, the Adenauer government first of all reacted slowly and cautiously over the vexed question of the border territory of the Saar, which France at first wished to incorporate into France, but subsequently saw as a quasi-independent buffer state between France and Germany. He also proposed a European army in which German units would participate, and which by inference would have been led by French generals, since France was traditionally the senior military power in Western Europe. And he also agreed to Robert Schuman's proposal that the iron, steel and coal industries should be jointly supervised by the Coal and Steel Community, a revival of the pre-war steel cartel, but arranged as an inter-governmental agency in 1951 on the proposal of Robert Schuman, a prominent French minister.

Meanwhile in France, Robert Marjolin had inaugurated the French system of indicative planning through Jean Monnet's Commissariat au Plan. This Commissariat, a joint effort of industry, the civil service and trade unions, indicated priorities for investment. Clearly, this basic approach to the economy influenced strongly Schuman's view that the right way to reconstruct the coal and steel industries of France was in collaboration with Germany and Benelux, which also had important installations, by making the pre-war private steel cartel a public international body. Monnet, another French planner, was convinced that the only way to prevent a fourth destructive war between France and Germany on the pattern of those of 1870, 1914 and 1939 was so firmly to cement the two countries that a war would be technically impossible. He therefore wished to enlarge the European Coal and Steel Community into a European Economic Community, covering all industries including agriculture, and embracing other countries. This idea was given its original boost in a famous speech by Churchill, in which he had advocated something like a United States of Europe. Churchill clearly had in mind, however, collaboration in defence and foreign policy, the traditional concerns of federal governments. Monnet's vision was predominantly economic. When Churchill was returned to office, in October 1951, he and Eden were so unenthusiastic about participation in European economic schemes, that they even failed to promote common European defence and foreign policy institutions. This was encouraged by the Foreign Office who had warmly embraced Churchill's view that the basis of British foreign policy would have to be a close link with the United States. This attitude had been justified both by the tremendous success of NATO, in apparently forestalling direct

Russian threats to Western Europe, and also of the Marshall Plan, which had reconstructed the European economy. Neither would have been possible without American and Canadian membership.

Participation in a much narrower European community seemed to the Foreign Office at that time against British interests, and Britain was prepared with the United States to sit benevolently on the sidelines as a non-participating senior partner, an attitude calculated to infuriate the French and Germans. Eden flatly refused to put British troops into the European Defence Community, whose principal force was to be a genuine mixed European army. The EDC proposal was accepted by the Bundestag in February 1954. The Benelux countries agreed, and Italy seemed certain to agree as well. Then in June the French National Assembly rejected the idea, mainly as a result of a Russian initiative to have four-power talks on the reunification of Germany. If Germany were neutralised, then France had no need to neutralise German power by having its own army in a 'mongrel' force. But the rejection led to the fall of the government of Joseph Laniel, and his successor, Mendès-France, was not an enthusiast. With Britain's participation also ruled out, the European army idea was dead. As a result Adenauer demanded full West German sovereignty with its own armed forces, which led to the entry of the German Federal Republic into the Brussels Pact, and in December 1954 to NATO with its own army, the very thing the EDC had been designed at all events to prevent. As a counterpart to the agreement to allow the Germans to rearm, Eden agreed with the Western European nations to keep four British divisions and a tactical air force in Germany for fifty years. Britain undertook an onerous, expensive, Continental military commitment in order to preserve its military autonomy. A similar short-sighted economic policy was followed.

The negotiations for the creation of the European Economic Community began in 1950, as part of Robert Schuman's proposals for the creation of the Coal and Steel Community. Eventually, in 1957, the Treaty of Rome was signed between Germany, France, Italy and Benelux. Britain stood benevolently aside. The Treaty proposed a fully integrated Common Market by 1972 with one labour market and one capital market, and a common external tariff but no tariffs or restrictions on competition and trade within Europe. As the movement towards the Common Market became politically important to France and Germany after the collapse of the European Defence Community in 1954, the critical years of negotiation were therefore 1955 and 1956. The arrangements of the Community were complex. A Commission was established, composed of two Commissioners from each of the three large countries and one Commissioner for the three small countries, each of whom would be responsible for initiating moves towards agreement on the implementation of the Treaty, itself a lengthy and legalistic document. An Assembly, whose members would be nominated by the parliaments of the countries concerned, was set up, though executive decisions of major importance were taken by the Council of Ministers. The Community's initial programme concentrated on the agricultural system, with an attempt to keep out cheap imports from overseas, particularly the United States, while supporting the peasant farming communities of France and Southern Germany, important electorally to the French and German governments. At the same time the Community created a large market throughout Europe for German industry which was reviving rapidly. Since the Common Market was built around the concept of free trade with no restrictions on competition, its close resemblance to the social market economy which Erhard had constructed in Germany was obvious. Ideologically the Common Market was capitalist. But it was capitalist with a difference. French indicative planning – setting targets for investment and using government power to see they were achieved – lay at the heart of the reconstruction of heavy industry throughout the Coal and Steel Community. Capitalism, too, was not synonymous with free trade. The external tariff against other countries was a reminder that both Germany and France had historically been high-tariff countries which had sought to defend their industries and above all their agriculture against British and American competition. It was thus to a very considerable extent a development of the original German concept of the *Zollverein*, or customs union, upon which the unification of the German Empire under Prussian leadership in 1871 had originally been based.

The impasse into which the world seemed to have settled in the early 1950s was apparently based upon aggressive Stalinism on the one hand and a powerful capitalist United States on the other. Both Russia and America were at the centre of alliances and both sets of alliances were in part military, in part ideological and in part economic. Each alliance suffered stresses and strains. The Soviet bloc countries were classic cases of occupation by a formidably powerful military and totalitarian victor. Despite their repressive regime, the East German workers initiated a wave of strikes in 1953. The Western alliance was far looser, and the opportunities for dissension were correspondingly greater. The Anglo–French invasion of Suez against strong American opposition was an especially vivid example of differences between allies that revealed profound conflicts of interest, and might well have brought the

alliance to an end – de Gaulle, a few years later, was indeed to take
France out of NATO whilst remaining firmly anti-Communist
domestically and internationally.

Nevertheless, despite these inherent strains in both sets of
alliances, and the profound antipathy between them, the election
of Eisenhower in 1952 and the death of Stalin in 1953 seemed to
mark the end of a period when war between the victors seemed
always imminent. The alliances seemed to guarantee security. A
period of peace – and prosperity in the West – was ushered in. But
once more an opportunity was lost to establish anything more than
stalemate.

As the Cold War persisted so the Western allies came to unify
their strategy and to some degree their commands in Europe. This
was formalised in the North Atlantic Pact, and the Paris accords of
1954 which established a Western European Union, for the purpose of allowing West Germany's armed forces to serve in NATO.
Russia, which was still uncertainly treading a path towards some
degree of liberalisation after Stalin's death, was obsessed by
German rearmament. It would go to almost any length to prevent
West Germany from having armed forces. But it would not go as
far as withdrawing from the conquered territories, a precondition
for a disarmed Europe. In November 1954 the Soviet government
asked for a European security conference, to include all European
states; when that proposal was rejected, it made clear that Germany would not be reunited (as Austria had been). In 1955 it
signed the Warsaw Pact. Yet another chance for détente had been
missed. If the USSR was acting in good faith, then perhaps 1955
should be seen as the year when a golden opportunity for a
complete peace settlement was missed.

The Warsaw Pact was of great significance in determining the
post-Stalin relationship of the Soviet Union to its European client
states. It had seemed at one time that several, or perhaps all, of the
Eastern European states would be absorbed into the Soviet Union
as the three small Baltic republics had been. But by 1948 it was
clear that they preferred that the countries should govern themselves, provided that they adhered pretty strictly to Stalinist-type
political, social and economic programmes and had no independent foreign or defence policy. Once the firm hand of Stalin
was removed, however, a problem of co-ordination remained.
Malenkov, the Soviet Premier who succeeded Stalin, and aimed
for a more moderate foreign policy, was dismissed on 8 February
1955. He was followed by Bulganin, with Khruschev as head of the
party; Molotov, Stalin's Foreign Minister, resumed his hard-line
policy. Nevertheless, the new leadership almost immediately be-

gan downgrading Molotov, and when the Eastern bloc countries
met at Warsaw in May 1955, the new line was 'peaceful coexistence'; and as part of this process, the Warsaw Pact was signed,
giving the countries formal independence of each other, united by
the treaty of mutual military aid, with a joint command. The
German Democratic Republic became a member of the Pact.

In 1955 the Soviet government gave cautious indications that it
might like to end the Cold War. The Austrian state treaty was
signed and Soviet troops withdrawn. A summit conference of the
big powers was called to meet in Geneva in July. In these circumstances, the Warsaw Pact was interpreted as (and was in fact) a
guarantee of the relative independence of its member states, an
interim step – at that stage of Soviet détente policy – before the
alliances, the Warsaw Pact, NATO and the Paris agreements
might be dissolved into a European security treaty. A disarmed
Europe was a genuine possibility. Although the armies of the
Warsaw Pact countries were moulded into an arm of the Soviet
army, with standardised equipment, a common early-warning
system and a centralised joint staff, the Warsaw Pact became a
central feature of Soviet détente policy, based upon the strength
of the independent but co-ordinated states of Eastern Europe – a
mirror-image of NATO. Molotov's warnings against détente resulted in his exile to Outer Mongolia.

The alliances thus took several forms – in the East, the Warsaw
Pact and Comecon, both coercive arrangements dominated by the
Soviet Union; and in the West, the North Atlantic Treaty, the
Marshall Plan (the Organisation for European Economic Co-
operation), and the Common Market. Though the United States
was the biggest member of the first two Western alliances and
largely paid for them, it was not politically dominant, though it was
extremely influential.

European prosperity, built around the enormous successes of
North Italian, German and French industry, and the growing
prosperity of European agriculture, was coincident with the development of the Common Market and its institutions. The Common Market had not itself caused the prosperity. Many countries
outside the Common Market shared in the prosperity – countries
as diverse as Sweden, Spain and Yugoslavia. Nevertheless coincidence was taken for cause. For many political commentators the
Common Market was seen as the cause of European prosperity.
Recurrent British difficulties were blamed on British failure to join
the European Economic Community in 1957. Its subsequent
attempts to do so were twice vetoed by General de Gaulle, in 1962
and 1967. The dismal failures of the 1960s, as they seemed to

British economic commentators, were frequently attributed to British isolation from the Continent.

The rejection of the British application stemmed partly from Adenauer's resentment at his treatment by the British in 1945 and his conviction that Germany could only be reconstructed by reliance upon American economic aid and French political support, and also from de Gaulle's resentment at what he saw as the patronising British attitude during his exile in London. This seemed to the British base ingratitude, since without Churchill's efforts France would never have been a permanent member of the Security Council of the United Nations, nor would France have been represented in the occupation zones of Germany. Both Adenauer and de Gaulle were right in thinking, however, that British membership would upset their apple-cart. In particular, Adenauer and de Gaulle would no longer be the joint leaders of Europe. And the British were committed, not to an integrated European community, with centralised institutions, but to a free-trade area, where trade took place without tariffs and without any European economic policy.

The re-election of Adenauer in 1957 left him even more powerful in Germany than before, and the patent success of both his foreign and domestic policies created a prosperous and formidable Germany. The SPD party, seemingly permanently in opposition, adopted at its Bad Godesberg Conference in November 1959 a new non-Marxist moderate policy document which effectively embraced the achievements of the social market economy, but called for a more moderate and Social Democratic solution to the problems of German society. It explicitly rejected state planning and nationalisation, opposition to rearmament and NATO, and it ceased to regard itself as either working class in its base or anti-clerical in its outlook. It thus became in some sense a mirror image of the CDU without the clericalism and capitalist support.

De Gaulle assumed power in France in 1958 as a result of the Algerian crisis, and was rapidly endorsed not only by the frightened National Assembly but by a popular referendum. De Gaulle had seen the non-Communist world as based upon three major powers – France, Britain, and the United States – though he was also convinced that in the long run the special relationship between France and Germany could form the basis of a reassertion of French strength in Continental Europe. In 1958, therefore, de Gaulle effectively jettisoned any idea of Britain as one of the major powers, substituting Adenauer's Germany. He invited Adenauer to Colombey-les-deux-Églises, his country house in Northern France, and on 14 September 1958 it was announced that France and Germany would unite to form a common front – implicitly against the United States. At a second meeting between Adenauer and de Gaulle on 26 November 1958, at Bad Kreuznach, they rejected the idea of a European free trade area, which was Reginald Maudling's proposal for a new economic status throughout Europe without supra-national authorities; in other words, Maudling's proposal was seen as an attempt to dismantle the integrationist structure of the Common Market. This led to a special relationship between Adenauer and de Gaulle, and the eventual signing of the Franco–German Pact of Friendship in January 1963. When de Gaulle withdrew from NATO in February 1959 he did so in the knowledge that though Germany remained within NATO, as was essential from the point of view of its relations with America, the German alliance with France was secure. De Gaulle's other major decision, also supported by Adenauer, was that Britain should not be allowed to join the Common Market, where it would threaten his leadership, while Adenauer was convinced that the Macmillan government would seek to weaken the Common Market. On 14 January 1963 de Gaulle announced that France would veto Britain's entry. This was followed immediately by the Franco–German Treaty of Friendship. It could have been called the We Hate Britain Treaty.

The Western alliance therefore became more diverse. The American economic and military preponderance was offset by a new French–German axis which developed a major economic bloc of its own from which the British were excluded.

A different sort of development took place in the Soviet camp. In February 1956 the dead Stalin was denounced by Khruschev at the Twentieth Congress of the Communist party of the Soviet Union, and Molotov and Malenkov were labelled as part of his entourage. In the Soviet Union the consequences of this denunciation were profound; in the Eastern bloc generally the shock was greater, since it was Stalin who had socialised them, and their parties and governmental apparatus were pure Stalin creations.

Khruschev tried to regain Yugoslavia for the new, milder Socialist camp, but in the process of de-Stalinisation a revolution broke out in Poznan in Poland that had to be put down by troops. It seemed as though the Socialist bloc as a whole might tread the Yugoslav path. By October Soviet troops had to move on Warsaw, and Khruschev and other leaders flew into Poland to strengthen the Polish party. In July Rakosi, the chief of the Hungarian Communist party, was dismissed, and a relatively liberal regime was formed under Imre Nagy. The Hungarians as a people rose in a move away from Communism and, in a panic, the Soviet Union invaded Hungary on 24 October 1956, sending Mikoyan and Suslov to supervise the restoration of an acceptable Communist government under Janos Kadar.

The illusion of independent but allied states was, for the moment, shattered. The Hungarian government had not asked for intervention, though a *post hoc* invitation was extended by the newly-installed government, nor were the other Warsaw Pact governments consulted or involved in the invasion. Oddly enough, however, on 10 October 1956 the Soviet Union made an unprecedented admission of errors and mistakes in its dealings with Soviet bloc countries, and implicitly prepared the ground for their growing diversity (within limits).

As a direct consequence of the Hungarian uprising, the USSR signed bilateral treaties providing for the stationing of Soviet troops in Poland, East Germany, Romania and Hungary. Interestingly enough this series of treaties did not include Czechoslovakia. This new set of arrangements replaced the Cominform as the means by which the USSR extended its influence and control throughout Eastern Europe, putting relationships upon a more formal and customary basis of inter-state negotiation, rather than the informal party network which had been dominant before.

The network of alliances was thus built around America and Russia, but in a way that was not a mirror image, and whose diversity reflected the economic and political diversity of the post-war world. The alliances were a form of guarantee of stability. But in at least two ways they were a source of instability. A European security treaty might have been negotiated in the mid 1950s, as was shown when the Russians agreed that Austria should be neutralised and independent. The Soviet Union might also have been willing to agree to an independent and neutral Germany if it were part of a wider scheme for a neutral and demilitarised Europe.

There were complex problems rending each alliance. For the Eastern states, the key question was whether or not non-Communist political and economic arrangements would be permissible. Hungary seemed to show that the answer was definitely not. Yugoslavia showed that independent action could occur but that it was fraught with dangers. In the West Britain beggared herself to preserve her military autonomy under the illusion that her special relationship with America was more important than participation with Europe. France and Germany set up their own bloc and, in the case of France, seemed more powerfully anti-American than committed to NATO. Britain, France and Germany all had separate and independent sets of interests, the

Americans had no power to negotiate on behalf of any of them.

All of these stresses and strains were to be made apparent first in the Middle East where rivalry between France and Britain as colonial powers, between France, Britain and America in pursuit of oil, fears of Soviet expansion, the growth of Communism, and lack of comprehension of the power of Socialist Muslim nationalism, all combined to make the Middle East the most touchy area of the emerging ex-colonial world.

It was lack of control rather than too much control that led to the waste of opportunities that the death of Stalin and the end of Truman's Presidency gave to the Western world. Such a proliferation of alliances left no one free to speak either for himself or for a group of others.

Chapter 15

Khruschev and the Hungarian revolution

The West supposed that the death of Stalin would lead to a struggle for the succession. They hoped that it would be followed by major changes in Soviet domestic and foreign policy, which might create an occasion for détente, but they did not take into account the legacy left by Stalin which thwarted liberal reform at every turn. The great bureaucratic Soviet state created by Stalin resembled the autocratic empire of the Czars in its monolithic stolidity. Both Holy Mother Russia and the USSR straddled the northern Euro–Asian land mass and this geopolitical set-up dictated foreign policy; in rhetoric and techniques of government, the mode of tyranny had changed little in a hundred years. Most of the people still lived in dire poverty, acutely short of housing, one family to a room, few clothes, scant food. Millions in camps were ragged, verminous and starving. Russia seemed stuck in a groove. De-Stalinisation would inevitably be fraught with repercussions.

The wounds created by tyrannical dictatorship of long standing cannot be healed overnight: they leave bitter resentment, and Stalin's final obsessive acts endeavouring to magnify Russian nationalism had created a backlash of local nationalistic fervour on the fringes of the empire which deterred his successors from ameliorating the old iron rule.

Stalin's purges, deportations, pogroms and excesses have been chronicled in Chapters 5 and 10. These tyrannical acts culminated in the unmasking of the Jewish doctors' plot of January 1953. Nine prominent professors of medicine working in the Kremlin were accused of attempting to murder the Bolshevik leaders of the Soviet Union. In the circumstances, Stalin's death on 5 March 1953, at the age of seventy-three, interrupted and ended what was perhaps the most extraordinary purge that the regime would have seen, the accused being charged with murdering many of the people whom Stalin had himself caused to be murdered.

There was no heir apparent – always, in any case, a difficult and dangerous job. The period of transition could indeed have been stormy but was in fact hardly felt by the ordinary people. Initially Malenkov took over, but he could not retain his hold on the levers of power and after two shaky years was obliged to relinquish his post to Nikita Khruschev. Khruschev came from a peasant family in the Donetz basin. A rotund sphere of a man with a potato face, he had become the Politburo's agricultural expert, enforcing Stalin's highly unpopular collectivisation of agriculture policies and encouraging the ploughing up of the virgin lands in Kazakhstan and Siberia with catastrophic results.

Khruschev soon made a number of key appointments, including Serov as head of the secret police, and established his cronies in crucial positions, but he lacked Stalin's absolute authority and was himself subject to severe criticism on many grounds, notably the failure of agricultural policy. Collectivisation was still hated; techniques of production were archaic. In 1953 agricultural production was no higher than it had been in 1913. Communism has never succeeded in coping with agriculture. For peasants to produce food there has to be a market. For a free market in food to develop, there have to be merchants, wholesalers, retailers. Rises in prices lead to higher output, and to technical progress. A centrally planned economy cannot allow this to happen by market forces; they have to be planned. Compulsion has to be used. And in the process, the peasants produce less, and keep their (illegal) surpluses for themselves. As a result while the East went hungry, the West had problems in disposing of its agricultural surpluses. In heavy industry, however, there had been substantial progress, and Malenkov tried to shift the emphasis of the programme towards light industry and popular consumer goods. Since Malenkov was responsible for industry, this weighted the political scales in his favour. But Khruschev supported the old Stalinist policy of priority for heavy industry at the request of the military, which feared it might lag behind America if the industrial policy was altered.

Khruschev's supremacy was achieved despite the opposition of virtually the entire heavyweight division of the Praesidium: Malenkov, Bulganin, Molotov, Kaganovich, Voroshilov and Mikoyan. It seemed as though they mutually disliked each other more than they disliked Khruschev.

Khruschev's political victory against Malenkov was followed by the Twentieth Congress of the Soviet Communist party, held in February 1956. In an unprecedented event in Soviet and Communist history, Khruschev denounced in detail many of Stalin's misdeeds, as well as announcing the adoption of a more sophisticated non-Stalinist line. The risk was considerable and Khruschev was almost overthrown by conservative groups who were threatened by the revelations of crimes in which they – and indeed Khruschev himself – had been implicated. Khruschev's speech had many purposes, one undoubtedly being to discredit Malenkov and Molotov; not only was the former blamed especially for his part in the Leningrad affair of 1948–9, and the latter for engineering the breach with Yugoslavia, but both earlier still, for the part they had played in Stalin's period of personal rule from 1934 onwards and especially in the Great Purge of 1937.

The new regime wished to follow a milder policy towards the satellite states but Khruschev found that he had inherited an explosive situation, for Stalinist extremists in the various states had embittered the people and alienated the milder Communists, particularly in Hungary. Yugoslavia was also a great worry to Khruschev since it offered an example of a Soviet-dominated country beginning to backtrack on its own internal Stalinist policies.

As the economy failed to prosper, Tito was obliged to run down the collectivisation of agriculture; industry was decentralised, at first gradually, and then by a full-scale shift into co-operative control; this was followed by a move towards a market economy, with the abolition of wage and price controls, and the re-establishment of profits as a guide to the allocation of resources. This shift in economic technique was accompanied by growing denunciations of Stalinism, and a modest return to some freedom from arbitrary arrest, tolerance of debate, and religious and artistic freedom. Thus Yugoslavia gained a not wholly unjustified reputation as a 'liberal' Communist state, though many repressive elements remained. Some rapprochement with Russia took place, however, culminating in a visit by Khruschev in 1955; at the same time, Tito began to take a leading role in a grouping of non-aligned Third World states, including India, Ethiopia and many other Asian countries. The extent of Tito's travels – eight months in Asia in 1954 – indicated the degree to which he trusted his security arrangements in Yugoslavia and the stability of the regime.

The reconciliation with the Soviet Union was underplayed in the West, but it was accompanied by a reintegration of large parts of the Yugoslav economy in Comecon, the East European economic alliance, and, following Khruschev's denunciation of Stalin at the Twentieth Congress in 1956, a sense that Tito's version of Communism had succeeded. Tito showed his steady commitment to authoritarian Communism. Milovan Djilas, a leading theoretician, published a series of articles on the democratisation of the party and the withering away of the state. In 1954 he was purged, with Dediyev, his leading supporter. Between 1954 and 1958 over two million Yugoslavs were imprisoned without trial.

A growing influx of Western tourists, and a steady exodus of

Yugoslavs to work in Western countries, meant greater contact with the West, and with it freedom of expression, than in other Eastern countries. Towards the end of the 1950s, the economic reforms began to take effect after a slow and hesitant start, so that in 1956 pre-war levels of agricultural output were at last achieved. Thus with a perceptible rise in the standard of living in the next ten years, sustained by emigrants' remittances, there was a movement of opinion towards reformist Communism.

Tito, however, persisted in keeping himself and his party prominent in the world Communist movement and, to that end, opposed the liberal reforms in Poland and Hungary and supported Soviet repression of the uprisings in Poznan and Budapest. The movement towards de-Stalinisation, accelerated as a result of Khruschev's speech to the Twentieth Congress, became alarming to the Soviet Union, whose leaders sought to use Tito's desire for rehabilitation in their eyes as a means of controlling the other satellites; and Tito was willing, indeed eager, to play this role.

In this context the Hungarian uprising was of crucial significance; it was especially serious for the future of Communism because it required severe Russian military intervention to put it down. In order to explain the background to the situation in Hungary, it is necessary to go back for a moment to the immediate post-war set-up there.

In the post-war elections for the provisional Hungarian legislative assembly, Communists had gained only 17 per cent of the vote. A coalition had been formed and a republic proclaimed. However, repeated Stalinist purges forced non-Communists out of the government and the middle-of-the-road Communists, under Imre Nagy, forcibly brought in land reform and nationalised heavy industry. The general secretary of the extremely popular Smallholders' party (which had polled 57 per cent of the votes), Bela Kovacs, was arrested by Soviet troops and subsequently murdered. The banks were nationalised, and a Three-Year Plan was introduced, taking the country further along the road towards Socialism. In August 1947, in fraudulent elections, the Communists still gained only 22 per cent of the votes. The following year the Social Democrats were forced to join the Communist party in a union, which led to a new government. In the purge of the Roman Catholic Church, Cardinal Mindszenty was arrested. This was followed in 1949 by new elections with the Communist candidates presented on a single slate, and a series of trials of potential Titoists, headed by Laszlo Rajk. All except the very smallest businesses were nationalised; a newly created security police system intensified the terror, and gradually many tens of thousands of former Smallholders' party and Social Democrat party members were arrested and put into concentration camps.

As the persecution increased a number of prominent Communists were imprisoned, including Janos Kadar, who was later to be Prime Minister. The high spot was the show trial of Rajk, a loyal Stalinist, on the grounds that he was a Titoist. The concentration camps by this time were brimming over, the Churches were increasingly persecuted and agriculture was forcibly collectivised. The Stalinist dictatorship in Hungary was at least as cruel and as arbitrary as that in the Soviet Union, and the General Secretary of the Communist party and Prime Minister was Matyas Rakosi, a hard-liner, whose orientation was so completely Stalinist that he was known as Stalin's best Hungarian disciple.

The death of Stalin in 1953 led to a summons for the Communist party leadership, including Imre Nagy, to go to Moscow to meet the new Soviet leadership. In June 1953, in a spirit of collective self-criticism and collective leadership, the party's former policies were criticised. In July Nagy replaced Rakosi as Prime Minister, and a new programme was announced in Budapest, including an amnesty for political prisoners and the abolition of the concentration camps, as well as some degree of liberalisation of the economy.

The limitations on this reform movement were great, however, since the tough Rakosi remained First Party Secretary. Although a small number of political prisoners were released, the savage repression continued, which began to stimulate resistance. The newspapers, which had once been full of contemptible attacks on the people who were now being released, changed their line, and journalists began to feel the need to speak with some degree of freedom about what had been taking place in Hungary. The huge industrialisation programme adopted under Stalinist guidance was slowed down; attempts were made to increase the flow of consumer goods and to raise the standard of living of ordinary people, though these changes were resisted by Rakosi.

In 1954 Rakosi once more became the Stalinist dictator of Hungary, although the new Prime Minister was, nominally, Andreas Hegedus. A new purge was initiated, but unfortunately for Rakosi, his new policy was undermined by Khruschev and Bulganin, who in May 1955 came to Belgrade, seeking to mend their fences with Tito. In the course of their visit it was announced that the charges which Stalin had made against Marshal Tito were false, and that the expulsion of Yugoslavia from the Cominform in 1950 had been a mistake. This exposed Rakosi, since he had been the most ardent Stalinist in the Eastern bloc, and had been

responsible for the show trial of Laszlo Rajk in 1949 which had
centred on Rajk being 'a Hungarian Titoist'. At this stage, therefore, sections of the Communist party in Hungary urged the
rehabilitation of Rajk. Rakosi, however, not only refused but
expelled the opposition from the Communist party.

The opposition to Rakosi's hard line was led by the writers and
journalists who first published indirect criticism of the government
and then, gradually, more open attacks, in which they expressed
the hatred of the simple working and peasant people for the
regime. At first everybody who so protested was attacked in public
by the state and party and some people were imprisoned. Gradually, however, they allied themselves to Imre Nagy as a reform
Communist group. It became clear that there were forces in the
Communist party, and even in the Soviet Union itself, who were
determined to get rid of Rakosi.

A group known as the Petofi Circle, after a young poet who was
the hero of the 1848 revolution in Hungary, met regularly in
Budapest to discuss developments in Communism. At its meeting
in June 1956, Mrs Rajk spoke and demanded posthumous justice
for her husband, Laszlo Rajk, who had been executed in the 1949
purges, and by the end of the month open political discussion was
taking place throughout Hungary. This coincided with Imre Nagy's
sixtieth birthday, an occasion for open political demonstration.
Rakosi banned the Petofi Circle and expelled large numbers of
people from the Communist party. Then Mikoyan came to
Budapest to visit Nagy and to remove Rakosi from office. He was
replaced by Erno Gerö, an old Stalinist who unlike Rakosi was
untainted by open bullying and terrorism.

Once one person had fallen, as so frequently happens, a series of
dominoes crashed in quick succession. By September the spon-
taneous criticism of Stalinism was stepped up, reinforced by the
people who had been released from prison, who demanded their
own rehabilitation. Imre Nagy once more was regarded as the
potential centre of the opposition, because he had earlier seemed a
likely Tito figure with a mind of his own.

Gerö and the new Hungarian party leaders, following Moscow's
instructions, made approaches to Tito, and a goodwill visit was
arranged to Belgrade. Before they left Hungary on 4 October they
announced that Laszlo Rajk would be reburied in a grave outside
the prison. This funeral became a political demonstration on
Sunday, 6 October 1956, with perhaps as many as two hundred
thousand people in the cortege. Significantly students in Budapest
also rose to march through the streets carrying banners and
chanting for freedom. Before long student meetings were held

continually in the provinces to demand freedom of speech and the end of Stalinism. Enormous popular support from other Hungarians swiftly followed, as meetings were held all over the country.

Nagy took no part in these demonstrations because he was on holiday. But when he returned to Budapest on 23 October, he found himself regarded as the leader of the revolution. A huge bronze statue of Stalin was hacked off at the knees and dragged through the streets of Budapest, and meanwhile the crowds surrounded the radio station and obliged the broadcasters to transmit the demands of the demonstrators. Gerö, on his way back from Yugoslavia, broadcast a hard-line, furious denunciation of the rising, which only fanned the anger of the protesters. A crowd appeared spontaneously on the streets, ransacked the Communist newspaper building and set light to books on Marx, Lenin and Stalin in vast bonfires, to which portraits of Stalin and Rakosi were added. The police began shooting and several demonstrators were killed, whereupon the workers themselves took arms from the security guards at the factories and began to fight.

On 24 October Soviet tanks entered Budapest, but the crowds built barricades across the city. The same day, Nagy, a conservative and somewhat timid figure, who was determined not to allow free trade unions or free political parties, became *de facto* the Communist leader and Prime Minister.

The following day Mikoyan replaced Gerö by Janos Kadar and the old leaders left Budapest under the protection of Soviet tanks and planes. At this stage Nagy decided that the rising was not counter-revolutionary, but full-bloodedly revolutionary. He said, 'In these stirrings a great national and democratic movement, embracing and unifying all our people, developed . . . with elemental force . . . in the course of these battles was born the government of democratic national unity, independence, and Socialism.' The revolution wanted the dissolution of the armed military police and the withdrawal of Soviet troops, and on 30 October Nagy announced that he approved of these demands, and moreover that he had decided to abolish the one-party system, to reopen the democratic coalition which had existed in 1945, and that he planned to withdraw from the Warsaw Pact. At the same time there were rumours of further Soviet invasion.

Behind this unrest lay deep dissatisfaction with Communism: the desire to withdraw from the Warsaw Pact was based upon the analogy with Austria, which had been neutralised by the Austrian State Treaty. The Hungarians desired a similar status for themselves. It was clear that the Soviet Union might have accepted some degree of liberalisation, but they would not accept the multi-party system, and above all they would not accept Hungary leaving the Warsaw Pact. On 3 November the Cabinet became a genuine coalition by including representatives from the Small-holders' party and the Social Democrats.

Though it was overtly committed to the maintenance of Social-ism in Hungary, the Cabinet made statements which could legiti-mately lead to fears of an anti-Soviet counter-revolution which would genuinely take Hungary out of the Eastern bloc into the Western camp, going further even than Tito in Yugoslavia. Mean-while throughout the country, as local councils were set up at the behest of the populace, it became clear that rural areas and provincial capitals were considerably more revisionist than the inhabitants of Budapest, since some of them obviously planned the dismantling of the Socialist system. This was particularly the case in western Hungary, on the borders with Austria.

Meanwhile fighting continued throughout Hungary between the so-called people's police or the AVH, and the revolutionaries. The reconstituted parties were active in the revolution, and besides those which participated in the government, a group of much smaller parties was formed similar to those in Western Europe, a Christian Democratic party based on Adenauer's CDU, and a Hungarian Radical party. Cardinal Mindszenty was liberated from prison, and though he refused to make any political statements, it was clear that he was potentially the centre of a radical movement in the country, in particular when he called for the restitution of the institutions and societies of the Catholic Church, which above all meant the right to teach.

On 4 November the Soviet army invaded Hungary and occupied it fully. The government was dissolved, Imre Nagy and much of his Cabinet sought refuge in the Yugoslav embassy, while Cardinal Mindszenty fled to the American embassy. Janos Kadar formed a government on the basis of Soviet support. Meanwhile Soviet troops were being opposed throughout the country with heavy fighting, which continued until 12 November, led by local workers' councils. As the revolution and fighting developed, a Central Workers' Council was created in the west of the country. Many of its members were arrested by the Russians, but the fight continued. The workers had a meeting with Kadar at which he agreed with the workers' councils' demands, namely that Imre Nagy should take part in the government and that elections should be held with several parties, and that Soviet troops should eventually withdraw. Nevertheless the workers did not believe Kadar, and negotiations were carried on with the Soviet army to try to release the Hun-garians who had been arrested. A general strike was threatened,

but as November progressed, large numbers of members of the
workers' councils and of the Central Workers' Council were
arrested; consequently only small-scale local strikes took place. To
make matters worse, Soviet troops opened fire on those who
demonstrated in support of the general strike. It was only a matter
of time before the uprising was over.

Under the Kadar regime, a puppet of the Soviet Union, repression was severe. By 5 January the death penalty was extended to
those who struck or those who incited others to strike. Thousands
fled from Hungary and thousands more were put into concentration camps and prisons. Nagy and his supporters were lodged in the
Yugoslav embassy where they tried to organise some sort of
resistance. His principal supporter, Gimes, having been allowed to
go to a press conference given by the Indian representative sent by
Nehru, was arrested as he left. Other people fled, but the resistance continued until February 1957. Nagy eventually quit the
embassy, was arrested, and like his supporters, was executed.
Their deaths were announced on 17 June 1958.

Just as Yugoslavia had been an affront to Stalin, who spared no
effort, short of armed invasion, to suppress Titoism, so Khruschev
stopped at nothing, not even armed invasion, to suppress Nagy. In
this he was supported by Tito and not opposed by America, which
was in the throes of a presidential election, nor the Western
European powers who were invading Egypt and capturing the Suez
Canal at this time. They were too busy with their own arcane
desires to care what the USSR was doing within its own sphere of
influence. The underlying Soviet theme from Stalin's time onwards
was fear of internal dissension leading to the overthrow of the
Communist system as a whole. The supremacy of the party was at
issue: institutionalised paranoia reigned.

The adverse consequences for Khruschev of the Eastern European troubles were further intensified by a slow-down of Soviet
economic growth – associated partly with the agricultural failures – and by Khruschev's attempt to reduce the power of the
Soviet centralised planning apparatus, to give more authority to
the regions. Here Khruschev was combining personal ambition –
for a decline in central authority would weaken his opponents –
with a genuine attempt to put the Soviet economy on a more
rational basis. This plan was announced in February 1957, and
Khruschev's principal supporters on the Central Committee over-
ruled opposition from the Presidium. Malenkov, Molotov and
Kaganovich were removed both from the Presidium and the
Central Committee, but unlike in Stalin's days, the fallen leaders
were not executed.

Molotov was made Ambassador to Mongolia and then to the International Atomic Energy Agency in Vienna; Malenkov was sent to run a hydroelectric station in Kazakhstan, and Kaganovich was made head of a cement factory in the Urals. Khruschev followed his triumph within the party by dismissing Marshal Zhukov (who despite everything had survived Stalin) from the Presidium in October 1957, in order to subordinate the army to the party's control, and throughout 1958 his rival Bulganin was gradually demoted, after he ceased to be head of the Council of Ministers. He was to be Khruschev's deputy until 1957, when he joined the so-called anti-party group, and was demoted and expelled from the Presidium of the Central Committee. He then retired. The process by which Khruschev came to power was gradual; nevertheless it ended up with a dictatorship, suggesting that Russia, at least under Communist rule, could only function with a dictator. Khruschev continued his anti-Stalin campaign in 1961 with another strong denunciation, ordering Stalin's body to be removed from Lenin's mausoleum in Moscow's Red Square.

Although Khruschev's rule was personal, he exercised it through the party and to some degree with the active consent of the party, who controlled the army and the state apparatus. But, unlike in the Stalin period, the party arrived at its decisions to some extent independently of Khruschev. However this independence was mitigated by the doctrine of unanimity, so that divergence from the agreed policy, once arrived at, was virtually unthinkable; Khruschev's strength depended ultimately upon the allies whom he had recruited and promoted within the party. In 1959 the Twenty-first Party Congress developed a new Khruschevian theory of where the Soviet Union stood, that it was on the verge of transition from Socialism to Communism, from the stage where people were paid according to their contribution to society to the stage where people were paid according to their needs. This theoretical position coincided, however, with an easing of the economic position of the country, so that substantial advances were taking place in the standard of living, and the economic system rested upon less arbitrary decisions than it had in Stalin's time. At the same time, too, the developments of a powerful though unorganised series of dissidents became a permanent feature of Soviet life. Some were immediately arrested and sent to labour camps, but a large number continued to function, more or less openly, and some of them had contact with the West. The range of dissidence was wide, from ultra-Marxist Marxism to extreme religiosity, but their very existence pointed to a deep well of disbelief in the reigning orthodoxy.

Thus Khruschev inaugurated a period of personal rule, far less terrible than Stalin's but hardly a great period of liberalism either. Rather, it marked a time of substantial economic and social progress, as the consequences of the wartime devastation were overcome, and as the rewards were reaped from the enormous investment in heavy industry of Stalin's period. The USSR, too, seemed to have shed some of its obsessive fear of the West, particularly, perhaps, because of its spectacular advances in military strength, especially with the atom and hydrogen bombs, and its first space vehicle, the Sputnik, in 1957.

The Sputnik, the first man-made object to leave the atmosphere, astonished the West, which had assumed that the Soviet Union was technologically substantially behind. Was the launching of Sputnik a sudden technological advance? Apparently not; the Soviet success owed much to German scientists captured at the end of the Second World War, as well as to the determination of the Soviet authorities to achieve this particular success, come what may. Enormous effort and expense had been devoted to space research and rocketry, much knowledge being made freely available by the Western scientific community with their liberal tradition that scientific knowledge should be given freely to all fellow-pursuers of the truth.

As an immediate result of Sputnik, influential circles in the United States became convinced that the Soviet Union had leapt substantially ahead, both in the technological capacity of its missiles and also in the number which it possessed. This formed a major plank in John F. Kennedy's campaign for the Presidency against Richard Nixon in 1960. In the event, this estimate turned out to be fallacious, as the United States was far ahead in the quality and quantity of its missiles. On the other hand, the Soviet Union had concentrated its education system on science and technology, whereas, it was argued, this had been dangerously neglected in the United States. Eisenhower's advisers in 1957 were convinced that the Soviet Union would pass the United States both militarily and economically, just as the United States had passed Europe in the past twenty years.

As a direct result of Sputnik, President Eisenhower appointed the President of the Massachusetts Institute of Technology, Dr James R. Killian Jr, as his scientific adviser, or Special Assistant for Science and Technology in the White House. Not only was the space programme substantially accelerated, but educational expenditure, already substantially up as a result of the population bulge which followed the end of the war, was further increased. Thus the United States entered a period of massive educational expansion, particularly in science and technology, as a consequence of a misunderstanding of Sputnik.

Sputnik was by any standards a Soviet triumph, if only because of its effect on America. It certainly made Khruschev seem successful. Like all Russian leaders, Khruschev developed an urge for a prominent place on the world stage. Initially seen in the West as a much easier figure to deal with than Stalin, the failure of the 1960 summit in Paris and the Cuban missile crisis made him appear both more erratic and less attractive than had been at first thought.

Khruschev's policy of opening to the West had collapsed with the U2 incident, when an American spy-plane was shot down over Russia during the Paris summit and Khruschev stormed back to Moscow, after humiliating Eisenhower. Brezhnev was then moved from the party Secretariat to an honorary post, but taking with him a number of his special officials, he began to travel throughout Africa, Asia and Europe, making himself an authority on international affairs. Khruschev's split with China also caused considerable difficulty. Then there was the failure of the agricultural programme; and the policy of regionalisation of economic control was accompanied by a faltering in economic growth. At the same time he attempted to reorganise the party and created considerable disruption, making many enemies; also his de-Stalinisation programme, and his lack of dignity, appeared to upset the conventional Russians.

Khruschev's downfall in 1964 had its origins in the fears that his policy over Cuba had generated. Khruschev, although viewed in the West as a notable liberaliser, was actually as zealous a persecutor of religion as Stalin. He was, however, a persecutor within legal limits. Though his successors, Kosygin and Brezhnev, relented from pursuing this policy to the same degree, they intensified the pursuit of dissent. It was however done within the limits of the law – admittedly Soviet law – and also with the awareness of the existence of Western opinion which had, to some degree, to be respected as a logical outcome of the policy of ideological co-existence. In 1961 the Twenty-second party Congress seemed, indeed, to promise a more liberal future, but ultimately was chiefly notable for the rise of Khruschev's successors, Brezhnev and Kosygin.

Brezhnev was born in Dniepropetrovsk in the Ukraine on 19 December 1906, studying at the Metallurgical Institute at Kamenskoye and the Land Utilisation and Reclamation Technicum at Kursk. He returned to the Ukraine and rose to a high position in the party there under Khruschev, after three successive levels of leadership had been destroyed in Stalin's terror. After the war, when he had been a political commissar in the Soviet army, he was put in charge of the reconstruction of Zaporozhe, a large area of the Ukraine. Later he became a powerful figure in the Communist party of the Soviet union, as party leader of Moldavia, which had been annexed from Romania.

A fanatical Stalinist, he moved to Moscow in Khruschev's wake, becoming Deputy on the Presidium. With Stalin's death he was demoted to a post of Deputy Defence Minister, then sent to Kazakhstan to implement Khruschev's 'virgin lands' policy. Three hundred new state farms, each with a minimum of 50,000 acres of land, were created in order to cultivate 6.3 million hectares between March 1954 and the end of 1955. Some output was achieved, although at immense cost, enabling Khruschev to claim that his virgin lands policy was a success, and in the process to demote Malenkov, replacing him by Bulganin. It gave Brezhnev a reputation as an agricultural expert, and though the yields from Kazakhstan have been erratic, they have in successful years been enormous and offset to some degree the recurrent crop failures in the Ukraine.

As Khruschev's most loyal supporter, Brezhnev returned to Moscow in 1956. He supported Khruschev at the meeting with Tito in September 1956, at which the suppression of Hungary was agreed, and after the crucial struggle of 22–30 June 1957, when Khruschev overthrew Molotov, Malenkov and Kaganovich, he became a member of the party Presidium, where he was as ardent a supporter of Khruschev in public as he had been of Stalin.

On 21 June 1963 Brezhnev was re-elected to the Central Committee Secretariat, together with Nicolai Podgorny, then aged sixty, the party leader of the Ukraine. Khruschev was removed from power by sending him on vacation to Sochi on the Black Sea on 30 September 1964, while Brezhnev was on a visit to East Berlin. A fortnight later Khruschev was dismissed, and Brezhnev was elected First Secretary of the Central Committee of the Communist party of the Soviet Union, with Kosygin as Prime Minister. It was not clear at first whether Brezhnev would be the new leader. The struggle was about so-called Libermanism, the theory that the Soviet Union should return to a market structure with independent centres of profit for each enterprise. Brezhnev was an opponent of what he called 'goulash Communism', as it would give independent sources of power in the state, thereby jeopardising the party's proclaimed leading role. Economism would prevail over Marxist–Leninist ideals.

At the Twenty-third party Congress in March and April 1966 Brezhnev became the Secretary General of the party, the title held previously by Stalin. Kosygin, a distinguished intellectual and a successful Premier, was the same age as Brezhnev. He had been Deputy Premier of the USSR at the age of thirty-six and became a full member of the Politburo at the age of forty-two. During 1965 there was a continual struggle between Brezhnev and Kosygin for leadership, which ended with power in Brezhnev's hands and Podgorny becoming President of the USSR, replacing the old-style politician, Anastas Mikoyan. Kosygin was not disgraced, however, as he would have been earlier.

The new leadership followed a more cautious and a more respectable foreign policy, though their main concern was the growing Sino–Soviet split, which led to occasional attempts to propitiate the Western powers in order to avoid a war on two fronts. Khruschev, according to his objectors, excessively personalised the leadership and reorganised institutions with great zeal, but to no very good purpose (rather like Mr Heath). The successor regime was by contrast impersonal, calm, legalistic and stodgy. Kosygin more than Brezhnev was in charge of the economy, and Brezhnev more than Kosygin of foreign affairs. But this rough generalisation needs to be qualified since the leadership was in all respects a joint one, and shared (to a lesser extent) with others such as Gromyko, the Foreign Minister, and Grechko, the head of the army. The phrase that fits is 'bureaucratic pluralism'.

Khruschev was retired in tolerable comfort and died in 1971, aged seventy-seven. In the thirteen years since the death of Stalin the Soviet system had evolved so that defeated leaders were not exiled or murdered, like Trotsky, yet they were not allowed just to retire; rather they had to be overthrown, but much of the mono-lithic stolidity of this autocratic state remained unchanged.

Chapter 16

America the prosperous:
the Eisenhower years

The old guard who had been present at Potsdam were departing
and their successors were about to grapple with the problems they
had left behind.

Government in the United States seems to come to a standstill a
year before a new President is elected and the world awaits the
outcome with bated breath, for so much depends on who is chosen.
In 1951 the American mood of the moment was clearly no longer
sympathetic to the old radical rhetoric, liberalism was unpopular,
Washington was felt to have become domineering and over-
bureaucratic; the outbreak of the Korean War, the development of
Soviet nuclear weapons, the Communist victory in China, the
initial defeat of UN forces and the intervention of the Red Army
from North Korea, made the Americans crave powerful leadership. But the greatest single influence on the minds of the populace
was a rage against Communism within as well as without, encouraged by Senator McCarthy.

In 1945 Elizabeth Bentley and Whittaker Chambers denounced
a network of Communist spy cells to which they had belonged
before the war. Their charges were at first ignored, but by 1948
several major persons had been convincingly accused – Harry
Dexter White, the American Director of the International Mon-
etary Fund, and Keynes' opponent; Alger Hiss, a senior State
Department official, present at Yalta and chiefly responsible for
America's attitude to the formation of the UN; and William
Remington, a senior member of the Commerce Department.
White died before serious investigations began, but Hiss and
Remington were convicted of perjury and jailed. In 1950 Harry
Gold, David Greenglass and a husband and wife, Julius and Ethel
Rosenberg, were convicted of passing atomic secrets to the Rus-
sians. It became clear that a network of Soviet espionage had
penetrated deep into the US government, as it had in other
Western countries. It was also clear that this network was partly
based on the American Communist party.

At the height of anti-Fascist feelings in the later 1930s, and
disillusion with capitalism, many liberals had seen no particular

harm in Communism, and many liberal organisations were penetrated by Communists who used them as fronts. The right-wing hawks, however, far from giving this natural tendency a sympathetic understanding, interpreted membership or sympathy with any of these bodies as support for Communism, and support for Communism as tantamount to treason. Membership of the Communist party had been made illegal by the McCarran Act, and from 1948 onwards the Congress, led by Congressman (later Senator) Nixon, and Senator Joseph McCarthy, held a series of publicised hearings which interrogated hundreds of people, and cast serious slurs on thousands of others, who instantly lost reputations, jobs and, on occasion, were indicted for refusing to testify.

The test case was Alger Hiss – a well-connected, senior official of the State Department, a friend of Dean Acheson, and a product of the most prestigious school and university. It became an article of faith among liberals to believe him innocent, and to believe that his accuser, Whittaker Chambers, was a lying paranoid tool of the FBI. Acheson and the President stood by Hiss. Yet it seemed clear that Hiss had in fact been guilty of handing secret documents to Chambers and others for use by Soviet intelligence. His conviction, after a second trial, made many people believe that the network of spies was almost as great as the most fervent anti-Communists said it was. Gradually a spirit of hysteria developed in which many hundreds of thousands of intellectuals, teachers, progressives, felt that their innocent association with moderately progressive causes had endangered their careers, perhaps their lives, while millions of other Americans were convinced of a vast conspiracy in their midst. Hysteria reached its peak in February 1950 when Senator McCarthy claimed to have a list of 205 (later 81, and then 57) Communists in the State Department, but it continued strongly for three more years and left a permanent mark on American life, of fear of political persecution.

McCarthyism became a by-word for political persecution, a savage irony, coinciding as it did with the second intensification of Stalin's purge, culminating in the doctors' plot, when millions were sent to the gulag, mostly to die, and hundreds of thousands were murdered.

In these circumstances Truman, at sixty-eight, was not a promising contender for a second elected term of office. As the primaries opened in 1952, Truman offered to support Eisenhower, whom he had made head of NATO. Eisenhower refused and subsequently accepted the Republican nomination. The initial Democratic favourite was Senator Estes Kefauver, but the ticket went eventually to Governor Adlai Stevenson of Illinois, a man of brilliance and sensitivity with a superb command of language.

In the 1952 campaign Stevenson distanced himself from Truman, and won the fervent and deep support of all liberal idealists. He became the most distinguished President never to hold office. Eisenhower won overwhelmingly, by the largest popular vote in history.

Dwight David Eisenhower, born in Denison, Texas, in 1890 and brought up in Abilene, Kansas, went to West Point Military Academy. His most important role before the Second World War was to serve General Douglas MacArthur when he became military adviser to the Philippines. Eisenhower took charge of the American landings in North Africa during the Second World War, where he showed outstanding political flair in handling the French and the British, and then became Supreme Commander of the Allied Forces in Europe. After the victory, he followed in MacArthur's footsteps as Chief of Staff of the US Army, served as President of Columbia University, and from 1951 to 1952 became Supreme Commander of the NATO forces in Europe (SHAPE).

It is almost impossible in America to have both political and executive experience in the national government before becoming President; although he had no political experience, for over twenty years Eisenhower had been near or at the top of a major part of the executive branch of the United States. Not only did he have an unequalled knowledge of North Atlantic strategy and diplomacy, but through his service with MacArthur a considerable understanding of Far Eastern affairs. He was immensely popular in Europe – where he was known as Ike – and among American troops. But his bluff, simple appearance and reputation disguised a tough and ambitious hard core.

Eisenhower campaigned that the Democrats had been soft on Communism, from Yalta to the loss of China; that the United States was militarily not up to scratch and that the Korean War should be ended.

In his autobiography Eisenhower wrote: 'By 1952 numerous instances of malfeasance in office, disregard for fiscal responsibility, apparent governmental ignorance of apathy about the penetrations of Communists in government, and a willingness to divide industrial America against itself, had reduced the prestige of the United States and caused disillusionment and cynicism among our people.' It will be seen how all aspects of Democratic inadequacy were linked together as an all-embracing character defect.

In Eisenhower's eight-year Presidency four issues dominated: race, economic policy, the welfare state and relations with the Communists. Race relations erupted into prominence with the

Brown decision of the Supreme Court, that segregation by race was unconstitutional. What began as organised sit-ins at segregated restaurants and on buses in the Southern states, grew into riots, such as those at Little Rock, Arkansas, where Eisenhower ordered the use of troops to defend black Americans. Although he remained personally an old-fashioned segregationist, Eisenhower led the way to the integration of the blacks, slowly but surely, non-inflammatorily and decisively – in contrast to his successor, Kennedy. He began desegregation with the armed forces, and moved on to veterans' hospitals and other federal institutions. Far more difficult was the sphere of individual and state activity, where the Supreme Court's decision only gradually impinged upon the collective consciousness of the American people. In the Civil Rights Act, 1957, which created the Civil Rights Commission, a main step forward was taken. But by the late 1950s desegregation was not enough: the new black leaders, such as Martin Luther King, were arguing for racial equality; behind the sit-ins, the picketing and the arrests lay threats of riots and of militant black consciousness which had not disturbed the Roosevelt era, despite the massive strains of depression and war.

One reason, though not the sole reason, for the emergence of black consciousness was the remarkable rise in the standard of living of ordinary American people in the years from 1945 onwards. America achieved year after year, with only two exceptions – 1948 and 1953 – an unprecedented rise in output and in incomes. Those were the miracle years of Western economic growth. The level of employment rose steadily, so that America was transformed into a middle-class mass-consuming society, well housed, well dressed, well fed, and physically mobile, with an abundance of consumer durables. It is at times of rapid income growth that hitherto submerged and marginal groups find the strength to protest, and this was the case with the blacks.

The affluent society faced two equal though different lines of attack, often from the same quarter – disaffected East Coast liberals based on the richer private universities, especially Harvard. On the one hand society was held to be crassly materialistic and neglectful of the broader and higher ends of humanity. On the other, it was acknowledged with growing embarrassment, groups of Americans, so numerous they must have been the great majority – the poor, the elderly, the blacks, the town dwellers, rural people – lived in grinding poverty and disgusting squalor. It grew fashionable to follow Galbraith's lead and to contrast private affluence with public squalor, when what the poor wanted was private (and not public) prosperity for themselves. Yet the argument that the growth of private expenditure was not accompanied by any parallel growth of public expenditure on health, housing, social welfare or education had little basis in fact and none in logic.

The Eisenhower administration saw the completion of Europe's post-war revival and the re-emergence of Japan as a major trading nation. The United States dollar was an overwhelmingly scarce currency on world markets from 1940 to 1952. But in the early years of the Presidency, the growth of international trade, the rapid rise of European and Far Eastern incomes, and the general reduction of tariffs and other trade barriers led to a stupendous outburst of world economic activity, with the logical consequence that the dollar lost its scarcity, but increased its value as a mechanism for the financing of world trade.

With an expanding economy to back him, President Eisenhower's view of government was based upon Lincoln's statement that 'the legitimate object of government, is to do for a community of people, whatever they need to have done, but cannot do at all, or cannot so well do, for themselves – in their separate, and individual capacities'. But Eisenhower refused to accept deficit-budget policies in order to encourage faster economic growth, even if that growth had been possible.

He was prepared, however, to support a growth of public expenditure in what had become 'acceptable' fields, such as education. School enrolments rose quickly as the children born to returning war veterans grew up and then flooded into higher education. Though the greater part of education expenditure was borne by state and local governments, federal funds were made available to fuel an expansion of education that was one of the most remarkable facts of the post-war world in which America (with Sweden) led the field. In creating the Department of Health, Education and Welfare, with a series of powerful Secretaries and Under-Secretaries, Eisenhower set up an institution which added impetus to the process of expanding the scope and size of welfare schemes, particularly for the self-employed and the disabled. By the time his Presidency ended, however, Eisenhower was being reproached bitterly for not extending 'medicare', or a public health policy. This criticism ignored the many millions of veterans (ex-servicemen) and their families with almost complete medical care, as well as many millions in tax-supported insurance schemes. Before Eisenhower the bulk of social welfare and education was a responsibility of state and local governments, the federal government being mainly concerned with defence and foreign policy, areas in which Eisenhower was exceptionally well qualified to offer leadership.

Eisenhower's first, somewhat flamboyant, act was to visit Korea before his inauguration. He had promised to do this, because it was claimed that Truman had neglected the war there and, by implication, that his firing of General MacArthur had been instrumental in allowing a stalemate to develop, instead of forcing an American victory. The trip was cosmetic, but it became a basis for the redemption of his pledge to end the war.

On the advice of the now retired MacArthur, Eisenhower reconsidered the use of atomic weapons to conquer North Korea, but rejected the idea, deciding instead to press for an immediate armistice and exchange of prisoners. The armistice was achieved within six months of his inauguration, on 27 July 1953, though the South Korean President, Syngman Rhee, tried to sabotage it by releasing North Korean prisoners who were to be exchanged.

Eisenhower lacked intellectual and aesthetic interests, his personal pleasure was playing golf. He chose inadequate associates without glamour or style, who had unsavoury reputations and committed financial indiscretions. As a military man, he delegated full authority to his Secretary of State, John Foster Dulles. This was a grave mistake for Dulles' massive tactlessness, self-satisfaction, arrogance and religiosity were major handicaps in the conduct of foreign affairs. Sir Alexander Cadogan, the British diplomat, meeting Dulles with Anthony Eden in London in 1942 described him as 'the woolliest type of useless, pontificating American'. Eisenhower's election and American strength gave him the power to pontificate without effective contradiction.

Dulles believed that the UN as a supra-national organisation should settle world policies on the basis of highly-generalised moral principles. Especially relevant to his later policy was his insistence on the rights of small nations, many of which had ethnic associations with electorally important parts of the United States. And it was the rights of the small Eastern European nations that triggered the Cold War. There has been much bitter controversy over the causes of the Cold War. The revisionist historian, Townsend Walter Hoopes, puts the most powerful case:

In the . . . Eisenhower presidency the cold war was pervasively institutionalised in the United States. Its chief manifestations were a strident moralism, a self-righteous and often apocalyptic rhetoric, a determined effort to ring the Soviet Union and China with anti-Communist military alliances, a dramatic proliferation of American overseas military bases, and a rising flow of American military officers and men to provide training and advice. The

posture of imperative, total confrontation thus came to full
development during the Eisenhower period.

As will have been seen, the origins of the Cold War are more
complex than is implied by Hoopes, and the fact of Soviet tyranny
and aggression is put by him on a par, morally and politically, with
the response of the liberal democracies.

Dulles had always led the Republican attacks on any attempt to
compromise with the Russians over Eastern Europe, during President Truman's and General Marshall's period of office. As an
international lawyer, and as adviser to the Republicans, who
controlled the Senate, Dulles was fully consulted. He was also
principally responsible for the Japanese peace treaty and during
those negotiations he was in Korea just before and just after the
outbreak of the Korean War. He therefore accepted and understood America's position and attitudes towards Communism but
he then proceeded to give them a personal twist of his own, which
coloured the whole Eisenhower period.

Truman had evolved a strategy of response to Communist
aggression wherever it occurred within the boundaries of the areas
that had not been put in the Soviet sphere at Yalta: it was a doctrine
of flexible containment. Whilst John Foster Dulles was committed
to international agreements in Europe to contain Communism, the
strength of the reaction against Truman's policy in China enabled
Dulles to push the view that the chief battle actually being waged
against Communism was in Asia, where America had a duty – an
inescapable duty – to act unilaterally, because it lacked powerful
allies. Above all, he distrusted deeply French, British and Dutch
imperialism – which made his attitude to Indochina, Indonesia
and Malaya ambivalent – and while he regarded Japan as potentially a powerful force against China and Russia, he thought the
Chinese civil war was by no means over – it could be won by the
Nationalists from Formosa, and by regrouping internal rebels. In
taking this attitude, Dulles was aligning himself with the 'America-
first' isolationists who, ironically, were great believers in the
special American relationship with China, which was largely mis-
sionary in origin. Dulles' religiosity, his vague idealism, and his
ethnocentric Americanism led him to take a view of world affairs
which emphasised his self-confidence in his own sanctimonious
judgments.

The bi-partisan post-war American policy therefore broke up, as
Dulles appeared to embrace a strong anti-Communist line which
was not pragmatic – that Communism was threatening America –
but ideological. And in that sense, he understood the view that

Yalta, and similar pragmatic settlements, were a sell-out to a monstrous conspiracy; McCarthy's line that Roosevelt, Marshall and their supporters had been systematically fooled, if not worse, by the Communists was not far from Dulles' own views. In fact, Dulles thought that Communism was weak, not strong, because it was overextended. When he eventually decided to back Eisenhower as Republican candidate for the Presidency, and Eisenhower accepted him, he veered to supporting a policy for the eventual overthrow of Communism, not by military threat, except for massive retaliation against aggression by threatening to use the nuclear deterrent, but rather by stimulating opposition within the Communist-controlled countries.

Ideologically, the difference between the policies of Truman and Eisenhower was small and operationally not greatly significant, but it seemed at the time as a far greater divide than had appeared for many years. Yet to many who had opposed the Truman Doctrine, the Republican version seemed even more reckless. When this was combined with a solipsist disregard for his allies' counsels, the antipathy to Dulles became easily comprehensible. Moreover, Dulles rapidly developed a close relationship with Eisenhower, who left him to get on with foreign affairs, provided there was daily consultation. Dulles' policies often seemed arbitrary and impulsive, they had not been widely canvassed, nor had they appeared as a result of discussion and compromise. Moreover, Dulles was neither liked nor trusted by his State Department officers whom he never defended from McCarthy, nor from any other attacks. As a result Dulles was blamed for the Cold War while Eisenhower, despite his vast international experience, was regarded as an amateurish, naïve front-man for his ideologically crude Secretary of State.

As Secretary of State, Dulles opposed any relaxation of the East–West confrontation, seeking rather to intensify it, and to this end he sought a united Western European defence system, a strong American presence in the Middle East, and an armistice in Korea enabling him to seize the initiative elsewhere in Asia.

Eisenhower trusted Dulles but he deeply distrusted the sophisticated civilians at Yalta and at earlier American–Soviet negotiations who had 'thrown away' a great part of the potential victory his soldiers had won. He regarded the State Department in particular and the East Coast intelligentsia in general as 'soft on Communism'.

Here then was the heart of the controversy about Eisenhower's Presidency and it deserves examination. The liberals deeply opposed Eisenhower for being slow in denouncing Senator

McCarthy, who had made his reputation by unprincipled and often unsupported allegations of Communism in the public service. McCarthy had been supported by Senator Nixon, Eisenhower's Vice-President, who, as a Congressman, was instrumental in beginning the process that ultimately sent Alger Hiss to prison. Eisenhower refused to reprieve Ethel and Julius Rosenberg, sentenced to death for passing atomic secrets to Russia. He believed that Harry Dexter White, opponent of Keynes and architect of the International Monetary Fund and the World Bank, had been a Communist agent. Further dissent and disapproval was caused by his administration's apparent sympathy to big business.

Though Eisenhower was not himself an active liberal he was a strict constitutionalist and therefore enforced the law impartially. This throws light also upon his reaction to McCarthyism. The actions of McCarthy and his supporters had undoubtedly helped Eisenhower's election by discrediting Truman and the liberal Democrats. Eisenhower rigorously enforced a system of security clearances for the federal administration, including the removal from office of Dr Robert Oppenheimer, the atomic scientist, on the flimsiest of grounds. On the other hand, once McCarthy had gone far beyond constitutional proprieties, in attacking an army dentist and humiliating the Secretary of the Army, Eisenhower reacted strongly. A series of hearings on the extent of subversion in the army was held, which ended with the censure of McCarthy by the Senate, and helped to reduce his future impact.

But all this was subordinate to his conduct of foreign and military policy. Eisenhower was convinced by the evidence of 1945 to 1952 that Stalin had one massive ambition: to take over the remainder of the world. The Soviet Union had scarcely demobilised after 1945 and had a huge military budget. In East Germany, Poland, Czechoslovakia, Hungary, Romania, Albania and Bulgaria the Communist governments became hard-line Stalinist, terrorist regimes. The Communist victory in the Chinese civil war and the invasion of South Korea seemed part of the same pattern. The development of Soviet nuclear weapons was particularly threatening.

Eisenhower had a deep hostility to Communism and a conviction that the military strength of non-Communist governments had to be built up, particularly through regional pacts such as NATO, CENTO and SEATO. He therefore set about reviving the NATO alliance which, as Supreme Commander, he found had feared American withdrawal through its preoccupation with Korea and the Far East. He was a strong supporter of the European Defence Community, a proposed merger of the French and German armed forces that collapsed when the French Parliament voted against it. But his concern for Western Europe was altered by the death of Stalin in March 1953. Eisenhower, seeing this as a possible turning point in world affairs, sought to achieve an understanding with the new Soviet leadership. It had already become clear before Stalin's death that world Communism had not been monolithic. The exiling of Trotsky and his subsequent murder in 1940 drew attention to the possibility of dissension even while Stalin's terror was at its height. Tito in Yugoslavia made his regime to some degree independent of Moscow, and survived. It became clear that China and even perhaps North Korea, while allied to Russia, were to some degree autonomous. Thus Stalin's death, it was supposed, would lead to a struggle for the succession and possibly a series of changes in Soviet foreign and military policy.

Dulles, however, regarded Stalin as an embodiment of basic Marxist–Leninist philosophy, rather than as a dictator with an autonomous policy which might be changed by his successors. He did not see Stalin's death as an occasion for détente, although Eisenhower, responding to apparent Soviet indications of a softening of attitudes in Malenkov's funeral oration for Stalin, made a speech appealing for peace. The Europeans, apart from Adenauer, agreed with Eisenhower, but a proposed Western summit meeting never occurred, partly because Churchill had a stroke, partly because Adenauer opposed it, but mainly because Dulles obstructed it.

Adenauer's opposition owed much to forthcoming West German elections. His Christian Democrats were demanding all-German elections, wholly unacceptable to the USSR, while the Social Democrats were seeking an agreement between the East and West German states. The German question immediately loomed large. On 16 June 1953 food riots erupted in East Berlin, Leipzig and elsewhere in East Germany. But Dulles did nothing to help the East Germans. He seemed to some a callous fraud, perhaps it was a shift back to his lawyer's sense of the possible tempering his enthusiasm.

Meanwhile American relations with Western Europe deteriorated, despite Eisenhower's popularity. The collapse of the European defence plan led to difficulties between Dulles and the French and, no less important, between Dulles and Eden, the British Foreign Minister who succeeded Churchill as Prime Minister in 1955. Britain had from the beginning declined to join the EDC, on the dual grounds that Britain's large military forces were deployed across the world, and that after the United States it made the biggest contribution to NATO defence anyway. This view was shortsighted, and led directly to de Gaulle's double veto a decade later of British applications to join the Common Market. But it was a cornerstone of Britain's foreign policy, widely understood throughout the West, although Dulles rebuked Eden for it. As a result Eden and Dulles rapidly grew to dislike each other. Having upset France and Britain, Dulles did not, however, fall out with all the European leaders, but soon became a firm friend of Adenauer. This was not wholly satisfactory. As Adenauer was a hard-line anti-Communist (or Cold-War warrior), and leader of a country still loathed and distrusted throughout Europe, the opportunities this gave for misunderstandings and misrepresentations of American policies were greatly enlarged.

The issues raised by the presence of the United States, its allies and its enemies in every corner of the globe raised problems of bewildering complexity for Dulles. Was Russia prepared to neutralise East Germany and withdraw its troops? Khruschev said later that it had been. On the other hand, the East German food riots were suppressed with strength. That was Russia in Europe. At the same time, the British were trying to evacuate their troops from Egypt, but were faced by riots which led to rapidly deteriorating relationships with the Egyptian revolutionary government of Neguib who soon gave way to Nasser. Dulles was opposed to British imperialism, and he wanted American oil companies' interests not only to be safeguarded, but increased. The Egyptians, however, were swinging towards Moscow for support. He was less than enthusiastic about Israel, but Israel depended almost entirely on American support. He wanted to end the Korean War, but to roll back Communism in the Far East.

Thus, all Dulles' policies involved compromise, on the part of an uncharacteristically uncompromising lawyer; but they also involved offending large numbers of people who thought they were being let down. It is this paradox which is at the heart of the mystery as to why so obviously intelligent and well-meaning a man should have been thought so disastrous a Secretary of State. In fact his policies were, within limits, successful. The Soviet Union's influence may not have been rolled back, but it was restrained. But Dulles did leave problems that escalated.

The lack of support, sympathy or even empathy by other countries led to a deep distrust of his massive retaliation policy – the 'bigger bang for a buck'. American military spending was large and growing, in view of its widespread commitments and the war in Korea. Eisenhower, desiring budgetary restraint, cut military appropriations, which led to an emphasis on nuclear weapons and planes to deliver them. Meanwhile, with the detonation of a Soviet hydrogen bomb in 1953, the American nuclear lead – which in 1945 had been four years – was rapidly wiped out. Thus, with Eisenhower's approval, by late 1953, of the use of nuclear weapons in limited wars, all future relations between the two countries were, inevitably, based upon a balance of terror, and a fear of escalation of a minor conflict, or even misunderstanding, into a terminal nuclear war. Dulles had stumbled, as it were, into the most terrifying possibility that the end of the world was literally just around the corner, having begun with a Wilsonian vision of a world regulated by universally accepted (and banal) principles of peace.

It was this apparent ruthless determination to use nuclear weapons that made him so dreaded a figure. The Russians did not arouse the same hostility among people of good will, such as Bertrand Russell and Jean-Paul Sartre. In a foolish speech in January 1956 Dulles referred to a new policy 'placing more reliance on deterrent power, and less dependence on local defensive power', and that America would 'depend primarily upon a great capacity to retaliate, instantly . . .' Recent 'local' actions, as in Korea, or in the Berlin airlift, had been expensive and dangerous; from now on, implied Dulles, the United States would deal directly with the source of the trouble – Moscow. It was not an insane policy, merely implausible and bound to be ineffective. Either every minor incident would become a nuclear confrontation (as in Cuba in 1962, under Kennedy), or America's bluff would be called (as in Hungary in 1956 and frequently later in Vietnam).

Dulles' policies were more than just words and he now proceeded to make two massive errors of judgment, affecting France and Britain, in Indochina and the Middle East.

Since 1945, the Communists had been waging a war against the French in Indochina, initially with American support, but later with Russian and Chinese arms and supplies. At Geneva, in 1954, Eden persuaded the French to accept a compromise with the Vietnamese leader, Ho Chi-minh, who was in turn urged to accept by the Russians and Chinese. Dulles disapproved of the French in general as colonialists and in particular as a result of their intransigence over the EDC; he also regarded Vietnamese nationalism as a purely Communist insurrection inspired by Moscow and Peking. The French had, in effect, lost the war with the fall of besieged Dien Bien Phu, as the extra military effort required in 1954 to win it was too divisive and too expensive. Nevertheless, Dulles insisted that to lose would be to capitulate to Chinese Communism, On Soviet initiative, a conference was called in Geneva to attempt to settle the Indochina question. Dulles, having opposed the confer-

ence, suggested a coalition of 'free' nations to intervene in Indochina, the sending of American arms and, possibly, American air
attacks on the Communists at Dien Bien Phu. Not only would such
a proposal have ended any compromise with the Communists, but
it could only have been effective if America had taken over the
conduct of the war with its own forces. Dulles was prepared for
this, if other Western countries agreed. He even deluded himself,
after a trip to London and Paris, that such agreement would be
forthcoming. Yet when a diplomatic conference was called in
Washington in April 1954 to prepare a defence pact for Southeast
Asia, Eden refused to allow the British Ambassador to attend.
This led Dulles to regard Eden as a double-crosser.

Dien Bien Phu fell during the Geneva conference, on 7 May
1954. Pierre Mendès-France succeeded Joseph Laniel as French
Prime Minister, and on 21 July 1954 the Geneva agreement
between China, Russia, Britain, France and America was signed,
Vietnam being divided into two states, and an armistice declared.
There were to be no foreign bases or troops; all-Vietnam elections
were eventually to be held; and a mixed supervising commission,
including Poles and Czechs, was set up to police the agreement.

This was a diplomatic triumph. It got the French off the hook,
and it seemed to settle Vietnam. It brought China into the world
diplomatic scene as a peaceful participant. It showed the USSR,
little more than a year after Stalin's death, as prepared to negotiate
for peace. The two active wars in Asia – Korea and Vietnam –
were now over. Limited peace seemed in sight.

Dulles, however, managed to upset this delicately balanced
apple-cart. In establishing a pact for Southeast Asia, SEATO, in
1954, which loosely linked the anti-Communist powers of the area,
but without any of the military unity and strength of NATO, he
caused grave disgust in Peking. Then the French finally rejected
the EDC in September 1954, which left Adenauer exposed, since
the rearmament of Germany was predicated on mixed European
military units. Eden thereupon formed the Western European
Union, which, unlike the EDC, contained a guarantee of the
continued stationing of British troops in Europe, and which
allowed the full entry of West Germany into NATO. Thus, Dulles'
talk of an 'agonising reappraisal' of American policies if the EDC
failed was seen to be empty; but the failure of the EDC and talk of
agonising reappraisal – which could only mean the rearmament of
Germany – further exacerbated relations with the Russians by
preventing any settlement in Germany.

The Americans' rift with Britain was, nevertheless, a fact, not
ameliorated by the Western European Union agreement. And the

French, already antagonised by the threat of the EDC, the failure to support them at Dien Bien Phu, and the constant criticism of their Algerian policy, were further infuriated when the pro-French Emperor, Bao Dai, who had a vague suzerainty over Indochina, was overthrown by the American-backed, violently anti-French Ngo Dinh Dieu. Dieu proceeded to turn South Vietnam into an American satellite by hastening the evacuation of French troops and the arming of South Vietnam by the Americans. Ho Chi-minh, a potential Asian Tito, was driven into a position where he was obliged to be hostile to the West and dependent on the Russians and Chinese; the French, who had hoped to trade with the whole of a peaceful, neutral and francophone Indochina, interpreted these events as naked American imperialism. Dulles, therefore, divided Vietnam when it might have been united and neutral. He also alienated his two most reliable European allies.

In 1955 Communist China threatened to seize the Nationalist Chinese islands off the China coast and to invade Formosa. Dulles struck a belligerent attitude, but was restrained by Eisenhower. But the American refusal to deal directly with Communist China was a serious threat to peace, especially when the world was under recurrent threat of nuclear war over minor clashes and misunderstandings. Churchill spoke of the 'balance of terror'. The USSR and the USA, with hydrogen bombs that could spread radioactivity over hundreds of square miles, were militarily equal. Just as significant, Dulles' hypothesis that Communism, being a hollow, rotten dictatorship, would collapse from within, was open to doubt, as the USSR grew in military and economic strength and Stalin's death relieved the worst excesses of the Terror. A reappraisal of foreign policy was cogent, in the French and British view the time was ripe. In Britain Churchill's retirement in 1955 was followed by elections, and in 1956 Eisenhower would run for a second term. With a new team in Moscow, was not now the moment for East and West to meet? A summit meeting, similar to Yalta and Potsdam, seemed in order.

The summit, however, was doomed to failure over Germany, since the Russians would agree to reunification only on the basis of an East–West federation and disarmed neutrality, while Dulles insisted on a reunified Germany based on free elections which would, naturally, have led to a Western-oriented and powerful Germany. Yet Russia indicated a less belligerent, more conciliatory posture when it agreed to the Austrian State Treaty, whereby the occupation was ended and Austria was declared neutral.

The summit was held in Geneva from 18 to 23 July 1955, with Eisenhower and Dulles, Khruschev and Bulganin, Eden and Macmillan, Faure and Mollet. But with no urgency to settle affairs, as at Yalta and Potsdam, the negotiating positions were irreconcilable. If Germany were to be unified, free elections would put it in the Western camp, and the other Soviet satellites would go the same way as East Germany. Russia therefore demanded a demilitarisation of the whole of Europe, in the sense of dismantling NATO, the Western European Union and the Warsaw Pact, and the removal of all foreign troops (meaning the Americans) before any German settlement could be negotiated. For the first time, disarmament by means of aerial inspection was raised as an alternative to visits to military sites. The Russians raised the issue of troop limitations.

Geneva had only two outcomes: the realisation that Eisenhower, who dominated the conference, wanted peace rather than war, and the recognition that nuclear war, if it occurred, would bring the world to an end. Thus both sides had an interest, ultimately, in preserving peace, which was to be a substantial bonus in the massive Middle Eastern crisis which developed over Suez in 1956 (described in Chapter 17).

The 1956 American Presidential election was a rerun of 1952. Eisenhower and Stevenson both stood, but Eisenhower was returned to office with an even larger majority. But the campaign was not without paradox, being accompanied by the Soviet occupation of Hungary and the Anglo–French–Israeli occupation of Suez, where the US appeared to fight its friends and condone Russian aggression. Yet Eisenhower's popularity in America was at a peak, just as Dulles' unpopularity was at its height abroad.

Was Dulles at this period 'one of the most unattractive figures in modern history', as Alastair Buchan, the British diplomatic correspondent, called him? That was certainly true of Dulles as a man, but his efforts to further American policies could hardly have been described as a deliberate attempt either to wreck the Western alliance or to enhance the risk of nuclear confrontation. His 'chilling dishonesty', another Buchan phrase, was remarkably unsuccessful in helping America, except that it enabled Eisenhower to campaign as a peacemaker, and stopped Adlai Stevenson from being President.

The rapid rise to prominence first of independent Asian countries such as India and Pakistan, and the important votes of the Latin American countries in the United Nations, gave a major political point to a humanitarian urge for substantial international aid, which was channelled mainly through the Point Four programme (so-called from Truman's inaugural address) and its successors, as well as through largely American-financed international agencies. It involved America, as will be seen, in conflict with the Third World, since the radical elements in those countries had been associated with independence and were for the most part Socialist and even Marxist. Dulles' policies, especially in the Middle East and Latin America, placed the United States (despite its generosity and genuine humanitarianism) in an increasingly reactionary position.

In 1957, with the Western alliance in disarray in the aftermath of Suez, the situation in Eastern Europe was also complex. In the Soviet Union's satellite states pressures not dissimilar to those that had broken out in Hungary were widespread, and although Khruschev was liberalising the regime in Russia, he was opposed by forces wishing to return to Stalinism. Thus a perilous path was trod between a move to a more peaceful world and one that though armed to the teeth was significantly less tense than it had been for a decade.

The first major issue was a test-ban treaty. The United States and the Soviet Union already had fully developed bombs, the British were conducting hydrogen bomb tests in the Pacific, and the French were developing an atom bomb. The pressure for a deal on nuclear weapons was therefore designed to avoid more atomic pollution by testing, to restrict nuclear proliferation, and to make America and Russia hydrogen-bomb monopolists. In the circumstances, a major deal might have been made, but Western policy shifted, mainly as a result of the disarray caused by Dulles' handling of the Suez crisis. The French, deeply engaged in Algeria, and the British, still regarding Nasser as a major threat, were disinclined to follow any American lead. In retrospect this period of frozen diplomacy may be seen to represent one of the lost opportunities for a high-level deal between America and Russia. Dulles also stalled on a second major issue, the possibility of a settlement with China. He was convinced that Chinese Communism had to be defeated and that Congress would not accept any new approach to the Chinese question. Khruschev, with the help of Marshal Zhukov, successfully fought off a return to Stalinism in June 1957.

Here, if anywhere, was the point at which the peace was squandered. Stalin was dead. Khruschev was a weird, odd, successor. He toyed with many ideas. The Chinese were a new and not necessarily friendly or hostile force for both the Americans and the Russians. The space-race was about to begin. Perhaps a deal could be imagined – an end to nuclear arsenals, a neutralised and unified Germany, a liberalised Eastern Europe. It was not to be.

Sputnik was sent up on 4 October 1957, and it was obvious that

Russia's world position had altered. This caused deep anxiety in the United States about its military unpreparedness, especially in missiles, and its relative scientific backwardness. As a result the American space programme was accelerated, culminating in the landings on the moon twelve years later, and the substantial expansion of federal aid to higher education and research.

Harold Macmillan, who had succeeded Eden as the British Prime Minister, requested a Western summit conference, which took place in December 1957 at the NATO annual meeting. NATO countries, it was decided, would be armed with medium-range ballistic missiles. This would lead to a direct threat by the Russians to Europe, where they were to be based. It was a risk worth taking, if the result was a serious American attempt to get a conference between the East and the West which would reduce armaments on a basis of mutual inspection, and so to a gradual de-escalation of nuclear threats.

While this move was being prepared, the Middle East once more came to a boiling point; there was trouble in the Lebanon, and the Americans promptly landed troops and sent the fleet to police the area in July 1958. This action, though at the invitation of the Lebanese government, seemed ironic after Dulles' attitude to Suez a year and a half earlier. The British sent troops to Jordan to protect King Hussein while their ally the King of Iraq, Faisal, and his family and government were murdered by left-wing forces. In all this flurry of activity, the USSR indicated it would not intervene. The strong American intervention in the Lebanon had been salutary but probably unnecessary. It was now clear that despite Nasser, or perhaps because of him, the Middle East was firmly in the American sphere of influence. The basic doctrine of Yalta still stood. This cast further doubt upon Dulles' hypothesis that any uprising was Communist-inspired or, even if it were not, that the USSR would seize the opportunity to expand its empire. An exercise in brinkmanship, as it came to be called, over the islands Quemoy and Matsu, off the China coast, when the Communists sought to defend them, led to a further abandonment of the Dulles position that nuclear war could be threatened at any or every comparatively small crisis.

This was particularly relevant to the Berlin crisis of 1958. Ten years before the Western allies had overcome a Russian blockade by an airlift. Thereafter, despite the establishment and arming of the Federal Republic, the Western enclave in Berlin had remained relatively untroubled. In late 1957 the Russians advanced a plan for a nuclear-free zone in Germany, Poland and Czechoslovakia; this was rejected by the Western allies, who saw it merely as a pretext to prevent missiles being placed in West Germany. The Americans still favoured the reunification of Germany after free elections, a proposal that the Russians would not entertain. The British and the French therefore favoured integrating West Germany into Western Europe, and leaving Germany divided indefinitely. When the United States followed Adenauer in refusing to recognise East Germany, Khruschev thereupon determined, in November 1958, that the rearming of West Germany broke the Potsdam agreement, and the stationing of Western troops in West Berlin was a consequence no longer acceptable. East Germany would become a sovereign state and regain the whole of Berlin as its capital. Alternatively Berlin could become a free city.

Berlin was almost indefensible. Indeed, if the Russians sought to overwhelm it, the only response was by nuclear war. It took some time for this truth to dawn. After a trip by Macmillan to Moscow in February 1959, where he was confirmed in his judgment that the real Soviet fear was of a rearmed and reunited Germany, the upshot was Western recognition of East Berlin and the maintenance of the Western zones of the city in Berlin.

By now Dulles was a sick man. Dying of cancer, he resigned in April 1959, and thereupon Eisenhower took charge of American foreign policy. He decided to reactivate the Western alliances, which had been jeopardised by Dulles' arbitrary actions and secretiveness, and to approach the Russians directly. The point was to re-establish mutual confidence. Eisenhower almost succeeded. He set out on a series of journeys throughout the world, and after a successful visit by Khruschev to America in September 1959, a summit meeting of de Gaulle, Eisenhower, Khruschev and Macmillan was arranged for May 1960. On 1 May, however, an American aerial reconnaissance plane, a U2, piloted by Gary Powers, was shot down over Sverdlovsk in Siberia. Eisenhower first denied and then accepted that he had authorised the flight. In consequence the summit collapsed, since Khruschev's approach to peace was dependent upon Eisenhower's integrity. This faith in American good intentions was much challenged by Khruschev's hard-line colleagues in Moscow. By late 1960, therefore, when the American Presidential election took place, John F. Kennedy opposed Vice-President Nixon on the ground that America's defence power was too feeble in the dangerous world position. Kennedy's inaugural address was worthy of Dulles at his most ferocious, and Khruschev's ultimate response was to station missiles in Cuba.

Eisenhower had brought the world nearer to peace than might have been expected. Dulles had disoriented the alliance with

Britain and France by his Middle Eastern policies, but Eden, obsessed by Nasser, can be blamed for that far more than Dulles (as the next chapter will show). The collapse of the Paris summit is still unexplained, but it was obviously caused by Khruschev, probably in response to strong pressure from Moscow. The Soviet Union had made overtures to ease tension over Germany but these had been haughtily dismissed by Dulles. If only Eisenhower had delegated less and controlled his Secretary of State more firmly . . .

Chapter 17

Israelis and Arabs

The area of the globe under greatest tension in the post-war world was the Middle East, where Zionism, burgeoning Arab national-ism, a resurgence of Muslim consciousness and the Western world's demand for more oil, created conflicting pressures. Here the interests of Britain and France clashed with those of America, and behind the scenes the Soviet Union – and Marxism – played a devious role which added to the turmoil. The whole area threatened world peace four times, in 1948 with the Israeli–Arab War and in 1956 over Suez (both of which are dealt with in this chapter), in 1967 with the Six-Day War and in 1973 with that of Yom Kippur which are discussed in Chapter 28.

The origins of these struggles lay in the collapse of the Ottoman empire in the First World War, after which a series of fragile new successor states was set up, all dominated by European powers and many sitting on vast reservoirs of oil. The Second World War saw much strategic fighting in the area, the eviction of the French from Syria and Lebanon, the Russians and the British forcing Reza Shah Pahlevi to abdicate in Iran, and the Americans trying to replace the British in Saudi Arabia. Inserted into this complex conflict came the establishment of Israel.

The invention of Israel was presented as a return, as a fulfilling of biblical prophecy, of manifest destiny. The Jewish race is not a race genetically; nor is it a religion in the proselytising sense; yet it is both a race and a religion, defined perhaps most by the antipathy that is felt by others towards it, so that in each country it is a minority and to some degree an irritant. Anti-Semitism and persecution of the Jews have been features of Western history since the Roman Empire, becoming especially acute in Russia, Poland and Germany in the late nineteenth century, at a time of growing national consciousness throughout the Western world. The vast emigration of the Jews from those lands – especially from Russian and Polish pogroms – to the United States and (to a much lesser extent) to Canada, South Africa and Australia, led to a wider Jewish consciousness of themselves as a separate nationality.

In most countries the Jews were a minority like other minorities, regarding themselves as citizens of, say, the United Kingdom, but with a special allegiance to their religion which gave them an added series of responsibilities towards Jewry as a whole.

The Holy Land was occupied by Muslims from the eighth century onwards, but not to the exclusion of Christians and Jews. As the Ottoman Empire gradually declined, so immigration by Jews and Christians increased. In 1896 Theodor Herzl founded Zionism with his book *Der Judenstaat*, which proposed the establishment of a Jewish state in the land of Israel. Zionism became a powerful movement, attracting the support of the Jewish community, though the majority of Zionists argued not for an independent state but a 'homeland for the Jewish people'. This distinction was to be of great significance subsequently.

Small groups of Jews began to settle in Palestine. In 1917 the British conquered Palestine and Arthur Balfour, the Foreign Secretary, wrote a letter to Lord Rothschild saying that the British government supported the idea of a Jewish national home there. In the years after 1920, when Palestine was a British mandate under the League of Nations, Jews continued to settle in Palestine; so, too, did Arabs, who resented Jewish settlements in lands which they believed were theirs.

In the Second World War the Jews rallied to the allies, and Palestine became an important British base throughout the Middle East campaign. But by the end of the war the old problems had reopened in a most severe form. The Arabs could expect the end of colonial rule, as each Arab state – including Lebanon and Syria – moved towards almost complete independence after allied occupation; independence within foreign and defence policy constraints. At the same time the horrors of the Final Solution in Europe, in which six million Jews were murdered, and the subsequent liberation of the survivors of the concentration camps, suggested the extent to which Palestine could expect a massive immigration of Jewish survivors. The British were caught in the middle of an increasingly ugly situation. If more Jews arrived they thought that the Arab world would explode; at the same time they feared that Jewish terrorism, directed against the British, would ultimately lead to a Jewish–Arab war. Meanwhile any hopes that immigration would fall once the defeat of the Nazis had removed the direct threat to the lives and property of the surviving Jews in Europe, ignored the tremendous psychological need of most of these Jews to leave the countries where the mass slaughters had occurred.

In 1945 Dr Weizmann moved to Palestine to assume the leadership of the moderate Jews. President Truman urged on Attlee, the British Prime Minister, at Potsdam, that as many Jews from Europe as possible should be admitted to Israel and, specifically,

100,000 immediately. David Ben-Gurion, the leader of moderate Jews in Palestine, the Haganah, asked the Labour government to accede to the request immediately. An Anglo–American commission repeated this request.

Bevin's rejection of the Anglo–American report was followed by Jewish violence in Palestine. On 29 June 1946 many moderate Jewish leaders were arrested and on 22 July the King David Hotel in Jerusalem was blown up by Menachem Begin, killing ninety-one Britons, Jews and Arabs. In October, in the middle of the United States Congressional elections, Truman announced his support for large-scale immigration and partition of Palestine; Bevin asked whether he was to force partition on the Arabs with British bayonets.

In 1947, the year of economic crises in Britain, and the granting of independence to India, Bevin decided that it was impossible for the British to find a solution to the Palestine question. He therefore asked the United Nations on 14 February 1947 to take back the mandate under which the British ruled. The United Nations appointed a Special Committee on Palestine (UNSCOP) of eleven states, excluding Security Council members, and set about negotiating a settlement. The British then announced that they were leaving Palestine regardless of whether a settlement was reached or not – a policy that had been applied in India – and the position was now of irreconcilable Arab and Jewish communities in Palestine, within a bitterly divided world, the two principal wartime Western allies deeply at odds as well. No agreed solution was possible. On 29 November the General Assembly adopted a modified partition plan.

After the UN resolution the Arabs attacked not only Jews in Palestine, but in Syria, Lebanon and Iraq too. The British nevertheless made no plans for the orderly transfer of power to any successors, whether Arabs or Jews, or to a UN peace-keeping force. The theory was that, as in India, the withdrawal would lead to a solution, although the Indian solution had been achieved with Lord Mountbatten's intense diplomacy, and the handover took place to two working governments, though with much bloodshed. Palestine had no successor administration, only groups of illicitly armed Jews and Arabs. The Czechoslovaks supplied arms to the Haganah while the Arabs relied chiefly on Britain, especially the Arab Legion, commanded by Glubb Pasha, in Jordan. In the early months of 1948 a fierce guerrilla war developed. The United States, concerned about the supply of oil for Europe, decided to oppose the UNSCOP plan and therefore partition; terrible rioting, terror and violence took place, and as a result over one hundred and fifty thousand Arabs became refugees. (These Arab refugees became the focus of the later 'Palestinian problem'.) This flight left whole areas of Israel virtually free of Arabs and made the creation of Israel possible; by the end of 1948 the 750,000 Arabs who had lived in what became Israel had fallen to 167,000.

On 14 May 1948 the British withdrew, and the Jews declared the state of Israel. At first the British and Americans regarded Zionism as to some extent Communist-inspired and it was thought that the Russians might be invited into the Middle East by the new state. The British still argued for an Arab Palestine, with Jewish enclaves, as an alternative, but President Truman, who was a great admirer of Dr Weizmann, decided, against State Department advice, to recognise Israel – as did Stalin – and to give aid. The idea of a bi-national state was considered and rejected. The Arab armies including Jordan's Arab Legion under Glubb Pasha entered Palestine and severe fighting developed. The Jews were forced out of Jerusalem and the Negev, but they conquered the whole of Galilee. The new state of Israel thus had two large enclaves jutting back from the sea coast of Palestine. The United Nations, having recognised Israel, sent a mediator, the Swedish Count Bernadotte, who arranged a truce on 11 June 1948. This broke down on 8 July, and was followed by ten days' further fighting in which the Israelis captured Lydda, Nazareth and Ramleh, and reached the outskirts of Jerusalem. A further truce was then arranged by the Security Council. In September Count Bernadotte was assassinated by fanatical Zionists. Occasional fighting took place throughout the rest of 1948, during which the Israelis defeated the Egyptians and captured Beersheba, the Negev, and the Red Sea port of Elath. Eventually, out of exhaustion, armistices were signed with Egypt, Jordan, Lebanon and Syria in 1949.

Israel then elected Dr Weizmann President and David Ben-Gurion became the first Prime Minister. The new state was desperately poor, but it encouraged unlimited Jewish immigration, and its army soon became easily the most powerful in the Middle East. The Western suspicions of Zionism's links with Communism were dispelled by show trials in Czechoslovakia in 1951, and the Jewish 'doctors' plot' in 1953 in Moscow, which showed that the Soviet empire was violently anti-Semitic. The United States remained a major supporter of Israel, but the British remained pro-Arab, for strategic reasons, despite their growing difficulties in Egypt.

Israeli governments were coalitions led by Mapai, the Israeli Labour party. Their ideology was linked to the kibbutz movements, although the great majority of Israelis were town-dwellers, or ordinary farmers; and the original kibbutz idealism (of shared resources, from each according to his abilities and to each according to his needs), became more and more a matter of rhetoric. So, too, with the religious basis of Israeli society. It became less a matter of a deeply religious people come home than a country which strictly observed Jewish religious laws in an otherwise secular society. Israel had a large Arab minority, largely disfranchised. On its borders, especially in the Gaza Strip, were large numbers of Palestinian refugees living in deplorable conditions: and from 1948 onwards a large number of 'oriental Jews' – Yemenis, Syrians, Iraqis, Egyptians, Libyans, Moroccans – arrived in Israel as Arab hostility to Jewish minorities grew to new heights. This profoundly affected the nature of Israeli society which up till then had been largely Ashkenazy (Polish and German Jews). By 1956, Israel's Jewish population had tripled since 1948 and nearly half the population was oriental in origin.

Help in financing this massive immigration and resettlement came from America and the West German government who now began to pay reparations. Nevertheless, the economic situation was profoundly difficult, and hindered by an Arab-organised boycott of Israeli exports. Defence expenditure was a major part of the Israeli budget, and a high proportion of the population served in the armed forces.

The Americans tried to influence Israel to grant concessions to the Arab countries for they feared that Israel, with fewer than two million people, could not hold out against forty million Arabs. Such gloomy prognostications drew Israel closer to France, which was fighting a bitter colonial war in Algeria, and was hostile to Egypt for giving assistance to the Algerians. Israeli and French physicists collaborated in developing an atom bomb, which the Americans and the British had denied to the French. Israeli–French accord deepened and the French shipped arms to Israel.

Israel was established by British decision and financed by American money against substantial Arab opposition. But however much American Jewry might rally to Israel and however many American politicians might need the Jewish vote, the United States also wished to guarantee her oil supply, to keep out the Russians and to end French and British colonial aspirations in the area. This meant also offering American support to the Arabs. But the Arab world itself was changing rapidly.

Arab consciousness had as its basis a common Muslim faith, allied to some concept of a common racial and cultural background. The Muslim faith had spread rapidly in the years before AD 1000, and had continued to grow until the seventeenth century, after which it declined. The Ottoman Empire had once included the whole of the Middle East, but piece after piece had gradually been picked off: the Muslims in India and the Far East fell under European control, and in the later nineteenth century the Arabs in Africa became part of French and British colonies. The First World War virtually finished off the independence of Muslims, as the Ottoman Empire was broken up and only Turkey and Saudi Arabia remained independent.

Thus Muslims were in a subordinate political position in almost every part of the vast empire they had at one time conquered. This deeply felt humiliation was accentuated by the patronising attitude to their faith adopted by those who regarded daily rules of religious observance and strict dietary and sexual laws as superstitious and out of date.

In addition Muslims were divided up by Europeans into good and bad. The good were healthy-living chaps who liked the desert, who were led by old-fashioned tribal leaders, the Bedouin, the Saudis and the Jordanians for instance, or who were great heroic fighters such as the Punjabi and Pathan soldiers of India. The bad lived in towns such as Cairo and Algiers, were non-military and were thought corrupt; the Egyptians, the Levantines, and Muslims not of Arab ethnicity were thought to play a diabolical role, were the negative side of the image and were felt to be dubious participators in nationalist movements. Virtually all the Western-educated leaders, such as Farouk, were considered unreliable.

At the end of the war in 1945 the Muslim world was showing signs of awakening politically. It was the increasingly successful attempt to overthrow European domination which attracted attention. Below the surface, however, especially in urban centres where it was least expected, there was a revival of religion itself which, in the long run, was to be most significant. Algeria and North Africa, Nigeria and West Africa, India, Indonesia and Southeast Asia also manifested a Muslim consciousness that spread from Morocco in the west to Indonesia in the east, from Turkey and Albania in the north to Nigeria and Tanzania in the south; the Muslims were party to warfare in the Philippines, in Mauretania and Nigeria; the Muslims were a major political fact in the southern part of the USSR and in the western parts of China. The Arabs were the most central part of this general Muslim movement, and were themselves divided between older authoritarian groups, Islamic revivalists, young Marxists and quasi-Marxists and those who embraced radical doctrines developed in Europe.

The Arab–Muslim Middle Eastern world was politically dominated by French and British interests. French influence ranged from

the almost completely absorbed Algeria, through the protecto-
rates of Tunisia and Morocco to the newly independent states of
Syria and Lebanon. British influence covered the quasi-
independent states of Egypt, Trans-Jordan, Iraq and Iran. As oil
grew in importance America too sought to exercise authority in
this area.

The spoils of Middle East oil had been divided between just
four companies – Anglo–Iranian, the Iraq Petroleum Company,
Aramco and Kuwait Oil Company – representing most of the
world's principal oil concerns, operating as a tight cartel. Throughout the world oil was virtually wholly controlled by this cartel. The
attempts of nationalists to escape from it explain many of the
subsequent events.

The concessions ran well beyond the end of the twentieth
century, and seriously limited the power of local governments –
for whom oil was the only major source of revenue – to tax the
companies' earnings. The oil companies represented complex
islands of modern technology, ruthlessly exploiting this source of
local wealth, amidst a quasi-medieval Arab and Iranian society
increasingly open to contemporary nationalist and even Marxist
ideas.

Growing nationalism led first to demands for the renegotiation
of the agreements with the oil companies and then to the nationalisation of oil concessions. This movement began in Iran, the most
modern of the oil countries. The British had exiled the dictator,
Reza Shah Pahlevi, during the war and installed a pro-allied
government. In 1951 the Prime Minister, Dr Mossadeq, nationalised the British companies exploiting Iranian oil without compensation. Britain refused to accept the decree so oil stopped
flowing. Mossadeq's moves were originally fanned by the Americans who thought they saw a chance for new profitable deals for
their own oil companies but when they saw the reality of Mossadeq, they changed their tune and arranged for him to be overthrown and for the Shah to be reinstated. This restored the position
of the Anglo–Iranian oil company. Loy Henderson, the American
Ambassador, now arranged a new agreement which gave 32 per
cent of the oil revenue to Iran, 40 per cent to the British, 14 per cent
to Royal Dutch Shell, 6 per cent to the Compagnie Française des
Pétroles, and 8 per cent to the five American Standard Oil companies. The American entry into the Iranian oil fields was rapidly
followed by a substantial number of other American companies.
Iranian oil sales were quickly restored and increased. Anthony
Eden, as British Foreign Secretary, negotiated an agreement in
July 1954 which, while giving British companies compensation,

and retaining Iranian ownership of the oil fields, established the Iranian–American–French and Anglo–Dutch consortium for the exploitation and marketing of the oil. The American government propitiated the new Iranian administration with a grant and a loan.

A major consideration which overshadowed the Iranian crisis was the fear of Soviet involvement. The Soviet Union had advanced into Iran in the early stages of the Second World War, and had then retreated, leaving Iran in the Anglo–American sphere. A further incursion in 1946 had been repulsed by Truman's threats. Iran's growing oil wealth would undoubtedly tempt the Russians again.

Another member of the oil cartel was the Iraq Petroleum Company which had obtained its concessions corruptly from the Turks and then maintained them whilst Iraq was a British mandated territory. The Iraqi government was paid a small fixed royalty in lieu of tax which was superseded in 1952 when a fifty:fifty agreement came into force. By various subterfuges, however, the government's total take from oil resources was reduced by the oil companies and by 1957, inspired by Iran's example, the Iraqis demanded a revision of their oil agreements.

The Saudi Arabian concessions had been taken by Aramco from 'an absolute monarch, unhampered by any of the paraphernalia of modern government, restrained only by Muslim customs and the advice of his tribal and religious leaders, making no distinction between the public and privy purses, badly in need of funds with which to meet the increasing cost of governing his loosely knit kingdom, unschooled in the ways of the West and ignorant of its technology'. The author of this trenchant statement, George W. Stocking, went on to remark that the king 'bargained as an Arab trader with sophisticated representatives of a modern oil company anxious to obtain a source of oil with which to supply its domestic needs and permit it to enter world markets'. As a result the oil companies were financially and economically in a strong position; though they worked in a desert, it did not blossom like a rose; their enormous profits came from low production costs and high prices in Europe and America, even though, in real terms, oil became ever cheaper to the world's consumers.

The Saudis adopted different tactics to increase their oil revenues. They introduced J. Paul Getty, a maverick American oil tycoon, into competition with Aramco, in a part of the country not hitherto conceded. This led to rapid exploitation of the Saudi oil fields which yielded a high-quality crude cheaply and easily. Other countries, meanwhile, sought to emulate Venezuela's decision in 1949 to impose a 50 per cent levy on the profits of the oil companies, which represented a big shift in favour of the Vene-zuelan government. Additionally, the big rise in output from the Middle East oil fields made the gross profit yields even greater, especially in the growing and developing fields of Saudi Arabia, where American influence was strongest, and in Kuwait. The Saudi Arabian arrangements were extremely beneficial to Aram-co, which deducted its Saudi tax payments from its American tax liabilities.

The arrogance with which the oil cartel interfered in their countries infuriated Saudi Arabia, Iraq and Iran and fanned the flames of nationalism. The Egyptians too deeply resented Euro-pean interference both over the Suez Canal's management and over the condominium of the Sudan. The Egyptians, with Amer-ican support, claimed the Sudan as an integral part of Egypt, partly from nationalistic reasons and partly because the control of the Nile waters was at issue. The British ruled the Sudan as an Anglo–Egyptian condominium because they saw it as the key to Africa which, in 1952, was still firmly and predominantly in British hands from Cairo to the Cape, and indeed was expected to remain so for at least two more generations. The Suez Canal, built by de Lesseps and opened in 1869, was owned and operated by a company which, although private, was in fact subordinate to the British and French governments. An Anglo–Egyptian treaty of 1936 gave the British the right to station troops in Egypt to protect the Canal, but in 1950 the Egyptian nationalist party, the Wafd, was returned to office with a massive majority, and with anti-imperialism sweeping the Arab world, it denounced the 1936 treaty.

In 1952 serious anti-British riots swept Cairo, and Britain threatened to intervene. The Egyptian army quelled the riots and the Wafd government fell. A new, more pro-British, government was formed but this too collapsed, taking with it the ineffective and profligate King Farouk. On 23 July 1952 General Neguib formed a military government. Neguib was half Sudanese and had been educated at Gordon College, Khartoum, so he was not wholly unsympathetic to British views on the Sudan, which was about to elect its first Parliament.

Neguib agreed to drop Egypt's claim to the Sudan if Eden gave it self-government. Eden accepted this; he also offered to withdraw British troops from Egypt, to maintain a base in the Canal zone, which could be reactivated if war broke out, and to offer economic aid, if Egypt agreed to join a Middle East defence organisation.

Eden's gestures had been made possible because Turkey had joined NATO, which meant that sites in Turkey, Greece and

Cyprus could now replace Egyptian bases, so Egypt had become less vital to British interests in Eden's eyes. Moreover the Prime Minister of Iraq, Nuri es-Said, had begun to initiate discussions for a pact between Turkey, Iraq, Iran, Jordan and Palestine to which Britain and the United States would accede and which Eden now hoped Egypt would join. This pact, which eventually became the Baghdad Pact, would effectively seal the southern frontier of the USSR by surrounding the Soviets with a Muslim crescent. There was a large Muslim population in the southern Soviet republics; it was hoped that they would revolt if their fellow Muslims over the border were attacked. Fear of internal disarray might deter Soviet advance.

Eden felt that he was about to bring off a spectacular diplomatic success: Anglo–American unity on Egypt and Iran, with all four states allied with the rest of the Middle East against Russia. The failure, when it came, was so sudden and so great a contrast to the potential success that Eden became enraged with the Egyptians and the Americans. The Suez affair was a direct result.

Meanwhile a new, powerful, patriot had been rising in the ranks of the Egyptian army, Colonel Gamal Abdul Nasser, more to the left politically and a stronger Muslim. Soon Neguib was under house arrest. The new Egyptian government pressed for total British withdrawal from Suez and the Americans, reverting to their view that Egypt was a victim of British colonialism, supplied Egypt with arms, diplomatic comfort and support. John Foster Dulles, as always, distrusted Western colonialism and thought that by his actions he would dissuade the Russians from interfering in an area where he was sure Stalin had designs. He was also motivated by a desire for peace before Eisenhower's 1956 election campaign. Dulles now began to negotiate with Nasser over the amount of American aid he would need in order to build the Aswan dam.

Nasser became identified in Eden's mind with Mussolini and Hitler, as an aggressive nationalist leader with unlimited ambitions to take over the Arab world. At almost any cost, therefore, Nasser must be resisted; the terrible examples of appeasement in 1936 and 1938, only twenty years before, were a warning. Eden saw Nasser buying more and more arms from Communist countries, especially Czechoslovakia and Russia, manifestly for an aggressive purpose, so he grew increasingly concerned to develop a common front against Nasser, bringing together as his allies Iraq (led by his favourite Nuri es-Said), the Israelis and the French.

Then three further incidents added to the tension. First there was an attempted uprising against the then British puppet in Jordan, King Hussein, which led to vigorous British and Iraqi intervention. The Saudis and the Egyptians threatened to become involved and Hussein was subjected to strong contrary pressures. On 1 March he dismissed General Glubb, the British head of his army, and other British officers. This maddened Eden, who saw the dismissal of Glubb as the 'jealousy of a younger man for an older one long established in a position of authority in the country . . . a personal dislike which had grown to something of a phobia'. (This seemed to stress Eden's remarkable lack of perspicacity about his own relations to Churchill.) Nasser, the Saudis and the Soviet Union offered to replace British aid to Jordan; Eden, meanwhile, consulted Iraq, but not the United States. Secondly, Nasser accepted an arms deal from the USSR. There is evidence that he had hoped for American arms but Dulles dithered so much that Nasser approached a somewhat reluctant Russia. Thus Dulles almost casually involved the Soviet Union in the Middle East. Thirdly, Nasser agreed to accept $270 million in loans and grants from the United States, Britain and the World Bank, ostensibly for the Aswan dam, although it looked as though this cash might be used for aggressive purposes. The Egyptians then asked for even more money, and on 19 July 1956 John Foster Dulles told the Egyptians that the whole deal was off. For seemingly financial reasons, the American government had plunged Egypt into a major confrontation with the West. Was this refusal to finance the dam a revenge for the Soviet arms deal? Whatever the motive it put Nasser against the West.

On 26 July, while King Faisal of Iraq was dining at Buckingham Palace, Nasser nationalised the Suez Canal, without compensation; 'Arab nationalism,' Nasser said, 'has been set on fire from the Atlantic Ocean to the Persian Gulf. Arab nationalism feels its existence, its structure and its strength.'

Eden lost no time. A secret treaty was concluded between Selwyn Lloyd, the British Foreign Secretary, the French Foreign Minister, Pineau, and the Israelis, that in certain conditions the Israelis would advance across the Sinai desert, the British and French would land troops in the Canal zone to secure the Canal and to create a barrier between Egypt and Israel. Every endeavour would be made, too, to rid Egypt of Nasser and replace him with an acceptable regime.

The nationalisation of the Canal seemed a threat to Western and especially British oil supplies, about half of which came through the Canal. Like Mossadeq's seizure of the Iranian oil fields, it was an example of the expropriation of a major asset without compensation. It seemed that Nasser would rally the Arab world against the French and the British. Finally, it was feared in London and Paris that he would let in the Russians.

Eden planned from the start to overthrow Nasser by force, but first the appearance of international consultation had to be gone through, not least because the British armed forces were designed to be used in Western Europe. Their nearest base to Egypt was in Malta, 1000 miles away, where there were scarcely any paratroopers. It would take at least three months to prepare for an effective invasion unless it were done directly from Israeli soil.

At America's suggestion, on 28 July 1956, Eden and Mollet agreed to seek a meeting of maritime powers whose ships used the Canal. The French government, which partly owned the Suez Canal Company, with its seat in Paris, was adamant for action. On 1 August 1956 Dulles told Eden that Egypt must be made to 'disgorge' the Canal. Throughout what followed, Eden was convinced this was America's true policy, and that other American statements were camouflage, largely made because of the impending Presidential election in November 1956 in which Eisenhower was again a candidate, running as the man who had brought peace to Korea as well as a more general settlement throughout the world. Support for a colonialist war would hardly be likely to appear as part of his electoral programme. Eden thought, however, that he knew Eisenhower's mind; Churchill had had similar delusions about Roosevelt.

Twenty-four countries who used the Canal – 'user nations' – were summoned to a meeting in London on 16 August and all except Egypt and Greece accepted. Eden believed he had American support for firm action to make Nasser 'disgorge'. After a debate in the House of Commons on 2 August 1956 he concluded that he had the Labour leader Gaitskell's support as well. It was thought that Russia would stay neutral, after ambiguous assurances from Shepilov, the Soviet Foreign Minister, to the British Ambassador in Moscow. Gradually, however, the realities of different attitudes became clearer, but paradoxically this intensified Eden's conviction that his analysis of the situation was correct and that he had to act by force, on a joint British–French–Israeli basis.

On 12 August Gaitskell and the Labour party began a campaign against British intervention in Egypt, and asked for the whole matter to be left to the United Nations. Since the Soviet Union would use its veto at the UN, this could have been seen as tantamount to acceptance of the Egyptian move and Eden refused. Behind this Labour agitation, which was strongly anti-colonial in character, was a sympathy for nationalisation as such, and a conviction that Egypt would not abuse its power. The same view of

Nasser was held by Dulles, who, when the user nations met in London, agreed with the setting up of a committee under Robert Menzies, the Prime Minister of Australia, which was to demand from Nasser a renunciation of his confiscation of the Canal, and to establish an international Canal authority.

Predictably, Nasser refused, on 7 September 1956. The United States would not go along with a British–French financial and economic boycott of Egypt, which now received substantial Soviet help for the Aswan dam, confirming Eden's view of the sources of Nasser's determination to defy the West. Eden's appeal to the United Nations was delayed while Dulles floated a proposal for a Users' Club with a merely supervisory and negotiatory role. On 19 September 1956 this proposal was discussed at yet another international conference in London, which agreed to Dulles' proposal. Eden persisted in his belief that, while the United States was weakening in its own attitude to Egypt, it would tacitly support the use of force against Egypt. Nothing was further from the truth. Dulles did not in fact regard Nasser's action as deeply dangerous to Western security; moreover, if the Canal were closed, there were substantial gains to be made by diverting European purchases of oil to North America. Eden and the French still refused to go to the United Nations and this exacerbated feelings throughout the world and especially amongst those, like Gaitskell, who thought that the major hope for world peace was to use international organisations, however imperfect they might be. There is little doubt that in the longer term he was correct, but such a course was still open to the objection that it effectively meant no action at all.

On 24 September the secret British–French–Israeli plan for invasion was finally agreed. The Users' proposals were taken to the United Nations and on a vote on 13 October they were vetoed by the USSR. It seemed to Eden and Pineau that the United States had now lost virtually all interest in the Suez question. On the same day Eden hinted to the Conservative party conference at Llandudno that force would be used, which led to redoubled protests by the Labour party and other groups in Britain. Secretly, too, Eden allegedly arranged for the British secret service to try to murder Nasser.

Meanwhile Egypt, Syria and Jordan began to co-ordinate a joint military command directed against Israel. Constant guerrilla attacks were launched from Egypt on Israel. It was agreed between Eden and Pineau in Paris on 16 October that the French, whose relations with Israel were close, would be responsible for informing the Israelis when the pre-emptive attack should begin. The Egyptians in their turn prepared for a major assault on Israel.

Lloyd, Pineau and Dayan met at Sèvres on 22 October; the Israeli attack on Egypt began five days later, their army advancing rapidly towards Suez and Ismailia, at either end of the Canal. Next day, Eden and Pineau announced that British and French forces would intervene to 'separate the belligerents' – a device agreed six months before with the Israelis. The United Nations and the House of Commons erupted with outrage, and the United Nations demanded an immediate Israeli withdrawal to the 1948 frontiers and a total British and French withdrawal. Britain and France vetoed the United States resolution at the UN calling for withdrawal, a wholly unprecedented and unforeseen division in Western opinion and action.

To add horror to this disarray, the Soviet Union proceeded to invade and bloodily to put down the Hungarian revolt against the Communist regime in Hungary. The apparent aggression of Britain and France against Egypt was used as an excuse for the Russian actions; the parallel that was drawn was an unfair but telling one.

With quite extraordinary military inefficiency (in striking contrast, for example, to MacArthur's Inchon landing in Korea in 1950, or the contemporary Israeli attack), the British and French forces began their attacks on Egypt, first by air on Egyptian air bases on 1 November 1956, then later by virtually unopposed paratroop and seaborne landings. This was during the week of the American Presidential election. These landings took so long to effect that virtually continuous sittings of the House of Commons and big public displays accompanied every move, both military and political, while the United Nations General Assembly adopted a United States motion on 2 November 1956 which required an immediate cease-fire and urged member states not to move military supplies into the Middle East. Not only Dulles, but President Eisenhower and Vice-President Nixon made strong attacks on British and French policy. Eden moved to new heights of fury. The action confirmed French distrust not only of the United Nations, but above all of the United States. Israel remained self-assured as always, and its troops seemed headed for Cairo – but their victory jeopardised the whole plot, since it was plain that had the Egyptians attacked they would themselves have been overwhelmingly defeated. The supposed Egyptian aggression plans were probably imaginary. The Israeli advance was so quick that the British and French troops might land behind the Israeli lines rather than in front of them, which would expose the whole plot for the lie it was. Eventually, on 5 November – three days after the UN resolution – British paratroops landed at Port Said and the Egyptians surrendered. Further French and British seaborne troops landed on 6 November.

Thus a defeated Egypt faced a victorious Israel, with a small and badly-led Franco–British force purporting to keep the peace. Meanwhile the United States, supported by Third World countries and the Soviet Union, was demanding British and French withdrawal. These threats could have been ignored. Withdrawal sprang not from political pressure but from the collapse of sterling. The victors were the Israelis who gained access to the Red Sea by their capture of Eilat. The defeated were the British and French who not only failed to seize the Suez Canal themselves but stopped the Israelis from capturing it and so making it free for world sea traffic. Nor did Nasser fall as a result of his military defeat, largely because the Franco–British intervention made him an anti-imperialist hero and won him American support. Indeed there was mounting evidence of stronger support for him and his ideas throughout the Arab world. With Tito of Yugoslavia and Nehru of India, he became a leader of the 'non-aligned states', which, on the principle that those who are not for you are against you, meant a substantial addition to anti-Western strength throughout the world.

In the American elections President Eisenhower was elected with an increased majority. He continued to be warm to the British in private, but hostile in public, insisting that any joint plan for the Middle East could not be discussed until the allies had withdrawn their troops. An international force was to occupy the Canal zone before it could be cleared of the twenty ships the Egyptians had scuttled after the cease-fire on 6 November. By 23 November allied troops began the withdrawal, which was completed within a month. All British and French assets in Egypt were gone; many people were killed in riots; the Canal was blocked; the extremely expensive British base at Suez – evacuated in 1954 but with the right to return – was lost; the Western alliance was bitterly divided; the reputation of the British army for efficiency and manoeuvrability was considerably lowered; the British balance of payments was severely damaged and petrol was rationed.

Eden collapsed physically and went to the West Indies. On 9 January 1957 he resigned as Prime Minister, on grounds of ill health. A year or so later, the Fourth Republic collapsed. Nasser stayed in office, until his death in 1970.

The Suez debacle has been described in such detail because it illuminates many problems of this period of shifting and changing alliances, not least too because it shows up the tangle of long-range attitudes and short-term objectives. Dulles was anti-Communist and against Soviet interference yet his actions in declining to finalise an arms deal or finance the Aswan dam encouraged Nasser to turn to the Russians and so drew them into Middle East affairs.

Thereafter the drama had a certain inevitability. Eden, following a row with Jordan when King Hussein dismissed Glubb Pasha, became obsessed with Nasser and proceeded to behave like Dulles on one of his bad days, only for nearly a year and with no President to control him. Dulles pontificated. Eden and Macmillan assumed that their old friend Ike privately supported them. The resulting muddle led to the Israeli invasion of Egypt, the long-drawn-out Franco–British operation to occupy the Canal zone, the intervention of the United Nations and the subsequent withdrawal, with Dulles appearing throughout to play a zealous, almost fanatical anti-British and anti-French role. The final tragic dénouement was armed Soviet interference in Hungary, and ruthless repression of their independence.

After Suez, Arab nationalism increased. But who should be the leader of the pan-Arab movement: Nasser of Egypt, Hussein of Transjordan, the House of Saud, the Shah of Iran or the ruler of Iraq? Who was sufficiently powerful?

Iraq's oil revenue fell by 1957 because the Mediterranean pipeline through Syria was destroyed during the Suez operation. Despite this Nuri es-Said and the young King Feisal II demanded a revision of their oil agreements to increase their revenues, but nationalisation was deferred because of the impossibility of selling the oil except through the oil companies' cartel. Nuri es-Said was a helpful member of the Baghdad Pact linking Pakistan, Iran and Turkey to Iraq and the pact seemed to elevate Nuri es-Said to a pro-Western leadership of the Arab states but then, in a coup d'état, he was murdered along with the young king and his family and replaced by an internal-looking Baathist – extreme Muslim – revolutionary government under General Qasim which was hostile to Egypt.

Iran was over-dependent on America who had accomplished a clever oil deal with the Shah. Two consortium companies produced the oil and sold it to the National Iranian Oil Company, who in turn sold it to the trading companies. The oil was sold at a 'stated' price, agreed by the international cartel, and 12½ per cent was paid to the producing companies. Half the profits were paid in tax to the Iranians, who also had access to a proportion of the total sales through the cartel. In 1957 the Iranians developed this share by going into partnership with the Italian state oil company, AGIP, then controlled by Enrico Mattei. The Shah's dynastic rule progressively expanded the share of Iran's own oil-producing and selling companies within the oil consortiums and exercised its power against the oil company cartel but the American, Dutch and British influence still shackled it too much for independent leadership.

The Suez debacle had left Transjordan with a serious refugee problem. Despite years of British aid, King Hussein had not held the Egyptians off during the war and later when Israel invaded Sinai, he had remained neutral. Transjordan was militarily weak and economically dependent on Britain and Israel; with no oil revenues and no independent economic strength, King Hussein had not sufficient individual charisma to be able to lead such a wayward group as the heterogeneous Arab nations alone.

Nasser seemed the strongest potential leader, for he had thrown off British interference and soon managed to extricate himself from Russian toils but 1956 had been a shattering military defeat for him, he had no rich oil revenues and so little to offer his fellow Arabs; he had ruled himself out.

The Saudi Arabians were the least politically involved, the most introspective of all the Arab states but the richest in enormous reserves of easily accessible oil, which placed them and Aramco in a very strong position. In June 1962 Sheik Yamani, the Minister of Petroleum, became a principal leader of the new cartel of native producers of oil, the Organisation of Petroleum Exporting Countries or OPEC, founded by Venezuela. Under Yamani, OPEC demanded higher oil prices and a more favourable royalty and tax arrangement for its member governments from the oil companies. Yamani immediately began to renegotiate Saudi Arabia's arrangements with Aramco. This led to a diminution in the area of the country where Aramco had concessions to explore for oil and exploit it, and a payment of $160 million by Aramco to the Saudis as a lump sum compensation in settlement of their claims.

Under Yamani's effective leadership, the oil-producing countries at last took control of their own oil fields and led by Kuwait and Saudi Arabia began to act in a unified manner. It was then seen that Arab unity did not require political leadership under one individual but that the Saudis, supported by Egypt and Iran, could effectively act as spokesmen for the Arab world.

OPEC in origin was Latin American. After a long and complex revolution, Mexico had nationalised its oil in 1938. A boycott by international companies followed, backed by the British government (which broke off diplomatic relations with Mexico), but the Second World War had made Mexican oil important to the American war effort. Venezuela profited by the war-induced shortages of oil to force through its first fifty:fifty profit-sharing agreement in

1943 and in 1949 to impose a levy. After the end of the war Middle Eastern oil flooded the market and prices fell, though oil producers' total receipts rose through increasing sales.

Rivalling the seven major international companies were independent oil producers, who largely grew up as a result of the United States anti-cartel laws which sought to break the vast American companies such as Standard Oil. By 1952, two thirds of American and Canadian oil was produced by independents, among them Getty, Howard Hughes and Richfield, who sought to break into the Middle Eastern oil-producing regions from which they were excluded. This suited the oil-producing countries.

The Venezuelans, however, refused to accept that their yield should fall and sought to stem the price decline. They also took the view that the Mexican and Iranian experiences of oil boycotts proved that the oil companies were all-powerful. OPEC was therefore sired secretly by Venezuela and Saudi Arabia in 1959 in an attempt to increase the power of the oil-producing countries – not the same as the oil producers since except for Mexico the producers were the international companies.

In September 1960 Iraq, Iran, Kuwait, Saudi Arabia and Venezuela met publicly in Baghdad to establish the new body. These five countries contained 67 per cent of the proved oil reserves of the world, 38 per cent of the production, and 90 per cent of the oil that entered into international trade. Opined the two founding Resolutions: 'The members can no longer remain indifferent to the attitude . . . adopted by the oil companies in effecting price modifications; . . . that members shall endeavour . . . to restore present prices to the levels prevailing before the reductions . . .' and 'If . . . any sanctions are employed . . . by any international company against one or more of the member countries, no other member shall accept any offer of a beneficial treatment, whether in the form of an increase of exports or an improvement in prices, that may be made to it by any such company or companies . . .' The original purpose of OPEC was thus defensive against the oil companies and the fall in oil prices. It was only subsequently that OPEC came to have more punitive functions.

This attitude developed partly as the membership of OPEC grew: Qatar in January 1961, Libya and Indonesia in June 1962, Abu Dhabi in November 1967, Algeria in July 1969. Thus OPEC united most of the major oil exporters whose 'petroleum interests are fundamentally similar to those of the founder members'. Countries such as Canada and the United States were therefore excluded, even though they were large oil producers.

But the oil producers, throughout the 1950s, were more concerned to avoid price reductions than to use oil as a political weapon; their main target was the oil cartel, and in their fight they allied themselves to the independent oil producers, even though they were themselves major Western capitalists.

Arab nationalism, far from being a rising of the oppressed, was partly an expression of militant Muslim feeling and partly a realisation of economic and military power by the oil states. It was pluralist and only loosely united. Prepared to be friendly with the USSR, Arabs did not accept Soviet suzerainty or godless Communism, preferring to align themselves with India, Yugoslavia and other neutralist forces.

Nasser, Syria, Libya under Gaddafi and Algeria, after independence, all flirted with the Soviet Union and sought support but the USSR never became actively involved in the Middle East despite Dulles' fears. Perhaps because such an involvement might well have been seen as a *casus belli* for the Americans but maybe also because the Muslim Arabs were too delighted with their newfound independence, pan-Arabism and religious zeal to want to become the satellites of another nation. Moreover the Arabs had the weapon of oil supply restriction which they soon discovered they could use with impunity.

America, Russia, France and Britain each had their own foreign policies, their own priorities and their own attitudes and goals but when they came up against each other in the Middle East, against Arab and Israeli nationalism, Muslim fanaticism and oil politics, each had to extemporise. In acting according to an immediate short-term expediency, perhaps hedged in by forthcoming general or Presidential elections, they jeopardised much else, particularly long-term alliances and goals.

Chapter 18

Algeria, de Gaulle and the Fifth Republic

The end of the wave of Western prosperity after the war came with the Arab oil boycott in 1973. In the emergence of Arab consciousness, Algeria played a crucial role.

In the late 1950s the war in Algeria overshadowed the steady, indeed remarkable, social and economic progress made by the French since the end of the war. It was not the economic or even the military burden of the war, for the kind of guerrilla and policing policy adopted by the French was not expensive in material, but the effect on French morale that mattered. France had never regarded its colonial people as autonomous, unlike the British. The French wished their colonial people to become French – the highest form of civilisation, in their view. In many respects this was an extremely successful policy; the black and Muslim graduates of the *grandes écoles* were in no respect inferior to their white contemporaries and, indeed, so it remains. Nevertheless, as a policy it was bound to fail with the millions of Muslims who found themselves, by accident of colonial conquest, French subjects. Neither Egyptians, Moroccans, nor Bedouins in Libya were required to become French. Why should the chance of being born in Algeria cause a man to sacrifice his Muslim identity in order to adopt a French one?

Chapter 11 discussed the post-war vicissitudes of the former French, Dutch and British colonies in Southeast Asia, from which it appeared that attempts by Europeans to control and organise far-flung foreign lands were doomed to failure and that independence was only likely to be successful if the native peoples had been allowed to plan towards the goal of freedom for some long time. Algeria however posed a completely different set of problems and their solution had far greater repercussions on the mother country than the struggle for independence elsewhere. This was surprising for Algeria was situated close to France, had been encouraged to think of itself as part of France and numbered amongst its population over one million *pieds noirs*, Christian French settlers, often in their fourth or fifth generation in Algeria, who had totally committed themselves to Algeria, although they had not lost their

French identity; their legal, social and economic conditions and ethnic consciousness made them for the most part a prosperous, privileged elite, yet a special sort of Frenchman.

The standards of the poor Muslims were considerably below those of the rest of the population, being mainly illiterate and landless. Nevertheless, their birthrate was high and, as mortality rates fell, their numbers grew rapidly. The population was therefore racially divided; and the Europeans and Muslims were suspicious of each other. With the rise of Muslim consciousness throughout the Middle East and, eventually, throughout the whole Muslim world, the French ideal of integration became not only an actual illusion (since it had never properly happened), but a cause for Muslim revolt. In 1947 the Algerian Statute in creating two separate political constituencies in Algeria, Muslim and European, finally abandoned the idea that one day the Muslims would become completely French; it retained the idea, however, that the Muslims would remain loyal to France within the French Constitution.

Algerian nationalism grew under the leadership of Ferhat Abbas and, from 1950, the more militant leadership of Ben Bella. The growing pressure for independence in Tunisia and Morocco, the French defeats in Indochina, ending in the final collapse in 1954, and the emergence of other countries in the Third World, led to a feeling that the lack of an Algerian identity was an anomaly. In 1954, when Nasser took office in Egypt, he gave support to Ben Bella, largely influenced by a group of Algerian revolutionaries in Cairo. The so-called 'club of nine' formed around Ben Bella, and a military insurrection began on 1 November 1954, with Egyptian aid.

The impact of this insurrection was substantial, since the French and most of the Algerians had convinced themselves that Algeria was completely immune to nationalist agitation. Pierre Mendès-France, the liberal reformist French Prime Minister, reacted at once by saying that there could be no compromise with sedition. The club of nine, who now called themselves the FLN (*Front de Libération Nationale*), divided into an External Delegation in Cairo led by Ben Bella, and an Internal Delegation of autonomous military commanders in Algeria, one for each Wilaya, or administrative zone, known as the *Armée de Libération Nationale* (ALN). This division into autonomous units proved a good basis for perpetual guerrilla warfare, and by early 1956 the ALN controlled comparatively large mountain and desert areas, with the French confined to military strongholds.

The French reaction was to strengthen the army and to speed up reform in Algerian agriculture, education, medical and social services, since it was believed that economic and social discontent underlay the insurrection. As the army struck hard at the guerrillas, so the civil power dispensed aid to the Muslims most liberally.

The Muslims in the towns then helped those in the country areas, which led to urban terrorism, then a relatively new development in post-war affairs. Thus the fight took on a straight Muslim against European character. There were, however, numbers of Muslims who remained loyal to France; and their very existence formed a moral challenge to those who saw the struggle as simply between nationalism and imperialism.

As the insurgency developed it was dealt with by the army and the police with considerable success. But diplomatically, a serious defeat occurred when the UN took Algeria 'under consideration' in September 1955 – a decision that considerably worsened the French attitude to the UN, as the Suez affair was to show a year later. And, as the Muslims became increasingly alienated from the French by terror, blackmail and domestic oppression by the security forces, so the spirit of pan-Arabism built upon itself.

The Algerian problem was further complicated by France's desire to keep Algerian oil resources in the Sahara, which also became a site for French atom bomb testing. In October 1956 Ben Bella and the FLN external leadership were kidnapped by the French while flying from Morocco to Tunis. This not only tilted the balance of power more firmly in the direction of those who were fighting inside Algeria, but it also caused the newly-independent governments of Morocco and Tunisia grave affront, and thereafter they were both strongly pro-Algerian. The kidnapping was undertaken by French military intelligence, and caused a furore in France as Ben Bella had been going to Tunis to meet representatives of France's left-wing government. Thus the revolution moved into a more extremist phase, dividing France between progressives and reactionaries; the Arab nationalists from the Algerian Europeans; and France from hitherto friendly governments.

Meanwhile the French decided to tackle the Arab world head on as they joined with Britain and Israel in a military venture into Egypt over Suez in October and November 1956. The consequence was a considerable reinforcement of pro-Arab feeling, and a growing sense of isolation among the French as their British and American allies deserted them. Suez reinforced the American conviction that the war in Algeria was being fought by imperialists against legitimate nationalist forces. In January 1957, after the votes of censure on Britain and France by the General Assembly over Suez, the UN voted in favour of Algeria.

Militarily, however, the French had not lost. Immediately after the UN vote, General Massu rooted the FLN out of the Kasbah (the native city) of Algiers in a carefully-planned and brutal operation, which was followed by a massive military sweep through Algeria; by November 1957 the cities, including Algiers, were effectively cleared of Algerian militants. The FLN meanwhile moved to Tunisia, which thereupon became the insurgents' main military base. The Algerians infiltrated and terrorised the countryside, and the war became a constant series of small but destructive attacks and counterattacks, which wore down the French army and tied it increasingly into a bitter struggle such as had been waged in Indochina. This time, however, the whole resources of the French army were at the disposal of the headquarters in Algeria and the French troops were usually successful. Moreover, in order to convert the Algerians to the French conception of an '*Algérie Française*', a sophisticated form of psychological warfare was initiated, that had a striking success, perhaps, because those who conducted it believed in the message that they were conveying. The army itself became heavily committed to this vision of a French Algeria, purged of dissident elements, and of France itself purified of partisan politics.

The *pieds noirs* French settlers wanted to keep their special privileged pre-war position, they also wanted the army to be tougher on the Muslim rebels. The FLN wanted the country for themselves and were receiving aid from other Arab states and from countries such as Yugoslavia. The French government hoped that the Algerian Muslims would be incorporated into greater France in the end so they used kid glove measures in an attempt to cool the fracas. The French army had views of its own and was becoming increasingly politically minded, tending to side with the *pieds noirs*. As the war intensified, so emergency measures in Algeria and in France itself made the country seem increasingly ungovernable by ordinary constitutional processes. Meanwhile at his small country house at Colombey-les-deux-églises, with a weekly visit to Paris, the brooding presence of de Gaulle seemed to offer the prospect of a government with more authority and enough political and military clout to resolve the Algerian conflict. It was assumed, especially by Jacques Soustelle, politically the most prominent of his supporters, that de Gaulle's Algerian stance would align him with the ultras of the *Algérie Française* type. De Gaulle had been bitter in blaming the Fourth Republic for the loss of Indochina, Tunisia and Morocco, and the abandoning of the Saar – a part of

Germany he had wished to incorporate into France. It was assumed, by Soustelle, a sometime Governor General of Algeria, that de Gaulle wished to keep Algeria, too, by force.

De Gaulle was an opportunist. He had a lonely, almost mono-maniacal vision of France, of which he was the voice, the personifi-cation. Made leader of France, largely by allied propaganda and by his own perpetual intrigue, he had walked off the political stage in 1946 at a time when France most keenly needed powerful and calm leadership. By keeping his brooding personality ever present, he had in no small fashion undermined the legitimacy and effective-ness of the Fourth Republic. It followed, then, that his return to power would be epic, but it would also entail the betrayal of his most loyal and prominent supporters.

By late 1957, despite the extraordinary success of the French economy, excellent relationships with Germany, and despite the major restoration in a dozen years of France's position inter-nationally, the defeat in Indochina, its rebuff at Suez, and its apparently interminable difficulties in Algeria, led to the wide-spread conviction that the regime, not just successive govern-ments, was doomed. The leading soldiers, Marshal Juin and General Koenig, were thinking of a military putsch; the ultras among the *pieds noirs* settlers in Algeria were seeking a white dictatorship in Algeria; Georges Bidault and Jacques Soustelle were thinking of a government of public safety. Those who wanted to keep France in Algeria, and those who wanted its independ-ence, such as André Malraux and François Mauriac, argued passionately that only de Gaulle's authority and political skill could save the situation. At the same time de Gaulle's political adher-ents, Debré, Soustelle and Chaban-Delmas, although in a small minority in the National Assembly, began urgently to negotiate for de Gaulle's recall.

In early 1958, however, it seemed as though militarily the tide was turning – despite two major propaganda setbacks when a Yugoslav ship carrying arms to the insurgents was arrested by the French navy, and the French air force bombed a village on the Tunisian border, Sahkiet Sidi Youssef, while an International Red Cross team was visiting the area. But a carefully orchestrated world outcry, led by President Bourguiba of Tunisia, isolated France from its friends.

This considerably worsened French–Tunisian relations and led to a fear in NATO that the spread of the war would cause France to weaken its forces in Europe still further. But in France itself, where the war was deeply unpopular, there seemed no conceivable manner in which it could be ended without giving independence to the Algerians, which would in its turn cause the Algerian Europeans to attempt to overthrow the French government.

After an enquiry into the bombing, the Prime Minister, Félix Gaillard, resigned, and President René Coty, head of the famous scent firm, sought to form a government among those, such as Soustelle and Bidault, who wanted to win in Algeria and who wanted a government of national safety, but they could not command a majority in the Assembly. General Salan, head of the army in Algeria, was then invited to come to Paris for consultations; Salan delivered an ultimatum instead – surrender of the rebels, followed by an amnesty and a new start. The policy could not possibly have succeeded, but it marked the emergence of the army as an active political force. On 10 May, Salan and his generals in Algeria publicly told President Coty, through the Chief of the General Staff, that the army would never consent to the abandonment of loyal Muslims and French citizens in Algeria. Behind the message to President Coty was a well worked out plot for the army in France to rise and occupy the country, with the help of General Massu's paratroops from Algiers. This plot was being translated into action when Pierre Pflimlin, leader of the Catholic MRP, formed a Cabinet on 13 May, which it was widely believed would negotiate a settlement with the FLN and 'betray' the settlers and the army.

The expectation world-wide was that a successful military rising in France would overthrow the Fourth Republic. In Algeria a general strike was declared, rioting students announced a committee of public safety and proceeded to take over the country under the leadership of the paratrooper, General Massu. The Commander-in-Chief, General Salan, was put into a difficult position. If he did not take power in Algeria, he might be replaced by the successful rebels; if he did take power, he was overthrowing the French Republic. In the event, on 14 May, he declared for de Gaulle – a signal to which de Gaulle responded the following day. France was plunged into political turmoil; the Communists and the left regarded it as a Bonapartist-type takeover; the army eventually agreed to serve under de Gaulle; and a number of parliamentarians, led by the Socialist Guy Mollet, agreed to support de Gaulle if he came to power constitutionally.

On 19 May, in an oracular press conference, de Gaulle indicated that he wanted a new Presidential constitution; that he would form a government with emergency powers; and that he was not seeking to be a dictator 'at the age of sixty-seven'; over Algeria he was cagey enough to give the impression that he wanted to maintain the French connection. It was a critical moment. De Gaulle's personality was powerful enough to meet the desire, widespread in France and Algeria, for a new start under a powerful leader and at the same time to reassure a substantial number of those who feared that a rapid descent into authoritarianism had become highly probable if not inevitable. Such a descent was indeed possible, because of the military plot to bring back de Gaulle, though had the plotters gone into operation, de Gaulle would very probably have come out against them. Nevertheless, it was a grave crisis not only for France, but for the rest of the Western alliance. German constitutional democracy was very recent; Spain was still authoritarian; and the suppression of the Hungarian rebellion in 1956 had shown the powerful nature of Communist repression. Had France slid into military government, it would have been a blow against constitutional government. Not only that, but the long colonial war in Algeria pointed to a series of confrontations with nationalist movements that could have become a perennial feature of the time, particularly as the army was assumed to support the settlers.

The growing stresses in France led finally to the collapse of the Fourth Republic and the assumption of power by de Gaulle. The main stress remained Algeria. The growing preoccupation of the army with Algeria, the apparently interminable war, the increasing fury of the European settlers all conspired fatally to weaken the French government. The army had virtually unlimited powers in Algeria, and a conspiracy developed for the army to take over the government in Paris; on 24 May 1958 paratroops flew from Algeria planning to occupy Corsica.

By 25 May 1958 the orders of the Pflimlin government to suppress the army-led revolt in Corsica were disobeyed; next day de Gaulle announced that he was himself forming a republican government, and on 1 June the Assembly endorsed his appointment. The planned military rising and the invasion of the paratroopers, on 29 May, was postponed and then cancelled, largely through the rebels' belief that de Gaulle supported their policies.

De Gaulle, therefore, played a difficult role superbly. He came into office constitutionally, at the request of the President and endorsed by the Assembly; by a series of referendums he received the approval of the French electorate for constitutional reforms; and he managed to avoid becoming a captive of the settlers and the army in Algeria. The result was to preserve not only the forms, but also the substance of constitutional and democratic government.

Two weeks later, after becoming President, de Gaulle went to Algeria and talked to the army. He appointed Salan as the French government's Delegate General in Algeria, and Soustelle was brought back to Paris as Minister of Information. In early July de

Gaulle returned to Algeria and made several gestures to the Muslims, establishing a uniform voting system and giving substantial additional grants for development.

Over the next few years de Gaulle negotiated slowly with different factions in Algeria – from his speech just after assuming office in which he said '*Je vous ai compris*', and his later use of the slogan '*Algérie Française*', he shifted from a position of complete integration of Algeria into France, with massive economic support to raise Algerian living standards to those of France itself, towards an eventual agreement with the FLN, still hoping that an independent Algeria would be closely associated with France. During this period his settler supporters moved towards total hostility, a hostility that endured as a million of them fled virtually penniless from Algeria to France; there were several attempts to assassinate de Gaulle; a bombing campaign was conducted in France, especially in Paris; and de Gaulle had to institute trials of many generals and other officers in the army for treason and rebellion, including his former supporters.

In the process of solving the Algerian problem, de Gaulle gained massive support for a restructuring of the French Constitution, around a President with executive powers, elected for a seven-year term, and an Assembly which lost almost all its powers to make and unmake governments. De Gaulle used his power as elected President in a restrained fashion, save in foreign affairs, where he withdrew from NATO, twice blocked British membership of the European Economic Community, and indulged his anti-'Anglo–Saxon' attitude to the full.

By early 1959 de Gaulle was President under his own new constitution. It became increasingly clear that his aim in Algeria was a military victory, by an army that was no longer involved in politics, and with a new Algerian state that would be independent but associated with France. The *Algérie Française* dear to the settlers was not de Gaulle's vision at all. Accordingly, he separated the military command under Challe from the civilian command under Delouvrier; the depoliticised army carried out its military duties effectively and inflicted severe defeats on the FLN army while the government seemed to draw increasing support for an Algerian–French alternative to an independent Muslim Algeria. On 16 September 1959 de Gaulle offered these choices to Algeria: secession (that is a Muslim Algeria), integration with France, or a French–Algerian state associated with France. This offer, implicitly a serious offer of the third choice, was welcomed internationally and it seemed likely to win wide support in Algeria itself. The FLN hesitated about accepting de Gaulle's offer of a negotiated peace on this basis, partly for fear that it would be rejected by the Algerians themselves in a free election.

The saboteurs of the solution were not the FLN, however, but the ultra settlers, together with parts of the army under General Massu, who returned to Paris in January 1960, after an indiscreet interview with a West German magazine, and was relieved of his command. There followed an uprising of settlers in Algeria, with the army looking on as neutrals. Challe and Delouvrier left the city, de Gaulle ordered the army to arrest the leaders of the revolt, and his orders were obeyed. Thereafter all the ultra sympathisers were weeded out of the army, police and civil administration in Algeria. This marked the culmination of the power of the settlers; and as if in response the FLN reduced its level of activity, in order to achieve independence by negotiation with de Gaulle and through international pressure. The French government, by its military success, and by its offer of independence, had gained its main objective. The FLN had gained its main objective by default – that is, free elections which would give Algeria a Muslim government, but it had lost the power to impose itself upon Algeria, resembling in this respect de Valera's IRA in Ireland in 1923.

In January 1960 the African People's Congress urged volunteers from other countries to fight for the FLN; and it became a race between the French government's policy of free elections – which were held in late May – and the FLN terrorism. In June 1960 talks between the French and the FLN were held at Melun in France, and broke down. What seemed to turn the tide was war-weariness in France. The intellectuals turned against the war – in September 1960 the Manifesto of the 121 was issued which urged the right of French conscripts not to serve in Algeria. It looked as though the army was once more to become politicised, despite de Gaulle's efforts. In December de Gaulle went to Algeria once more, in preparation for a referendum on his programme. The FLN organised savage Muslim riots, and the ultra settlers huge anti-de Gaulle demonstrations, which led de Gaulle publicly to abandon their cause. The army now had to maintain peace in order to prepare for an independent Algeria; and in January 1961 both France and Algeria voted overwhelmingly for self-determination, despite FLN terrorist attempts to prevent Muslims from voting since they held the referendum to be illegitimate. In April 1961 negotiations were to begin at Evian for a cease-fire.

In that month, four leading French retired generals led a revolt in Algiers – Challe, Salan, Jouhaud and Zeller – and it seemed for a while that they might succeed, even perhaps invading France by air to depose the President. But de Gaulle and his government acted swiftly. The army in France and Germany rallied to support the government, and a massive general strike showed that the French population as a whole supported de Gaulle. The conscripts in the army in Algeria refused to obey their officers, and after three days the revolt began to crumble. Some rebel generals went into exile and Challe, Guerand and Zeller surrendered and were tried for treason. A purge of the army was immediately undertaken.

The Algerian settlers now joined the OAS – the European terrorist organisation, *Organisation Armée Secrète* – in considerable numbers, and began a terrorist war in France against the Muslims. It was led by those ex-generals who had escaped arrest, especially Salan. Meanwhile de Gaulle's government began negotiations at Evian with a delegation led by Belkacem Krim; a virtual cease-fire in Algeria was ordered, and the army was kept short of ammunition and fuel as it was deeply distrusted by the French government. A complex terrorist civil war began between the OAS, the FLN and the French army which continued until a cease-fire agreement was signed between the French and the FLN on 18 March 1962. The French electorate overwhelmingly endorsed the agreement, which was for a French withdrawal, in a referendum on 8 April. Salan was arrested in Algiers on 20 April, and the OAS set about a scorched earth policy and stepped up open terrorism in France. Meanwhile, the settlers began to leave Algeria in huge numbers, and on 3 July 1962 the Provisional government of the FLN took office in Algiers. The French army was withdrawn and *Algérie Française* was over.

Algeria's battle for independence rocked Europe for it showed how precarious Social Democratic constitutional government was if a fanatical group of religious zealots could so easily undermine France. Terrorism, bombing of civilians, shooting and civil violence also now entered the West, hitherto only encountered from the IRA. But perhaps the most important immediate effect of the Algerian war was the return of de Gaulle to power: a man who felt it was his destiny to raise France's self-respect, to return to a narrow nineteenth-century concept of patriotic nationalism; a man who would go to surprising lengths to achieve this goal of *la patrie* even if it meant overthrowing alliances and loyal supporters. The longer-term consequence, however, of the Algerian war, was the rise of Muslim feeling throughout the Middle East.

Chapter 19

Mao Tse-tung

The proclamation of the People's Republic of China on 1 October 1949 was clearly an event that qualified for the label 'epoch-making', but the nature of the epoch was unclear. The Indians and the British extended a cautious welcome. Stalin was mistrustful and patronising for, from his point of view, Mao was a heretic who might become another Tito; however, a Sino–Soviet pact of friendship was signed that February and Stalin proceeded to flood China with Soviet 'experts' who infiltrated the key positions in the administration. Soviet troops were not however evacuated from Manchuria nor was North Korea denuded of its Soviet controllers. The United States accepted Mao's government as the *de facto* government of mainland China without according it recognition. Instead Americans continued to put money on Chiang Kai-shek in Taiwan. The Korean War had caused Americans to regard the Chinese as Communist aggressors, especially as allies of the Russians, whilst the Chinese now pictured the Americans as imperial invaders of Asia. Both views had an element of truth, but the truth was more *post hoc*; in the event both parties came to act upon preconceived ideas and to provoke each other into expected behaviour patterns.

The followers of Mao now set about transforming China into a Communist society. Foreigners, landowners and bourgeois groups were persecuted. Many were executed, many millions more were sent to forced labour camps. The population was put under constant police and party supervision, civil order was restored and a new currency was successfully introduced along the lines of the currency reform which had worked so well in Germany. By mid 1950 the country was more peaceful and more stable than it had been for a century.

Such industry as remained after the Japanese occupation and the civil war was socialised; it was hardly surprising therefore that industrial output was very low in 1950 and 1951; equally, the yield from the harvest was especially poor as collectivisation proceeded and former owners of peasant farms were 're-educated' or executed. A trade boycott imposed by the United States was only partially compensated for by trade with the USSR, who also gave substantial technical aid. In 1953 China adopted its first Five-Year Plan on the Soviet model, which followed orthodox Stalinist lines – collectivised agriculture, electrification and an emphasis on heavy industry, coal and nuclear power.

In the cities a ruthless programme of 'de-Westernising' took place, involving the elimination and resettling of millions of urban 'parasites'.

There were mass trials of former officers in the Kuomintang, and the elimination of the rural landlords. Some estimates suggest that up to twenty million people were resettled or executed; in such huge numbers vagueness seems to mask the size of the tragedy. Others were put through a process called 'the reform of thinking', otherwise better known as brainwashing. The trials were accompanied by substantial land reform, as promised early on in the civil war. Over one hundred million acres were divided up into very small holdings, but the peasants – each of whom had a landholding – were then compelled to join together in mutual aid teams, for communally planned planting and the simultaneous harvesting of adjoining fields. In 1953 the village units were amalgamated into one communal farm, although the peasants still had nominal title to their own land. This co-operation undoubtedly raised output significantly.

By 1956 the division of land into individual units of ownership was abolished, communes were established and the allocation of output was determined principally by the number of days worked by each peasant, and to some extent by his status in the party hierarchy. Throughout this agricultural reform, Mao and his comrades relied upon the high discipline and fervour of the Communist party. As each commune was led by a party cadre, there were no exceptions to the land reform and opposition was swiftly suppressed. This land reform was accompanied by a substantial development of irrigation and of water conservancy. Output yields rose significantly, and the threat of famine and starvation was removed. In the great drought of 1960–2 for the first time in Chinese history no famine was experienced.

Mao's solution to the land problem was not only the most radical in China's history, but the most radical yet tried in an Asian country. Its immediate productive effectiveness immensely strengthened China and in particular the hold of the Communist regime over China. Industrial China had been completely devastated, and the Russians had looted Manchuria; the Communists then proceeded to nationalise most of the important industrial enterprises without compensation, the former owners having fled abroad, for the most part to Formosa with Chiang Kai-shek. The smaller manufacturers and professional people who had stayed in China were put under the control of the local party cadres.

In early 1951 the Three Antis campaign was launched against

corruption, waste and bureaucracy; capitalist merchants and businessmen were denounced, as were officials and even Communist party members. But these people were not, for the most part, executed, being put instead through a prolonged form of indoctrination in Communist ideology in order to change their attitude to the regime. In 1952 the campaign was stepped up as the Five Antis – tax evasion, fraud, the breach of state and industrial secrecy, theft of state property, and bribery.

In this campaign all former private enterprises, including the smallest, were in effect nationalised, and all economic policy was organised through the distribution of raw materials, the marketing of the finished product, and the allocation of finance during its manufacture. Each enterprise was controlled like the communes.

Thus, within a year after his victory, Mao Tse-tung had re-established order and communications throughout China; within two years had begun massive land reforms; and within three years had launched the Five-Year Plan. The *Thoughts of Chairman Mao* became a basic text for all members of the party, and thus one of the major controlling devices of the regime, since dissent from its tenets was not permitted. It emphasised the extent to which Mao Tse-tung had become a major Communist leader in his own right.

Mao was the sole source of authority for Communist doctrine, for though the works of Marx, Lenin and Stalin were cited frequently, they remained for the great part unread.

Mao's achievements were all the more impressive for taking place despite growing Soviet hostility and in the teeth of American opposition. Mao's greatest triumph however had been to force back the UN troops when they overstepped the Yalu River frontier in the Korean War, thus achieving a massive military victory against, in effect, the United States, who were the dominant part of the United Nations force. As the first major post-war victory of a non-white people against whites, it had an electrifying effect in the Third World.

The People's Liberation Army developed a new professionalism in the use of advanced technology, and, in consequence, by the Korean armistice China was an equal power with Russia in the crucial area of Manchuria, adjoining Siberia. The Russians subsequently relinquished such rights as they had previously held there, with a consequent deterioration in Chinese–Soviet relations, as the Soviet Union reluctantly accepted China's new role.

The Chinese intervention in the Korean War, although it strengthened the People's Liberation Army, and consolidated Mao's position in China by giving him a further great victory, also led to a frenzied anti-Chinese policy being adopted in the United States

Congress. In a tide of conservative opinion Eisenhower was swept into office in the Presidential election of 1952, following alle- gations that General Marshall, Truman's Secretary of State, had been instrumental in causing Chiang Kai-shek to be defeated when he failed to insist that the Communists should be destroyed in 1945 and 1946. In fact, such an insistence would have been impossible; much the wiser course would have been for the United States to come to some agreement at that time with Mao Tse-tung. It was also assumed in the United States, incorrectly, that the Chinese and the Russians were close and powerful allies, sharing a common doctrine. This was false.

One further consequence of the Chinese army's Korean success was a significant softening of the terror in China. Executions virtually ceased, great emphasis instead being placed upon re- education. American prisoners of war, for example, were indoc- trinated for long periods, some even successfully. Brainwashing, as it came to be known in the West, was regarded by international authorities as a form of psychological torture, and as such outlawed by various international codes. Nevertheless, the principle of re-education was less offensive than the previous mass executions.

When Stalin died in 1953 Mao and Chou En-lai, the Prime Minister, remained loyal to his ideas, despite the difficulties which he had created for them. Mao was promoted almost to Stalin's status as a world figure, not only in China, but in the Soviet Union too. The new Soviet leadership stepped up aid to China, and implemen- ted the agreement to withdraw troops from Port Arthur and Dainan in Manchuria. In a real sense, therefore, China and especially Mao became Stalin's heirs. At the Geneva conference, which ended the Franco–Indochina war in 1954, China was accorded world power status, not only by Russia but also by Britain and France.

Mao had sent Chou En-lai to Geneva in 1954 even though China remained unrecognised by the United States and many of the major Western powers. China continued to assist the Communist regime in North Vietnam, but was in no sense responsible for that regime's attempt to advance further south.

China was not, however, present at the subsequent Geneva summit meeting between Russia, America, Britain and France in June 1955, to discuss world peace. Nevertheless, Chinese Com- munism had arrived as a serious force in world affairs. Mao and Chou En-lai began to devise an independent foreign policy, first of all using their Indian connections to gather favour in Asia, reaching a high point at the meeting of Asian and African powers at Bandung in Indonesia, which affirmed the essentially neutralist principles of 'peaceful coexistence'. Mao's China was recognised as a leader at this conference, with Nehru's India, and although the immediate tangible result was to rally opinion against the 'imperialist' powers, it had a longer-term effect of suggesting that the Afro–Asian group – to which China allied itself – was also independent of the Soviet Union.

Mao felt himself to be a dominant figure in world Communism and the leader of China; he did not therefore much care for Khruschev's denunciation of the cult of personality and his censure of Stalin at the Twentieth Congress of the Communist party in 1956. China's immediate reaction was to adopt principles of collective leadership which Mao then used to overthrow the pro-Russian element in his hierarchy.

The Chinese continued in many respects to support Stalin's policies despite Khruschev, notably the building of Socialism in one country, and the emphasis upon heavy industry and collective farms. Though Mao and Stalin had clearly differed on almost all major points of doctrine other than these, and Stalin had clearly taken the view that Mao was potentially another Tito, Mao was unprepared for a denunciation of Stalin to become official Marxist doctrine. This remained the basis of China's ideological split with the Soviet Union from that time on, to which other splits were added. One such was caused by Tito's speech at Pula on 11 November 1956, both condemning and accepting Soviet intervention in Hungary in the previous month, but arguing that Titoism represented an evolution from Stalinism that all Communist states would follow. The Chinese judged this view as rank heresy – there could be only one road, the Stalinist (for which read Maoist) one. Their earliest significant break with the Soviet Union was therefore late 1956, though Mao had successfully pursued an independent line, for many years developing an identifiable 'Chinese' Communism based on the Communist conquest of China and the subsequent peasant revolution, all of which was contrary to Stalinist teaching.

In November 1957 Mao went to the World Congress of Communist parties in Moscow, which excluded Yugoslavia, and delivered a speech which included the phrase 'the East Wind prevails over the West Wind', one of his gnomic utterances, which was later interpreted to mean that the Chinese path to the revolution would be the successful one. The Moscow declaration of unity was based on a fight against 'revisionism'. Here was an attack on Khruschev's attempts to conciliate Yugoslavia and a reaffirmation of Mao's hard line in China, based on unanimity and Leninist principles of leadership by one man from the top. Mao and Khruschev became bitter personal enemies, on the Russians refusing to supply China with the airborne missiles which the Americans had supplied to

Chiang Kai-shek. The Russians also refused to support the development of the Chinese atom bomb, for they felt that if they offered aid at great cost to themselves, then China should be obliged to follow Soviet international policies, as well as internal economic and social developments on orthodox Soviet lines.

As the Chinese Communist regime entrenched itself, with communes in the countryside and workers' enterprises in the towns, Mao inaugurated the Hundred Flowers movement in 1956. This came from a classical quotation in Chinese literature, 'Let the hundred flowers bloom, let the hundred schools contend', that is to say, let different forms of art and philosophy flourish simultaneously. Mao had come to believe that the revolution had been so successful and the main tenets of his teachings universally accepted, that he wished to see 'Communist' freedom of expression, within the narrow confines of Marxism–Leninism. But when freedom of speech was permitted the regime itself was attacked and party members lost control of large areas of public opinion.

The Central Committee of the Communist party and Mao himself were alarmed by what they had unleashed so they immediately reversed their policy and suppressed those who had come out openly against the regime. Dissidents undertook arduous manual labour in remote communes. It became a tenet of the new Mao philosophy that purely intellectual labour was not permitted but that each Chinese should do his share of hard physical labour. Thus significant members of intellectuals and managers were dispersed from the cities to toil in the countryside.

Overtly the regime remained favourable to Russia; Chou En-lai and then Mao himself went to Moscow; Voroshilov and Khruschev came to Peking. Nevertheless anti-Russian demonstrations took place in Peking, including demands for the return of territory 'stolen' from China by the Czars. The ideological struggle between the Soviet view that in building Socialism power lay with the working class, and the Chinese view that revolutionaries had to be like fish in a sea, that is, absorbed into peasant life, was of fundamental importance, since at issue was the bureaucratic nature of the Soviet state and its revolutionary leadership in Asia. China was rapidly moving to an anti-Soviet line.

Between the early 1950s and 1958, the Chinese economy made significant steps forward. Agricultural output from the communes increased and industrial production concentrated on steel works, heavy engineering, shipyards and electricity stations with great success despite the United States blockade of China, fear of possible invasion from Chiang Kai-shek in Formosa (Taiwan), and the Vietnam conflict. Internationally China joined non-aligned countries at the Bandung conference and appeared to be settling for a moderate role.

Meanwhile Mao was developing his own form of village Socialism. He argued for the development of a rural society which carried out its own agricultural processing and for the same degree of light as heavy industry. Behind this view of balanced development was the realisation that countries with huge labour reserves like China should make full use of their labour power rather than concentrating on capital-intensive industries. There was also the need to tap the enthusiasm, the local initiative and the resources of the people themselves. Mao argued for the rapid diminution of central bureaucracy and the over-extended state apparatus, which was a radical departure, not only from Stalinism, but also from Marxist thinking from the time of Lenin. Mao became a truly revolutionary innovator. Not only Russia and its satellites had followed Stalin's line, but India as well in its earlier Five-Year Plans, and so in a modest fashion had France.

In 1958 the second Five-Year Plan was adopted of the 'Great Leap Forward'. Industrial output was to be multiplied 6.5 times and agricultural 2.5 times. This leap was based on self-help in the villages and the towns; on simple backyard furnaces to produce pig iron and the use of elementary cultural techniques adapted to the realities of China's technological backwardness and its enormous reserves of manpower; and on barefoot doctors using traditional peasant remedies instead of modern technological medicine, Soviet-style. This would end the alienation of the worker caused by industrialisation, in which the techniques of production entailed a managerial class and a proletariat.

The initial impact of the enormous shift of emphasis, to communes in the countryside, led to a decrease in production, which resulted in yet further efforts by the Chinese to free themselves from reliance upon Soviet technology. The new programme marked a tremendous divergence from the agreed norms for development which had been laid down in Moscow for all Soviet bloc countries; and it caused considerable intellectual as well as political shock in Moscow. The Chinese elaborated a theory of three types of Socialism – those proceeding quickly to Communism (China), those stuck at a Socialist stage (the Soviet Union), and those returning to capitalism (Yugoslavia). The Chinese detected in the USSR attempts to revert to the Yugoslav model, and used Russia's alleged benevolence towards Tito as proof of the decay of Soviet Socialism. These attacks on Russia were broadcast to the world.

The Great Leap Forward was based upon the harnessing of individual energies in small collectives. Although it had an economic rationale, because China had a large labour surplus and an acute shortage of capital goods, it was presented chiefly as an ideological step towards Communism. At the same time the commune idea became a central feature of the regime, with its members, in principle, living communally, sleeping in dormitories, eating in mess-halls, as in the most advanced kibbutzim in Israel, and abandoning all private property, while the children were cared for in crêches and schools.

Mao's experiment in agriculture was a major break with Russian experience. There was to be a giant leap forward to 'Communism', in the Marxist sense of from each according to his ability and to each according to his needs, by establishing the communes. By 1961, it was argued, the Chinese countryside would be a place of abundance of food and clothing, where the old pre-Communist habits of mind would have been eradicated. The communes were to be collectively governed, under the leadership of the Communist party, with a quasi-religious, semi-mystical sense of participation in the collectivity of the people. It was an act both of political and social advance from Stalinism, and also a once-for-all solution of the problem of agricultural production. In forty years the Soviet Union had failed on both counts; it had not achieved Communism in the Marxist sense, and its agricultural record was lamentable. So here were the two big Communist powers – one organising its agriculture like factories, and the other adopting a utopian rural ideal. This was accompanied by a renewal of the policy of industrialisation.

The Great Leap Forward marked the final collapse of Sino–Soviet relations. All Soviet technical advisers were withdrawn and many Soviet-financed industrial enterprises abandoned, often unfinished. In July 1959 Khruschev denounced the communes as ideologically naïve, and emphasised that each Communist country had to progress through all the stages that the Soviet Union had followed to achieve its economic, social and political levels of achievement. In practice, the extreme development of the commune rarely if ever happened, but it represented a major break with Russia's concept of collective farms. By mid 1959 it was clear, however, that the Great Leap Forward had not substantially increased industrial production, but had instead diverted urgently needed resources to what became a great failure, while the egalitarian excesses of the commune system probably caused output to fall. Certainly, with the onset of the great drought of 1960–2, the intensification of the commune programme stopped to enable people to work by traditional methods. The harnessing of local knowledge was regarded as important. In the event, agricultural output was sufficiently high to prevent any form of starvation.

In 1960, as the polemics between Khruschev and Mao intensified, as Russian experts were withdrawn from China and in
consequence much orthodox industrial production suffered severely, Mao was forced rapidly to develop Chinese science and
technology to such effect that by 1964 the first Chinese atom bomb
was exploded, and agricultural output had risen above the level
reached in 1959. But Mao's identification with the Great Leap
Forward and with the intensification of the commune had caused
dissension, and he resigned as President of the government,
although remaining Chairman of the Communist party. His position in the government was taken over by Liu Shao-chi, one of
those who advocated the strengthening of the orthodox path of
developing heavy industry. In August 1959 the Politburo met, and
Peng Te-huai, the War Minister, was expelled and imprisoned
because of his opposition to Mao's disputes with the Soviet Union.
Meanwhile Mao rebuilt his position as Chairman of the Communist party, strengthening it against the state apparatus. The theoretical point at issue was Mao's conviction that social change must
take place continually, while Liu was convinced that economic
development must take priority, even if it meant delaying certain
social changes. In Mao's view, this had led to the revisionism of
which he accused the Soviet Union, which he thought had relapsed
into a form of state capitalism, sacrificing the achievements of the
Socialist revolution. In particular, Mao disapproved strongly of the
creation of elites which in China would, he thought, lead to the
re-creation of a mandarin society. Consequently he was continually strengthening party power at the expense of the state.

As Sino–Soviet relations worsened, Khruschev sought some
accord with the West, while the Chinese attempted by force to
conquer some offshore islands remaining in Nationalist hands,
Qemoy and Matsu, which led to a threat of American naval
intervention. Chou En-lai and Khruschev toured the Third World
to draw support for their own camps.

In June 1960, at the Romanian Communist party's Third Congress, Khruschev reasserted the Soviet Union's leadership of the
Socialist world, and argued that peaceful coexistence was not just a
tactic, but created conditions in which the Socialist world would
strengthen itself and would lead to the collapse of capitalism.
Nationalist governments, for example, though not Socialist,
weaken imperialism, he asserted, and disarmament agreements
would limit capitalist militarism.

Relations between China and the Soviet Union were effectively
broken off in April 1960 when Mao refused to visit Moscow, and
Long Live Leninism was published, with its thesis that imperialism

was not in decay, but must be fought by wars of national liberation, in particular that nuclear weapons, however devastating, would not lead to the defeat of Communism, even if China lost 300 million. In China, Mao was deified, as an equal of Marx and Lenin; Soviet imperialism was denounced; and the idea of peaceful coexistence between the West and Socialist countries was declared impossible. In return, Russia accused China of deviationism, and of attempting to revive a Chinese imperial past that had been broken by over a century of foreign invasions.

Despite the collapse of the Soviet and Chinese alliance, China was a Marxist and totalitarian power. Its role in world affairs was bound to grow; in part, as an opponent of the Soviet Union it served Western interests, but its basic philosophy was a seductive one to the poorer nations, especially in Asia. It seemed that China had solved the problems of production and poverty in agriculture, that it had invented a system of self-help which eliminated dependence upon Western imperialism, and that it provided a model for Asian countries such as India that wished to be powerful and alleviate their poverty. Implicitly, then, China was a massive threat to liberal values in large parts of the world.

The grand coalitions that emerged in the 1950s, NATO on the one hand and the Warsaw Pact on the other, were more durable than the wartime alliance. It proved a mistake, however, to think of them as two monolithic blocs. In 1948 Tito proved that it was possible to leave the Soviet group, albeit in extreme circumstances and at great cost, and though his example was not followed by any other country, the years after Stalin's death showed a great loosening up of the Soviet sphere. Though none of the countries abandoned state Socialism and one-party authoritarian government, the worst of the excesses of purges stopped, and differences between countries emerged. The limits within which variation could occur were fairly strict, however, as the Hungarian rising in 1956 showed. The West was preoccupied with Suez, and consequently would in any case have been unable to intervene, even if it had been prepared to risk a world war to do so, but the Russians used as the pretext for their invasion the threat of Hungary's leaving the Eastern bloc and reverting to capitalism.

The Western alliance was far looser, and for that reason easier to break out of. France, for example, left NATO in 1958, and Cuba was to join forces with the Soviet Union. Moreover, the entire Third World started as colonies or client states of the Western powers and, for the most part, moved into opposition to Western aims. The creation of India, Pakistan and other newly independent nations was not without trauma, but it was brought about easily and with little opposition by the metropolitan powers, who in particular for the most part did not seek to control the foreign and defence policies of the successor states. The exceptions, like Algeria, stand out because they were exceptions, and in Algeria there were special reasons for the slowness of the realisation that a break had to be made. A million French people provided a major reason for France to seek to continue its control of Algeria. Elsewhere in Africa and Asia there were not such established colonies (in the original sense of the word).

There was thus a major difference between East and West in the attitude to weaker client states. The Soviet Union could not abandon its centralist and authoritarian policies without threatening the survival of Communism in the Soviet Union itself. Had free elections been even remotely possible not a single Communist regime would have survived. Stalin's legacy – indeed Lenin's legacy – was a regime that in essence was unalterable. Stalin's death was followed, however, by a thaw. The mere cessation of terror was itself a relief. The amazing stability and endurance of the Soviet Union cannot be understood without realising that though there was a thaw, the apparatus which had sustained the Terror survived – the secret police, the detailed control of people's lives, and the centralisation of authority in a society where freedom of expression was denied.

The liberal ideas of the West were encouraged by the outburst of prosperity that transformed the industrialised countries in the 1950s. Yet China, the world's oldest civilisation, set out on a Stalinist path, wilfully choosing, as it were, the less successful of the two model societies on offer. The brilliance of Mao's military victory and his direct confrontation with the Americans in Korea led to the adoption in China of his extreme philosophy. Yet, Stalinist though he was, he had not been Stalin's protégé, and the Soviet Union saw with regret, but not with great surprise, China's emergence as an autonomous centre of Marxist practice. The tenets of Lenin and Stalin did not allow for a bipolar world. The conflict between Russia and China was written in the stars.

The 1950s, then, began with the confrontation between two armed camps. That conflict remained. But each camp lost supporters: the West, as its colonies drifted into neutralism, non-alignment and, eventually, in Cuba's case, Communism; whilst the Soviet camp began to break up and, eventually, China seceded. The 1950s gave way to a more complex period. Yet the 1960s early on saw the most dramatic confrontation between Russia and America, over Cuba, which led to the very edge of nuclear war.

PART THREE

Progress

Chapter 20

Technological and economic growth: a gale of creation

Everybody knows that it is science and technology that has changed the world in the past eighty years. The application of the rationalist mind to nature and society which began tentatively in the thirteenth and fourteenth centuries became widespread in the nineteenth century and universal in this. Steam, electricity, oil, the internal combustion engine, aircraft, the computer, the radio, above all the pill and the injection have made the world one; after all a civilisation is a society that uses the same things. They have subjected society after society to the same stresses and strains of change, as well as enabling them to reap the benefits of material and intellectual improvement.

Despite the spread of authoritarian and specifically Marxist authoritarian rule, the consequence of the scientific and technological revolution has been a diminution of ignorance and a spread of informed inquisitiveness about the natural world.

Marxism is one of the consequences of the scientific revolution, since it is an attempt to understand the world scientifically; though by the canons of natural science it is an aberration, a heresy. Nevertheless, Marxism was one of the means by which the scientific and technological revolution was carried to new countries.

Capitalism carried itself forward by what Schumpeter called 'gales of creative destruction'; after a destructive and disruptive war an apparent miracle took place. Capitalism was not artefacts, but ideas.

By 1950, compared with pre-war, output had increased in the United Kingdom and France by one-tenth, in Ireland by one-fifth, in the Netherlands, in Denmark and in Norway by slightly less than a third, in Finland by a quarter, in West Germany by one-sixth, in Italy by one-fifteenth, in Austria by one-twenty-fifth and in Switzerland by a quarter; while in Sweden and in the United States it had increased by two-thirds, in Canada by four-fifths, in Australia by three-quarters. Output had doubled in Mexico and increased in Argentina by a half, in Brazil by two-thirds and by one-tenth or so in mainland China. In Greece it reached approximately the pre-war level, but in East Germany it was only three-quarters.

Had Europe not recovered so swiftly, then it would indeed have seemed that capitalism was over, had run out of steam, and the American experience would have been its sole monument. As it was, the great burst of American prosperity that came with the war continued, and was soon being perceptibly emulated by the Europeans; Europe was, therefore, restored to its former position as a twin pillar of prosperity and technological innovation.

The beginning of the great post-war boom was associated with exceptionally high economic growth rates, especially in those countries where there was a shift out of low-productivity agriculture into manufacturing industry – Italy, then Spain, Yugoslavia and Greece, and subsequently Japan and other Far Eastern countries such as Korea, Taiwan and Singapore. In a burst of agricultural innovation, new plant strains, improved fertiliser and pest control (including herbicides) doubled, tripled and in some cases quintupled the yield of grain crops, whilst machinery rapidly diminished the demand for labour. Thus in the developed non-Communist world and an increasingly large part of the Third World agricultural abundance became the norm. Hunger, even famine, was confined to a declining, though still important, group of really poor countries. The surplus of labour thus generated flocked into manufacturing where productivity also rose because of heavy investment in plant and machinery, and the development of new products.

The substantial growth of economic activity in the former colonial countries, too, led to what the great economist Simon Kuznets calls an increased 'capacity to generate economic growth and to make decisions regarding nonpolitical ties with the metropolitan country'.

At the same time the war gave large areas of the world to the Communists, who adopted economic organisation that led to substantial industrial growth, even though agricultural output remained at an extremely low level. As Kuznets says, 'Given the capacity of Communist rule to mobilize the energy to build up economic power, although at great sacrifice and with considerable waste, and the Hobson's choice offered by the Nazis to the Soviet people' it was almost axiomatic that industrial recovery and growth took place, though agriculture never recovered from Stalin's policy of collectivisation.

Paradoxically the end of imperialism coincided with the creation of international economic and technological order, which united the non-Communist world in an upward swing of prosperity that managed to overtake, in most cases, one of the consequences of its own success – the population explosion.

Twentieth-century innovators in physics and biology gave the opportunity for unprecedented changes in two fields – war and medicine. War acted as a catalyst for atomic energy and atomic weapons. The basic advances in nuclear physics had taken place in Cambridge and Copenhagen in the 1930s; just after the outbreak of war it became apparent that it was possible to use the energy released by nuclear fission in a controlled manner to create a bomb. In less than five years a workable bomb had been invented and tested. The harnessing of energy for peaceful purposes followed, though this took significantly longer to apply. By 1970, something like one tenth of electricity supplies in the United Kingdom and the United States was being generated from atomic power stations. But it was nuclear weapons which offered literally unrivalled opportunities for destruction and threatened the survival of life itself.

Technological advances were also taking place in other fields, innovations that came, without exception, from the capitalist countries. A characteristic example was the jet engine developed in Britain by Frank Whittle, which came into use at the end of the Second World War for fighter aircraft. The jet engine was also the basis of the rocket technology which fuelled the V1 pilotless missiles that the Germans began to use by 1944 soon after the invasion of France by the allies. Developed fundamentally as a means of speeding up aircraft, it reduced the journey across the Atlantic, for example, from twelve to six hours during the 1950s.

The most spectacular technological development was the conquest of space. This effectively began with the V2, the German missile at the end of the war which was fired by a rocket motor. Werner von Braun, the chief scientist in charge of this mission, went to the United States with his team, while other German scientists and engineers were captured and set to work by the Russians. Following the initial Russian space orbit of Sputnik, in 1957, the United States put a substantial effort into its space aviation programme, and a subsequent series of launches during the 1960s culminated with the landing on the Moon, followed by a series of space shots going to the outer planets.

The space race was not, however, merely for the greater glory of mankind. The necessary technology enabled the development of a profusion of intercontinental ballistic missile systems which rendered the entire world open to almost instantaneous nuclear attack. Even without nuclear weapons, the destructive force of explosives already well known would have been of great significance, but the fact that they required more effort to construct than nuclear weapons would probably have favoured the USSR, with its slave labour.

Spinoffs from the defence effort supported the long-term economic boom, the most significant innovation being the great acceleration in the rate of discovery of computer technology. Twenty years after the first computers came into operation at the end of the war, their power had been transformed to speed up computations that brought further advances in science. But more important, the programming of hitherto unachievably complex decision-making – for instance the control of military technology of all kinds – as well as the programming of industrial and commercial processes, became possible for the first time. As a result of these developments only two powers could mount the 'ultimate' military effort – the USSR and the United States. But, as change occurred in other branches of the economy, so different countries emerged as economic giants – Japan and Germany – whilst others, like Britain, lagged behind.

The technology of space involved the use of enormously strong, lightweight materials and the micro-processor. These accelerated in their turn the developments which were already taking place in communications. Radio had been a significant advance in the First World War, and it was an essential tool of all the armed forces in the Second World War. The development of radio systems throughout the world, accompanied by the transformation of the telephone system, was accelerated by the invention of the transistor, which enabled small portable radio sets to be manufactured and made available throughout the world, including some of the most remote and poor areas.

But radio paled when compared to the rise of television, which had been invented in the United Kingdom before the war by John Logie Baird, and was then rapidly developed after the war primarily for entertainment and news purposes. Thus from the 1950s television became the normal means of communication in the industrialised countries, a revolution greater even than popular newspapers and the use of radio for news and entertainment. With the development of artificial satellites in the 1960s, world-wide television became possible, so that by the end of the 1960s its use was also widespread in the Third World countries.

Several consequences of all this development stand out. Advanced economies like Germany, Japan and America jumped ahead, followed by those like Taiwan and Hong Kong, that adopted the new technology. And, increasingly, the world was unified by the use of these artefacts.

Long-distance travel changed out of hand as aircraft took the place of passenger ships. The cost of air travel steadily fell in real terms as larger and faster airliners took to the air. Passenger ships,

Luton Sixth Form Col
Library

except on very short sea routes, became uneconomic, and the massive arrival of air travel itself caused fundamental social change, making foreign holidays feasible for the newly affluent population of Western Europe and their more established cousins in North America. Migration, no matter the distance, also became much easier and more feasible; hence the arrival of substantial numbers of West Indian and Asian immigrants in the United Kingdom. Thus the acceleration of technological change led to major social change. Hitherto migration had been from Europe to America, Australia and Africa. Now the flows became more complex. The 1950s and 1960s saw some of the biggest migrations in history, from East Germany to the West, from the fringes of Europe to Germany, from Southern Italy to Northern Italy, from the Southern United States to the North. Above all, however, and cumulatively, the cost-reducing consequences of innumerable innovations played a major part in the development of the great industrial and consumer boom which dominated the post-war era until the early 1970s. Particularly important was the spread of the car, a consumer durable that became almost universal among families in North America, large parts of Western Europe, and in the urban areas of many other countries, which led to the enormous growth in the demand for oil. The huge rate of increase in output of basic materials to be used in the industrial processes substantially increased the volume of world trade. Those countries that exported raw materials prospered; and markets were in turn created for industrial products.

Major new products depended upon steel, newly-usable metals, upon chemistry and plastics: these new lightweight, heat-resistant materials led to further developments in areas as diverse as clothing and packaging. The result was not only a series of changes in textiles and consumer goods, but above all in the processes of other industries, for example electricity transmission and medicine. The old industrial centres declined and new regions emerged, especially in the Pacific from California to Japan and Singapore, and also around Dusseldorf in Europe.

The plastics industry was based on derivatives of oil, and it was oil which was the great fuel of the age. The internal combustion engine, the basis of the motor car, the truck, the bus and engines large and small, marked the most significant increase in the use of energy available to man since the steam engine. Steam created the basis of modern civilisation, but what caused that civilisation to knit together was electricity – generated originally from coal and then from oil – before oil came to fuel the great transport explosion.

The geopolitical consequences of the dependence upon oil were of fundamental importance in the new world power balance, for an oil-based economy made America and Europe dependent upon the Arab states for their basic fuel; and this resource had a limited life – in a couple of generations it would run out.

Meanwhile massive innovation was transforming medicine and agriculture. The basic infectious diseases were conquered, both by immunisation and by substantial therapeutic programmes, and surgery was revolutionised by modern anaesthetics.

The scientific and technological revolution grew from the enormous burgeoning of education which was one of the major phenomena of the post-war period. In North America, the universal secondary education provision to the age of sixteen was boosted at the end of the war by the GI Bill of Rights, which gave most veterans free access to universities and colleges. This snowballed into an enormous higher-education boom, culminating in the late 1960s with something like 80 per cent of high school graduates proceeding to some form of college. The European countries followed the same cycle a generation later, beginning with the universalisation of secondary education in France and Sweden, and a little later in the United Kingdom, culminating in the raising of the school leaving age to sixteen in 1973. The Third World in the meantime went through the primary-school revolution. Thus the rate of growth of world education at all levels was phenomenal, and more than matched the explosion in population. The newly literate peoples became politically conscious as colonialism ended.

World population had been rising noticeably since the beginning of the Industrial Revolution, but it was not until after the Second World War that the numbers soared. Better health care was chiefly responsible as improved feeding and rising standards of hygiene substantially reduced infant mortality rates throughout the world, and increased the survival rate of adults. This required no great technological breakthrough, just better food and more education. As one other immediate result the upward movement of the population graph accelerated, only to be followed by a decline in the birthrate in the more prosperous countries. No such decline took place in the poorer countries, thereby causing a shift in the balance of world population – one of the most fundamental trends in the period – and the growing pressure of population on resources in Asia, and in some parts of Africa and Latin America, was a source of instability and of anti-imperialist feelings, arguments and measures.

Nevertheless as a result of the rise in output in the advanced countries, by the later 1950s the weight of the world, measured in economic terms, had shifted dramatically towards the United States and Western Europe. In 1958 total world output was estimated at $1,075 billion. Of this, $436 billion was generated in the United States and Canada, $145 billion in Northern and Western Europe, $85 billion in the rest of Europe, $14 billion in Australia and New Zealand, and $36 billion in Japan, making a total of $716 billion for the non-Communist developed countries. The USSR had $144 billion, Eastern Europe $68 billion, China $46 billion, and the rest of Asia $1 billion, making a total of $259 billion for the Communist countries. In the less developed countries, the less developed European countries had $14 billion, Asia $30 billion, India $27 billion, Africa $27 billion, making a total of $175 billion. The United States therefore had over a third of total world output, while the USSR, with roughly the same population, had only about 12½ per cent. The non-Communist developed world produced over two thirds of world output. The position ten years before, in 1948, was even more heavily weighted in the direction of the non-Communist world, and by 1968 the balance was once more even more heavily in the direction of the prosperous West. This imbalance was in itself a source of instability. Far from Communism 'burying' capitalism by its own success, as Khruschev had threatened, the West swamped the world.

Change was not just economic and technological. Social change was based upon education, and upon more fundamental attitudes to race, sex and class.

The urge towards equality, which had been endemic in Western liberal optimism, was far more realistic as an objective in an era of technological abundance. The commitment to racial equality became a major factor in the United States, but elsewhere it fuelled xenophobic nationalism – the Asians were expelled from Uganda, the whites fled from Algeria – and it led to the black-Asian power bloc in the United Nations. Similarly, attacking the bourgeoisie was adopted as part of the litany of bastardised Marxism, quickly turning into an attack on 'imperialism'.

It became popular to argue that technical progress and the consequent affluence would lead to more equality and to a growing convergence of different social systems. But this was emphatically not the experience of the years after 1950, quite the reverse. The distances in income between rich and poor are greatest in countries with poor agricultural sectors – the Soviet Union and many Third World countries – and privilege is most deeply entrenched in tyrannies. Social mobility is greatest in Western Europe, paradoxically and specifically the United Kingdom.

The Communist world did not achieve affluence, though in the

towns certain basic amenities – education, rather poor health
care, crowded housing, poor food, sports facilities, public transport – were widely available. This was partly because centrally
planned command economies are less efficient than market economies and partly because the effort of the Soviet Union and its
allied countries was devoted overwhelmingly to defence and to
internal security. By contrast, the seemingly ever-growing wealth
of the market economies, which spilled over to many of the Third
World countries, was accompanied by what the Soviet Union had
sought to achieve: growing social homogeneity, and equality in
race, sex and class. The richer a country the more equal its income
distribution tends to be.

Yet the propaganda, which became received opinion, asserted
exactly the opposite. It was the lineal descendant of the argument
that capitalism inevitably widened the gap between the
bourgeoisie and the proletariat, as exploitation developed, and
that the system would collapse through the poverty (the 'immis-
erisation') of the proletariat. The nineteenth century disproved
Marx, as the living standards of the working class steadily rose with
industrialisation – even though the size of the population grew
rapidly.

The persistent hope of Marxists that the final crisis of capitalism
had come – the slump of the 1930s, the Second World War, the
post-war economic collapse, and the economic difficulties which
began with the oil price rise of 1973 – all these were seen as the
final crisis. But each such capitalist 'crisis' coincided with a crisis in
Communist countries – the famine in the Ukraine, the war, the
Stalin post-war persecution, and the growing economic failure of
the Eastern bloc countries in the 1970s. Nor did Communist
countries have any golden age of prosperity like that of the 1950s
and 1960s in the West.

The technological revolution coincided, then, with vastly increased prosperity and a general reduction of social distance, or
growing equality, within the West. But it did not lead in any sense
to a growing together of the Marxist and non-Marxist worlds.

Chapter 21

Nuclear weapons

Technological advance had created prosperity but it also increased the possibilities of utter destruction. The emergence by the mid 1950s of new nuclear powers, France and China, upset the polarity that had been maintained from 1945. The race between the super-powers (as Russia and America were now known) for leadership in armaments took the form of ever more complex weapons systems (based upon nuclear energy) and missiles, from which stemmed the space race.

After the United States lost its absolute nuclear dominance in the early 1950s, a dual nuclear threat existed, from both America and Russia, and the hope for peace rested ultimately either upon a nuclear stalemate or the negotiation of an agreement between the two sides. The West's policy of containing Soviet aggression, which evolved in 1948, was replaced by a threat of nuclear assault from United States air bases maintained in a perimeter round the Soviet Union. This set a premium upon high-altitude, high-speed, long-distance bombers and missiles.

The wars that were fought in the Middle East in 1948 and the rearmament which began in 1948 were largely dominated by weapons which had been in use in the Second World War, though the Americans were rapidly developing high-altitude long-range bombers, as were the British, and a missile capability. The crucial concept in the American thinking was that the capability of delivering nuclear missiles on Russia counterbalanced the numerical superiority of the Soviet conventional forces.

Nuclear strategy, at this stage, stemmed from the Second World War, when the Germans had bombed the countries which they subsequently occupied, as well as the United Kingdom. The United Kingdom had begun retaliating by bombing 'strategic' targets in Germany, but as they were only able to bomb by night, and as the accuracy of the bombing was low – bombs often falling five miles or more from the target – the RAF turned to saturation bombing of industrial and other cities. This eventually became a form of retaliation for the bombing of Britain, which in turn led to indiscriminate bombardment by the German missiles, the V1s and the V2s. The Americans, having begun with more precision in daylight raids, also succumbed to the temptation to go in for mass bombing of German cities, and when their bombers were able to fly sufficient distances, mass bombing of Japanese cities, culminating in the destruction of Nagasaki and Hiroshima by the atom bomb.

Consequently between 1945 and Korea, the American tactics for the long-distance bombing of the Soviet Union were to send bombers first to industrial targets, then to transport links such as railways and road bridges to slow down the Soviet forces and finally to the bases of the Soviet air force; the primary threat, clearly, was the destruction of Russia's industrial cities, including Leningrad and Moscow.

The American nuclear deterrent rested upon overseas bases which were within striking distance of the Soviet Union. The Soviet Union was not within striking distance of the United States, but it could have destroyed the bases overseas, and it was possible that even with its early missile technology it could have hit the continental United States.

By October 1953 tactical nuclear weapons were already in position in West Germany, and in 1954 the United States Congress amended the Atomic Energy Act to permit America's allies to use American nuclear technology. The British had already developed their bomb, between 1949 and 1952, followed by the French in 1960. Nuclear proliferation was at hand.

As nuclear stockpiles of East and West increased and were diversified, the possibility of an almost accidental nuclear war became increasingly worrying. Worse still were the dangers of proliferating nuclear weapons to more and more states which would use them for localised conflicts, dangerous enough in themselves, but entailing the possibility of wider conflict through their alliances or assumed alliances. Supposing, for example, that Britain had used an atomic weapon in Egypt in 1956; the Soviet Union might have considered it was doing so with the connivance of the United States, and a world war might have been precipitated.

By 1954 NATO's strategy was firmly based on atomic weapons, as the Supreme Commander, General Gruenther, stated that year: 'Our strategy . . . requires the use of atomic weapons, whether the enemy uses them or not.' Field Marshal Montgomery, his deputy, added, that 'We at SHAPE are basing all our operational planning on using atomic and thermonuclear weapons in our own defence.' This strategy was however already outdated: the hydrogen bomb test on Eniwetok Atoll in the Pacific on 1 November 1952 had completely destroyed a mile-long island, and had been followed in August 1953 in the Soviet Union by the explosion of several more advanced hydrogen bombs than those held by the Americans. The contamination of some Japanese fishermen in the Pacific in March

1954 made it clear that the use of atomic devices would probably be fatal to humanity itself; and the development of Soviet long-range bombers made all parts of the United States vulnerable to nuclear attack.

In this context, while the United States could conceive of tactical nuclear weapons being used in a European war, but hoped for agreement that long-range missiles would not be used by the US and the Soviet Union against each other, for Europeans this clearly involved nuclear destruction for allegedly tactical reasons. No wonder that a split developed between the European members of NATO and the Americans. It also became clear that tactical nuclear weapons, far from economising in the use of conventional forces, actually required more (through greater casualties and complex logistics), and that nuclear weapons were in fact part of the steady growth in the cost of war to which technological progress contributed.

With the development of much faster and high-flying long-range bombers the invulnerability of the continental United States was rapidly disappearing, and with the launching of Sputnik in 1957 the development of Soviet missile technology demonstrated that the United States was clearly within range. In the thesis of nuclear war at that stage the existence of vulnerable nuclear forces held by both the United States and the Soviet Union gave a premium on the first power to strike, and therefore destroy the strategic forces of the other. The first-strike theory held for some time, but it was followed by the realisation that unless all enemy nuclear missiles were destroyed, almost instantaneous nuclear retaliation would be inevitable. Thus in a new thesis the balance of destruction was now considered crucial; a loss of forty million Russians would be offset by the deaths of twenty million Americans, and in such circumstances the Americans would be held to have 'won'. The horrific nature of this concept, and the cost of the forces entailed by it, caused a revulsion in societies which were free to express such revulsion.

In Europe strong pressures developed for unilateral disarmament, and for the neutralisation of Europe, a course favoured in the Soviet Union and strongly sustained by its propaganda. In Britain and France, the capability to threaten independently the Soviet Union with nuclear retaliation was used to encourage Soviet and American missiles to bypass Britain and France. World-wide demands grew for disarmament by both the USA and the USSR as a recognition of the stalemate. The almost unthinkable calamity of a nuclear war, once thought about, led to a diminution of defence effort since, eventually, it seemed hardly worth while defending

Europe against the Russians if the result were complete devastation.

In 1957 British defence policy was realigned, with a reduction in expenditure on conventional defence, the abolition of conscription, and a greater reliance upon the nuclear deterrent. In the course of this review the armed forces were to a great degree integrated, and a primary role was assigned to the Royal Air Force as the nuclear strike force. Yet it was appreciated that the nuclear weapon could not be used. As Montgomery said, 'When both sides have nuclear sufficiency, the deterrent will merely serve to deter each side from using it as a weapon.' This of course left the nuclear force as a threat, particularly against non-nuclear powers, but even this threat was never used.

The distinction between tactical and strategic use of nuclear weapons was soon seen as narrow, especially for countries such as Belgium, which would be entirely devastated by tactical weapons, or for Britain which might lose the whole of London or Birmingham in a 'limited strike'. From 1957, too, with the launch of Sputnik, it was clear that the whole world was vulnerable to missile attack, and that the missiles could carry nuclear weapons. Initially, however, NATO strategists were not fully aware of the implications, being concerned instead with the 'missile gap' and that the Soviet Union appeared to have far more, and far more effective, missiles than the United States. It was this missile gap, subsequently discovered to be largely imaginary, which John F. Kennedy used in his 1960 Presidential campaign against Richard Nixon, accusing Eisenhower of leaving the United States dangerously under-defended.

This was to lead Kennedy, once elected, to accelerate the space programme, and in 1963 to the test-ban treaty which forbade atmospheric testing of nuclear weapons – a treaty to which neither the French nor the Chinese adhered – but which drove future Soviet and American tests underground. The Strategic Arms Limitation Treaty of 1972 was designed to lead to a banning of the development of launchers of ballistic missiles. Therefore by the mid 1960s the problem, clearly, was not closing the gap between the United States and the Soviet Union, but rather of trying to limit the arms race altogether. Up to Kennedy's election, however, it was the missile gap hypothesis that prevailed.

While this summit diplomacy between the superpowers rumbled on, the French withdrew from an active role in NATO and the Chinese widened their split with the USSR. The nuclear bombs exploded by the French in tests in the Sahara in 1960 were under their exclusive control, and as de Gaulle declined to have American anti-ballistic nuclear missiles on French soil, the headquarters of NATO was transferred from Paris to Brussels.

In the United States a system of continental air defence, requiring a wide range of air, missile and civil defences, began to be constructed under the Eisenhower Presidency. As it was still not possible to use atomic weapons in limited situations for battlefield targets, the defence of Western Europe depended, ultimately, upon the capacity of the United States, and to a lesser extent of the United Kingdom, to deliver atomic weapons on Soviet cities.

As the development of the hydrogen bomb made it possible to destroy entire countries, it became quite clear that however strong the anti-nuclear missile defences, even if only one or two missile bombers got through with hydrogen bombs, the number of dead would be dramatic. By the late 1950s the United States had about five hundred B-52 long-range bombers, about fifteen hundred B-47 and RB-47 medium-range bombers and seven hundred medium-range missiles. At the same time the explosive capacity of United States nuclear weapons had increased twentyfold in six years, which meant that over half the Soviet Union's cities and towns could be destroyed. Thus it was impossible to argue any longer that the purpose of nuclear war was to attack the strategic installations of the enemy, but was nothing less than the total destruction of the enemy. The only United States deterrent, therefore, to a whole series of possible Soviet threats was a complete and crushing blow against the Soviet Union. This was the Strategic Air Command (SAC) doctrine developed by General Curtis Le May. The logic of Second World War thinking had reached its ultimate conclusion.

In the late 1950s the development of the Polaris submarine fleet, with its ability to launch nuclear missiles at the Soviet Union, meant that the offensive capacity of the United States would not be affected by the destruction of the United States itself. According to American strategic thinking this would stimulate the Soviet Union to spend more on nuclear weapons, at the expense of conventional forces. At the same time, if the United States concentrated on building Polaris and similar offensive capabilities which could not easily be destroyed by a Soviet first strike, it would be possible for the United States to develop its conventional forces, particularly the aircraft carriers and the army, which would enable them to fight limited wars without resort to nuclear terror.

Another theory, one of controlled response, supposed that the first attacks on the Soviet Union would be entirely outside the urban areas, to demonstrate America's power, and so alarm the Russians that they would make a controlled response by similarly bombing empty areas in America. This implied that the first strike would not inevitably tempt the Soviet Union to escalate the conflict immediately by the destruction of United States cities. Here was a return to the original idea of war, that major civilian targets would be left unharmed, as they were worth capturing and preserving, and that the destruction would concentrate on the armed forces. But if the civilians were destroyed then the war itself would either have no purpose or become an end in itself. And that, it was thought, was illogical.

Thus, after Khruschev took power, it was clear that a balance of terror existed in which both the Soviet Union and the United States had the capacity to destroy each other. At the same time both countries were developing large conventional forces which were capable of waging limited conventional wars. The Kennedy administration strengthened deterrence by having a more credible nuclear deterrent as well as more limited non-nuclear deterrents for smaller provocations. It was argued that this would give an alternative between suicide and surrender.

Less than two decades after the end of the Second World War, therefore, the Soviet Union and the United States both possessed the capacity largely to destroy the major cities of their enemies or of third parties. The material civilisation which had enabled the technological advances to take place had created the possibility of utter destruction. It was a far cry from the peace with security and freedom from fear of war which the United Nations Charter laid down.

Chapter 22

Non-aligned and Third World nations

The failure of the United Nations to achieve anything like the role envisaged for it by romantic, liberal optimists at the San Francisco conference in 1945 could hardly have been more self-evident. By 1947 it had become a forum for confrontation between the Soviet Union and the West. Having been designed to be powerless when the great powers were in conflict, as a positive peace-keeping institution its role was minimal. The accident of the Soviet boycott of the UN after its refusal to seat Mao's China had enabled the United States and its allies to wage the war in Korea under the guise of United Nations forces, but once the Soviet Union returned to the United Nations, conscious of the serious error of its withdrawal, all further votes of this kind were blocked. Moreover they gained a deep distrust of the Secretary General, Trygve Lie, a Norwegian whose reappointment by the Security Council they vetoed. Thereafter he was re-elected by the General Assembly. This was a departure from the original concept of the charter and further weakened the authority of the United Nations.

Meanwhile the McCarthy committee of the United States Senate, seeking Communists in the State Department and other parts of the American government, turned its attention to the UN and its agencies. Lie inevitably sought to defend his staff. Thus, when Lie retired in 1952, both the United States and the Soviet Union distrusted the United Nations. Any attempt by the UN to become less obviously dominated by the Americans increased Washington's distrust.

In March 1953 Dag Hammarskjöld, a senior official of the Swedish Foreign Ministry and son of a former Prime Minister of Sweden, succeeded Trygve Lie as Secretary General. The Russians had been pressing for the Secretary General to be replaced by a troika of three Secretaries General appointed by the three big powers, who could only proceed by a rule of unanimity. The decision to support Hammarskjöld, therefore, was a surprise, apparently representing some slight degree of Soviet moderation. When Stalin died, therefore, the UN became a forum where Soviet efforts towards softening the Cold War could be seen. But, far more significant, the rapid arrival, too, of substantial numbers of Third World delegates, and the emergence of the non-aligned states as a positive force in world politics, made the UN once more a centre for active diplomacy, especially as every nation kept a permanent delegation in New York, often of senior career diplomatists who were in continuous contact with each other.

The first of the Third World countries to emerge was India. Prime Minister Nehru distanced himself from both East and West blocs, even though India remained a member of the Commonwealth and closely tied to the United Kingdom, and received substantial aid from the United States. India was soon joined by Yugoslavia following Tito's break with Stalin which created another country of Socialist inclinations aligned neither with the Soviet Union nor with the West. The emergence of Nasser as Egypt's leader created a third country in this so-called non-aligned camp, and there were others such as Burma and Ethiopia which felt that they were outside the orbit of what had become conventional Western or Eastern blocs.

Haile Selassie, Emperor of Ethiopia, visited Yugoslavia in 1954, and Tito paid a return visit to Ethiopia a few months later. The following year, at a conference at Bandung in Indonesia, Nehru, Tito and Nasser formulated the non-aligned principles of the Asian and African governments. They condemned colonialism, emphasised the importance of peaceful co-existence and of further international co-operation, and the strengthening of the United Nations. In a fascinating paradox, they all embraced some form of centralised planning and the ideology of Socialism whilst dependent upon American aid and military support.

Tito organised a further meeting at Brioni in Yugoslavia in 1955 with President Nasser and Prime Minister Nehru, and this non-aligned group thereafter became a powerful influence in the United Nations, as more and more countries became independent. With its emphasis chiefly upon anti-colonialism and the promotion of Socialism, its vote, therefore, often supported Soviet bloc motions, such as on Algeria and on the intervention in Suez. Indeed it was argued that Tito was, in his foreign policy, aligning himself closely with the Soviet Union in order to mend his fences, and that the non-aligned group was in reality nothing more nor less than a Soviet front. It is, however, worth noting that the development of anti-imperialism and the argument against neo-colonialism implicit in much Western aid, and its use to bolster centralised planning and large projects, was a powerful force in the Third World. It was a cause to which the Soviet Union may have lent its support rather than orchestrating the campaign, which its ideology certainly did not envisage.

Faced with these three blocs, the NATO countries, the Soviet countries, and the non-aligned states, Hammarskjöld concentrated on trying to build the UN into an effective, international and neutral administration, by trying to create a body of staff-members who were of high quality and dedicated to the UN ideals and policies. Unless one has experienced an international organisation, it is almost impossible to imagine its complexity, with its diverse administrative styles, the political pressures from diplomats, the blatant careerism of people from poor countries seeking high tax-free salaries and security in New York, Paris or Geneva, and the naked corruption, all clothed in a miserable rhetoric of empty pro-Communist platitudes about racialism and colonialism. In view of the tremendous pressures on Hammarskjöld, it was astonishing that he was so successful.

The early months of his term of office were marked by the truce in the Korean War negotiated by Eisenhower and the lowering of tension following the succession of Khruschev. The US intervened in Guatemala in 1954, maintained a stern position against Communist China, and was tough in its line at the Geneva peace negotiations on Indochina. As Hammarskjöld appeared to be less than enthusiastic about Dulles' position, the UN began to be widely perceived as neutralist and even anti-American. Its role as a focus of anti-Western propaganda and resolutions was well established by the mid 1950s. In defiance of the Americans, Hammarskjöld was the first Western world leader to make official and personal contact with China, through Chou En-lai, and he was much impressed; eventually such meetings were to lead to the entry of China into full contact with the West, especially after the Sino–Soviet split. But Hammarskjöld faced a major crisis when Egypt was invaded by the British, French and Israelis.

To the club of non-aligned nations, of which Egypt was a senior member, the United Nations was rapidly becoming identified as the forum where they could present their anti-colonialist case; sixteen new members were admitted in 1955, mostly from Europe, but they were followed by a flood of Asian and African countries. The initial debates at the UN in the later 1940s between Vishinsky and Gladwyn Jebb, on the evils of Communist aggression, were now replaced by diatribes against colonialism and racialism from the Third World and Communist delegates.

In this context, therefore, the British refused to take the Egyptian occupation of the Canal to the UN, since it was clear that the UN majority would support the Egyptians. The non-aligned nations and Russia were eager to take the issue to the UN. With a show of neutrality, the UN's first posture was one of fact-finding: a mission was sent to the Middle East to survey the Arab–Israeli armistice agreements, which had followed the 1948 war. These had been supervised by a small UN force, whose activities had been increasingly circumscribed as tensions built up in the Middle East. As the Suez crisis deepened, the British and French asked for the Security Council to be convened to examine the question of an international board to supervise the Canal. The expected failure of the Security Council to agree to the proposal was to be the basis for unilateral action. In the event, after Egyptian concessions, the original motion was pressed and vetoed by the USSR. In the British view this proved the impotence of the UN in a position which was a 'danger to peace', and left them free to act in self-defence of their interests. At this stage Britain still counted as a great power; and the Suez situation showed that the UN was impotent in any matter that affected a great power.

The Suez crisis became indissolubly linked at the UN with the Soviet invasion of Hungary which began the same week. The US produced a motion of censure on Britain and its allies in the Security Council and Yugoslavia (under the unity for peace procedure devised to cope with Korea and to bypass the Security Council) moved for an emergency session of the General Assembly. The Security Council motion was vetoed by Britain and France, but on 2 November 1956 the General Assembly adopted a motion calling for a cease-fire; Hammarskjöld helped to negotiate the cease-fire and arranged with the government of Canada for a UN force to be sent to police it.

A United Nations Emergency Force, of troops from Canada, Colombia, Denmark, Finland and Sweden, under the command of the Canadian General Burns, arrived on 13 November, only eight days after being invented – a remarkable exercise, especially as it had taken ten weeks for British troops to get to Suez for the invasion. The UN force remained in the area for eleven years; and the US, in a remarkable volte-face, attributed the rapidity of the cease-fire negotiations to Hammarskjöld, having previously been bitterly opposed to him. The speed of the British withdrawal, however, was largely determined by the economic crisis precipitated by the United States failure to support British foreign policy.

In the parallel case of the invasion of Hungary by the Soviet Union, the General Assembly passed a motion of condemnation, but no more. By the time the resolution was adopted, the Russians had installed the Kadar government in Budapest, which requested that Hungary be taken off the UN agenda. That Hammarskjöld did not persist illustrated, admirably, the double standards of the UN and the Third World countries.

From the time of Hammarskjöld's re-election, in late 1957, for a second five-year term, he relied more and more upon the uncommitted and smaller countries – especially Canada, Ireland, Tunisia and Poland – for his majority, and consequently for the tasks of international policy formation. This coincided with the rapid growth in the number of member states and the consequent shift of opinion in the UN towards Third World questions and Third World concerns. As the UN itself became increasingly anti-Western, so the struggle between the United States and the Soviet Union shifted increasingly from Europe to one of influence in the Third World.

Hammarskjöld was a product of Scandinavian high-mindedness, a depressed and ambitious man given to quasi-poetic mystic musings on life, death and peace. He had great delusions about his mission to humanity, to bring peace and prosperity through a secular church. In the process of developing a 'UN presence', however, he offended both Russia, in the person of Khruschev, and France, in the person of de Gaulle, and would have offended America had the Americans not been by this time punch-drunk from sneers and attacks by their client states. Partly in consequence most initiatives in what was to be called détente took place outside the UN: disarmament and the nuclear test-ban treaty became bilateral or multilateral conferences with only the relevant states participating in them. The UN was therefore confined to what were essentially minor disputes between minor powers. These minor conflicts were liable of course to become matters of great significance.

Such an issue was the Congo. In 1960, when Belgium decided to evacuate its African colony, the Belgian Congo, little or no preparations had been made for its native population to take responsibility. Education in the Congo had been minimal and it was one of the African states least ready for independence. Hammarskjöld had deeply involved himself in African affairs and had liberally offered UN assistance to many of the new states. In so doing he aroused expectations which could hardly be met, and not by a small and relatively impoverished body such as the UN. The Congo, as Belgium's only colony, was not able to benefit, as were the French and British possessions, from wide experience by the imperial country in the process of handing over power. Moreover the Belgians in the Congo, especially in the copper-rich province of Katanga, were deeply hostile to the idea of independence, freely prophesying bloody chaos after the handover – prophecies which proved correct. The civil service, the army officers and virtually the entire school-teacher class consisted of white Belgians.

Patrice Lumumba, who became Prime Minister of the new state in June 1960, was determined to govern with as little Belgian aid as possible. The army was soon in revolt against its Belgian officers, and Belgian troops had to intervene to protect white civilians. The Congo Cabinet, led by President Kasabuvu and Prime Minister Lumumba, asked for UN military assistance. Meanwhile the province of Katanga, headed by Moise Tshombe, declared its independence, with the support, it was assumed, of the Union Minière, the Belgian-controlled copper company. When Belgian troops were sent to Elizabethville, capital of Katanga, to protect the whites, this was interpreted as Belgian support for Katanga; they also occupied the airport and European quarters of Leopold-ville, the Congolese capital, and this led to a Congolese demand for UN intervention.

On his own authority, Hammarskjöld decided in early July to send UN forces to the Congo, a move supported on 14 July by the Security Council who condemned Belgium (which had no veto) and agreed to send troops from Ethiopia, Ghana, Morocco and Tunisia. Belgian troops were gradually evacuated as the UN force arrived, eventually remaining only in the seceding province of Katanga, while Lumumba, young and inexperienced, threatened to call in Soviet help to end the secession, a proposal completely unacceptable to the Western nations. Hammarskjöld declined to recognise Katanga as an independent state, and the Belgians said that the arrival of UN troops to annex Katanga would lead to a European exodus, as Lumumba was bent upon a racialist blood-bath. Henceforward the UN was to be identified with black racism; all whites were imperialists and their deaths did not count. In September 1960, under international pressure, Belgian troops were withdrawn from Katanga and were replaced by UN troops. But Tshombe was still in charge, and no serious Congo force was available to push him out. The Congo deteriorated into tribal warfare; Lumumba, who belonged to the Lulua tribe, ordered the massacre of the rival Baluba tribe by the Congolese army, and requested (and got) Soviet support for his growing role in Con-golese life, as a preliminary to ousting all Western and UN influences and overthrowing his rival Kasabuvu. His pretensions were not immediately supported by the UN, which led to strong outbursts by Khruschev, who returned to his idea of a troika to replace the Secretary General, abusing Hammarskjöld as a col-onialist tool (a charge that upset pro-Soviet 'neutrals'.)

The Congo situation deteriorated still further, when, in a coup on 1 December 1960, Lumumba was arrested by the head of the Congolese army, Mobutu, who then made himself head of state. Kasabuvu, however, remained recognised by the UN as the effec-tive head of state, but his writ ran only in areas where the UN had its forces. On 17 January 1961 Lumumba was sent by Kasabuvu to Elizabethville, where he was held prisoner by Tshombe and then murdered, probably on the same day. The death of Lumumba caused uproar in the Third World, and therefore at the UN, and the Soviet Union ceased to recognise Hammarskjöld as Secretary General on the ground of his alleged complicity in Lumumba's murder. A university in Russia for the education of mainly black and Asian students was named after him.

On 21 February 1961 the UN Security Council passed a resolution to enforce the unity of the Congo, but like most UN resolutions it was ambiguous. The UN had a small military force in the Congo, commanded by the Indian General Dayal who, having lost the confidence of the USSR, was replaced by General Sture Linner, from Sweden. Into this troubled situation, which threatened to disrupt the UN itself, Hammarskjöld sent a senior official of the Irish Department of External Affairs, Conor Cruise O'Brien, to be the UN presence in Elizabethville. Dr O'Brien interpreted his role more positively than was customary among UN officials, and was soon at loggerheads with Tshombe, France, Britain, Belgium and the United States. Hammarskjöld, in a passion of restraint, ordered O'Brien to desist and set out for the Congo himself. On 17 September 1961 Hammarskjöld was killed in a plane crash. O'Brien left for a professorship in New York.

Hammarskjöld was replaced by U Thant, a Burmese who specialised in inscrutability. The Congo War dragged on, the Katangan secession finally ending in January 1963, with Tshombe becoming Prime Minister of the Congo in July 1964. In October 1965 he was succeeded by Mobutu. Tshombe was kidnapped by the Algerians in June 1967, and died in 1969.

The UN continued to dabble in peace enforcement, especially in the Middle East and Cyprus, but its role was minor. The Congo had shown conclusively that the UN could not exercise an independent and neutral power in any conflict without getting drawn into major dissension and being regarded as a tool of one or other of the great powers.

Nevertheless, as it had a membership drawn from nearly every state, large and small, and as it was predominantly ruled by African, Asian and Latin American politicians, the UN and its specialised agencies became an important diplomatic forum, and the specialised agencies a useful channel of American and European aid to the Third World, aid which (it was claimed) was more acceptable and more usefully given by multilateral agencies than on a bilateral basis.

The post-world-war era was dominated by technological progress. The engineer Kondratieff speculated in the 1920s that history consisted of alternatives of forty-year-long periods of boom and slump, whose ultimate cause was technological change, the boom being when the change occurred, and the slump the period when it was absorbed. The 1950s and 1960s were a characteristic Kondratieff boom. The process of change associated notably with the growing use of oil, and the innovations in radio, television and telecommunications, led to sustained surge of economic growth. This surge brought with it tremendous benefits in the standard of living of ordinary people, but as all change has its own disadvantages, the problems of change emerged – of migration from the country to the town, of the rapid decline of older industries and the rapid build-up of others, of tension between different social groups, age groups and races as they responded in different ways to change. A strong and fashionable school of opinion emerged led by people like J. K. Galbraith, which argued that the crass materialism of the economic miracle was more destructive of values than it was beneficial to the standard of living, that people's desires for goods were unnaturally stimulated by capitalism, particularly through advertising and the media. The affluent society, it was argued, was a bad society.

For the most part this attitudinising by the privileged, who may perhaps have resented the prosperity of their social inferiors, could be ignored, and was. But of one thing the world could be certain. The application of technology to war, epitomised in the proliferation of nuclear weapons, carried the genuine possibility, even the probability of a wholly destructive war which would end civilisation finally. In such circumstances there was a tendency to say a plague on both your houses, and to regard the Americans and the Russians as no better than each other, and to avoid moral condemnation of the Soviet system and its lack of freedom and its economic failure. This was especially the case with the Third, or non-aligned, World, which chose a path of moral superiority over America, while relying to a large extent on its aid, and wholly on its trade, for its own economic development. America chose the role of protector of the smaller nations, and was constantly attacked for so doing, because (it was alleged) it was itself spreading its imperialism. Certainly, in driving the British from the Middle East and using its influence on Saudi Arabia and Iran, to gain oil concessions, and in its intervention in Vietnam, it did not (to put it mildly) show itself in its best light. But in the vast majority of cases its influence was both disinterested and generous. The natural protector of small nations was the United Nations. And the United

Nations was itself a major failure. The more it became a forum for the Third World, the less it became a forum for resolving disputes between the United States and the Soviet Union.

PART FOUR

Mounting Instability

The 1960s

Chapter 23

America the glamorous: Kennedy

The election of John F. Kennedy in 1960 symbolised the success story of the United States. The 1950s had given the country unprecedented prosperity which spread throughout the Western world; it was also at the head of a strong defensive alliance, apparently loosely united by certain common ideals. The Soviet Union, though powerful militarily and, at that moment, ahead in the space race, was not in the same league ideologically or materially. Although the Soviet political system had been lightened after Stalin's death, the Hungarian rising had been ruthlessly put down. In contrast to America, the appeal of Communism ought to have been limited.

But within ten years the United States appeared to be defeated in Vietnam, its youth demoralised and the Soviet Union was posing an even greater threat militarily and politically than ever before. The Third World and large parts of Europe seemed committed to one version or another of Marxism. The United States was labelled imperialist and a failure.

The reason for this extraordinary swing did not lie in Soviet military victories, nor in any great economic success. It was, rather, a failure of Western nerve and the Western capacity to organise itself.

Kennedy was the first media President. His predecessors, Truman and Eisenhower, had used speech-writers to prepare run-of-the-mill official addresses, but their personal appeal was as men speaking directly to the nation and Congress. Kennedy's national appeal was not, however, based mainly upon his political skills, but upon a series of television advertisements, debates with the Republican candidate, Vice-President Nixon, and speeches which were written by professionals in a debased Demosthenean vein. In his inaugural address, Kennedy's speech-writers continually coined banal phrases.

'Let the word go forth from this time and place to friend and foe alike, that the torch has been passed to a new generation of Americans, born in this country, tempered by war, disciplined by a hard and bitter peace, proud of our ancient heritage, and unwilling to witness or permit the slow undoing of those human rights to

which this nation has always been committed, and to which we are
committed today at home and around the world.

'Let every nation know, whether it wishes us well or ill, that we
shall pay any price, bear any burden, meet any hardship, support
any friend, oppose any foe to assure the survival and success of
liberty . . . and so, my fellow Americans, ask not what your
country can do for you; ask what you can do for your country.

'My fellow citizens of the world, ask not what America will do
for you, but what together we can do for the freedom of man.'

Similar empty rhetoric echoed throughout his other major
addresses. Nevertheless, despite this packaging, a genuine intelligence and some degree of sincerity seemed to come through and
proved to be attractive, especially to non-Americans.

The myth of John Fitzgerald Kennedy and his family was a myth
in the proper sense of the word, with magical properties, based
upon a highly distorted version of fact.

Here were three brothers, handsome, clever, brave and sexually
attractive. They set out to conquer the most powerful nation on
earth and to use its power for good. The older two were murdered,
brutally, insanely and mysteriously, and the third disgraced. It
was, it seemed, symbolic of America itself.

The father, Joseph Kennedy, was among the earliest Boston
Irish to be sent to Harvard. A self-made millionaire, his business
and political careers were fairly unsavoury. Through his friendship
with Roosevelt, and his financial support for the Democratic party,
he had been made United States Ambassador to London, where he
was unpopular as he was anti-British and neutralist at the time of
the fall of France, in 1940. He was powerfully and passionately
ambitious for his sons. The eldest, Joseph, was killed in the war.
His second son, John (known in the family as Jack), was almost
killed when his ship was sunk in the Pacific, leaving his back
severely damaged; he also contracted Addison's disease, an afflic-
tion of the glands. His third son, Robert, enjoyed rude health, as
did his youngest, Edward. Old Joseph Kennedy set his sights on
the Presidency for Jack, and probably for a Kennedy Presidential
dynasty.

In 1947, aged thirty, Jack was elected to Congress as a Democrat
for Massachusetts, and in 1952 he moved to the Senate following a
campaign, in which he was heavily supported by his father, against
the Republican Henry Cabot Lodge, a Boston brahmin. Jack
failed in an attempt to become Adlai Stevenson's Vice-Presidential
nominee in 1956, but built up a strong base to fight Richard Nixon,
Eisenhower's Vice-President, for the Presidency in 1960.

Not only was he at forty-three considered young to run for the

Presidency, but he also had the great handicaps of being a Roman Catholic, his family's reputation for ruthlessness and, in the case of his father, for corruption. His fight for the nomination against two Democratic stalwarts, Hubert Humphrey and Lyndon Johnson, was bitter, but he finally won by shrewdly exercising his money and his patronage at the Democratic convention in Los Angeles. Astutely, he then chose Lyndon B. Johnson from Texas as his Vice-Presidential nominee, thereby helping to ensure the Western and the Southwestern vote. His campaign was organised around the traditional Democratic stronghold of the South, and the Roosevelt coalition of the Irish poor, the blacks, and the Hispano–Americans. He was also overwhelmingly the choice of the press and the intellectuals.

Vice-President Nixon, running with somewhat less than President Eisenhower's full support and against a campaign organised by the Kennedy forces with ruthlessness and skill, made an unexpectedly strong showing. The election in November 1960 was an extremely narrow one, eventually turning on the votes in Cook County, Illinois, which included Chicago, where it is now known that the corrupt votes ensured by Mayor Daley turned the scales. In consequence, although Kennedy was elected President when Nixon finally conceded, it was clearly a highly contentious election.

A new era had dawned. The brightest and the best arrived in Washington. The new President was impressive; his relative youth – he was a generation younger than Eisenhower, Macmillan and de Gaulle – his enthusiasm, and his very effective publicity machine made it seem that a new spirit had entered the United States.

It was on this basis that the White House became known as Camelot, partly for the style in which President and Mrs Kennedy entertained distinguished visitors, a style which had become uncommon in Washington, and also as a result of Mrs Kennedy's redecoration of the White House in an attempt to give to it the kind of meretricious glamour which other presidential houses had elsewhere.

Kennedy's Cabinet choices centred partly upon his own family; his younger brother Robert was made Attorney General, and other friends and relations were given junior office, and remained close to him; but he also brought in a group of gifted people often from the foundations and the universities, who gave his administration an aura of respectability. They included Dean Rusk, the Secretary of State; the controversial economist J. K. Galbraith as Ambassador to India, Ed Murrow as head of USIA and Robert McNamara, as Secretary of Defense. All in all, wrote historian

Theodore Sorensen, himself Kennedy's head speech-writer, 'the Kennedy cabinet was a group of gifted men'.

This brilliant team came into office pledged to rearm the United States, President Kennedy having alleged during the election that the Sputnik and associated developments of missile technology, such as putting the first man into space, Yuri Gagarin, had put the Soviet Union substantially ahead. It was also pledged to raise the standards of minorities, especially the blacks, to stimulate economic growth after what was regarded as the quiet do-nothing years of the Eisenhower regime, and to stimulate the world economy in order to give substantial aid to the poorer parts of the world.

Since the economy was not really in a parlous state, the blacks were not especially violent and the Russians were behaving themselves, it was an aggressive policy destined to stir up trouble. Kennedy wanted to convince the world that he was a great President of a great nation: in his search for greatness he brought the world nearer to nuclear war than at any time since 1950.

Kennedy accepted, almost unthinkingly, a plan originally inaugurated by the CIA in Eisenhower's time, for a small group of anti-Castro Cubans to invade Cuba. Fidel Castro had come to power in Cuba by overthrowing the corrupt Batista regime with a handful of men. The CIA thought that Castro was a Communist who would give Russia a toehold in the American continent and would spread sedition throughout Latin America. The CIA also thought that he could easily be overthrown by an equally small group of men backed by United States money and arms.

On Monday, 17 April 1961, a mere three months after Kennedy's inauguration, where he had spoken of 'a beachhead of co-operation' which 'may push back the jungle of suspicion', just under fifteen hundred anti-Castro Cubans landed at the Bay of Pigs on the Cuban coast, where they were met by a force of 20,000 Castro troops. They were defeated and all but 100 were taken prisoner. The landing was not covered by United States aircraft, and the invasion's main supply ship was sunk by the Cuban air force. The United States government pretended that it had no knowledge of the invasion, and Adlai Stevenson, its Ambassador in the United Nations, denied American complicity before the Security Council, a denial which was almost immediately disproved by evidence. In view of the resulting furore, it was decided not to send in American troops and aircraft to follow up the invasion. There was no evidence to support the view that the landing would enable the invading force to join a successful guerrilla movement in the mountains. There was in fact no such guerrilla movement for it to join.

The defeat was an appalling setback to anti-Castro hopes in Cuba and the failure of the United States attempts to topple Castro gave him a great boost as the leader of an independent Central America seeking to escape from American domination. President Kennedy finally had to assume responsibility for the invasion, which undoubtedly led to deterioration of the United States' standing in the area and marked a major reversal for Kennedy in his relations with Russia. The Bay of Pigs fiasco had to be followed by victories if Kennedy's aggressive stance was to seem valid; this meant that he quickly bristled with defiance at every encounter with Khruschev.

Khruschev was particularly scathing about the American Cuban fiasco, alleging that Castro was no Communist, but that these American escapades were likely to drive him into the Communist camp. Khruschev was also most concerned at Kennedy's inexperience and youth, at his prancing prickliness, for he wished to reach an agreement with America over Germany. Khruschev wanted a German peace treaty which would accept the division of Germany and end all Western allied rights inside West Berlin. It was within this context that the Russians were prepared to agree to a neutralising of Germany as they had agreed to a neutralising of Austria five years before. On the other hand, the Western allies were not prepared to give up their position in Berlin, nor were they prepared to neutralise West Germany, since West Germany was a more integral part of the NATO defence arrangements than East Germany was of the Warsaw Pact.

To back up his words Khruschev imposed limitations on freedom to travel from the West through East Germany to Berlin. Kennedy reinforced the American garrison in Germany, partly as a precaution and partly as a response. On 25 July 1961 Kennedy, in a broadcast, said, 'We cannot and will not permit the Communists to drive us out of Berlin, either gradually or by force.' This speech was regarded by Khruschev as a challenge.

Khruschev now said that he was determined to 'eradicate this splinter [West Berlin] from the heart of Europe'. At issue was the signing by the wartime allies of a peace treaty for Germany, failing which the USSR would sign a treaty with East Germany, turning it into a sovereign state. The consequence, according to Khruschev, would be the end of the Four-Power Agreement on Germany, which had been made at Potsdam, and subsequently the breaking of the road link from West Germany to West Berlin. Kennedy decided that this approach was unacceptable, and that he would defend the right of free access to Berlin, if need be by means of nuclear war, a course of action that did not gain the support of the

French, the British or the Germans. Nor was this threat of nuclear war believed by Khruschev, who on 13 August 1961 began the building of the Berlin Wall, which cut the city in two and prevented the East Germans and East Berliners from leaving. President Kennedy reinforced the American troops in West Berlin and then added to those in West Germany. The American military budget was increased, and the 160,000 additional men in the reserve were called up.

Berlin continued to be a major source of difficulty in American–Russian relations until President Kennedy's visit to West Berlin on 26 June 1963, when he made his position clear; he addressed the Berliners with the phrase, 'I take pride in the words *"Ich bin ein Berliner"* ', thus assuring the Germans in public that the United States would go to war over access to Berlin. In this particular context, therefore, Kennedy, for the second time in two years, threatened nuclear war over the relatively limited, minor issue of access to West Berlin because he thought that Berlin was a symbol of confrontation with the Soviet Union.

Berlin was not, however, the most dangerous Kennedy–Khruschev confrontation; that distinction was reserved for the Cuban missile crisis. In the first aerial photographs of Cuba on 31 August 1962 Russian anti-aircraft surface-to-air missiles and missile-equipped torpedo boats were identified, followed on 5 September by MIG-21 fighter aircraft. There was strong pressure on the United States for a pre-emptive strike at Cuba, but Kennedy regarded this as another possible Khruschev trick in order to make American relationships with Latin America more difficult while he was engaged in the confrontation over Berlin. On 14 October an American intelligence aircraft, the U2, flew over Cuba, and the next day it was obvious that Soviet medium-range missile bases were almost ready. Kennedy wondered why these missiles had been sent. Were they to test America's will in order that Khruschev could subsequently move in West Berlin? Were they for the defence of Cuba against a hypothetical attack? Were they a bargaining counter with which to force Americans to withdraw from some of their overseas bases? Did the Russians think there might be a growing gap in the missile race which favoured the Americans, in which case the Cuban bases, being so near to the United States, would considerably enhance Soviet power?

In mid-September Kennedy warned the Soviet Union that he would not allow the development of a Russian base in Cuba. The Soviet Union responded that any American attack on Cuba would lead to nuclear war. By Monday, 22 October 1962, when Kennedy broadcast on television at 7 p.m., it was known that a fleet of

Soviet missiles was in mid-Atlantic, sailing to Cuba. Kennedy said on television on 22 October: 'We will not prematurely or unnecessarily risk the costs to the world by a nuclear war in which even the fruits of victory would be ashes in our mouth, but neither will we shrink from that risk at any time it must be faced.' The President announced an American blockade of Cuba to stop missiles being sent there. He was supported in this action not only by his political opponents (the biennial Congressional elections were being held) but by all his allies, including Macmillan in Britain and de Gaulle in France. But this moment of genuine confrontation terrified the people of Western Europe and had important consequences for the alliance.

Some ships were stopped, searched, and being without missiles were allowed to sail on to Cuba. The Security Council met, where Adlai Stevenson produced the aerial photographic evidence which the Russian Ambassador, Zorin, said was fabricated. A large American fleet took up station in mid-Atlantic, where eighteen Soviet dry-cargo ships were heading towards the United States, escorted by Soviet submarines. By 24 October the ships stopped dead, and then during the following two days they turned round and began to sail back to Soviet ports, followed by United States aircraft. Nevertheless, in public and in private, Khruschev continued to threaten Kennedy, and to try to bargain the Cuban bases against bases in Turkey, or for other objectives of Soviet policy. On 28 October, however, Khruschev backed down and agreed to dismantle the bases, withdraw the missiles and allow inspection to make sure that the withdrawal was in fact complete. In return America agreed never to invade Cuba and to withdraw the blockade.

Were Khruschev's threats serious? Was Kennedy determined to interpret everything in the worst light in order 'to earn his place in history'? Perhaps something of both, but more probably it was Khruschev's recklessness that caused the crisis. In any case, after the Cuban confrontation, moves towards conciliation were started.

During the crisis the world remained in combat readiness, however, and planes with primed nuclear weapons were actually flying. This was the nearest the world came to nuclear war at any stage in the post-war period, including the crisis in Korea, when MacArthur advanced to the Yalu River, threatening to drop atom bombs, and also the Yom Kippur War between Egypt and Israel in October 1973.

Less dramatic as an issue but one which dominated Kennedy's Presidency was his involvement in Asia, first in Laos, then in Vietnam.

The Geneva Accords of 1954 made Laos neutral under a coalition government, but, despite this, the country was gradually torn between Communist insurrectionary forces in the North, the Pathet Lao, supplied with arms from North Vietnam, and a Southern pro-Western government supplied with equipment from America. Kennedy decided to abandon the idea of neutrality, support the pro-American forces, and not to conquer all Laos but to divide the country, as with Vietnam and Korea. But this option proved unacceptable to the Southern Laotians; Kennedy changed his mind and after the damage was done, strove for a neutral coalition government by calling for a cease-fire. The collapse of the Bay of Pigs invasion a month later made the President suspicious of further military intervention in Laos, though the advice which he received was that the collapse of any part of Southeast Asia to Communist control would lead sooner, rather than later, to the collapse of neighbouring states – the domino theory.

On 15 May 1961 a major Pathet Lao attack led Kennedy to send 5000 marines to Thailand and to move them up to the Laos border. In this move he was supported by Britain, Australia and New Zealand. As a result of this threat of American intervention, a Laotian coalition government of national union was formed in June 1962 and the following month a new Geneva Accord was signed by fourteen governments, guaranteeing the neutrality of Laos. But supplies still continued to reach the Pathet Lao from North Vietnam. Despite this, by the time Kennedy died, Laos seemed reasonably peaceful.

The domino theory suggested that the fall of Laos would lead to the loss of Thailand and South Vietnam but the hypothesis was questionable at that time and the definition of 'fall' was also in doubt, since a country that was neutral was not necessarily anti-American. Khruschev, however, had been rattled by the Bay of Pigs and was belligerent over Berlin; thus it was assumed by the Americans that throughout the world there was a constant search for weak points in the American system of defensive alliances.

The Laos crisis temporarily ended, the action moved to South Vietnam. Following the victory of Mao Tse-tung, the Korean conflict, and the fall of Dien Bien Phu, the Americans regarded Asia – which Potsdam had put in their sphere of influence – as a continent where they were prone to defeat. Some of the newly-independent countries, especially India, had disappointed the United States by adopting an aggressively neutralist stance in the Cold War; consequently those countries which, like South Korea and South Vietnam, adopted a vigorously anti-Communist line, were regarded as important allies, fighting in the front line of the

Cold War. The validity of these governments, their legitimacy, their prospects of survival without substantial United States military support, were consistently exaggerated. Neither South Korea nor South Vietnam – especially the latter – were viable allies in the manner of the United Kingdom or (increasingly) the Federal Republic of Germany. Nevertheless, it was not only the hard-line anti-Communists and military establishment who were committed to South Vietnam; if possible, Kennedy and his liberal foreign policy experts were even more aggressively committed to limiting the spread of Communism, and to so doing by encouraging new types of warfare, especially anti-guerrilla activity, which the British had used so successfully in Malaya, and the Greek government (with American help) in their civil war. The idealism of Kennedy's advisers was harnessed to a vision of converting the Third World to self-defence based on prosperity and democratic governments, both achieved with abundant American aid.

The initial American position in Vietnam had been anti-colonialist, supporting Ho Chi-minh. By late 1945, however, the predominant American view (and there were always many strands) had swung right round to support the French. At Potsdam, Vietnam had been divided at the sixteenth parallel, the Chinese were to liberate the North from the Japanese and the British the South. Following the victory of the Communists in China in 1949, the division of Vietnam took on a political nature, with a Communist North and non-Communist South, whose independence was agreed at Geneva. American advisers had been helping the President of the South, Ngo Dinh Diem, although he was a dictator and opposed to all Vietnam elections.

With South Vietnam an ally of the United States and a member of the South East Asia Treaty Organisation (SEATO) President Diem fought bitterly against the infiltration of Vietcong Communist guerrillas. The United States was in a classic dilemma in that opposition to Diem was obviously legitimate, but it was also supported from North Vietnam, in breach of the Geneva Accords, and moreover, Diem was a reliable ally and his overthrow would mean that the United States guarantee of the security of small independent countries which were its allies would be in danger of being shown as invalid.

The Vietcong continued to attack throughout South Vietnam, and to terrorise the rural areas, some of which they occupied. The American choice of response was difficult, as to support Diem suggested that it identified with the dictator of South Vietnam. Nevertheless the Americans opted for a military solution, whereas the British, in their fight against Communist infiltrators in

Malaya, had strengthened the local forces in their resistance, emphasised the responsibility of the local leaders to the local population, and trained the British troops in guerrilla warfare rather than massive-scale invasions in the Korean style. The Americans, however, were only trained for massive action.

President Kennedy accelerated the American military commit- ment in the hope that with a Southern victory a negotiated settle- ment would become possible. He was convinced that the North Vietnamese and the Chinese were allied in a substantial attempt to conquer South Vietnam, and that unless they were repulsed by the Americans they would win. Initially, in May 1961, he tripled the number of American military advisers to South Vietnam and sent Vice-President Johnson on a tour of Southeast Asia, which in- cluded a substantial stay in Saigon to show solidarity with Diem. Johnson's public commitment to Diem as 'the Winston Churchill of Southeast Asia' was to have a fateful result when he unexpect- edly became President. Despite Johnson's visit, which accepted the hypothesis that the fall of South Vietnam would be followed by the fall of other Southeast Asian countries to the Communists, the situation continued to deteriorate. In October 1961 Kennedy's two expert advisers, General Maxwell Taylor and W. W. Rostow, visited Vietnam and recommended that American troops should be committed in substantial numbers to Vietnam in order to stiffen the South Vietnamese forces which, although substantially larger in number than the Vietcong, were inefficient and not strongly motivated. Despite this strong advice Kennedy never ordered the commitment of combat troops, though by the time of his assassin- ation the military assistance mission had reached 15,000 men and the supply of war material had become substantial. In Kennedy's opinion, however, Diem became more and more out of touch with the people, and more and more dominated by his brother, Ngo Dinh Nhu and his wife, Madame Nhu. This sinister pair were Catholics who persecuted the Buddhists. This attitude by his co-religionists annoyed Kennedy, as the Nhus were driving the Buddhists willy-nilly into supporting the Vietcong.

The more American aid came, the more powerful the Nhus, the more unpopular the regime, the greater the insurgency, re- quiring (in turn) more American aid. Thus, once Kennedy had taken the decision to approve advisers, and had sent as advisers some of the most conventional military minds in America, he had determined the subsequent course of the war.

The arrival of substantial numbers of Americans in Saigon in early 1962 led immediately to an escalation of the overt conflict; South Vietnam troops (known as ARVN, Army of the Republic of

Viet Nam) massed against the Vietcong, who were already in control of large areas of the countryside. Helicopters, supplied by the Americans, made a difference, but the power of, and probably the support for, the Vietcong was growing, while the Diem regime was becoming more and more unpopular. Its army simply was not fighting. But the American propaganda commitment was so deep that doctored reports of the conflict, ludicrously favourable to the ARVN, were sent back to Washington and to the rest of the free world. American colonels and other officers who reported that the South Vietnamese troops would not fight, that the Nhus and Diem were unpopular and that the corrupt local regime was just not worth supporting were ruthlessly fired or side-tracked. The atmosphere became reminiscent of the McCarthyite period and was furthered by the blatant favouritism of the Kennedy entourage and the President's commitment to 'positive' news. The real heroes of the war, apart from those who died in action, were men such as Colonel Vann, a fighting officer, who told the truth to men such as McNamara who did not wish to hear it. (In the First World War Haig had played exactly the same game during the dreadful battles in France and Belgium.)

Journalists in Saigon and Washington gradually learned at least some of the truth and it was from them that the beginnings of serious opposition to the war came; at first their criticism was of Diem, but by late 1964 their entire understanding of the war differed from the Pentagon. The President himself firmly believed his own propaganda; when Senator Mansfield, after a visit to Saigon, tried to hint at the truth he was rudely dismissed. Kennedy approved the use of napalm and defoliation – both barbarous methods of warfare – reluctantly; nevertheless he approved them on a limited scale. The limitations were of course soon forgotten. McNamara, the Defense Secretary, was put fully in charge of the Vietnam operation and from then onwards, until well into the Nixon Presidency, it was primarily a military affair. Attempts to negotiate a settlement were perfunctory; the United States was caught between the assumption of deference towards the South Vietnam government whose policy was no surrender and no compromise, and its own military establishment's concern at achieving 'victory' – an increasingly imprecise objective. McNamara was a typical corporation executive, from the Ford Motor Company, with little human or political sensitivity, interested only in success, and success in statistical terms – body counts, people resettled in camps – all of which added a peculiarly inhuman horror to the war.

Early in 1963 the war reached a stalemate, even a pause, but in

May a riot erupted on the occasion of the religious festival of Buddha's birthday, which led to a Buddhist uprising against the predominantly Roman Catholic government of Diem. As the crisis grew, Kennedy appointed his old Boston opponent, Henry Cabot Lodge, as American Ambassador in Saigon – a leading Republican, his appointment helped to ensure a bipartisan support for the war. Diem and Nhu violently crushed the Buddhist rebellion; and Buddhist monks began to burn themselves to death in demonstrations. The regime was harsh, oppressive and unpopular. Civilian morale had collapsed and the country was united in fear and detestation of the regime. This put the Americans in an ever more difficult position. To win politically it was necessary to get rid of Diem; the military regarded Diem's strength as essential to victory. Lodge was instructed by Kennedy to organise a coup by the predominantly Buddhist Vietnam army against Diem and the Nhus, a coup which at the last moment failed, largely because the American Defense Department supported Diem and the Vietnam Army refused to move. Finally however an American-backed coup was successful: Diem and the Nhus were murdered. Less than three weeks later Kennedy was assassinated and Lyndon Johnson, who had been publicly committed to Diem, became the new American President.

Kennedy had arrived in Dallas on 22 November 1963 to gain support from the Texan Democrats for his forthcoming Presidential campaign. As he drove through the centre of the city, a series of shots, fired from the sixth floor of the Texas Book Depository, blew off the top of his head and wounded the Governor of Texas, John Connally. The assassin was identified as Lee Harvey Oswald, a man of poor education who had served in the Marine Corps, at one time at a U2 base, and then gone to the Soviet Union where he had married a Russian wife and returned to Texas. On the way there he had been arrested for distributing pro-Castro pamphlets in Florida. He was at the same time in active contact with low-level FBI agents. It also appeared that he had attempted to murder a prominent local general.

It appeared that Oswald was mentally unbalanced, though the connection with the Soviet Union led people to suspect that he might be a Soviet agent, or alternatively, that he might be connected with the Cuban anti-Castro exiles who resented President Kennedy's failure to invade Cuba at the time of the missile crisis.

The assassination was further obscured by the murder of Oswald himself, while in police custody, by a local friend of the police, one Jack Ruby, who subsequently died of cancer. A large proportion of the witnesses of the assassination also died mysteriously, though it was never established whether or not there was a conspiracy. Certainly, it was thought that two people were involved in the murder, since a significant number of witnesses claimed that a bullet was fired from a gun on a grassy knoll opposite the Texas Book Depository, though this theory was discounted by the commission set up by President Johnson under Chief Justice Warren.

Kennedy's body was flown back to Washington and in a world outburst of mourning at the death of a brave and much admired young statesman, his body was buried in Arlington National Cemetery. His successor, Lyndon B. Johnson, having been sworn in on the plane carrying Kennedy's body, inherited the Presidency and subsequently fought the 1964 election to gain the largest majority of any President.

The sudden death of Kennedy made an assessment of his Presidency inevitably partial. He had served only three years of the eight that he might reasonably have expected. He had brought the world near to nuclear war. His international record had been hair-raising, moving from the prospects of an understanding with Khruschev to the Cuban and Berlin crises; and his involvement in Laos and Vietnam was to lead to a decade of disastrous defeats for the United States. Domestically his achievements were small. Little of the legislation he proposed was enacted by Congress. His lust for a laurel wreath led him into thoughtless pugnacity. He displayed remarkable lack of perspicacity and judgment when dealing with Soviet taunts, which reflected his immaturity.

But the glamour, star-like in its quality, persisted. And the tragedy attached to his family pursued him beyond the grave. His brother Robert, seeking the Presidency in 1968, was murdered in Los Angeles. And in 1969, after a drunken party, his younger brother, Teddy, was in a car accident at Chappaquiddick in which his girl companion was drowned. By death, misfortune and scandal the Kennedys became a royal line with the magic that tragedy brings attaching to them. And in the process America lost much of the position it held in the world in 1960.

Chapter 24

Liberalising Socialism:
the Prague Spring

In 1964, not long after Kennedy's assassination, Khruschev was succeeded by Brezhnev and Kosygin. The basic characteristics of Soviet dictatorship in the USSR itself remained unchanged but during the next few years each satellite country in Eastern Europe tried to manoeuvre some small individuality for itself, some slight deviation from the overpowering Soviet apparatus of control. Each tried to lessen the rigid uniformity of ideology and organisational structure imposed from Moscow.

The Soviet empire remained in essence unchanged. The worst of the terror was over. Gradually the sheer scale of the Leninist–Stalinist horrors emerged. But there was no sudden shock of revulsion, no sense of a sleeping giant waking up from its nightmares. Freedom was not even a distant dream and the prosperity of Western capitalism was unimaginable.

Communism was not overthrown but – and it is a profoundly significant exception – the Terror came more or less to an end. Arbitrary arrest was now rare; the labour camps were slimmed down; the systematic use of torture was reduced. In the 1960s the number of political prisoners was perhaps of the order of a million. Freedom of expression was limited, but illegal typescripts – *samizdats* – circulated. Religion was practised, under severe restriction. There was no freedom of movement within the country and little emigration from it. But compared with the first thirty years of Soviet rule, life was easier.

Reform was not possible because there was no institutionalised procedure for change – elections, freedom of expression, public discussion – and the concept of 'democratic centralism' gave all power to the party, and no alternative sources of authority (except perhaps for the army) could develop. The party, in power year after year, grew out of touch with reality, and deeply corrupt. The economy, with few market influences at work, was arbitrarily planned, and grossly inefficient – especially agriculture, which was a permanent, lamentable failure.

To the Soviet Union, safety since Yalta had lain in the total domination of the satellite states. As Communism had not endeared itself to the people of Eastern Europe, they had to be ruled by force and repression. Had they been independent and had shared interests with Russia, then indeed they might have formed a useful buffer region, but domination without consent had made them a permanent area of risk, insecurity and trouble. In 1956 the Hungarians rose to overthrow Communism. Soviet troops moved in to repress the revolt. In 1968 Czechoslovakia sought to reform the system from abuse and Soviet troops moved in to stop the reform. In 1981 the Poles reneged. The fundamental change the Soviet Union wished to avoid at all costs was the restoration of individual political rights and individual property rights. The Soviet Union lived in perpetual fear that political and economic changes in the balance of power in these states might weaken external alliances and so threaten Russian overall military control and safety.

In the 1950s, each Soviet-occupied country had a Communist party organised along Stalinist lines. The party represented (according to its own evidence) the organised and conscious working class; and the Politburo expressed the collective wisdom of the party. Each Politburo deferred to its General Secretary who was in fact dictator of the country, owing allegiance in turn to the Soviet Communist party and its General Secretary. Each shared an apparatus of thought whereby Marx, as interpreted by Lenin and Stalin, had discovered the laws of history; these laws show that Socialism would succeed capitalism, and that Socialism would be entrenched by the dictatorship of the proletariat, its consciousness embodied in the Communist party of the Soviet Union.

No more thorough apparatus of control has been discovered; without terror, however, and the continual pressure of the secret police, show trials, total censorship and continuous propaganda, this common system of thought could not have continued amongst sophisticated Europeans such as the Poles, the Czechs and the Hungarians, not to mention the Prussians who formed the bulk of the East Germans.

Since the option of choosing non-Communist governments was closed, the question was how far any party might deviate from the Soviet model. For this reason the question of Yugoslavia continued to dominate Eastern European affairs long after Tito had broken dramatically with Stalin and his defiance proved successful. The violence of the Hungarian rising in 1956 showed the Russians and orthodox Communists elsewhere that any country might at any time follow the Yugoslav example. But Hungary seemed to demonstrate that Yugoslavia was unique, because of Tito.

Tito, while managing to unite the Yugoslav party and probably much of the nation behind his line, maintained, for a considerable part of the time, a degree of personal freedom and prosperity in Yugoslavia which silenced much internal dissension. He also had the ultimate backing of the Western powers and of the non-aligned movement which he helped to found, but above all, he had his own remarkable personality.

The new economic system in Yugoslavia, with its emphasis upon autonomous enterprises and free agriculture, regulated according to certain basic national criteria of investment, of payroll funds for wages and of indicative planning of output totals, led to a substantial increase in the standard of living. At the same time, millions of Yugoslavs went to work in Germany, while large numbers of Western tourists visited Yugoslavia for their holidays. Yugoslavia thus became one of the least despotic Communist tyrannies in Eastern Europe, and one which had a fair element of capitalist structure in its organisation.

The development of a genuine local government in Yugoslavia was an important break with the Stalinist tradition, implying no further use for democratic centralism which was the foundation of autocracy in the Soviet Union. Nevertheless, Yugoslavia did not go so far as to have a multi-party system. Its Communist party was built upon small local units with genuine representation of different groups of people.

This degree of participation led to a growing belief that Yugoslavia had found an autonomous road to Socialism which became known as Yugoslav Socialist consciousness. The system had a pyramidical series of institutions, culminating in a President, who was Tito, and the federal government became a Federal Executive Council which ruled collegially – that is by discussion and agreement, not by accepting the rule of the party secretary. But the other Communist countries lacked to a greater or lesser extent the special characteristics that ensured Yugoslavia's independence.

Hungary had been occupied by the Red Army. Although its people were strongly opposed to the Russians and to Communism, Imre Nagy had been no Tito; Nagy was executed after the 1956 uprising. Earlier emphasis on collectivised agriculture and heavy industry had led to collapse of productivity and depressed the standard of living which, after the invasion, fell steeply. Faced with economic failure in 1966, the Hungarian Communist party adopted a New Economic mechanism which, from 1968, marked a shift to a market economy, although state ownership of enterprises was maintained. But Hungary did not become Titoist.

Similarly in Poland, though its people were passionately anti-Russian, anti-Marxist and for the most part ardent Roman Catholics, revolt proved impossible because of relentless repression by the secret police. The Poles were completely dominated by the Soviet Union in both external and internal affairs. During the Hungarian revolution, the Poles supported the Soviet Union in order to retain the few minor elements of liberalisation they had been able to secure from Gomulka. Gomulka had in fact handed over four fifths of the collective farms to the peasants, which led to substantially increased agricultural output and he had put less emphasis on heavy industry. At the same time, the economist Oskar Lange, who had previously been disgraced and imprisoned, developed a market type of Socialism, with state ownership. Eventually Gomulka compromised with Cardinal Wyszynski: a large number of priests and bishops were amnestied, and in December 1956 a limited amount of Church teaching was allowed in schools, and Catholics were allowed to become supporters of the Communist party.

But that was the extent of Poland's liberation.

The position was even worse in Bulgaria and Romania, inescapably in the Soviet orbit and without strong national traditions or allegiance to Catholicism to give focus for resistance. East Germany was treated as a Soviet colony for many years. After the Hungarian uprising, the regime under Walter Ulbricht grew even more repressive and over three million people fled to the West. On the night of 13 August 1961 the GDR frontier was sealed and a wall built dividing East from West Berlin. The whole frontier was mined and boobytrapped and became effectively impassable.

Titoism, therefore, did not provide a model for the rest of Eastern Europe to follow. Nor did it remain true to itself, as a new philosophical and organisational form of Marxism. Titoism was, rather, a deviation from the Soviet model, not a substitute for it. In any event, the Yugoslav case was soon overtaken by the problem of the Chinese heresy.

Moscow's quarrel with Yugoslavia was related to its dispute with China, and it was clear that in the eyes of the Soviet Union Tito was concerned with the developing autonomy of China, while Khruschev had convinced himself that Yugoslavia was prepared to repent and to accept a Polish solution to its problems, that is to say, the right to determine its own domestic policies in return for complete solidarity with the Soviet Union in foreign policy and in dogmatic terms.

The Chinese regarded Tito as a Trojan horse in the Communist camp and distrusted his influence on Russia, insisting, at the 1957 fortieth anniversary of the Russian Revolution, on a resolution which opposed 'revisionism' – the code word for Tito. Hence the

Yugoslavs could not sign the declaration. By mid 1958 Tito was back in the doghouse, as he had been ten years earlier. For two more years Tito tried to work his passage back, but by 1960 the Chinese had managed to provoke the Albanians into an open split with Yugoslavia and when, in 1961, the Russians split with the Albanians, this in turn led to difficulties with China – all these permutations and combinations emphasising Tito's role as a source of dissidence in Eastern Europe.

The Sino–Soviet split (see Chapter 9), first identified in 1956, developed rapidly and in 1960 the Chinese openly took a hard line at the Warsaw Pact meeting, in contrast to the still emollient Soviet line. Albania, where Hoxha remained a Stalinist, moved from the Soviet to the Chinese camp; Hoxha boycotted the Warsaw Pact meetings, Soviet submarines were withdrawn from Albania, and in 1961 Albania broke off diplomatic relations with the USSR, following effective expulsion from the Pact. The fact that the USSR did not invade Albania was probably due to its geographical isolation, surrounded as it was by Yugoslavia and Greece.

The effect of the polemical attacks on Albania, however, was to emphasise the break elsewhere with the Stalinist past and to emphasise, despite the interventions in Poland and Hungary, that the Eastern bloc was a diverse group of countries. This was especially the case in Romania which combined a hard line domestically, while retaining links with China and developing relations with the West, notably West Germany. In 1958 Soviet troops were withdrawn from Romania. This enabled the Romanian government to follow a more independent line in foreign affairs, but (ironically perhaps) it became more authoritarian at home – not unlike Albania, save that it was not following a Stalinist line. The USSR was plainly worried lest Romania defect to the Chinese camp, and tried to avoid such a defection by treating Romania softly. Russia also needed Romanian agricultural products and oil.

In the revamping which followed the upheavals in Hungary in 1956, Comecon became a vehicle for the supranational planning of the Eastern European economies, and the direction of commodities to Russia on terms unfavourable to its satellites. It was this hegemony and exploitation to which Romania objected, while arguing for a world Communist movement that included both Yugoslavia and China.

In 1964 Brezhnev and Kosygin signed a major economic agreement with Romania which led to increased industrialisation and considerable economic freedom from Soviet interference. The Romanian leader, Dej, died in the spring of 1965, and the Soviet

Union made friendly gestures to his successor, Ceauşescu, which led to a rapprochement, and apparently left the Eastern bloc countries free, to some extent, to follow their own paths, domestically, as long as there was external unity. But Ceauşescu then received Chou En-lai of China in Bucharest, in July 1966, and proposed a liquidation of all military pacts. Russia also had reason to fear that Romania, as well as other Eastern bloc countries, was going to seek the return of territory lost at the end of the Second World War. Romania appeared determined to go its own way. In February 1967 it recognised the West German government, and appeared to have withdrawn from Warsaw Pact manoeuvres.

These complex manoeuvres by different countries within the Soviet bloc arose from different perceptions of national interest, and also from debates about the nature of Marxism.

The attempt to keep Communism together was threatened first by the Yugoslav breakaway in 1948 and then by the Sino–Soviet split. Meanwhile the Communist movement had held three world conferences, in 1957, 1960 and 1969 (this last not attended by the Chinese), and two European conferences in 1967 and 1976. During the span of these conferences major divergences took place between the Communist parties within the Eastern bloc and the parties in Western Europe, identified by so-called Euro-Communism, a name first coined in 1965 to describe the Italian movement. Membership of the Communist party in Italy, the largest outside Eastern Europe, had reached 2.3 million members, but had stabilised at about one and a half million. Drawing from the whole range of Italian society, including a high proportion of intellectuals and people from the middle class, as well as from the traditional red belt of industrial workers, it had aimed at presenting itself in many respects as a normal democratic party. In 1968 its leader, Enrico Berlinguer, sought political power, by announcing that the Communists wished to become the governing party, *partito de governo*, developing this further in autumn 1973 through a 'historical compromise' with the Christian Democrats. The party freely criticised the Soviet invasion of Czechoslovakia, and also criticised the Portuguese Communist party for failing to take part in the Portuguese government after the revolution in 1974. They also took note that the collapse of the Allende regime in Chile in 1973 showed that a plurality or even majority of 51 per cent of the votes – and Allende never even got a majority – was insufficient in order to achieve democratic consent to the changes. Its constant attacks on NATO were replaced by a plan for a gradual withdrawal, but even this was modified since it was argued that to withdraw from NATO would be to slow down attempts towards détente. Furthermore, the Communist party developed in Italy a new theoretical structure based on its own background and in particular the work of Gramsci, the most important Communist theoretician of the inter-war years.

Possibly Europe's most intellectual and certainly its most argumentative Communist party was in France which followed a hard line. Despite its mass appeal in 1945 and 1946, and despite, too, the fact that it had a high proportion of intellectuals in its membership, it slavishly followed the Soviet leadership. When Thorez gave up in 1964, the party became more liberal and took a more independent stand, though they supported the Soviet invasion of Czechoslovakia. The Russians put in as the leader of the French Communist party Georges Marchais.

In this complicated and largely Moscow-dominated Marxist camp, Euro-Communism played little part in practical politics. Tito, the chief heretic, was driven by the need for self-preservation to seek diplomatic support from non-Communist states, because only they possessed the power to come to his aid. Almost inevitably, therefore, Tito was increasingly dedicated to neutralism and non-alignment. In September 1961 a world conference of non-aligned states in Belgrade gave Tito the position he had sought for many years as the equal of Stalin and Mao.

The emergence of Tito as a leader of the non-aligned states therefore reflected less an ideological stance than the logical outcome of a complex series of relationships beginning with his quarrel with Stalin. Yet the Yugoslavs were themselves Marxist and pro-Soviet as became evident in several major confrontations between East and West, notably the Cuban missile crisis, and in the Sino–Soviet split. This coincided with a series of attempts to put Yugoslavia's internal policies on a systematically more repressive and orthodox Marxist basis; in the 1958 'election', for example, Tito gained 99.3 per cent of the votes. Despite this, and despite its acceptance into Comecon in 1964, Yugoslavia became associated with OECD, GATT and the IMF, because of its potential bridging role in East–West relations.

The actual economic policies Yugoslavia now adopted were a reversion to the centralist planning which characterised the other countries of Eastern Europe, and were equally unsuccessful, despite substantial elements of Western aid and support, and some credits from the USSR, following the Sino–Soviet split in October 1961, when Tito came out in support of Moscow.

Tito's personal power, his quasi-monarchical rule, was exercised in a fashion that was characteristically Stalinist, but less oppressive and cruel, and Tito himself was probably more genuinely popular.

Titoism, nevertheless, was widely interpreted as a liberal form of Communism, partly due to effective propaganda, partly to a need on the part of the West not to drive Yugoslavia fully into the Moscow camp, and partly to wish-fulfilment, similar to the reports of left-wing tourists from Russia in the 1930s who, despite the known horrors of the purges, described an idyllic land of happy brotherhood – the exceptions being André Gide, the French writer, and Walter Citrine, the British trade union leader. But 1964 onwards saw a genuine shift to locally-controlled enterprises and to decentralisation of the Yugoslav state itself into constituent republics. These reforms were fully endorsed in June 1965, with a full-scale entry into Western international trade, a devaluation, and a shift to a basically market economy. The basis for private enterprise was agriculture and tourism, and to these were gradually added small business enterprises and, most important, co-operatives. These were singled out in propaganda as the key to the nature of the Yugoslav experiment in Socialist democracy, which was so great an exaggeration as to be an untruth. Inevitably disruption and confusion followed so substantial a reform and there was even a reaction in favour of traditional Communism. Rankovič, a close ally of Tito, was purged in 1962 in order to put a stop to this movement; likewise a group of intellectuals advocating yet more liberal policies.

In the 1960s Yugoslav output grew rapidly. As the economy developed, there were accusations of totalitarianism, signs of inefficiency and of corruption in the party, and a stop put on all ideological and theoretical discussion. The problem of the distribution of income became more serious, since the more backward areas remained backward, while Serbia and the coastal areas shared in the prosperity of Western Europe.

'The economists' debate' was concerned with the way in which the economy should be run, in particular the use of decentralised market systems to allocate resources. The theme was no longer decentralisation, but a hybrid word, 'de-étatisation', meaning the anti-statist line of the Yugoslav Communist party. These debates rejected centralised planning, and endorsed the liberal economic line. Thus Western economic thinking was adopted as the basis for organising the Yugoslav economy and the final abandonment of all allegiance to the Soviet system of planning. Yugoslav Socialism could now be called *laissez-faire* Socialism.

The reconciliation between Yugoslavia and the Soviet Union, which took place first under Khruschev and then with Brezhnev, was formally completed when Brezhnev visited Yugoslavia in 1962. It was not, of course, an ideological agreement but a burying of hatchets. The West, perceiving the non-aligned nations, and in particular Yugoslavia, as reasonably loyal allies of the Soviet Union, became increasingly distrustful of Tito. At the same time the non-aligned movement itself grew more interested in the long-term problems of the developing countries and agreed to hold the first United Nations Conference on Trade and Development (UNCTAD) which took place from March to June 1964 in Geneva. As the number of small independent states, particularly in Africa, proliferated, ultimately two more United Nations agencies were created, the Special UN Fund for Economic Development (SUNFED) and the United Nations Industrial Development Organisation (UNIDO).

The development of the Group of 77, which put forward a co-ordinated point of view of the less developed countries, was growing embarrassing for the West, particularly with the original UNCTAD developing into UNCTAD II in New Delhi in 1968. Over the Egyptian–Israeli War of 1967, Tito supported Moscow's line and broke off diplomatic relations with Israel.

Although it was clear that Tito felt his national problems were solved, it became equally clear that from the point of view of two of Yugoslavia's indigenous nationalities, the Croats and the Slovenes, this was by no means the case, and their difficulties were accentuated by the levels of economic development achieved in different parts of the country, with Slovenia and Croatia much ahead of Bosnia, Herzegovina, Macedonia and Montenegro. As the 'Liberals' began to win, Yugoslavia's 1961–5 Five-Year Plan was cancelled. Nevertheless the Centralists mounted a strong counterattack. The upshot of the economic crisis of 1964–6 was the reassertion of the principle of self-management which Tito eventually supported. Subsidies on many commodities, such as bread, milk, coal and electricity were reduced, and prices rose. The rate of inflation and the Yugoslav balance of payments deficit increased.

By 1966 there was – for Yugoslavia – a considerable economic crisis which could neither have led to greater centralism nor to more emphasis on reform; in fact the reformers won. The crisis coincided with the visit to Moscow, for a Soviet Congress, of Rankovič, the Vice-President of Yugoslavia, who was responsible for the organisation of the Yugoslav Communist party and the secret police. In his absence Rankovič was disgraced on the grounds that he had been secretly tapping the phones and installing bugging devices throughout the senior echelons of the Yugoslav party, including that of Tito himself. The theory went that Rankovič was supporting the Soviet line, that economic reform would strengthen Yugoslav ties with the West, and that, therefore, the pro-

Cominform members of the Yugoslav party would be opposed to reform. Rankovič resigned from all his party offices and was succeeded by Popovič.

Reform, when it was implemented, was a tremendous success. National income rose dramatically, the balance of payments deficit disappeared, and trade with the West increased enormously. Particularly significant was the growth in tourism and domestic car ownership. As censorship was eroded, so considerable freedom of the press grew alongside comparative free debate in the federal and republican assemblies. But there were limits, as for example the trial in 1965 of Mihajlo Mihajlov, a lecturer in the faculty of philosophy in Zagreb. A new Marxist journal, *Praxis*, was established (it had connections with *New Left* in Britain), and this also was attacked. Djilas was released from prison in 1967, in order to reconcile Western Labour and Social Democratic parties to the Yugoslav regime.

Nevertheless, for Tito, the behaviour of the Soviet Communists made rapprochement difficult. The Yugoslavs welcomed the Prague Spring, so the Soviet invasion of Czechoslovakia caused outbursts of anti-Soviet feeling, particularly as the Yugoslavs were ever fearing Soviet intervention into their own country. But as détente blossomed the position of Yugoslavia became easier, particularly with the appointment of Willy Brandt as Chancellor of the German Federal Republic, which enabled Brezhnev to pursue an active *Westpolitik*, in which Yugoslavia played an important part.

Within Yugoslavia the Croatians developed a strong nationalist line, reaching the point of demanding near independence except in defence and foreign affairs.

Yugoslavia, like China, had broken away from the Soviet Union because it was not occupied by Soviet troops. In both cases there had been an ideological split as well. In countries outside the Soviet orbit, especially Italy, new forms of Marxism emerged within the Communist party.

But in 1968 Czechoslovakia demonstrated, as Hungary had done in 1956, that in a country in which Soviet troops were stationed, ideological divergence was strictly limited.

Czechoslovakia became the most rigorously orthodox Stalinist state of the Soviet bloc other than Russia itself. In a major show trial in 1952 Clementis, Slánský and twelve other prominent Communists had been charged with being traitors, American and British spies, agents for international Zionism and Titoists. Eleven were hanged and three others sentenced to life imprisonment. It subsequently emerged in 1968 that they had all been deprived of food, kept in solitary confinement, interrogated standing at attention for sixteen hours a day, woken thirty or forty times a night and made to learn by heart the confessions which they had made. Such trials had continued throughout the 1950s under the hard-line Stalinists Gottwald and Novotny. Thousands of Czechs were jailed and hundreds executed. Stalinisation went further here than in Poland or elsewhere and since the Roman Catholic Church was weak in Bohemia, there was no natural focus for inner opposition to the regime.

As Novotny was the most Stalinist ruler in the Eastern bloc, serious problems were raised within Czechoslovakia by the denunciation of Stalin by Khruschev and the Hungarian uprising. The Czechoslovakian Communist party did not begin its slow process of de-Stalinisation until late 1962 when a demand was accepted for the study of the Slánský trials. Then in April 1963 Alexander Dubček became the First Secretary of the Slovak Communist party. Dubček's important post enabled him to attack the Novotny regime and in June he announced, on behalf of the party, that Clementis and other Slovaks had been illegally convicted; in August Slánský was declared innocent. It followed therefore that the trials which had been conducted during the Great Purge were now admitted to have been show trials. Consequently the whole process by which Novotny had come to power was called into jeopardy.

Novotny himself survived and tried to appease the discontent in Czechoslovakia by slightly lifting censorship. An international jazz festival held in Prague in 1964 was seen as a sign that a great liberalisation of the arts was under way and that Czechoslovakia, from being the stuffiest and most repressive of the regimes, would become intellectually, socially and artistically the most progressive country in Eastern Europe and a source, therefore, of anxiety to other regimes.

To some degree, too, the economy began to improve and there was a major reform of the allocation system by adopting some modified market economics under the direction of Ota Sik, who was a director of the Economics Institute of the Academy of Sciences. Sik was much influenced by Yugoslavia and attempted to introduce similar reforms to those which had succeeded in raising its output and productivity. Whilst there was a paradox in that the most hard-line head of a Soviet regime was presiding over a cultural and economic reform, this process could not endure, since it was essentially unstable.

In early 1967 a step forward to freedom of speech began to be taken: the radio joined with the press in freely discussing ideas. As large numbers of foreign tourists began visiting Czechoslovakia so Czechoslovaks travelled abroad. With output diverted from investment in heavy industry once more to consumer goods, the standard of living substantially improved. Nevertheless, hard-line Stalinists still opposed the liberalisation, and in particular the secret police continued to arrest and harass in large numbers. The Soviet Union's trial of Sinyavsky and Daniel in 1966, and the attack on Solzhenitsyn and the closing in January 1967 of the first modern art show in Moscow, were all signs that the Soviet Union was distressed at liberalisation within its borders and in the Soviet satellite countries.

The Middle East war of 1967, which the Israelis unexpectedly won, disconcerted the Czech regime, an ardent supporter of Egypt and Syria, and deeply anti-Semitic. The Jewish community in Czechoslovakia was powerful in intellectual and media circles, therefore an immediate conflict developed between their enthusiasm for the Israeli victory and the official dismay.

At that year's Czechoslovak Writers' Union dissidents came out into the open to challenge the whole basis of the Communist state. A particularly outspoken novelist, Ludvik Vaculik, for a long time a member of the Communist party, denounced the regime, and demanded freedom, and went on, 'It is necessary to understand that in the course of twenty years no human problem has been solved in our country – starting with the elementary needs such as housing, schools and economic prosperity and ending with the finer requirements of life which cannot be provided by the undemocratic systems of the world . . .'

Then, in the same September, Dubček drew attention to the way in which Slovakia was getting less than its fair share of investment and expressed deep dissatisfaction with the way that the New Economic Model was working. By this time discontent was clearly centring on Novotny, who could neither go forward nor back. Dubček, in an unprecedented move in October, claimed that Novotny had always cheated Slovakia, whereupon Novotny attacked Dubček for bourgeois nationalism. This ensured that the Slovaks would rally round Dubček.

The Central Committee then adjourned until early December, but on 31 October 1967 students marched towards the President's palace, the Hradcany Castle, carrying candles. They were brutally dispersed. This was followed by a meeting on 8 November of students from the philosophical faculty of Charles University, accompanied by a rising of the students of the Prague Technical University, and on 20 November a mass meeting developed into a sit-in which led to further police violence, but sympathetic treatment by the university authorities. The students were demanding academic immunity and protesting about police brutality, and demanding some degree of freedom of speech.

In the meantime Novotny tried to have Dubček removed from his post. This caused further trouble with the Slovaks who thereupon demanded considerable autonomy for Slovakia and in particular a splitting of the parties into a Czech and a Slovak Communist party, without a Central Committee. Novotny also appealed for help from Brezhnev who came to Prague on 8 December, in order to see all parties.

Eventually Dubček was nominated as First Secretary of the Party; Novotny retaining the Presidency, a ceremonial post. On 5 January 1968 therefore, Dubček became the leader of Czechoslovakia. He was congratulated by Brezhnev, who clearly hoped that trouble could be contained. Dubček, who was born in 1922, had been educated in the Soviet Union, having gone there with his parents in 1925, had returned to Czechoslovakia in 1942, fought with the Communist partisans, and had then gone back to Moscow to the Higher Party School, from which he graduated in 1958. Since Dubček had survived the Stalin purges, the Soviet Union had no reason to suppose that he was unreliable; indeed, Novotny's replacement by Dubček may have seemed to Moscow a purely internal matter not affecting Czech relations with the Soviet Union.

For some time Dubček kept his profile low and it was thought that he might be a secret follower of Novotny. In fact Dubček was surrounded by Novotny supporters, and in particular faced pressure from the Soviet Ambassador to follow the old policies. There is little doubt, too, that although he had been an active supporter of Slovak national efforts for reform and improvement, he had no serious proposals at that time for the reform of the entire Czechoslovak party and state apparatus.

Novotny was quick to retaliate. Jan Beneš, a liberal leader, was tried for passing on information to the West, and sent to jail for five years. This suggested that Novotny was going to revert to the show trials of the early 1950s to enforce his will on the people. Foreign journalists were harassed and expelled. Then the most popular novelist in Czechoslovakia, Ladislav Mnacko, defected to the West and decided to emigrate to Israel. In his statement he said, 'It is impossible for me to support – even through silence – a policy which leads to the eradication of a whole people and to the liquidation of an entire state.' This was a reference to the attacks on Israel, and he continued, 'The system in Czechoslovakia must be changed to a very considerable degree if we want to continue as a healthy Socialist humanitarian country.' This was broadcast to Czechoslovakia by the Western radio stations. The importance lay in the fact that Mnacko was not Jewish, and wrote in Slovak. Mnacko was immediately deprived of his Czechoslovak citizenship and expelled from the Communist party.

Novotny continued to seek to repress the intellectual ferment, but then in September Jan Prochazka, who was a candidate member of the party Central Committee, published a tribute to Thomas Masaryk, in which he was violently critical of Novotny. On 26 and 27 September Prochazka was removed from the Central Committee, while Vaculik and others were expelled from the party. The Writers' Union lost its literary magazine to the Ministry of Culture, which caused a furore.

The Czech people's real feelings were shown for the first time on 15 February 1968 when its ice hockey team defeated the Soviet Union in the Winter Olympics at Grenoble. An explosion of joy in Czechoslovakia stimulated those who were opposed to the Soviet Union to come out into the open. A fortnight earlier Dubček had spoken to a meeting of the agricultural co-operatives in Prague and chosen to make a speech defending democracy and freedom of speech. In late February he began to remove a number of hard-line Communists from various positions in the hierarchy, and in particular to remove the Security Chief, Mamula. Dubček, it transpired, was concerned to increase freedom of speech and to liberalise the economy while at the same time maintaining the strongest possible links with the Soviet Union, since the failure to do this had brought about the downfall of the Hungarian revolution in 1956.

Dubček not only visited Moscow to reassure the Soviet Union of his loyalty, but also established good relations with Kadar, the Hungarian leader, and with Gomulka in Poland, though he was unsuccessful in achieving any kind of rapprochement with Walter Ulbricht of the German Democratic Republic. In many respects Hungary represented the model on which Dubček was basing his reforms. Those who had been concerned with Imre Nagy had been rehabilitated and Hungary went through an economic reform very much along the lines advocated by Ota Sik in Czechoslovakia.

Novotny and his son resigned on 22 March 1968, thus the entire Communist apparatus which had been installed in February 1948 was rapidly falling apart. The Masaryks were rehabilitated, particularly Jan, who, according to the official report, had been murdered by the Communists, and was now elevated by Czech students to join his father, Thomas Masaryk, as a national hero.

The unrest in Czechoslovakia spread rapidly to Poland, where Gomulka clamped down on liberalism. The Soviet Union became

increasingly anxious, and Dubček and his colleagues were summoned to Dresden on 23 March to meet Warsaw Pact members.
Only the Romanians declined to go. The *Tass* communiqué said that
'Confidence was expressed that the working class and all workers
of the Czechoslovak Socialist Republic, under the leadership of the
Czechoslovak Communist party, will guarantee the further development of Socialist construction in the country.' The Soviet
party, supported by other parties, argued that Dubček had lost
control of the situation. Dubček strongly disagreed.

Demands now sprang up for free political parties and for the
ending of the Communist monopoly. These demands were led by
former political prisoners and by students, and were debated on
the radio and television and at mass meetings. On 1 April 1968
Dubček published the Action Programme of the Communist party
in Czechoslovakia, 'The Czechoslovak Road to Socialism'. It was
intended as the compromise programme around which all Czechs
could unite to attack the past and argued that there could be
freedom for Czechs and Slovaks to work together with free expression, while at the same time maintaining a Socialist state. It
also said that the Communist party need not be the monopoly
political party, but it spoke strongly in favour of support for the
Soviet Union, and its foreign policy, though it was no longer an
anti-Zionist party.

The document was unacceptable to Moscow, and on 9 and 10
April Brezhnev denounced it, among other matters, to a Soviet
Central Committee meeting in Moscow, claiming that the pro-
gramme broke the agreement which had been reached in Dresden.
Meanwhile *Pravda* attacked the Czech line.

This was the beginning of what became known as the Prague
Spring in which the dictatorship established in 1948 was abandoned
at an ever-accelerating pace. The central issue was the investigation of Jan Masaryk's alleged suicide in 1948. It became clear
that there was evidence that Stalin had personally ordered the
murder of Masaryk, and that it was Soviet secret police who had
assisted the Czech secret police in dragging Masaryk from bed and
throwing him out of the window after he had been shot behind the
ear. It was then revealed that the Slánský trial had been ordered by
Stalin through Mikoyan, who had come from Moscow to order
Gottwald to conduct it. Previously Beria had been blamed for
these actions, but Mikoyan was still a powerful figure in Moscow
and a friend and colleague of Brezhnev and Kosygin. The inference was clear, that both Brezhnev and Kosygin were also implicated in the Stalinist excesses which led to the Slánský trial and
later to the trials in Leningrad and Moscow.

The Soviet Union continued its attacks on the Dubček leadership and also applied economic pressure. The United States remained completely silent throughout this extraordinary outburst and so the Czechs were left to struggle alone, as the Hungarians had been in 1956. As the spring developed, the mass demonstrations grew larger, culminating, on 3 May, in Old Town Square, in a massive anti-Communist demonstration.

Dubček and Smrkovsky then flew to Moscow, where they were given the warning that an intervention along the lines of 1956 in Hungary would take place unless the liberalisation was stopped. Dubček gave no hint to the Czechs of the likely intervention of the Soviet Union, and consequently the popular fervour continued.

Meetings took place in Eastern Europe between Brezhnev and Kosygin, and Ulbricht, Gomulka, Kadar, and Zhivkov of Bulgaria, and on 17 May Kosygin came to Prague, presumably to attempt to negotiate with Dubček. The rumour was spread that Kosygin represented the more liberal element of the Kremlin leadership. He arranged economic support and also that Warsaw Pact manoeuvres would be held in Czechoslovakia in June.

The Communist party in Czechoslovakia itself began to split and hard-liners emerged to negotiate with the East German Ambassador. The liberals under Dubček and his Deputy Prime Minister, Ota Sik, pursued economic reform, including Western capital investment, and the development of Czechoslovakia into the Federal Union of Czechs and Slovaks, as well as substantial indemnities to the hundreds of thousands who had been unjustly imprisoned. Plans for heavy industry were severely cut back with an emphasis instead on consumer goods output.

The Yugoslavs announced their support for the Czechoslovaks, as did the Italian Communist party, while West German and American businessmen were welcomed in Prague. Moscow was considerably alarmed, seeing this as the beginning of Western orientation in Czech policies.

On 27–28 June, at an extraordinary session of the Communist party Presidium, feelings hardened against the statement issued by Ludvik Vaculik and signed by seventy people, called '2000 Words', which demanded that the revolution must continue and that the development of a hard-line Communist reaction to the revolution must be stopped.

The arrival of Warsaw Pact troops on the pretext of taking part in manoeuvres was regarded amongst the Czech people as a prelude to a full-scale military occupation of the country. Ota Sik continually denounced the economic position of Czechoslovakia, which was undoubtedly very poor indeed. West German aid and a small amount of American support were promised, thereby pre-cipitating the decision by Moscow that there must be an interven-tion, either by a military invasion or by an internal coup d'état to eliminate Dubček.

On 3 July Brezhnev and Kadar spoke at a Hungarian friendship meeting in Moscow in which they denounced the United States and made it clear that they would restore order in Czechoslovakia. Kadar said that the Hungarians expressed 'full solidarity with the Communists, with those who defend the power of the working class, the cause of Socialism against the encroachments of dogma-tists, revisionists, the class enemy. We understand the sense of the struggle, and we are prepared to extend international aid by all means.' The Czechoslovak Presidium was ordered to attend a meeting to discuss the '2000 Words' manifesto, but declined. Though the Warsaw Pact manoeuvres ended on 30 June, Soviet troops did not leave the country; and in July the Czechs formally demanded that they should.

A meeting of the Pact, which Czechoslovakia did not attend, was summoned in Warsaw on 15 July. In an ultimatum the Central Committee of the Czechoslovak Communist party was ordered to reverse the Prague Spring measures and give 'a rebuff to the anti-Communist forces'.

The issue was now one of Czechoslovak sovereignty. The War-saw statement made it clear that each party was responsible not only to its own working class, but to the international working class, and therefore national sovereignty had no place in a Com-munist world. The reply from the Czechs was a statement that Czechoslovakia regarded its national sovereignty as paramount. The Czechs also requested a revision of the Warsaw Pact. It was clear that the vast majority of the Czech people strongly supported Dubček. The entire Presidium of the Czechoslovak Communist party was summoned to the Soviet Union to meet the entire Politburo of the Soviet Communist party. Fearing that they would be kidnapped, the Czechs insisted that the meeting should be held in Czechoslovakia. Jan Hus, the leader of the Reformation in Czechoslovakia, had been tricked in 1415 and invited to the Council of Constance, where he was arrested and burnt at the stake as a heretic. The Czechs were determined this trick would not be repeated.

The meeting of the two Communist parties was held at Cierna and Tisou in Slovakia on the Soviet border. The meeting ended in apparent amity, though Dubček claimed afterwards that the Czechoslovak party had been given authority to continue on its own line. He also said that Czechoslovak sovereignty was not

threatened. A further meeting took place at Bratislava with Dubček and Smrkovsky, Brezhnev and Kosygin, Ulbricht, Gomulka,
Kadar and Zhivkov.

On 3 August Soviet troops withdrew from Czechoslovakia. Tito
came to Prague on 9 August to indicate his support for Dubček,
and freedom of expression continued. Ulbricht came on 12 August
and was received correctly, but not warmly. Attacks then started in
the press of other Communist countries. Nevertheless, when
Ceauşescu of Romania came on 15 August, he was given a warm
welcome, though less enthusiastic than had been given to Tito. On
19–20 August reports began to appear of Soviet and other Warsaw
Pact troops massing on the borders of Czechoslovakia. On 20
August 1968 troops invaded from East Germany, Poland, the
Soviet Union and Hungary. The violence, hostility and resistance
that greeted them were filmed by Czech and Western reporters and
transmitted to the rest of the world. The Soviet plan for Dubček to
be overthrown by the Presidium failed; instead Dubček and his
colleagues were taken prisoner by Russian soldiers and flown to
Slovakia. President Svoboda, however, refused to sign a proclamation to appoint a new government, and the position became
extremely embarrassing for the Soviet Union.

A special session of the UN Security Council was called, where
the Czech Ambassador protested about the invasion. On 23
August Svoboda was flown to Moscow to negotiate, and in the
meantime the Western European Communist parties declared
their support for the Czech Communist party. Dubček and his
colleagues were then flown to Moscow where they were treated
humiliatingly with threats and violence. On 26 August an agreement was announced, actually a capitulation to the Soviet demands. On 27 August Dubček broadcast a tragic speech, but
hinted that some room for manoeuvre still remained. The Party
Conference held secretly just after the Soviet invasion was declared illegal, and a new Party Conference was called, which
included, as well as Dubček, Svoboda and his supporters, some
pro-Russian members.

For ten days the United States had remained aloof, but on 30
August it was warned that the Russians might be about to invade
Romania. 'So let no one unleash the dogs of war,' cried President
Johnson, who warned that the United States would not stand idly
by. On 13 September censorship was reimposed in Czechoslovakia, and in October, Kosygin came to Prague and signed a treaty
which legalised the occupation. The stalemate lasted until well into
the winter, with Dubček and Svoboda still in office, and with
no persecution of the liberals. But finally, in the spring of the

following year, Dubček and Svoboda were disgraced and exiled.

Once more the Warsaw Pact was used as a means of suppressing any deviation from the Soviet line. Brezhnev reiterated the 1947 position that the world was divided into two, and that the USSR had to assume the leadership of the Socialist camp. But even Communists themselves could no longer disguise that the invasion of Czechoslovakia was an invasion and the imposition of a dictatorship was a dictatorship. As in the case of Hungary in 1956, the world Communist movement lost prestige and credibility by this act.

The result of all these moves – and others which will be described in subsequent chapters – was to maintain Soviet control of Eastern Europe, though in a less tyrannical form than in the 1940s and early 1950s. This was probably due to a greater sophistication on the part of the Eastern European Communist movement, and also to the influence of Communist parties operating in Western Europe and in former European colonies and in Latin America, where the Soviet military presence was absent or less dominant. In Africa, Asia and Latin America, however, as the West withdrew so the Soviet empire sought to expand. Its most formidable expansion came in Cuba and Chile.

The attempts to reform Communism had failed. Perhaps all revolutions conceived in terror always end in absolutism – the French revolutionary terror being the exemplar. But, in any case, so long as Soviet power was there, and could be used (as it so frequently was) no nation could escape from its grip.

Nevertheless, Communism still exercised a fascination, not only for the Blunts, the Burgesses, the Hisses, but for Sartre, for the trade union leaders in the West, and for the Castros and Allendes.

Chapter 25

Latin America: Castro and Allende

South America was the scene of two startling Marxist successes, Fidel Castro's revolution in Cuba and Salvador Allende's election in Chile, the only Marxist ever to win by an open democratic free vote. Why then did Communism not sweep through South America? Was it the influence of the United States and CIA plotting or was it the tortuous course of Latin American politics in each country?

Mexico was no stranger to Communism for it had provided its own alternative to Marxism and Latin America had its own Socialism, APRA, the American Popular Revolutionary Alliance, founded by Haya de la Torre, a Peruvian, in 1924. De la Torre argued that Latin American capitalism, developing in a feudal context where the impulse of capitalism came from overseas, caused a basic disequilibrium in Latin America. In this argument the external impulse to capitalism gave particular importance to imperialism which, far from being the last stage of capitalism in Europe, as suggested by Lenin, was in Latin America the first stage. APRA policy was against Yankee imperialists who controlled the export trade and extractive industries and for the reunification of Latin America with gradual nationalisation of land and industry, internationalisation of the Panama Canal and solidarity with all oppressed people. APRist parties developed in Peru, Mexico, Guatemala, Costa Rica, Puerto Rico, Bolivia, Chile and Argentina, offering a Socialist alternative to Marxism and Leninism. In Venezuela, two APRist leaders founded a party which alternated the Presidency with the Christian Democrats, but in Peru, the original home of APRism, it was unsuccessful and overborn by the military.

The two biggest countries in South America, Brazil and Argentina, both with a high level of economic development, were ruled in a way where classic Marxist–Leninism seemed inapplicable. They were examples of Caudillo-ism or dictatorship by a leader.

Brazil outlawed the Communist party in 1947 and governed through a series of deeply conservative Presidents who controlled an increasingly prosperous society of over seventy million people with cautious liberalism. Argentina was governed by a series of military-dominated juntas whose periods of office usually ended in coups d'état. The first of a series of populist nationalist dictators was Juan Perón who, with his wife, Eva, were extremely popular with the workers and the *descaminados* or shirtless ones, but loathed by the middle class. According to Perón himself, Perónism was a form of Fascism, a mixture of Mussolini-style personal dictatorship and militarism. The standard of living of the labourers, the factory workers and the peones was substantially raised, but liberal elements were firmly suppressed.

Perón was the archetypal modern Latin American dictator, of whom many lesser examples were to be found in Central America. In Cuba a new-style dictator emerged, who challenged the United States from a Marxist standpoint and brought the Soviet Union to America.

Cuba was a relatively prosperous state with a corrupt and dictatorial government aligned with the United States. In 1959 a small group of guerrillas led by Fidel Castro successfully deposed the local dictator Batista and entered Havana in triumph. The Soviet Union gave Castro the support that it habitually extended to 'anti-imperialist' governments but there is little evidence that Castro's movements were linked to any Moscow-based programme. However the nationalisation of American companies, especially oil companies, in 1960, led to Russian promises to make up the Cuban shortages of imports. In consequence Cuban sugar exports to America were forbidden by the US government. The consequent disruption of trade added to the serious and growing problems of the Cuban economy.

After the American failure to invade at the Bay of Pigs, the Cuban economy continued to deteriorate, but so too did the American position in Latin America; at the Punta del Este inter-American conference in Uruguay in August 1961 the Americans inaugurated a major aid programme for Latin America through Kennedy's Alliance for Progress.

It was nevertheless obvious that anti-American feeling was widespread throughout Latin America and that Castro might be the first of many anti-American, perhaps Communist, dictators there. On 1 December 1961, in one of his longest speeches – at midnight before a multitude of people – Castro declared himself a Marxist–Leninist. This was probably a surprise to the Soviet Union. After a delay this declaration gained support first from Peking and then from Moscow.

In early 1962 Castro initiated, in classic Communist manner, a purge of his closest associates. In May Khruschev admitted Cuba to the Soviet camp and decided to position missiles on the island. The bases were the price Castro had to pay for the substantial

Soviet aid he needed to replace Western imports. On 14 October a U2 aircraft took photographs that identified the missile sites and two days later Kennedy accepted the evidence. There followed the Cuban missile crisis that brought the world to the brink of nuclear war, ending when Khruschev agreed to withdraw the missiles from Cuba. It was clear that Khruschev had not expected the strength of the American reaction and, further, that he had expected at some time a second Bay of Pigs to avenge the failure of the first. In both assumptions he was wrong. On the other hand, Kennedy should not have assumed that Khruschev was taking a deliberate step into confrontation with the United States and doing so at Cuba's behest.

Khruschev's withdrawal left Castro exposed, in the sense that the Soviet Union clearly recognised Cuba as part of America's strategic zone. On the other hand, Castro had Kennedy's guarantee that there would be no further American invasions of Cuba. Castro was therefore to a considerable extent a free agent, free of both great powers. The United States kept up its blockade, but after a period of coldness the Soviet Union stepped up its aid and support. In 1963 Castro declared himself an orthodox Marxist and became First Secretary of the United Party of the Socialist Revolution.

The consequence of Castro's successful revolution and even more of his successful defiance of the United States led to renewed confidence by Nationalists and Socialists throughout the Americas and in Africa and Asia, where Castro became a hero of the non-aligned movement. Yet in the major Latin American countries the direct consequences of Castroism were small.

Why did Castroism not sweep to power throughout Latin America as some hoped and many feared? Was it American influence? Or was it that the local varieties of Caudillo-ism and Marxism, with APRism as the indigenous political movement, and Christian Democracy occasionally practised both in Venezuela and Chile, meant that there was no striking original Latin American contribution to ideas about political structure and political initiatives? The APRist model was an important one and it created a climate where Castroism might in future flourish.

In the year before Castro's amnesty a rising took place in Argentina against Perón, who was labelled a Fascist and a tool of reactionary elements. His populism was certainly reminiscent of Mussolini's appeal to the underdog; his militarism, his vulgarity, the superficiality of his social reforms all seemed a familiar Latin pattern which created conditions ripe for a more radical revolution.

On 16 June 1955 the navy and air force attempted to overthrow Perón; and the Church, which had been especially favoured by Perón, reacted against him. The army helped Perón to put down the revolution, but only three months later it combined with the Church to overthrow him. The middle class and the big landowners appeared in the ascendant.

Successive civil and military governments were formed after Perón's fall, all of which followed severe economic policies, and asked for American capital to develop oil and natural gas. But far from a shift to Castroite Socialism, the difficulties led to a revival of Perónism and a military dictatorship, although this was loyal to the populist principles that Perón had embodied. Argentina thus 'chose' populism.

Peru seemed obviously open to Castroism. The regime was punctuated by the armed coups, pronunciamento alarms and excursions that had always marked Peruvian political life. A local guerrilla leader, Che Guevara, became a world-wide symbol of youthful revolution. At the same time the United States repeatedly pressed for free democratic elections. In 1962 an election was called in which the old popular APRist leader Haya de la Torre stood. The Indians had no vote as they were illiterate. Nevertheless the election began to excite passions among the poor Andeans. It seemed that Haya de la Torre might win the election and the army, fearing him to be on the left, aborted the elections. The American government protested and the elections were held again in June 1963, with the same candidates. Fernando Belaúnde Terry marginally won but any proposals for reform were blocked by his opponents' supporters, who themselves still sought power. Politics continued to be about the pursuit of individual authority.

Che Guevara's influence remained powerful among intellectuals, but after his capture and death in the Colombian Andes, the Peruvian development took a militarist direction, and a group of radical colonels took office. Once more, a military coup had aborted any genuine social reform; the colonels merely acquired a new form of Socialist rhetoric, known as the 'Peruvian road to Socialism', and APRA was banned.

Central America fell more completely than any part of Latin America within the United States sphere of economic and political influence, and was tied to the American economy by its production of minerals, principally bauxite and copper, but above all by coffee, bananas, cotton and meat exports. It was divided into six small states. Guatemala, Honduras, El Salvador, Nicaragua and Costa Rica, with Panama split into two by the Panama Canal Zone which belonged to America. It was there that the United States earned its worst reputation for propping up bad guys and opposing the good guys.

Substantial urban development meant a growing proportion of the population was involved in the revolution of rising expectations which affected the Western world. Yet in 1950, of some seven million inhabitants in the region, probably about two hundred and fifty thousand were literate. The rural areas remained backward, the middle class was tiny, and the countries were ruled by military governments, largely tools of the proprietors of large estates, and they were often in turn dominated by American companies such as United Fruit, and the State Department. The only revolutionaries were the university students.

No Central American dictator, with the exception of Figueres of Costa Rica, was seriously concerned with improving the lot of his country. Caudillos preferred to stay in office and to become, or remain, rich. Even when a dictator was deposed the government which replaced him owed little more than a rhetorical duty to liberal or Socialist ideals.

In June 1954 Jacobo Arbenz of Guatemala was overthrown by Guatemalan exiles from Honduras, assisted by the US Marine Corps. Since this was to form the basis of a major myth about the United States, it is important to establish that the intervention by the United States came after the decision by the Guatemalan army to overthrow Arbenz, a decision taken on purely political grounds. Nevertheless the United States was prepared, in 1954, to help overthrow a government which had become Communist-dominated. It was a year after Stalin's death, which had been greeted with eulogies in the Guatemalan press, and before Khruschev's denunciation of Stalin; it was also two years before the Soviet invasion of Hungary. It was alleged that the United States was not prepared to see the expropriation of the United Fruit Company, a corporation with which John Foster Dulles had close connections. The United Nations did not debate the invasion, and Arbenz resigned, to be replaced by Carlos Castillo who had helped to lead the invasion. This had been organised under Nicaraguan and Honduran auspices, but planned by the CIA.

In Guatemala, Nicaragua and El Salvador reactionary and corrupt regimes prevailed, the United States seeking to protect its interests. Only in Honduras was Kennedy's suggested Alliance for Progress successful in supporting, for a brief period, a liberal and moderate president. But in Brazil, a country much influenced by the United States, though there was little political progress there was substantial economic growth. In the 1950s Brazil's agricultural output grew by over half, and industrial output by 140 per cent.

Vast schemes were begun, including the new capital of Brasilia, 600 miles from the coast, and massive highways linking all the states. On the other hand inflation reached ever greater heights, and the speed of urbanisation led to vastly increased social problems. Urban violence and unrest were perennial features of Brazilian, as of other Latin American, society. In 1964 the installation of General Castelo Branco as President marked a sharp move to the right and to orthodox economic remedies for what were seen as Brazil's problems. A series of military regimes then followed which were opposed by the Church, intellectuals and, probably, many of the workers and peasants, as the leaders became more oppressive and conservative. But the rise in the prosperity of the middle and business classes continued and the revolution, long predicted, never came.

Similarly Mexico, long regarded as the home of Latin American intellectual radicalism and the site of an earlier major Latin American revolution, settled down to bourgeois conformity.

During the 1960s, a substantial increase took place in output levels, the standard of living and in consumption, as well as in the social services, despite the rapid rise in population. Mexico became, therefore, one of Latin America's more stable and prosperous societies; neither democratic nor Castroite, but reasonably liberal.

The most extraordinary and sad change in Latin America took place in the hitherto stable and progressive country of Chile. Paradoxically its very stability enabled the country to elect the only Marxist ever to win a free election and in so doing to destroy the country's prosperity and its political institutions.

Chile was a prosperous Latin American country largely populated by immigrants. Its main exports – fertilisers, wine and other agricultural produce, as well as copper – gave it a substantial level of foreign earnings and the standard of living was among the highest in Latin America.

Chile had a long tradition of constitutional rule, with a two-chamber Parliament and an elected President. The armed forces had scarcely ever intervened in politics. Chile, a highly politicised country with elections every two years, had a sophisticated electorate, even when extended to include illiterates in 1970. But the proportional representation system encouraged the proliferation of parties and meant that few Presidents had a majority in the legislature.

In 1958 the three leading candidates for President were Arturo Alessandri, a lawyer and a businessman who ran on a very conservative ticket; Eduardo Frei, a Thomist scholar who supported the sort of Christian Democrat programme which had been very successful in Germany and Italy; and Salvador Allende, a committed Marxist who was, however, also deeply committed to parliamentary politics and whose bourgeois background and tastes seemed to make him an attractive and non-totalitarian leftist figure rather than a committed Comintern agent.

The votes in 1958 were split almost equally, with Alessandri winning the election by less than 3 per cent of the vote over Allende. Chile, like other Latin American countries, had a rule that a retiring President could not be re-elected so the two main candidates in 1964 were Frei and Allende. The Americans, through the CIA, financed one half of Frei's campaign, whilst Allende received Castro's support. Frei won with 56 per cent of the vote in an 88 per cent poll, an enormous victory by any standards. The country then drifted towards the left and Frei lost support as part of an anti-American slide associated world-wide with the years 1967–8. Despite success with his agrarian reform, with nationalisation of the copper mines and reduction of union power, the middle class lost confidence in Frei and began to support Alessandri as his successor. The country was polarising into left and right, in the midst of substantially deteriorating internal conditions of urban violence. The 1970 elections were between Alessandri, Allende and a Christian Democratic candidate, Radomiro Tomic. The campaign was conducted in an atmosphere of heady violence with strikes, bank raids and armed attacks. All candidates secretly asked for American financial support and investigations revealed large sums from the great American combine ITT and the CIA for anti-Castro and anti-Allende propaganda. Allende gained 36.2 per cent of the vote, Alessandri 34.9 per cent and Tomic 27.8 per cent. Had there been a run-off open to the whole electorate, it is certain that Alessandri would have won, because the majority of Tomic's supporters would have voted for him. Allende had not gained anything like the predicted overwhelming victory, but in the absence of a run-off, Allende became the first Communist in the world to take office as the result of a free election.

He could take over only after the Congress had chosen him; under the constitution it had to choose between Allende and Alessandri fifty days after the election. This extraordinary choice of a Marxist whose support was thirty per cent, and whom over sixty-three per cent of the electorate opposed, was made because the Christian Democrat candidate, Tomic, threw in his lot with Allende. So Allende came to power on a minority vote with

Christian Democrat support. Whatever mandate he had it was certainly not to introduce full-blooded Socialism. The process by which he was chosen was indicative of the disastrous course that Chile was now set upon. Tomic's wheeling and dealing gave the Marxists the opportunity to claim they were the national choice.

In the seven months before the Congressional vote took place, there was an enormous flight of capital from Chile; the right wing sought to gain the support of the Christian Democrats for Alessandri, but Allende offered a statute of guarantees of freedom in return for their support, which was accepted. ITT and the CIA renewed their anti-Allende campaign, overtures were made for a possible military coup and plans were drawn up for economic disruption. In fact these plans were never implemented, but they gave a legitimate excuse for the left to accuse the United States of seeking to overthrow a democratically-elected government.

The Statute of Democratic Guarantees was watered down, but passed by the Congress, in order to prevent Allende from turning Chile into a second Cuba. At the same time General Viaux organised a military coup, which was frustrated by the police, though General Schneider, the head of the armed forces, was murdered. This assassination gave the Christian Democrats the determination to vote for Allende, and he was elected President by the Congress on 24 October 1970. The Statute of Democratic Guarantees was incorporated into the Chilean Constitution on 9 January 1971.

Even now it seemed that Chile was the great Latin American success story. Frei had been one of the most progressive and democratic South American Presidents, and Chile was a prosperous country with relatively advanced social services. Despite covert American involvement in plots to overthrow him, Allende had been elected freely, and the Americans welcomed further proof that Chile remained a constitutional democracy.

Though Allende was an atheist and a Marxist, the Roman Catholic Church in Chile welcomed his election and Allende attended an ecumenical *Te Deum* in Santiago Cathedral. Despite his recognition of Communist regimes such as North Korea and North Vietnam, he remained on good terms with the United States, and Castro did not fly immediately to Chile to welcome an ally at the other end of the continent, as had been feared. Allende spoke frequently of the 'via Chilena', which was to be a democratic Marxist solution to Chile's problems, a regime unique in the world, and far from Cuba's chosen path. He openly accepted that other Communist regimes were tyrannies, and he appeared to accept that democratic politics would continue, with the possibility that he might be succeeded by a right-winger in the 1976 election, when he would be ineligible to stand. He was anti-imperialist, he said, but not anti-American. Nevertheless, his resolve to nationalise American firms carried with it the possibility of conflict with the United States. He also faced a Congress that contained no majority and would be difficult to manage.

Allende began at once to use the President's emergency powers to nationalise the banks. The Christian Democrats supported the nationalisation of foreign banks, and also of the remaining foreign-owned copper mines. A takeover of land in the south by illegal land seizures was denounced by the Christian Democrats but they supported Allende's further proposed agrarian reform.

In 1971, in his first budget, Allende increased the deficit, bringing dire prophecies of economic doom, but the inflation rate fell dramatically and the country seemed prosperous. As often in Latin America, when all seemed bad, fair weather set in, only to be followed by storms. There were even then signs of trouble to come; the foreign exchange reserves began to run down rapidly and the export prices of copper fell, while foreign investment dried up. This external trade deficit became a cause of worry, and severe restrictions on overseas trade were introduced, offering a prospect of characteristic Communist restrictions on freedom of movement abroad.

The regime's first major crisis arose in agriculture. The redistribution of income raised the demand for food, and the illegal seizure of nearly fifteen hundred farms in the south of Chile in 1971 by peasants and by left-wing agitators and students threatened to reduce agricultural production. That year's harvest, planted before Allende took office, was fairly large, but successive years showed serious falls and mounting rural violence. The issue of revolutionary violence or 'bourgeois legalism' came to the fore as leftist groups seized farms, houses and factories.

Nevertheless, despite the problems of public order, the municipal elections in April 1971 gave Allende's parties a 1 per cent lead over the combined opposition – his share of the poll had therefore risen from 36 per cent to 49 per cent, if these elections were regarded as a referendum on his Presidency.

The large cloud on the horizon was widespread violence. The Christian Democrats then split, their left wing seceding in order to support Allende, which made the party leaders more strongly opposed to him than would perhaps have been the case if the party had remained united. The Radicals also split, with their members of the Cabinet offering to resign. Politics increasingly took on a pro- or anti-Allende aspect, with the President becoming, as it were, the embodiment of the Revolution. Despite his democratic assurances, the government became increasingly personalised.

In the course of 1971 and 1972 the attempt to nationalise American copper concerns with little or no compensation was offset by major American counter-claims on Chile. Ford and General Motors joined the copper firms in putting pressure on the US government to stop the wholesale confiscation of foreign-owned assets in Chile. Allende's government then moved to take over the paper industry, in which Alessandri's firm was important, raided opposition newspapers and attacked Frei for corruption. The Christian Democrats became convinced that the Allende government was now a Communist-dominated body determined to suppress its opponents by the familiar tactics of character assassination, violence and terror.

On 10 November 1971 Allende sent to Congress a draft constitutional amendment designed to abolish the Senate. This meant that if his party could gain control of the single lower chamber, he could govern dictatorially, since the President could dissolve Congress at will and hold elections when it suited him. The amendment further weakened Congress by making its members eligible for re-election only once; and it subordinated the Supreme Court to the President. It seemed that Allende's pretensions to support normal constitutional procedures were no longer valid. On the other hand, some constitutional reform was essential if political stability were ever to be restored.

On the day that the constitutional amendment was presented, Fidel Castro arrived in Chile and stayed for three weeks. Castro described Chile's free elections, free press and representative institutions as 'condemned by history as decadent and anachronistic'. To his rage he was subject to hostile criticism for his totalitarian views, his calls to revolution, and his alleged homosexuality.

Meanwhile the Senate moved to impeach the Minister of the Interior, José Tohá, for infringing the constitution. In an act of defiance Allende made him Minister of Defence. In January 1972 Allende lost two by-elections, and it was clear that if free elections were held Allende and his supporters would lose. He therefore sought to broaden the basis of his government. But whatever political moves he made, he was faced by mounting revolutionary violence and above all by a growing collapse of the economy – roaring inflation, a loss of all overseas reserves, and a decline in agricultural output. Throughout that summer of 1972 and on into 1973, political and social life was dominated by strikes, demonstrations and protest marches until virtually the whole of the middle and professional classes were on strike, together with 100,000 peasants.

During the rest of the year conditions deteriorated still further: most people in the towns could only get food on the black market, inflation increased to 300 per cent with a 3400 per cent increase in the money supply in two and a half years and a 25 per cent fall in agricultural output.

By early September 1973 it was clear that the air force and large parts of the navy were prepared to consider overthrowing Allende. Then the carabineros (armed police) agreed that they too would join other military leaders in overthrowing Allende. Their reason was the undeniable fact that the revolutionary workers were already taking over the state, with Allende's connivance.

At seven a.m. on 11 September the army began to move; by eight-fifteen a.m. Concepcion had been peacefully occupied; the navy occupied Valparaiso (the main port) at six-twenty a.m.; an hour later Allende was offered an air force plane to take him into exile which he refused. By nine-thirty a.m. Allende broadcast a defiant message, and most of Santiago was occupied. The Presidential palace was bombed by the air force at eleven-fifty-five a.m. and at one-thirty p.m. the defenders and politicians surrendered and Allende shot himself, or was shot, by a submachine gun.

At ten p.m. the military junta, led by General Pinochet, with the support of Gustavo Leigh of the air force, Admiral Merino of the navy, and General Mendoza of the carabineros, appeared on television to announce their policy ostensibly to restore constitutionality. The Supreme Court approved their action under article seventy-two of the Constitution, though the Church was more reserved. The Eastern bloc countries, except for Romania and China, immediately broke off diplomatic relations. On 29 September the Christian Democrats denounced the new regime as a dictatorship.

In the repression which followed the coup, many Communist foreigners were interned and then expelled whilst some three thousand Chileans were executed. Marxist organisations were dissolved, and the universities 'reorganised'. Thousands of people were interned in the National Stadium; censorship and other repression were rampant; and politics discontinued. On the other hand, the new government had a major task in disarming the thousands of people who had been armed in order to wage civil war.

It was also proved beyond doubt that Allende had planned to murder generals, admirals and other high officers, and most of the opposition leaders on 19 September. The allegations that the

Pinochet coup had been organised by the US were without foundation, though it was clear that from 1963 to 1973 the CIA had played
some part in Chilean politics, including support for Allende in the
1970 election. Aid was not extended to the Pinochet regime,
though its acceptance of Chile's foreign indebtedness enabled
credit lines to be reopened from the Export–Import Bank, and the
International Monetary Fund.

The new regime was intensely patriotic and moralistic; it stopped the enormous corruption of the Allende regime, and 'cleaned'
up' pornographic activities. Its economic policy was to dismantle
the newly-socialised sector, to eliminate controls, to free the
exchange rate, to expand agricultural output and to reduce the
public sector deficit. Professor Milton Friedman's influence was
powerful.

Allende's Communist regime had not begun a reign of terror,
nor had it banned freedom of expression but it had not succeeded
either, though excessive interference by the United States seemed
to give Marxism the propaganda victory. The Euro-Communists of
Italy and France and the Third World of Africa and Asia watched
happenings in Cuba and Chile with unfeigned fascination.

Chapter 26

Asian troubles

The newly emergent independent Asian countries of India, East and West Pakistan and Indonesia battled to raise their standards of living but were nearly overwhelmed by huge populations, magnified by a fall in the infant deathrate through advances in primary medical care and increased longevity, by poverty, political rivalry within and without, internal dissension and heavy military commitments but they did not fall prey to Marxism or desert the Western alliance. China too suffered many of the same problems but her ways of dealing with them were very different, culminating in the Cultural Revolution. However after its excesses had been overcome, she too swung towards the West.

Pakistan's Western wing based on Karachi and Lahore developed industrially at the expense of the poorer, more populous East, centred on Dacca. Pakistan was the favoured country for Western aid, which added substantially to economic growth there. Politically however the country never settled. To say that the parliamentary system was unruly would be an understatement: on one occasion the Speaker of the lower house of the Eastern wing was hit over the head by a chair, and killed. In 1958 the Pakistan army overthrew the civilian regime and Field Marshal Ayub Khan became President.

Pakistan had joined the Baghdad Pact in 1954 with Turkey, Iraq, Iran and Britain; four years later, when the revolutionary government was installed in Iraq, the treaty was formulated as CENTO, the Central Treaty Organisation, and included Turkey and Iran, forming part of the 'containment policy' by which the United States both sought to preserve Asia from further Soviet penetration, and provide itself with bases for nuclear strikes against the Soviet Union and China. In 1955 Pakistan also joined SEATO, with Britain and the United States, which linked anti-Communist states across Southeast Asia. In the 1950s therefore Pakistan was firmly allied to the United States, who found this doubly valuable because India's fervent neutralism appeared to favour the USSR and China.

As Pakistan moved emphatically into the American sphere of influence US aid enabled it to build up a strong army and air force, as part of America's strategy for deterring the Russians and

Chinese. The forces were officered largely by Punjabis, the traditional officer class, and many of the army's most prestigious units
continued to recruit from the Muslim warrior tribes.

Punjabi officers were given all the plum jobs and ran both wings
of the country with repressive ferocity. The Bengalis in the poorer
Eastern wing became restive. In 1971 they won a majority of seats
in the Pakistan constituent assembly but their leaders were assassinated, whereupon the Bengalis rebelled: they wished to become
independent. The rebellion was repressed with great violence and
millions of refugees fled to India. Mrs Gandhi's government
prepared to support the rebels, for which she gained Soviet backing, and the Indian army invaded. The Bengalis of East Pakistan
finally became independent and called themselves Bangladesh –
perhaps the poorest country in the world, with a massive population fighting for a living on frequently flooded muddy flat lands,
permanent recipients of international aid. The remaining rump of
West Pakistan reverted to authoritarian rule, first under Zulfikar
Ali Bhutto and then under General Zia, both of whom nurtured a
growing relationship with China. As a result of being allied to both
China and the United States, Pakistan became the catalyst for a
rapprochement between these two great nations.

India, which had inherited the bulk of the very strong army built
up by the British – the fourth strongest in the world in 1945 –
carried its own military preparedness to a high standard, importing
arms both from Britain and the USSR and using its own large
industrial base to build much of its own equipment. Its strength did
not however prevent an ignominious defeat in border clashes with
China in 1965. Then, as Pakistan became more bellicose, in the
early 1960s, India and Pakistan went to war in August 1965 with a
dramatic Indian victory. China at first threatened to intervene on
Pakistan's side, but 'world opinion' – that is joint pressure by the
Americans and the Russians – enforced a cease-fire through a
Security Council resolution. The USSR, through Kosygin, then
negotiated a peace treaty between Shastri, for India, and Ayub
Khan, for Pakistan, in Tashkent in January 1966. This treaty put
the Kashmir question into abeyance, and obliged both parties to
seek peaceful solutions to disputes.

Nehru's successor, Shastri, had only been Prime Minister for
eighteen months when he had a heart attack and died. In the
political crisis that followed he was succeeded by Nehru's daughter, Indira Gandhi. Born in 1917, she had been educated in
England and had married, against her father's wishes, Ferozi
Gandhi (no relation to the Mahatma), by whom she had had two
sons. President of the Congress Party in 1958, she had been

Minister of Information in Shastri's Cabinet and was elected Prime
Minister on 19 January 1966. Later she turned her elected government into a dictatorship. This affronted the people of India, for
although they may not appear to be democrats in the Western
sense of that word, they do have a deep sense of constitutional
propriety and respect for law; India remains a deeply caste-ridden
society run by Brahmins. Hinduism too seems to produce lawyers
who respect the law and law-making processes. Moreover Britain
had most successfully trained – perhaps even brainwashed – the
official classes and left behind strong institutions, such as the army
and the civil service, which had remained subordinate to ministe-
rial control. India was thus paradoxically by far the most Western
country in the Third World, paradoxical because it was culturally
profoundly oriental. When Indira Gandhi therefore finally allowed
free elections to be held again, she was heavily defeated.

After the Indian army had invaded East Pakistan (Bangladesh)
in 1971, and the UN assembly had called for a cease-fire, India
prepared to invade West Pakistan. Late in December the remaining Pakistani forces in East Pakistan surrendered, and a cease-fire
was called on the India–West Pakistan front. Meanwhile American
threats of intervention in this war were interpreted by India as
support for Pakistan, thus throwing Mrs Gandhi towards the
Soviet bloc, whilst trying to remain neutral.

India emerged from her various frontier conflicts much the
stronger of the two states, easily capable of defeating Pakistan and
with all threats on her eastern borders eliminated by a new client
state Bangladesh, which was rapidly reduced to starvation. Mrs
Gandhi had now firmly established her boundaries with her neighbours and India had come into her own as a neutral non-aligned
nation of considerable potential power.

Whereas India had become a major nation, the giant republic of
Indonesia in Southeast Asia was always on the brink of dissolution,
yet it survived, despite being the target for the biggest Communist
effort outside the Soviet bloc and China. The Communists, however, were overwhelmingly defeated.

A military uprising in West and North Sumatra led to the
complete collapse of the government's authority in Sumatra in
March 1957. Sukarno, the 'father of his people', thereupon ceased
to be a figurehead, took control and instituted a system of what was
called 'guided democracy', in other words, a form of dictatorship
based on Lenin's concept of democratic centralism. Sukarno
formed a cabinet in April 1957 with the help of the Chief of Staff of
the army, General Nasution. It seems that Sukarno was supported

by John Foster Dulles with military aid, and also to some degree by the CIA. A people's consultative assembly was called in order to evolve a more workable constitution, but it was clear that this constituent assembly suffered from many of the problems associated with the previous parliamentary regime, and Nasution used his martial law powers to ban all policital activity. Since that time there have been no free elections either to the people's consultative assembly or to Parliament itself. Sukarno tried to develop the country socially and economically, regarding the question of constitutional progress as utterly dependent upon social and economic reform. In this he was to be followed by other Asian leaders, notably Lee Kuan Yew in Singapore and Marcos in the Philippines, both of which were to become remarkably prosperous.

Indonesia however was still desperately poor, despite its great natural wealth, but Sukarno was keen to cut a figure in the United Nations. He therefore called a conference at Bandung in April 1955 where India and China got together to form the first Afro–Asian conference. Indonesia therefore seemed on the surface to join India and Yugoslavia as one of the leading 'non-committed' nations which had originally been brought together by Tito and Nehru at Brioni. But that was a delusion of grandeur. In reality Indonesia relapsed into chaos, unrestricted turmoil and outrageous corruption.

Sukarno's dictatorial powers were limited by Islamic fundamentalist forces, by the Communist party of Indonesia, the PKI, which had been stimulated by the success of the Chinese revolution to prepare to take over the country, and by the army under Nasution, Sumitro and Suharto, generals greatly conscious of their potential power. Despite the Communist party's plans to overthrow Sukarno, he was in fact toppled in 1965 by a coup organised by the non-Communist military under Suharto.

As Suharto started to restore order, with Sukarno still the apparent leader, large numbers of people were arrested and a tremendous explosion of anti-Communist feeling broke out, including rioting against the three million Chinese who lived in Indonesia. Probably between one hundred and sixty thousand and two hundred thousand people were killed in the massacres, which were led by the Muslims, who showed an astonishing degree of ferocity. Hundreds of thousands of former PKI members, or people who were assumed to be PKI members, were also rounded up and sent to hastily improvised prison camps. Behind the massacre lay action by the British and the Americans to destroy Communist power, though the massacres themselves were never envisaged; certainly Indonesia ceased from that time forward to be a pillar of Communism.

From March to December 1967 Sukarno struggled to hold on to power but eventually Suharto became Commander in Chief and placed Sukarno under house arrest where he died of chronic kidney disease on 21 June 1970. Despite all the rivalries, Suharto was preferred to Nasution, although the latter was Chief of Staff of the armed forces and a vigorous and active man of forty-seven. Suharto now proceeded with what were called 'mopping up operations' during which all those opposed to him were killed or locked up. Meanwhile the corruption and disreputableness of his Indonesian government were spectacular, particularly a scandal over the state-owned oil corporation. Corrupt elections were held in 1971 giving a majority to Suharto and the military junta. Suharto was appointed President. In 1974 ferocious students' riots led by Nasution and Sumitro took place but Suharto managed to hang on to power.

With the discovery and development of oil, Indonesia became potentially a rich nation which, combined with its large population and its enormous geographic spread, made it one of the most powerful in the world. Its lack of organisation, however, held it back. Smaller nations in Southeast Asia – Thailand, Malaysia, Singapore and the Philippines – achieved faster rates of economic growth. But they all had one facet in common, being modified forms of dictatorships resting on quasi-democratic plebiscitary constitutions, with parliaments that were for the most part representative of only one party. In all of them Communist parties were illegal and in opposition. The prosperity of these nations, who were all linked in an ASEAN pact, depended upon almost uncontrolled capitalist development. Like Brazil and Venezuela, they represented the most successful developing nations economically, and were an oasis of political stability.

The extent of Communist subversion was limited; the defeat of the Communists in the Malayan emergency and their overthrow in Indonesia showed that China was to follow a lonely path in Asia. Mao Tse-tung would have to seek allies, to proselytise elsewhere.

Mao Tse-tung did not believe in grooming a successor but by the 1960s Liu Shao-ch'i was thought to rank second in the hierarchy. Liu had been born in the same province as Mao and his career had followed similar lines. In November 1961 Liu represented Mao at a meeting of leaders of Communist parties from all over the world in Moscow, which included Khruschev, Western and Third World Communists. The Chinese maintained that Lenin was still relevant; that the struggle between Socialists and imperialists was continuing; that although Communism would win, it would only do so by continual struggle; and that for this reason they opposed peaceful coexistence and disarmament. The Soviet Union, apart from asserting its own historical primacy in the world Communist movement, took an entirely different view, notably that world war would destroy Communism as well as capitalism. As a result of this split. Khruschev sought reconciliation with Tito whilst Albania, hostile to Yugoslavia, adopted the Chinese line.

The Great Leap Forward was now admitted to have been a failure and the Chinese economy was in a poor state. Millions of tons of grain had to be imported from Australia and Canada but the failure was attributed more to lack of enthusiasm and skill than to any defect in the orientation of the policy itself. By 1963 the Chinese were setting up Maoist Communist parties of their own all over the world, and seeking to capture existing Communist parties and other left-wing organisations. Their biggest success was Albania, which became completely Maoist under its dictator Hoxha, annoying equally Tito and Khruschev. In particular, China felt able to extend substantial aid to the newly independent African countries for example, building a railway in Tanzania from Dar-es-Salaam into Zambia.

In 1962 the Chinese demanded rectification of the Sino–Soviet border; and in 1964 they exploded an atom bomb, following the signature of the Test-Ban Treaty the previous year and at the same time as the Presidium of the Soviet party was renouncing Khruschev and promoting Brezhnev, who (it might have been assumed) would be favourable to some rapprochement with China. The Chinese were soon denouncing the Russians as the enemies of peace and Socialism, and pointing out (with considerable effect) to the Third World the dangers of Soviet participation in the affairs of developing countries.

After the breach with the Soviet Union, China fought a brief but bitter war with India, in which it occupied areas of Indian territory on the border which had historically belonged to China. India was supported in the conflict by the USSR, and its defeat was therefore humiliating for the Soviet Union. Meanwhile, the Chinese occupied Tibet, which caused further conflict with India. As a result China was now isolated from the Soviet Union and its satellites, and from the United States; it had also antagonised India, a leader of the neutral powers, and its traditional allies, such as the United Kingdom. Despite this isolation the rapid development of Chinese industry and the explosion of the atom bomb showed clearly that China was capable of autonomous development.

To Mao it appeared that the revolution was not going fast enough, whereas Liu thought that stability and the development of the authority of the regime were paramount. Liu was, it seems, opposed to Mao's personality cult and a supporter of some form of bureaucratic centralism. Mao would have none of this; he argued that only by reviving the class struggle could the revolution be maintained, otherwise counter-revolutionary forces would succeed and capitalism would be restored.

Mao now returned to active power and with his wife renewed revolutionary vitality in a tremendous wave of fervour. Shock troops of young Communists, the Red Guards, were sent into pitched battle with the aim of eliminating the entire upper echelon of the Communist party through violent public abuse and forced self-criticism. At the same time the *Little Red Book* was published as a means of codifying Mao's ideology through excerpts from Mao's writings and maxims from the Long March. Most of these utterances were gnomic in form but revolutionary in intent.

The Cultural Revolution began in the army and was followed by Mao's emergence, in July 1965, from semi-retirement to swim fifteen kilometres along the Yangtse at Wuhan in sixty-five minutes, a dangerous river with strong currents. This symbolic swim, which was much photographed, indicated Mao's strength and his return to active life, and demonstrated his revolutionary theory that 'the fish swims with the current'. He wrote a letter to the Red Guards in which he said, 'I give you my warm support. Your revolutionary actions are a sign of anger and condemnation towards the exploiting classes, the revisionists and their henchmen.' Mao's swim was followed by the denunciation of Wu Han, the Deputy-Mayor of Peking, which marked the beginning of the actual purges. In the Central Committee meeting in September 1965 Mao and his wife, Chiang Ching, were in a minority, but following the old doctrines of I-Ching, the 'correct line' was thought by Mao to lie with the minority.

The official opening of the revolution was on 1 June 1966. Wall posters were put up throughout the universities. The posters spoke directly to the rank and file of the Communist party without addressing directly the hierarchy. The rising was modelled on the Paris commune of 1871 for Mao believed that the commune's source of strength had lain in the enthusiasm and revolutionary initiative of the masses. Liu Shao-ch'i dismissed the Mayor of Peking, reorganised the Communist party secretariat and removed the President and Deputy President of Peking university from their posts. The Red Guards, mainly schoolchildren, but also some university students, emerged, after much careful rehearsal, shouting, threatening people with violence and putting up wall posters; the guards spread like some feared microbe so that by August, Mao and Lin Piao could inspect over a million of their 'troops' in Peking. Other guards rose throughout China, supported and to some degree organised by the army and the persecution began of a large number of people who hitherto had been highly regarded, including Liu Shao-ch'i, who was now called the Chinese Khrushchev.

Thus Liu, who was actually Prime Minister at the time, was prevented from exercising any of his functions. The former Mayor of Peking, and numerous other prominent officials, including the Chief of Staff, were all described as revisionists who had taken the capitalist road. The victims were paraded throughout China from the backs of lorries, wearing dunces' caps and with placards round their necks. Soon the Red Guards were denouncing millions throughout the country. All schools and universities were suspended and many factories were closed while the workers were sent into the towns to activate the masses. Only simple training courses in Marxism were allowed and brief lessons in practical methods, done by self-help and self-criticism, in which students went out and worked in the fields and in the factories. Professors and teachers were subjected to trial by the masses and then sent to work in farms in remote parts of the country.

By early 1967 China was in confusion, with young people trekking across the country, seeking out bourgeois elements to purge wherever they might be found, without any attempt to discover whether those denounced had been 'guilty' or not of any 'crime'.

Later the Cultural Revolution was to prove a powerful influence throughout the world, since young people everywhere were stimulated to copy the behaviour of the Red Guards. Students throughout Europe waved the *Little Red Book* as they marched and rioted in Paris in May 1968, in Germany, in Britain and in Italy.

Thus by 1967 Mao had not only eliminated his rivals in the party and state hierarchies, but also inspired the young Chinese to shift the direction of the revolution into the way that he thought best. But in the process the country's economic and cultural life had been almost completely disrupted. The army was called in to restore order, but to distinguish between genuine Red Guards and false agitators. This gave the military and Lin Piao the power to have a selective purge. It seems possible that Lin Piao was planning to succeed Mao by extending the revolution to its ultimate, a sort of perpetual cultural revolution. That is to say, true Communism would be achieved, where the problems of production would have been overcome, and everybody's needs were met, mainly because people's false wants had been eliminated by the changes in their personalities, and they only required what they truly needed.

The revolutionary developments in Shanghai represented the culmination of the extreme left element of the Cultural Revolution. On 10 April 1967 the 'monsters' of the old bourgeois general staff were humiliated at Tsing Hua University before 200,000 workers. A central symbolic role was given to Liu's wife, Wang Kwan-mae, who was accused of having a weakness for jewellery and bourgeois clothes; at the public humiliation she wore a necklace of gilded ping-pong balls, high-heeled shoes, an old robe and a Koolie hat from colonial times. The Minister of Higher Education, the Minister of Forestry, and three other leaders stood by her side wearing placards of humiliation. As the revolutionary committees spread all over China, Mao criticised the army, including the marshals. Only Mao was sacred. At the end of April, Chou En-lai was attacked and the Red Guards killed over sixty-three thousand people in violent attacks, leaping from trucks and cars and beating people to death in the streets. Chou En-lai was described as half dog and half sheep, and an expert in trickery. The files in the ministries were thrown open and frequently destroyed, and the Ministry of Foreign Affairs in particular was put out of action.

Mao Tse-tung's wife, Chiang Ching, soon began to emerge as a leader of the more violent parts of the revolution when she said 'you must attack with words but defend yourselves with weapons', which was an open invitation to the far left to arm themselves against the regime. Throughout August hundreds of thousands of young demonstrators camped out in the streets and parks of Peking and kept up a continual chanting and screaming, marching and counter-marching in demonstrations. Foreign embassies were attacked, including the British Embassy, which was stormed and burned.

The Hot Summer of 1967, as it was known, was the culmination of the first stage of the Cultural Revolution. Mao Tse-tung toured the provinces issuing a 2000-word statement to the Communist party, which appeared in Red Guard posters. His main theme was unity, though he expressed great satisfaction with the Cultural Revolution, saying that 'there has never been such a broad and deep mass movement as this in the factories and the countryside. In the schools and the army units, and the whole nation everyone is talking about the Cultural Revolution and feeling involved in national affairs.' He saw the main achievement of the revolution as the unification of the cadre with the masses.

By 1 May 1968 the student leaders were less popular, and leadership was seen to begin a boycott of the Revolution. At this stage Mao intervened to call the revolution to order, and Chiang retracted her cry for armed rebellion.

The students were sent into the provinces to work on communes on 7 May 1968. In July the universities were occupied and the Red Guards completely crushed. The party began to be rebuilt. Three millions at least were sent to work on virgin lands in the remote districts, while gradually the former teachers and students were brought back to the deserted schools and universities.

The Cultural Revolution, despite its devastating consequences, was limited by the fact that the main organs of the state were not disrupted, and significantly the province of Sin-Kiang was not affected because it was too close to Russia and the site of the main missile bases. It was thought that the defence of this state apparatus was the achievement of Chou En-lai, who remained throughout in full command of his area of authority despite the attacks on him. In April 1969 the Ninth Party Congress of the Chinese Communist party met in Peking. It declared that the Cultural Revolution had been brought to a triumphant conclusion. Lin Piao was called 'Mao's close comrade in arms' and therefore probably his successor. By the end of 1969, therefore, relative calm had been restored to China. It is clear that during the Cultural Revolution the opportunity had been seized to reorient foreign policy in such a way that the quarrel with Russia became permanent and sharp, with the possibility of war being regarded as likely, and that secret moves were made towards some kind of agreement with the United States. Meanwhile, the Chinese army remained unaffected, and the development of the missile and nuclear programme was accelerated.

At this stage the degree of dissent in the leadership was revealed. It seems that Lin Piao had been organising a rising with the Acting Chief of the Army General Staff, the Political Commissar of the Air Force, and the Commander of the Peking Garrison. Chou En-lai began to interpret the anti-party struggle as emanating from Chiang Kai-shek Kuomintang supporters who had infiltrated the Communist party, a preliminary to reversing the Cultural Revolution.

By this time Chou En-lai's line seemed to be adopted as the correct one, and he became clearly Mao's chief heir. It was subsequently argued, after Mao's death, that the work of the Cultural Revolution was almost entirely that of the Gang of Four, led by Mao's wife, Chiang Ching, and Lin Piao, though whether or not the conspiracy against Mao actually existed, or whether it was retrospectively invented, remains unknown.

Lin Piao having been on the extreme left, now found himself in grave difficulty, and he sought, but failed to get, a guarantee from

Luton Sixth Form College
Library

Mao that the party cadres that had been purged and banished to the provinces would not be brought back. In August 1968 Chou En-lai attacked the Soviet Union for invading Czechoslovakia.

Chinese relations with the Soviet Union deteriorated when on 3 March 1969 there were some border clashes in which China sought to rectify areas lost to the Czars when it was weak. Meanwhile, secret diplomacy had been taking place in order to enable a rapprochement with the United States, which culminated in a state visit by President Nixon in 1972. Dr Kissinger, the American Secretary of State, had made several secret visits to China, which rapidly became almost an anti-Soviet ally. Technologically the Chinese were making rapid strides; the atom bomb test of 1964 was then followed in July 1967 by a hydrogen bomb test, and it was clear that these weapons were being developed not against the Americans nor to support Hanoi in the Vietnamese War, but for fear of a Soviet invasion. Lin Piao gradually switched from attacking the United States and the Soviet Union equally, to stepping up his attacks on the Soviet Union alone, almost to a pitch of violence, obviously envisaging the possibility of war. Whereas Lin Piao declared that the excesses both of the Russians and of the Americans would cause the collapse of their policies of aggression, Chou En-lai was aiming at a rapprochement with the Americans. In September 1971 Lin Piao was purged and fled to the Soviet Union in a plane which crashed or was shot down near the Soviet border.

China fully came in from the cold when it joined the United Nations in October 1971. Before he died in 1974, Chou En-lai saw the Communist-inspired revolution in Sri Lanka against Mrs Bandaranaike's government put down, and stood by while the Indians crushed the Pakistanis in East Bengal and created the state of Bangladesh. Hitherto China had been opposed to India and in favour of any revolutionary movement. Now China withdrew from active participation in Africa to become a law-abiding and respectable member of the world community.

As the Cultural Revolution drew to an end, Mao was obviously ailing, and he died in 1976. His wife Chiang Ching sought to take over the leadership of China with three colleagues, but the Gang of Four was arrested as soon as Mao died, and Hua succeeded. With Mao's death, China returned to an orthodox and non-revolutionary path.

Mao Tse-tung had brought peace and unity to China for the first time in a hundred years; he then proceeded to create mass participation in total revolution in order to overcome all opposition. He believed that city dwellers should go to work in the countryside, side by side with peasants and soldiers, a revolutionary policy which ensured mass support and harnessed surplus labour, unlike many other developing countries, in order to create an industrial base for the transformation of society into true Communism. Mao picked and chose the bits of Stalin's doctrines and practices with which he agreed. He never attributed infallibility to Stalin, nor did he regard the Soviet Communist party as the guiding light. Mao thought that the Chinese Communist party should 'walk on its own legs', a view offensive to those Soviet leaders who shared the assumption that the Russians were the natural and inevitable leaders of Communism. In the Kremlin and its European satellites, this view remained unchallenged.

The Chinese road to Socialism was therefore different from the Soviet Union's, which depended upon the tight dictatorship of a small centralised Politburo and avoided any kind of 'mass participation'. The roads diverged, and ultimately careered off in opposed directions, the catalyst being the Cultural Revolution. The Sino–Soviet break may also have arisen originally, at least in part, from the disharmony between Mao and Stalin, the mutual dislike arising from Stalin backing the wrong horse in the early days of the Chinese revolution, then in advising Mao, wrongly, to seek a coalition with Chiang Kai-shek after the end of the Second World War and, finally, in invading North Korea without first seeking Mao's full support and agreement.

The rise and fall of China as a revolutionary power marked several major changes in the world. China became the predominant threat to the Soviet Union, and from being a bitter enemy of the United States it was regarded *de facto* as virtually an American ally. Perhaps most surprising of all (because after all radical shifts of alliances were a familiar part of diplomatic history) was revolutionary Socialism's decline as a model of Asian development. Japan, South Korea and the ASEAN countries were all examples of countries that achieved astonishing economic growth by the capitalist road, and political stability as well. Even India, which had seemed in the 1950s in the grip of a virtually insoluble and chronic economic problem, began to make steady progress, and to combine it with a great degree of political stability; despite Mrs Gandhi's period of dictatorship, India had well-established parliamentary, judicial and executive machinery. What had seemed the inevitability of a victory for the Chinese way of revolutionary Socialism appeared increasingly as a mirage. Was there another route?

Would Socialism spread in Asia through war and American military defeat in Vietnam? In the event the defeat weakened America far more than it strengthened Socialism.

Chapter 27

Vietnam: an American tragedy

The Vietnamese War was run by the generals. It had no place in either Kennedy or Johnson's overall world or domestic strategy: it never had political logic. It formed a sad threnody throughout the 1960s, threatening to obscure all President Johnson's positive achievements.

Lyndon Baines Johnson was sworn in as President of the United States on 22 November 1963 in an aircraft at Dallas, Texas, carrying the body of the murdered President Kennedy, about to take off for Washington DC. He could hardly have been more different from Kennedy. Born in 1909 to a poor Texan family, he became a schoolteacher, entered politics, made money by wheeling and dealing; was elected a Senator for Texas and later a successful Senate majority leader. In succeeding Kennedy he became the first President from the South since the Civil War. During the Kennedy Presidency, he had felt socially at an enormous disadvantage; that he and his wife were patronised, condescended to and excluded by the Kennedy clan. This feeling was intensified by the aftermath of the assassination when almost all the Kennedy associates regarded him as an impostor, the illegitimate successor of the adulated President. L.B.J. decided, therefore, to be President in his own right and to differentiate his term from that of his predecessor. But to do that he had to go cautiously.

His first task was to reconfirm all President Kennedy's appointments, including Robert Kennedy as Attorney General. It must be seen that the United States government continued, when the nation and the international community were shocked and puzzled by the assassination. Then, following the murder of Kennedy's murderer, Lee Harvey Oswald, and the widespread belief in a conspiracy to murder Kennedy while he was in Texas, Johnson set up a Commission of Enquiry under the chairmanship of the Chief Justice, Earl Warren. The new President showed amazing energy and, domestically, it soon became clear that President Johnson had skills and the knowledge in dealing with the Congress that Kennedy had lacked. Within months not only the civil rights legislation became law, but a tax-cuts bill and a major overseas-aid bill too. Johnson worked hard and energetically at establishing a consensus for radical measures that had not yet passed through the Congress and which, in a sense, had been accumulating since the end of President Truman's period of office some fifteen years before. This programme, which became known as the Great Society, arose partly from legislation prepared during Kennedy's period of office, but mostly from recent studies of poverty which showed that low income, racial discrimination, unemployment, bad housing, in-adequate medical care, delinquency and poor schooling were associated with each other, especially in areas of urban depriva-tion. The war on poverty announced by Johnson in the 1964 State of the Union message was begun under Sargent Shriver, Ken-nedy's brother-in-law, for the urban problem seemed, and was, serious. In the summer of 1964 there was serious rioting by blacks in the major cities across America, despite the passage of the Civil Rights Act.

If the greater part of the President's attention was concentrated on domestic matters, his Achilles heel proved to be foreign affairs, specifically Vietnam, which was still being masterminded by Dean Rusk and Robert McNamara, both of whom had been in Ken-nedy's Cabinet, as well as by the specialist adviser in the White House, Walt Whitman Rostow, who made the war his principal preoccupation, using the Presidency to intensify it and add to it the whole strength of America.

As Vice-President, Johnson had been sent to represent Kennedy on a mission to South Vietnam and he had ardently identified himself with the cause. He was deeply distressed when Kennedy allowed the Diem regime to fall in November 1963; three weeks later Johnson was President. 'Vietnam and the consequences of Diem's murder became mine to deal with,' he later wrote. By late 1964 the North Vietnamese had moved from guerrilla war to a more general and conventional offensive and McNamara, after several visits, urged that more and more American troops and material should be sent to Vietnam. Johnson construed the failure of policy so far as a failure to recognise the Vietcong as part of the North Vietnamese strategy, and American failure fully to support the South Vietnamese government.

In June 1964 General William C. Westmoreland was made American commander in Vietnam; a distinguished general, with the complete confidence of Johnson and McNamara, his posting was an indication of the degree of American commitment. Johnson was now running for the Presidency and Vietnam, far from proving an electoral liability, seemed to be an asset; Johnson, the Demo-crat, could now rely for votes on the hawkish America-first senti-ment which had so bitterly criticised Truman and Acheson for the loss of China, the dismissal of MacArthur, and had so strongly supported Dulles. Thus L.B.J.'s hawk-like opponent, Senator Goldwater, had his main electoral thrust hi-jacked. The remaining obstacle to full-scale war, that without overt Congressional support the President might be exceeding his powers, was overcome in August 1964 when the so-called Tonkin resolution authorising American military action was passed. It arose from covert naval operations by the United States navy off the North Vietnamese coast. On 31 July 1964 the US destroyers *Maddox* and *C. Turner Joy* were attacked by the North Vietnamese whilst covering South Vietnamese attempts to land saboteurs, and trying to identify North Vietnamese radar equipment. American naval planes immediately destroyed or damaged large numbers of North Vietnam naval bases. Congress passed a resolution authorising American military involvement in Vietnam because of the attack on the US vessels; the resolution was proposed by Senator Fulbright, a liberal Democrat, and fully supported by the Republicans. It passed the Senate with only two dissentients. Later Fulbright was to discover how misled he had been in proposing the resolution, since the attacks on the ships had not been unprovoked, and he was to become a leader of the movement in America against the war.

In the 1964 election the Republican Senator Goldwater was the 'war' candidate, and Johnson was the 'peace' candidate. This may seem paradoxical, but it was the case; and it considerably strengthened Johnson's inclination to step up the war, since he could be seen to be doing so out of necessity, not out of hawk-like passion. He also did not want to be thought a weak President. Yet by February 1965, chiefly from Moscow and Peking, but also by Communists throughout the world, L.B.J. was denounced as a major aggressor. This view was soon widely accepted by 'liberal' opinion in Western Europe and the United States. This was the greatest Communist propaganda campaign since the adulation of Stalin during the purges. The non-aligned nations, led by Yugoslavia, also appealed to the United States to withdraw.

In July 1964 General Maxwell Taylor, the prominent soldier and former Chairman of the Joint Defense Staffs, had been appointed to succeed Cabot Lodge as US Ambassador in Vietnam and he and Westmoreland became aggressively dominant in the prosecution of the war. Hitherto an opponent of bombing in the North, Taylor became convinced that he could only succeed in the South if the North were forced to withdraw its support for the war. On 1 November 1964 the Vietcong destroyed the greater part of a squadron of American bombers stationed at Bien Hoa in the South, a direct challenge, Taylor felt, to the prestige of the United States. He returned to Washington, where President Johnson had just been elected with his record-breaking 61 per cent of the vote. In South Vietnam the government was rapidly losing control, with its authority now restricted to the towns alone. In December 1964 Khan, the South Vietnamese leader, and his lieutenant, Air Marshal Ky, arrested large numbers of their allies and dissolved South Vietnam's High National Council, turning the government into a straightforward dictatorship. In the circumstances, President Johnson felt its prestige could only be assured by a decisive attack on the North, though still he hesitated. On 7 February 1965 the Vietcong attacked the American barracks at Pleiku in the Central Highlands and on 11 February at Qui Nhon. This was the last straw and retaliatory air raids were authorised on 13 February.

The bombing was first confined to strictly limited military objectives, and on 8 March two Marine battalions were sent to South Vietnam, to defend American installations. As the war escalated, the bombing became more intense; known as Operation Rolling Thunder, it spread to Hanoi and Haiphong. On 1 April 1965 it was decided to send great numbers of American troops in order to undertake missions to search and destroy Vietcong throughout South Vietnam's jungles and mountains. In a meeting at Honolulu on 20 April Westmoreland, Taylor, McNamara and Bundy decided on all-out prosecution of the war. Initially this involved 82,000 American combat troops, several other divisions (including one from South Korea), and substantial increases in air force missions – including bombing runs amounting to over six hundred sorties a week. In the process President Johnson committed the whole United States armed forces to the war. The Americans replaced South Vietnamese – known as ARVN – in almost all combat roles and the extent of the involvement became a tactical decision for Westmoreland (and, behind him, McNamara), rather than a matter for the President and the Secretary of State. It was this decision which was to destroy the Democratic administration since there was never to be a fundamental political reassessment of Vietnam and its place in America's world strategy and domestic policy. Vietnam was seen as a military question. At the behest of General Westmoreland, the number of American troops gradually increased; by July 1965 the target of soldiers in the American forces in Vietnam had begun to be thought of as 300,000 and the Joint Chiefs of Staff were thinking of up to a million men to achieve victory. By late August the immediate target figure had already reached 200,000 and by the end of the year the number of American troops actually in South Vietnam had passed 175,000. The analogy of the British, French and German generals on the western front in 1915–18 was alarming.

The huge expenditure on the war drove the federal budget further into deficit than had been expected; and by December 1965 McNamara was already envisaging 600,000 troops by the end of 1967. In other words the Defense Department was envisaging a lengthy and major land war in Asia, of the kind from which Eisenhower had withdrawn the United States in Korea.

The build-up of American troops was met by a corresponding build-up of North Vietnamese troops. In their first major battle, in November 1965, the North Vietnamese won (or at least did not lose). Even as late as early 1966, however, the extent of the American commitment was hidden from the American public, even though it was the overt intention of the Johnson administration to bomb Hanoi to the conference table. In late 1965, however, there had been a 'bombing pause', to see whether the North Vietnamese would negotiate; then the bombing was resumed and became steadily intensified. As deputy to Rusk, and an ally of McNamara in planning the war, Rostow advocated bombing 'economic' targets, especially electrical and petroleum installations. The war therefore spread to the whole of Vietnam. By the end of 1966, over 570,000 American troops were designated – approaching the original McNamara target for mid 1967.

Throughout 1966 Senator Fulbright conducted Senate hearings on the war, and came to the view that it was both illegal and disastrous. On top of serious civil rights disturbances in the cities, American university campuses erupted as more and more students realised that they would be drafted to Vietnam.

In February 1967, after pressure from Harold Wilson, the British Prime Minister and L.B.J.'s principal overseas enthusiast, L.B.J. assured Kosygin, the Soviet Prime Minister, that a bombing halt he had ordered would be extended to allow for direct negotiations with Ho Chi-minh, the North Vietnamese leader. Ho Chi-minh refused – demonstrating that he was clearly not acting directly under Soviet instructions – and the bombing was renewed and intensified. A meeting between L.B.J. and Kosygin in Washington in June 1967 led to the same result. In July 1967 the authorised number of American troops in Vietnam was again increased, to 525,000; and once more the assurance was given by the Vietnamese and by Westmoreland and the other American leaders in Saigon that the war was on the point of being won.

In the meantime, opposition to the war developed in the United States, with riots, demonstrations, and trouble on college campuses, where the draft (conscription) continued to be felt to be most unacceptable. The North Vietnam winter offensive of

September 1967, followed by the Vietcong infiltration of South Vietnamese cities in October, set the Americans back severely. McNamara lost heart at this point and recommended the end of bombing and a stabilising of the numbers of Americans in Vietnam, implying a shift to the South Vietnamese forces for their own defence. On the latter point Rostow agreed, but favoured continuing the bombing; while General Taylor correctly interpreted McNamara's memorandum as a move that would 'probably degenerate into an eventual pull-out'. Rusk shared Taylor's opinion, and L.B.J. decided not to accept McNamara's advice. McNamara resigned and left to become President of the World Bank in March 1968.

In January 1968, on the Buddhist festival of Tet, the Vietcong launched a major offensive, with an uprising in all the major cities, capturing Hué, the imperial capital, for twenty-six days. It was now perfectly clear that the bombing, the arrival of massive numbers of American troops and the equipping of ARVN had had little effect on the Vietcong.

By this time America was passionately, deeply divided. The President's domestic programme had been halted. His economic strategy was in ruins as military expenditure grew, unbalancing the budget, and the dollar weakened internationally. The government was unable to deal effectively with other international crises, such as the Six Day War in the Middle East, and the recurrent Berlin crisis. Opinion polls showed the depths of L.B.J.'s unpopularity, and the unlikelihood that he would be re-elected in 1968.

Senator Eugene McCarthy now entered the Presidential election campaign against Johnson on an anti-war ticket. Johnson was defeated in the first primary, in New Hampshire, and withdrew in Wisconsin, when it was clear that he was losing. On 31 March 1968, less than three and a half years after his record-breaking electoral victory, he announced that he would stop the bombing and not run for re-election. He now became an impotent, lame-duck President with six months in office still to go. Robert Kennedy seemed his likely successor, but in June 1968 Robert was assassinated in Los Angeles by a Palestinian, Sirhan Sirhan; a few weeks later the black leader Martin Luther King was also murdered. Johnson's initiative towards a great society seemed to have petered out into unimaginable and apparently futile military violence abroad, and riots and assassinations at home.

The year of youthful uprisings was 1968. In China the Red Guards trekked across the countryside waving the *Little Red Book* of Chairman Mao, as did the students in Paris in May, which led ultimately to the fall of the Gaullist regime. There was unrest amongst students all over Europe. In America many repercussions from Vietnam rippled through the country. Many tried to escape from the draft, others opted out of everyday life through drug use or by joining 'flower power' pacifist communities; new religious cults grew up with their own life styles.

In Czechoslovakia a reform movement gathered way under Dubček; the Prague Spring led to the remarkable experience of a Soviet-controlled regime with, briefly, relative freedom of expression. However by August the Soviet Union had reoccupied Czechoslovakia and suppressed the Dubček government and its supporters. The United States was too enfeebled to be able to do anything, physical or moral such was the impotence of the successor to President Kennedy who had pledged in his 1961 inaugural address to brave any peril in the defence of freedom. For the sake of one corrupt puppet regime in South Vietnam the whole power of the United States was immobilised throughout the world.

Johnson's explanation to himself and to the country for not running again was his health, but the true reasons were the Vietnam War and the violence in American cities and on American campuses. He had had enough. The Democratic candidate was the Vice-President, Hubert Humphrey, who had to defend Johnson's record while trying to distance himself from the unpopularity that it caused. Demonstrations dogged the Democrats' Chicago convention in August, and amid astonishing scenes of police brutality Humphrey was nominated.

Richard Nixon, who had been Eisenhower's Vice-President, was adopted as the Republican candidate. It was clear that whether Nixon or his Democrat opponent won, it would be part of the process of bringing the war to an end. The question was not a simple one, however. How was it to be ended without a huge American defeat?

In May 1968, as a result of the US bombing 'pause' on North Vietnam, peace discussions between the Americans and North Vietnamese began in Paris. Humphrey announced he would stop all bombing if elected; McGeorge Bundy, a leading hawk, called for American troops to be withdrawn from Vietnam; Nixon argued for a short sharp war for victory. The Vietnam war, by the time of the election, had cost 29,000 American lives and $75 billion.

Earl Warren's resignation as Chief Justice in the summer of 1968 gave L.B.J. the opportunity to nominate Abe Fortas, his liberal lawyer. The nomination was rejected by the Senate. This marked a major swing to the right in America that culminated in Nixon's election in November 1968 when Humphrey, L.B.J.'s Vice-President, was overwhelmingly defeated.

The tragedy of L.B.J. – and no other word will do – was his high ambition for the United States and his commitment to its essential virtues, of generosity and openness, which became enmeshed in the Vietnam failure. The American virtues of passionate commitment to an ideal of high-principled behaviour then led to a repudiation of the commitment to Vietnam. In the collapse of American foreign policy that followed, in the dissolution of the American army's reputation as an effective fighting force, in the loss of respect for the Presidency and its collapse in recrimination and scandal, there were the seeds of a victory for Marxism which had been repudiated by every country the Soviet army had conquered.

From 1947 to the mid 1960s Asia and Africa and Latin America went through the trauma of 'liberation' from imperialism. The Soviet Union secured few footholds in the new countries, except for Cuba and, briefly, in Chile and – somewhat later – in Angola and Ethiopa. In Asia it seemed, for a while, as though Communism was the way of the future. But India, Pakistan, Indonesia and Japan chose quite different paths and even China, which became a completely Communist society after Mao's victory in 1949, broke with the Soviet Union. In Europe, where the building of the Berlin wall symbolised the deep division of the Continent, Communist governments were confined to those countries which had been occupied by the Russians as a result of their victory and the decisions at Yalta. Even there, however, Yugoslavia had broken away and major revolts erupted in East Germany, Poland, Hungary and Czechoslovakia – all of them initially accepting both the unalterable character of their Communist regimes and the indissolubility of the military alliance with the Soviet Union, but shifting in the Hungarian and Czechoslovak cases to demands for ordinary constitutional liberties. In Western Europe, the French and the Italians voted in large numbers for the Communist parties, yet there was no sign that either might shift into the Soviet camp. Even Portugal and Spain, long under right-wing dictatorships, did not veer far to the left when their dictators died and were succeeded by ordinary constitutionally elected, parliamentary regimes.

In these circumstances, with Russia apparently on ideological retreat, the calamitous involvement of the United States in Vietnam led to military defeat, to the loss of Indochina to Soviet-style Communism, and widespread disillusion with Western (and specifically American) society. The eruption of the Middle East War between Israel and its neighbours in 1973 and the subsequent end of the Western economic boom because of the rise of oil prices led to renewed fears throughout Europe and America of a collapse of the West similar to those prevalent in 1947 when the European economy seemed to have failed. For this series of defeats President Johnson was unfairly, but perhaps inevitably, blamed. The collapse of America's reputation – and above all the morale of its army – began in his Presidency.

PART FIVE

Diversity

The 1970s

Chapter 28

The Middle East

The Middle East after Suez was the epicentre of several further conflicts, the Arabs and the Israelis, old-style Arab leaders like Hussein and new patriots like Nasser, the Russians and the Americans, the oil cartel and OPEC, all these clashed, sometimes simultaneously, to keep the area in uproar. To them were now added fanatical religious extremists and Palestine Liberation guerrillas. This heady and explosive mixture was ignited by oil and nationalism. Oil was the fuel of the prosperous years and its abundance the basis for the affluent society. Nationalism led to the disruption of the peace: the loss of oil to the dissolution of prosperity.

In 1958 Syria had joined with Egypt to form the United Arab Republic (UAR) but withdrew four years later to become a violently leftist regime engaged in supporting fanatical terrorist attacks on Israel. Israel had received massive economic aid after the Suez War, becoming an important Middle Eastern state, with a high technological base and a powerful army. Nevertheless, being surrounded by deeply hostile neighbours, it could not relax its military effort. Jordan and Lebanon kept their hostility quiescent but Nasser waxed violent in speech though not in action, except that the Suez Canal was permanently closed to Israeli shipping. Syria, led by the militant Ba'athists, had now decided that hostility to Nasser was less important than hostility to Israel, so Egypt and Syria agreed to co-operate again and were supported in their aggression by the Soviet Union.

It will be remembered that after the Arab–Israeli War of 1948, between 900,000 and 1.3 million refugees had been left in makeshift camps in the Gaza Strip and on the West Bank. They had been left there by Arab governments pending the reconquest of Israel but Israel's repeated victories put off resettlement day; neither the Syrians nor the Egyptians wanted these refugees moved for their unrest made them a potent breeding ground for terrorism and their settlement outside Palestine would have been equivalent to rejecting their claims for a return to Palestine. The refugees camping round the Israeli border formed into many groups, the most militant being the Palestine Liberation Organisation, the PLO, with its army in the Gaza Strip and in Syria under Egyptian officers. The PLO linked with the Fedayeen, the original

Egyptian-backed Palestinian terrorist group, and its military wing, Fatah, which was modelled on the Algerian FLN, and led by Yasir Arafat and two other Palestinian student leaders. Fatah became the centre of terrorist attacks inside Israel, using tactics similar to those which had been used by the Algerians against the French and the Zionists against the British. The remoter kibbutzim were subject to attack, and there were also gun battles inside Tel Aviv itself.

The PLO and Fatah were also concerned to overthrow the so-called reactionary governments in the Arab states, including King Hussein of Jordan. In 1967 Egypt itself was exceptionally badly off, with the economy suffering as Nasser continued to build up armaments. At the same time Egypt's relations with most other Arab countries, notably Tunisia and Jordan, were deteriorating, because the rest of the Arab world resented Nasser's desire to dominate them. There were also attacks on him from Saudi Arabia and Kuwait. The Egyptian army, however, was exceptionally strong in hardware, being heavily supplied by the Russians and to some extent by the British and the French. It had 1200 tanks, 70 bombers, 130 MiG-21 fighters equipped with air-to-air missiles, 280 MiG-19 all-weather fighters and a further series of missiles and other equipment, whereas Israel had 800 tanks and 350 aircraft in total, supplied partly by the United States and partly by France. Its army, however, was better organised than that of the Egyptians.

Consequently, early in 1967, not only were two powerful armies opposing each other but there existed all round the borders of Israel a series of armed camps housing terrorists. Syria was in a state of revolutionary aggression, and two weak countries, the Lebanon and Jordan, were hesitant about taking part in any war, but prepared to allow their territory to be used. The position was poised for a major crisis. In May the Syrians claimed that the Israelis were building up an attack against them, and the Soviet Union chimed in that there was a major conspiracy by the Israelis, supported by the Americans, to overthrow Syria's Socialist government.

That there was something in this charge was a possibility, though it was certainly not an American conspiracy, but rather a growth of Israeli confidence. Eshkol, the Prime Minister of Israel, had suddenly announced that the major danger to Israel came from Syria where, the Israelis were convinced, the Fatah terrorists were organised by the Syrian High Command. A pre-emptive strike by Israel was, therefore, possible. Apparently what the Israelis intended was more modest than the Russians expected – an invasion of Syria to stop the guerrilla activities but not necessarily to overthrow the government in Damascus. Eshkol also believed that Egypt was unprepared militarily to launch an attack on him at that time.

The Syrians were prepared for civil war as well as a possible Israeli invasion. The Syrian government was exceptionally unpopular, and there was a plan by some army officers, who had fled to Jordan after an unsuccessful coup in 1966, to return and overthrow the Ba'ath regime. The Soviet Union was more concerned in helping the Syrian government resist any Israeli intervention, with Nasser determined to offer a show of strength on Israel's southern frontier. He may also have had a broader objective, to renew the 1956 war and to defeat Israel.

Egyptian troops advanced towards the Israeli frontier in early 1967 and in May Nasser unilaterally requested the UN to withdraw its observers and troops who were policing the Israeli border. It was held by some members of the Security Council that any unilateral request from either the Israelis or the Egyptians automatically obliged the force to withdraw; and the Indians and the Yugoslavs, whose troops were in the zone, particularly accepted this doctrine. U Thant, Secretary General of the UN, ordered a withdrawal of the troops, as he was bound to do, which may not have been what Nasser immediately wanted, since he was as yet militarily unprepared to mount an invasion of Israel. U Thant made no serious attempt to reach any other peaceful solution. The opposition to what seemed to be U Thant's hasty and precipitate action was based upon the fact that the Israelis had received assurances from the United States, the United Kingdom and Dag Hammarskjöld that President Nasser would never again make war in this particular area. On the basis of these assurances the Israelis had withdrawn their troops from the occupied Egyptian territories as part of the cease-fire settlement. There was therefore, it was argued, a bilateral agreement between the UN and Egypt and a further bilateral agreement between the UN and Israel which could not be broken by one side alone. Certainly the acceptance by the UN of the unilateral demand of Egypt for UN withdrawal made the UN seem the creature of Egypt. The Israelis were convinced that war with Egypt was inevitable. The threat of war steadily grew as Nasser claimed that he had mined the Tiran Straits, which gave access to the Israeli port of Eilat. It was at this point that he decided that he was going to invade Israel. In retrospect, the irrevocable act was the order to remove the United Nations emergency force.

By 21 May 1967 the Egyptian forces in the Sinai had taken over Sharm El Sheikh, the peninsula that dominated the entrance to Eilat, and clearly preparations were being made for a war against Israel. In a violent propaganda attack Cairo radio screamed: 'It is our chance, Arabs, to direct a blow of death and annihilation to Israel and all its presence in our Holy Land. It is a war for which we are waiting and in which we shall triumph. Allah Akhbah, Allah Akhbah, Allah Akhbah.' Such broadcasting was typical of the Egyptian radio during Nasser's regime, but it reached a crescendo. On 23 May Nasser closed the Gulf of Aqaba to Israeli shipping, which meant that the access to the Israeli port of Eilat through the Straits of Tiran was no longer merely difficult but impossible. This had been the precipitating cause of the Israeli intervention in the Suez affair of 1956, so it was possible, almost certain, that it would in fact lead to an Egyptian–Israeli war. The Straits of Tiran were not actually of vital economic importance to Israel, since most trade came to the Mediterranean ports, but they represented a symbol of Israel's access to the Red Sea and the outside world, making it not dependent entirely upon the Mediterranean.

Israel ordered a general mobilisation. Abba Eban, the Foreign Minister, set out on a journey through Europe to the United States to seek international support for Israel. The King of Jordan, Hussein, invited Iraqi troops to come across Jordan to the Israeli border, and King Feisal of Saudi Arabia revived an Arab united command. The United Nations, dominated by an anti-Israeli majority, entered a long and pointless debate and it was clear that the United States, Britain and France would still not support Israel. The Prime Minister of Israel, Eshkol, was undecided, but the Israeli mood hardened.

Nasser, too, was now reaching new heights of popularity in the Arab world because of his bellicosity, and delegations began to arrive from many of the states which had hitherto been extremely critical. On 29 May Nasser announced that he was ready to confront Israel. He would go to war with Israel, he said, in order to settle the matter of the refugees and the rights of Palestine, and his aim was to abolish Israel by Arab strength alone. Nasser said that he did not need the active intervention of the Soviet Union, and he denounced the United States as one of the major supporters of Israel. Saudi troops were sent to Jordan, and King Hussein came to Cairo on 30 May to negotiate.

Meanwhile Israel prepared for war under the leadership of Eshkol, who relied upon General Rabin as the Chief of Staff to prepare a lightning campaign. Would the Israelis make a pre-emptive strike? This the Soviet Union warned them against, supported by President Johnson, who had also been warned by the Russians that an Israeli attack on the Arabs would be regarded by them as a *casus belli*.

On 5 June 1967, early in the morning, the Israeli air force almost completely destroyed the Egyptian air force on the ground, bombing 300 planes and shooting down twenty. Iraqi planes in Jordan, and Syrian planes in Syria, were similarly attacked and most of them destroyed on that and the following day. Israeli troops entered the Sinai, capturing Gaza on 7 June. The Jordanians invaded Israel, began to shell Tel Aviv and attacked the Israeli enclave in Jerusalem. The Israelis counterattacked and by 7 June had reached the Jordan, captured Jerusalem, Jericho and Hebron. This action, against stern warnings from both the Soviet Union and the United States, was unprecedented. The Security Council was in continuous session, but it failed to find agreement on the British government's proposal for an international free waterway through the Straits of Tiran. Eighty per cent of the equipment of the Egyptian army was destroyed, over ten thousand soldiers were killed and over five thousand soldiers captured. The Israeli army advanced to the Suez Canal and, with no opposition, could have sped straight to Cairo and Alexandria. The Suez Canal was blocked by the fighting, and the whole of the Sinai peninsula was in Israeli hands.

On 8 June Nasser asked for a cease-fire between Egypt and Israel, and offered to resign. King Hussein, who had lost half his kingdom, and had also lost virtually his entire army, was also forced to ask for a cease-fire. On 9 June Dayan attacked the Syrians, entrenched on the Golan Heights overlooking the Sea of Galilee, and after a bitter battle the Israelis broke through and advanced towards Damascus. The Israeli army occupied the Golan Heights from which the kibbutzim in the valley below had been continuously shelled, and the Syrians fled. In the evening the Syrians also asked for a cease-fire, but the Israelis continued advancing until the following evening, when what was called the Six Day War ended. Egypt, Jordan, Iraq and Syria had lost almost their entire armies, their 450 planes and 1000 tanks. Israeli losses, though serious, were small in comparison.

The military victory in the Six Day War was so complete that it radically changed the balance of power in the Middle East. The Americans tried to insist on direct Arab–Israeli negotiations to achieve a lasting settlement, while the Russians tried to secure UN condemnation of Israeli aggression. On 22 November, however, largely under British influence, the UN adopted Resolution 242, which called on the Israelis to withdraw from their occupied territories in return for full recognition of the right to statehood, a guaranteed peace, and freedom of passage for their ships. This became the basis for the negotiations for a settlement which were to last on and off for the next twelve years. Israel was now militarily powerful; but it had over a million Arabs within its new borders, including almost all the former refugees; the two large Arab enclaves of Gaza and the West Bank were to represent substantial military and policing problems. Jerusalem was reunited as the capital of Israel. The border with Jordan was effectively opened with Hussein, to a degree, dependent on Israeli support. Nasser, however, after recovering from the shock of his defeat, left the Suez Canal blocked, and substituted oil from other Arab states for the lost Sinai oil fields. His army was re-equipped by the Soviet Union. Meanwhile, the Lebanon, Israel's one neighbour uninvolved in the Six Day War, began to be disrupted by a civil war. It had Palestinian forces, especially the Fatah, and large enclaves of Christians under Israeli protection on its southern border.

In 1967 the Syrian pipeline was once more shut by the Syrians. This helped to drive Iraq into strong measures to find alternative markets and outlets, culminating in a law which effectively nationalised Iraqi oil through the Iraq National Oil Corporation, and broke the cartel by a twenty-year agreement to sell its oil to France, and to receive technical and trade help from the Soviet Union. The power of the oil companies as distributors remained. Their position as monopolist producers was continually weakening.

One of the consequences of the Arab defeat was the rise of Arab extremism. In 1968 the Iraqi government of General Abdul Rahman Aref fell, to be replaced by a revolutionary Socialist regime, and the Syrians became once more aggressive under a new government led by General Hafez Al-Assad.

Despite UN Resolution 242, calling for a negotiated peace in which the Arabs recognised Israel and Israel withdrew from the occupied territories, the majority of Arab states were unwilling to negotiate. Nevertheless, they were also unable to wage war. Israel continued, therefore, to be surrounded by war-minded enemies. In Lebanon and Syria, and to a lesser extent in Jordan, the Palestinian Liberation Organisation developed a strong guerrilla force and attacked Israelis and their supporters all over the world, especially by hi-jacking aircraft and by terrorist attacks on civilians. Israel responded to the Palestinian attacks by air raids on the Nile valley, and by raids into Lebanon and Syria to suppress the guerrillas. In the circumstances, the PLO became a less coherent force; Shukairy was forced out of the leadership, his place being taken by Yahya Hamonda. Splintered as it was, it became paradoxically a more dangerous enemy. The Syrians encouraged the PLO to wage war by guerrilla tactics, using Yasir Arafat of Fatah as its leader. The Syrians trained Fatah, which collected abandoned Arab weapons from the battlefields, acquired arms from Communists states, and adopted some of the hit and run terrorist tactics perfected by the Vietcong. Their raids on Israel were mostly foiled by Israeli intelligence, which had acquired Arab intelligence files after the Israeli victory. Nevertheless attacks from Jordanian and Egyptian territory led to a permanent state of active hostility on these borders, chiefly artillery exchanges and sorties by Israeli aircraft on Fedayeen bases. This culminated in a full-scale attack by the Israeli army on guerrilla bases in Jordan, where the King was securely in control. In a clash at Karameh the Israelis were defeated by Fatah. Fatah thereupon became the heroes of the Arab world. Yasir Arafat had organised the various Arab terrorist groups – especially the PLO and the Marxist Popular Front for the Liberation of Palestine – into a unified command structure, operating through the PLO organisation of which he now took control. Nevertheless, Hussein attempted a clamp-down on the Fedayeen, which led to a civil war, in which King Hussein was successful.

The main terrorist bases were in South Lebanon, on the Syrian border. The PLO forces were disruptive of their unwilling hosts; they were active in the Lebanese civil war, and they provoked a major civil war in Jordan which they lost. Thus they were a potent factor in the instability of the Middle East.

But their most notorious accomplishments were the frequent hi-jacking of commercial aircraft (initially Israeli, but subsequently without discrimination) and terrorist attacks abroad on Israelis and anyone suspected as a Zionist sympathiser. This virtually continuous terrorism, linked as it was (through Libya) with the IRA in Northern Ireland, the Basque terrorists in Spain, and other foreign groups, led to an atmosphere in which international security against terrorism was in striking contrast to the happy-go-lucky years of the 1950s, when people had walked on and off planes as casually as they had boarded their local buses. As a technique of drawing world attention to their existence it could hardly be bettered.

In the aftermath of the Israeli inquest on the preparations for the war, which they had won, but which they had not been fully prepared for and which had cost them dear, Golda Meir became Prime Minister in March 1969, and pursued a policy of strong military preparedness and uncompromising resistance to Arab aggression. Golda Meir had been born in Russia, but had then lived for fifteen years in America before returning to Palestine in the 1920s to settle on a kibbutz. Under her government, Jewish settlement in the Arab-occupied territories was encouraged and

Israel began to identify itself with a new geographical shape. This was a dangerous policy as it left a million Arabs permanently within Israel, as a source of disaffection and as an excuse for Arab military intervention.

In the late 1960s Israel's Jewish population continued to grow, especially after renewed anti-Semitic persecution in Argentina and the Soviet Union. But, paradoxically, the army was weakened by its leadership problems and corruption in government. Israeli intelligence and security fell from its previous high standards, hence the massacre at Lod – Tel Aviv airport – and the murder of Israeli athletes at the Munich Olympics in 1972.

Egypt, meanwhile, grew more efficient. In September 1970 Nasser died and was succeeded by Anwar Sadat, who broke previous close ties with the Soviet Union and reoriented Egyptian policy towards the Arab world. He made a close alliance with Syria and Jordan, and received substantial Saudi aid.

Arab resentment against Israel continued, as did their bitterness about America's pro-Israeli policy. The Arabs had for long operated a boycott on states and companies trading with Israel, but had hitherto not used the threat of diminishing oil supplies. In the spring of 1973 the Arab states, in a rare act of union, agreed that they would support an oil boycott of Western countries unless there was some change in American policy towards Israel. They also prepared a plan, fomented by Egypt, for a concerted attack on Israel. On 6 October 1973, the eve of Yom Kippur, the Jewish Day of Atonement, the American CIA discovered that Syria and Egypt were about to attack the Israelis, it being the day the Jews were least likely to be prepared. In the United States President Nixon and his Secretary of State, Henry Kissinger, contacted all parties and the Soviet Union to try to stop the war.

Israeli intelligence had in fact learned of the invasion plan on 5 October and asked Mrs Meir and General Dayan for mobilisation and a pre-emptive strike. This was refused, save for the assembly of the armoured corps reservists.

The Syrians launched a massive attack on the Golan Heights which lasted for four days and captured the Israeli radar installation on Mount Hermon, which allowed their planes to fly into Israel. SAM missiles and tanks bombarded northern Israel in large numbers, virtually eliminating the northern Israeli army. At the same time, 600,000 Egyptians, with 2000 tanks, 160 SAM missiles and 550 planes crossed the Suez Canal and penetrated the eastern bank to a depth of thirty miles. The Israeli tanks were on the other side of Sinai and had to cross the Gidi and Mitla passes to reach the Egyptians. The Israeli defensive line, the Bar–Lev fortifications, had been completely overrun and, for the first time, Israeli troops surrendered.

The plan had been for the Syrians and the Egyptians to attack jointly: the Egyptians advancing beyond Suez into the Sinai, while the Syrians attacked over the Golan Heights. This time initial Israeli losses were large, including a third of their tanks and well over one thousand men.

By 9 October the Israelis seemed defeated. Mrs Meir and General Dayan had been caught completely unprepared and their initial bravado soon turned to despair. They were, however, saved by the Chief of Staff, General David Elazar, who organised the counterattack, first on Syria, whose oil terminals and power stations were bombed. By withdrawing tanks from other fronts, he counterattacked on the Golan Heights and pushed back the over-extended Syrians. By 10 October the key town of Kuneitra was reconquered and over eight hundred Syrian tanks were destroyed. By 15 October the Israeli troops were only twenty-two miles from Damascus and were shelling the city. The attack was then directed against Egypt.

As the United Nations, led by Kissinger, sought a cease-fire, the Russians sent by air and sea vast quantities of weapons to Egypt and Syria. On 12 October President Nixon ordered a massive airlift of advanced military equipment to Israel.

Ensured of this support, Israel launched an attack in the Sinai on 14 October which became the scene of the biggest tank battle since the battle of Yursk in the Second World War. A magnificent plan for crossing the Canal was prepared and on 15 October the Israelis mounted an amphibious operation well behind the Egyptian lines, leaving almost all Egypt's armour encircled in Sinai around the Mitla and Gidi passes. The road to Cairo was open and the Egyptian army was lost.

The Soviet Prime Minister, Kosygin, flew to Cairo on 15 October to see Sadat, to press for a cease-fire followed by an international peace conference guaranteed by the Soviet Union and the United States.

The Israeli advance to the Suez Canal and their overwhelming victory on the Golan Heights restored the 1967 position; the Arabs had had Israel's defeat snatched from them, as they saw it, by United States material help. On 17 October 1973 the Organisation of Arab Petroleum Exporting Countries agreed to reduce oil production, and Abu Dhabi, Libya, Saudi Arabia, Algeria and Kuwait imposed total oil embargoes on the United States, followed by similar embargoes for Western Europe. This created a major oil shortage throughout much of the Western world in early 1974.

The Egyptians continued to fight, though the Egyptian army was fast disintegrating. Sadat appealed for a joint American–Soviet force to intervene; and Kissinger and Nixon threatened to move against the Soviet Union if Russian troops were sent to the Middle East.

The Egyptians were at first not prepared to accept, but on 18 October, when Sadat realised the full extent of his defeat, he feared that the Israelis might not accept the cease-fire. Nixon sent Kissinger to Moscow on 20 October and on 22 October the United Nations adopted Resolution 338, calling for a cease-fire, based on the full implementation of Resolution 242.

This cease-fire was violated by Egyptian troops and the Israelis advanced and captured the entire Egyptian third army on the east bank of the Suez Canal. It was once more clear that the Israelis were in a position to capture Cairo. On 24 October Kissinger and Brezhnev agreed on another Israeli–Egyptian cease-fire, though the war continued with Syria. By this time a large Soviet force had sailed into the Mediterranean, including eighty-five ships with landing craft and troop helicopters, while 50,000 airborne troops had been put on alert to intervene. The Soviet Union called for a joint American–Russian force to police the cease-fire, which Nixon and Kissinger opposed in order to prevent a permanent Soviet presence in the Middle East. Thereupon Sadat and the Israelis agreed to a renewal of the UN mandate for a peace-keeping force. On 24 October a cease-fire began, and Kurt Waldheim, the Secretary General of the United Nations, offered a UN peace-keeping force to police it.

But the war was still not yet over. On 26 October the Egyptian army tried to fight its way out but was defeated by the Israelis. On 28 October the army was evacuated under UN auspices, in return for Israeli prisoners of war.

Israeli troop losses were heartrendingly large; and its depletion of equipment was serious too. It became clear that Israel's most costly victory was its last; henceforth, the sophisticated technology available to the Arabs meant a war to the death, and final holocaust. As the price of oil quadrupled following the OPEC oil export embargo, the Third World turned decisively against Israel, branding Zionism as racism, and regarding Israel as an American tool.

By the time the war ended, the Syrians and the Egyptians had lost almost all their Soviet equipment, and seen an Israeli advance over its frontier with Lebanon, which promptly disintegrated into a civil war between those parts occupied by the Palestine Liberation Organisation and the Christians, who were broadly speaking sympathetic to Israel. The Syrians sought to separate the two sides. After further negotiations, Henry Kissinger launched what became known as his shuttle on 5 November, in order to secure a permanent settlement in the Middle East. He had a remarkably free hand, for the Vice-President of the United States had resigned after being convicted of conspiracy, extortion, bribery and tax fraud and the President was in the throes of Watergate.

Flying between Jerusalem, Cairo and Damascus, for four months, Kissinger eventually succeeded, in March 1974, in persuading the Arabs to drop their oil embargo, though their prices continued to rise, and the Israelis to withdraw across the Canal, while a UN buffer zone was drawn up between the two countries. War flared up again on the Golan Heights between Israel and Syria, but eventually a similar buffer zone proposal was also adopted.

The position in the Middle East, then, was one of embittered enmity between the Arabs and the Israelis, reduced to a stalemate and to a degree a settlement through United States negotiation, with deep divisions between the Arabs, chiefly the Egyptians on one side and the more extreme Arabs, such as Fatah and the Syrians, on the other. Though the Soviet Union had intervened frequently, its interventions had not led to any permanent presence in the region, save in Libya, a country of doubtful stability and of little strategic significance for the Arab world as a whole. But for the West the loss of influence was significant. It had lost its former complete control of its major source of oil and of a key region, and the profound hostility of most Arab governments to America and its allies was a potent source of danger, as the later troubles in Iran were to prove.

World terrorism, largely initiated by the Palestinians, had spread to many areas outside the Soviet bloc. So all told, though it was not a Soviet victory, it was a victory for nationalism and to some degree for unreason. Western loss of influence and loss of real power was directly attributable to the lack of a coherent policy for oil and for the Middle East. The oil companies had played a role in the Middle East often at variance with true Western interests. The British, French and Americans had often been at loggerheads. The West veered between strong support for Israel and support for the Arabs. The Arabs whom they supported were often overthrown, and their successors were regarded as enemies and (more important) distrusted the West. For an area which was the major supplier of oil, and of fundamental strategic importance, the muddles and incoherence of Western policy were as dangerous as they were unsuccessful.

Chapter 29

Western Europe: liberalism and the fear of reaction

The OPEC oil embargo of 1973 interrupted twenty years of economic boom. This miracle of affluence had been astonishing and quite unexpected. Western Europe's recovery had been marked by a shift of population from the countryside to the towns, a rapid increase in agricultural output and a vast growth in manufacturing, especially in engineering products. In every country more and more people went to live in houses and flats with central heating and bathrooms, with radios, television, in many cases telephones, cars, plenty of holidays, a forty-hour working week, considerable savings and a choice of jobs available: all backed by social security, health care and universal education. Prosperity and freedom seemed to have brought liberal political regimes. But how secure were these? When the boom collapsed, would Italy, Spain, Portugal and Greece remain liberal or would Fascism reappear? How strong was Germany's Social Democracy and France's new constitution after her Algerian trauma? After all, in 1944 every major country in Western Europe, except the United Kingdom, had been under an authoritarian government.

This chapter looks at the way in which Italy, Spain, France, Germany and Greece gradually swung away from authoritarian regimes to more liberal ones and ponders the stresses and strains attached to constitutional democracy.

The Roman Catholic Church's unremitting hostility to Communism, Socialism and liberalism – interpreted in its pluralist anti-confessional sense – led to the view that it would be among Catholics especially that the seeds of Fascism were likely once more to sprout. During the earlier part of this century the Vatican and the hierarchy were deeply reactionary and anti-Socialist; it would have been hard, but not impossible, to find any substantial movement of leftist-leaning social Catholicism. The Italian bishops strongly backed Mussolini; most German bishops supported Hitler; all Portuguese bishops were behind Salazar, and Franco had virtually unanimous and strenuous clerical aid. Catholic Ireland was neutral under President de Valera but he presented his condolences to the German Ambassador when Hitler committed suicide.

The Catholic vote in the American Presidential election of 1940 was fiercely anti-British, as was Joseph Kennedy, Roosevelt's Boston–Irish Ambassador to London.

Pope Pius XII had been reluctant to support the allies. Whilst he was alive, the Catholic Church remained authoritarian and Mariolatry became an effective substitute for social philosophy. Pius, like Franco, survived the downfall of Hitler and Mussolini, and achieved a triumphant revival of the Church, politically and to some degree spiritually. He reiterated his detestation of godless Communism, abandoned right-wing absolutism and rapidly embraced the form of social liberalism embodied in the Christian Democratic parties which took office in Italy and West Germany, in Opus Dei (operating principally in Spain), and in the Mouvement Républicain Populaire, in France. There was however always the problem of how a Catholic party was to operate in a laicised and pluralist society where not everyone accepted Catholic dogma on censorship, contraception and other social issues as was done in Ireland.

The Catholic revival was advanced, especially spiritually, by his successor, John XXIII, who added a radical social philosophy to his predecessor's piety. John, an Italian peasant's son, was a conservative pietist practitioner of the faith, but impressed the world by his radical innovations in the Church's structure, notably by calling the Second Vatican Council and, above all, by seeking to break with the obscurantist and Fascist past, to bring the Church up to date in the world – *aggiornamento*, as it was called.

De Gasperi was the first practising Roman Catholic to be a leader of a free non-Fascist Italian government. He took part in the Marshall Plan, joined the OEEC and NATO, and cemented the country firmly into the Western camp. When he retired in 1953, after the second election, his government had seen the beginning of the economic recovery and the subsequent boom, but above all seen the power of the Vatican and the Catholic vote switch firmly to parliamentary democracy rather than to authoritarianism. The Communist party had pulled out of the government in 1947, partly because they were expelled by their moderate coalition partners but partly as a general move by Communist parties throughout Western Europe to withdraw from coalitions. The Marxist vote remained large, at about one third of the electorate, predominantly in the Northern cities. During the years of boom, the Italian workers remained firmly attached to a Marxist party, and authoritarian in outlook, for while Nenni was highly regarded as an anti-Fascist, Togliatti, who had spent the war years in Russia, remained an orthodox Stalinist.

The boom was based upon manufacturing, cheap energy – for natural gas and oil had been found in the Po Valley – allied to cheap and competent labour. But prosperity coincided with corruption and political instability, which became endemic. The Christian Democrats were obliged to form coalitions with smaller parties and though the personalities remained the same, the number of governments multiplied, closely resembling the experience of France under the Third and Fourth Republics. The democratic parties seemed corrupt and their regimes unstable, there were growing scandals involving industry and the Mafia. But the left was little better. The Hungarian uprising affected them. Nenni broke with the Communists, who were also faced with the problem of Khruschev's revelations about Stalin. It is from this period, 1956, that Euro-Communism dates, associated in Italy particularly with a return to the ideas of Gramsci, one of the founders of the Italian Communist party. The intellectuals who rediscovered him felt less dependence on Stalin or even Lenin, which gave the large Italian left considerable latitude for manoeuvre.

The left accepted the rise in the standard of living but blamed capitalism for the by-products: vast fortunes, corruption, and a disagreeable and polluted environment. But they had no possibility of forming a left-wing government since the Communists could never gain a majority by themselves and the central parties would not join with them at this time. Mattei, the head of ENI, and other industrialists, notably Fiat, argued for accommodation with the left and the Christian Democrats endeavoured to bring about indicative planning, regional reform and better education, health and housing. Italy seemed to be gently changing her mood. In March 1963 Pope John XXIII received Khruschev's daughter and her husband in audience, and on 10 April 1963 his encyclical *Pacem in Terris* accepted the Communists, recognised freedom of conscience among Catholics, and the peaceful coexistence of different political and intellectual systems. In the same month the Communists (with 166 seats) made major gains in the general election – the Christian Democrats now had 260 seats in the chamber, the balance of power being held by the Socialists. It seemed distinctly possible that the Communists might enter the government.

The death of Pope John in 1963 and the succession of Paul VI could not stop the *aggiornamento* of the Roman Catholic Church that was occurring because of the Second Vatican Council, any more than the death of Togliatti in late 1964 made any significant difference to the apparently growing liberalism of the Italian Communist party. The result was a combination of a Marxist-led working class, with a highly cultivated Marxist intelligentsia, political instability, economic prosperity and free exchange of ideas, a Church that almost despite itself was being led mainly by non-Italian Cardinals into an ecumenical world of peaceful coexistence between Marxism and liberalism. Prosperity and instability became an Italian hallmark and, interestingly enough, a forerunner of much of the future of other countries in Western Europe – Spain for example – and indeed, to some degree, of Latin America. Yet despite these apparent contradictions Italy remained a loyal member of NATO and the EEC – with Communist support.

In December 1963 Aldo Moro formed a government allied to the Socialists (the PSI), with Nenni as Foreign Minister and an ex-Communist, Antonio Giolitti, as Minister of Planning and the Budget. The government lasted five years, with Fanfani succeeding Nenni in 1964, who in turn returned to the Foreign Office when Mariano Rumor became Prime Minister in 1968. The Italian game of musical chairs with Cabinet posts continued. Public disorder, however, became a new factor, spreading from the universities into the streets and the factories. From the mid 1960s on, Italy ceased to be a low-wage industrial country and one of the principal engines of economic progress was lost.

With the election of Paul VI, the Vatican moved more to the centre and though the 1968 general election slightly improved the Christian Democrats' position, political crises continued with a rapid turnover of governments, while the social problems of the country became more acute and the economy entered a serious depression between 1969 and 1971. In common with other Western European countries considerable student violence and workers' sit-ins in 1969 were common, accompanied by demands for new regional governments, which were established after the elections held in 1970, and for the reform of the divorce law and the development of women's rights.

An uncertain Presidential election in December 1971 was followed by even more political intrigue and disturbance, representing, to a considerable degree, the final collapse of the Christian Democratic party as an effective political machine with coherent ideas about the development of Italian policy. The Christian Democrats, who fought the 1972 elections on an anti-Communist ticket, retained their vote despite their political failure in government. After a Centre–Left coalition, a Centre–Right experiment was tried, which also failed. This was succeeded by a further Centre–Left government with the Communist party deciding to support the government.

In 1974 the governments, successively headed by Aldo Moro

(twice), who was later kidnapped and murdered, and by Rumor, followed each other in quick succession. All had failed, and with the collapse of Socialist support in January 1976 Italy seemed to become almost impossible to govern.

The crucial question was how the Christian Democratic party, which had been in office continuously from 1944, either alone or mostly in coalitions, could form a stable coherent government. How could it reform the economic and social position of Italy, and above all the civil service, and continue to seek to establish its independence from the Church while gaining the Church's support in the elections? The declaration of the Communist party in 1973 that they were in favour of the 'historic compromise' whereby they would support the Christian Democrats, faced the Christian Democrats with an acute question: they condemned Marxist atheism but governed with Communist support, and by so doing showed the Communist party to be *de facto* a respectable, almost bourgeois, party.

The dilemma of the Christian Democrats lay particularly in the struggles within the party itself for leadership, together with the peculiar system of proportional representation in Italy which yielded a multiplicity of parties who wheeled and dealed in and out of shifting coalitions. The Christian Democratic party, embracing as it did a wider range of opinion, had at least six major factions, being parties within the parties, with their own organisations. This factionalism led to differences on the question of centralisation versus the regions, and especially on the issue of reform and the relationships of the party with business and with the Church. Thus it was despite the firm convictions of large numbers of Christian Democrats that divorce reform was accepted by referendum. This continual development of factionalism made it impossible for successive Christian Democratic governments to organise the reform of Italian society which was throughout this period urgently required.

Italy showed the success of capitalism economically. It was a liberal and free country. It was loyal to the Western alliance. It was the source of high art and popular fashion. Though it seemed in some respects ungovernable, the original home of Fascism was prosperous and liberal. The arch-fiend himself, the Pope, paid lip service at least to liberal Western shibboleths. This victory was moral as well as material and the Euro-Communists were the doves in some intellectual circles.

The other major Catholic nation in West Europe was Spain. Like Italy it had once had a great liberal and anti-clerical tradition but this had been ruthlessly broken by the Civil War.

In July 1936 the greater part of the Spanish army followed a group of generals headed by José San Jorjo and Francisco Franco in a revolt against the Liberal Socialist anti-clerical Republican government elected only five months before. The Republic, which replaced the monarchy in 1931 with the abdication of King Alfonso XIII, had begun as a fairly conservative and cautious regime. But the left had soon made substantial electoral advances. Franco rallied to his cause the Roman Catholic Church, the land-owners, the middle classes and much of the army. He was supported by Hitler, Mussolini and the Catholic countries, headed by de Valera's Ireland. The Republicans, a heterogeneous group of ordinary Constitutional Republicans, Socialists, Communists, Anarchists, as well as Basque and Catalan Nationalists, often fighting among themselves, were supported by the international left, especially Soviet Russia.

In the less than three years of Civil War over one million people died in intensely bitter fighting. By April 1939 Franco had won a complete victory, becoming a dictator of a theocratic state, organised on corporate lines, somewhat like Mussolini's Italy.

Despite support from Mussolini and Hitler during the Civil War, Franco chose not to involve Spain in the Second World War. His neutrality grew steadily more neutral, like that of Sweden, as the allied victory grew nearer. Even so his failure to join the war was undoubtedly a factor in Anglo–American success.

After the war Spain was excluded from the United Nations, ostracised, but left in peace. The victorious powers had not the energy to invade, nor did they want to see the Civil War renewed, nor add to their many other difficulties. Isolated, with some of the lowest living standards in Europe, the country made little progress. Franco's government could achieve little with real wages of industrial workers only about half what they had been in the 1930s and genuine starvation frequently a fear up to 1952. Education and social progress had been set back a generation and the people lived under a pall of dark, oppressive, ruthlessly imposed Catholicism. The economy was autarchic, with private monopolies in industry and large estates in agriculture. Trade unions were prohibited except for government-organised syndicates.

In the face of such immobilism, there seemed little hope for change. But as the European economy recovered, so its trade links with Spain developed and stimulated trade, particularly when the beginning of tourism on the Costa Brava began to increase Spain's

foreign exchange reserves. Then the cumulative pressure of the
Christian Democrat form of Roman Catholicism now dominant in
Rome itself had an effect and Spain saw how out of step it was with
Christian Democracy. The accumulation of capital in the hands of
industrialists, large farmers and banks provided the basis for the
beginnings of a significant economic upsurge.

A major Cabinet reshuffle on 19 July 1951, which led to the
introduction of a number of Opus Dei specialists as ministers who
were pro-American, led also to a gradual winding down of the
significance of the Falange. The direction of economic policy was
radically changed. A major programme of industrial investment
was undertaken; imports were enlarged to overcome shortages;
and prices were decontrolled, though wages and salaries were let
off the leash only gradually. The process of economic improvement was at first slow – 1935 output levels were only achieved by
1954 – and balance of payments difficulties continued throughout
the 1950s, together with noticeable inflation (by the standards of
the time).

As the revival of European tourism gave a substantial stimulus
to the Spanish economy, so industrialisation followed, led by a
quasi-Fascist organisation similar to that of Italy, called INI
(Instituto Nacional de Industria). This built steelworks, tripled the
output of electricity, began a small motor-car industry in Barcelona, and built several oil refineries.

The boycott of Spain, initiated after the end of the Second World
War, was rescinded by a UN General Assembly resolution on 5
November 1950. The Western majority was a consequence of
manoeuvring in the UN over the Korean conflict. New ambassadors therefore went to Madrid, and Spain negotiated the establishment of United States military bases on its territory. Final agreement was confirmed by Eisenhower, as one of the first acts of his
Presidency.

Spain applied to join the OEEC, having been in receipt of its
forerunner, Marshall Aid. Following a substantial devaluation and
a liberalisation of foreign trade, the peseta went into surplus and
economic growth made substantial advances. After an initial
hesitancy industrial output grew by 11 per cent a year, and by the
early 1960s the rate of growth of the economy was running at the
level of that of all Southern European countries. Consequently
national income per head rose between 6 and 11 per cent a year
throughout the period from 1956 to 1967. Nevertheless many
Spaniards emigrated, chiefly to Germany and France, but also to
Latin America and Australia.

A wave of strikes in 1951, at first in Barcelona, led to the burgeoning of a semi-recognised opposition hitherto repressed by terror. With Spain's accession to OEEC a recognisably liberal attitude to the censorship of foreign books, newspapers and magazines became apparent. The millions of tourists were themselves liberalising, as were the millions of expatriate workers, who went to liberal societies and liked what they saw. This, and the death of Pope Pius XII, led to a more open regime in Spain, with the government adopting a less rigid attitude to liberal ideas, the Church no longer identifying itself so closely with the ideology of clerical Fascism, and the army being influenced by the democratic pressures of its American ally. Economic success and social change made all the difference.

Franco remained an absolute dictator, however, though he shrewdly manipulated the members of the various groups with which he had to deal. By adopting a potentially monarchical form of government he gave his regime a legitimate successor. He chose Don Juan Carlos, the son of Don Juan, the Bourbon pretender king who lived in exile in Estoril to be trained as his own heir. This provided the bridge by which after his death Franco's regime would move to constitutional democracy and full membership of the international community.

The later 1950s were also marked by a radical shift in Spanish opinion brought about by the election of Pope John XXIII and his radical and liberal declarations. In particular the encyclical *Mater et Magistra* was followed by a series of strikes which led to the revision of Spain's labour laws. Spain joined the United Nations and associated United Nations agencies, and it became standard form for Spain to belong to every international organisation except the EEC, to which it began to make approaches in 1962.

Spain, symbol of the victory of Fascism, had become a prosperous, acceptable and relatively liberal country. Yet this great victory for the West was rarely if ever celebrated.

The two other major Continental European nations, West Germany and France, remained firmly attached to constitutional democracy despite considerable stresses and strains. In France, for example, the preoccupation with the Algerian War led to the return of de Gaulle, but he came to power constitutionally and the new Constitution of the Fifth Republic was adopted and maintained in a strictly legal and democratic manner.

De Gaulle's foreign policy was based upon a deep concern for narrow French interests. He bitterly opposed the Americans and the British, whom he regarded as American stooges. French strength, as he perceived it, depended upon a firm alliance with a strong West Germany, an alliance 'of equals' with Russia and China, and a development of a world of separate but equal sovereign states. Nevertheless de Gaulle supported the Western Alliance – for example in the Cuban missile crisis – but he was never a 'slavish' adherent of a Western bloc. He regarded the division of the world into 'free' and 'unfree' states as a hopelessly romantic vision. France would form alliances as it suited him, not as it suited pragmatic political advantage. Consequently he withdrew from NATO and vetoed British membership of the EEC. France was only safe when it was supreme.

After settling the Algerian War, de Gaulle had a steady eight years of government marked by diplomatic success and economic prosperity. But in May 1968 the wave of student unrest that burst upon Peking and broke in America with the student reaction to the Vietnam War, arrived in Paris. The universities were occupied and Marxist and Trotskyist mobs took to the streets, led by ephemeral leaders like Rudi Dutschke and Danny Cohn-Bendit. France seemed on the verge of insurrection but the student revolution proved short-lived, despite the significance given to it at the time by the press.

De Gaulle's power was reaffirmed by an election and by massive demonstrations in the streets but he was growing old and his political acumen was beginning to slip. He was seventy-seven in May 1967 when he visited Canada on a state visit and shouted to the crowd '*Vive le Québec libre!*' This caused an official protest from the government of Canada and led to growing rumours that de Gaulle was losing his grip. The Prime Minister, Georges Pompidou, began to negotiate the succession.

When de Gaulle's desire to build up regional assemblies in France was rejected the following year in a referendum, he resigned. He was too old to stage a comeback. Pompidou stood as a Gaullist against François Mitterrand, the eventual Socialist candidate; after two ballots, Pompidou was elected President.

Pompidou, a lawyer, a businessman and a banker, was no less conscious than de Gaulle of the high office to which he had been called, but less mystical in his relationship to 'la France'. He immediately changed Gaullist policy in several directions, by becoming less arbitrary internally and internationally, and by retreating from some of the high points of Gaullist arrogance. He devalued the franc, and dropped some of the more prestigious expensive technological schemes which de Gaulle had introduced. As a result of Pompidou's policies the economy surged upwards substantially, a boom only brought to an end by the OPEC crisis of 1973.

At the same time Pompidou made a major effort in the Common

Market, beginning at The Hague Conference in 1969 when he pushed for three aims: *achèvement* – the completion of the Common Agricultural Market; *approfondissement* – the development in depth of the Common Market so that it included banking and monetary policy, the harmonisation of taxation and of social security administration, and the ultimate development of speaking with one voice in foreign affairs; and *élargissement* – the inclusion of the United Kingdom, Ireland, Norway and Denmark as members. In 1972 a referendum in France agreed by two to one that the United Kingdom should join. This was agreed at a summit conference of the Six and the Three, Norway deciding not to join, on 19 October 1972, in Paris. Enlargement was achieved on 1 January 1973.

To a considerable degree, too, Pompidou modified the anti-American stance of the Gaullists, though he failed to move the position of France in any major direction. At the time of his death from the type of cancer Kennedy had suffered from, on 2 April 1974, the Fifth Republic had survived the passing of de Gaulle and not proved to be a one-man band like the Second Empire. Nevertheless, Pompidou's death occurred after the Yom Kippur War and the impact of the oil price rise which created a serious political and economic crisis in France. He was succeeded by Giscard d'Estaing who scraped in by a narrow margin to govern strictly according to the Constitution.

The Fifth Republic had been founded upon the collapse of the Fourth. But though France changed regimes – five republics, two monarchies, two empires and Vichy in less than two centuries – it remained basically a liberal, constitutional, democratic and prosperous country. Even so, the fashionable intelligentsia was either Marxist or sympathetic to Marxism, and the threat of tyranny was seen to be from the right, from Fascism, not in the actual tyranny only a few hundred miles away on the banks of the river Elbe, the frontier of East Germany. France was allied to a free and liberal West Germany. Intellectually, however, its sympathies were often with the East.

West Germany was an artificial creation, invented largely by the Americans. Under Konrad Adenauer, its first federal Chancellor, a period of prosperity and stability ensued. At the same time, the experience of the Berlin airlift and the Communist suppression of the 17 June 1953 rising in East Germany had made the German voters terrified of Communist advances. Nevertheless, Adenauer consistently attempted to form coalition governments with Liberals and also paid particular attention to the needs of the refugees represented by the German Party. This policy paid off handsomely in electoral politics, but Adenauer had no wish to create a one-party state by his overwhelming electoral successes.

Adenauer remained in office until 1963. His achievements were immense. Constitutional democracy, not previously considered a particularly German form of government, became deeply embedded in West Germany. His administration provided the basic economic policy for the German economic miracle which led to the highest national income per capita in Western Europe, except for Switzerland, by the end of the 1960s. Germany, too, became deeply entrenched in NATO and the Brussels Pact, but above all the Treaties of Rome and Paris. Franco–German rapprochement formed a major bloc around which other European nations aligned themselves. The historic enmity was ended and a historic friendship begun.

Hovering over all German politics, however, was the unspoken question – was German reunification either possible or desirable? Was neutralism a price worth paying even if it meant the liberation of East Germany?

No peace treaty was ever signed between Germany and the Second World War belligerents. World-wide fear of a German military revival was genuine, and opposition to a united Germany was the unspoken common platform of the three countries most affected, France, Poland and Russia. The border between the two Germanies and divided Berlin formed a potential flashpoint.

With the launching of Sputnik in October 1957 the prospects of nuclear warfare on a global basis became technically far more likely than before. World nuclear war loomed seemingly ever closer. The Rapacki Plan advanced by the Foreign Minister of Poland on 2 October 1957 at the United Nations proposed a nuclear-free zone, initially including both Germanies, Poland and Czechoslovakia, which would bring to an end the threat of nuclear war. At the same time a substantial anti-nuclear campaign was mounted – probably under Communist auspices, certainly with Communist support – throughout the world, with perhaps its most prominent manifestations in the United Kingdom, the second Western nuclear power. The proposals for the Rapacki Plan were, however, rejected by Adenauer on the grounds that it would leave Germany without its own troops, and therefore defenceless, and without recourse to the American nuclear umbrella. His Defence Minister, Franz Josef Strauss, was also deeply opposed to the plan, and wished to arm German troops with tactical nuclear weapons, a view supported by the Bundestag.

In May 1960 the Paris Summit between Eisenhower, Khruschev,

de Gaulle and Macmillan collapsed when the shooting down of an American U2 spy plane over Russia gave Khruschev the excuse to break up the summit, since he was obviously not achieving his aim of a reunited Germany at the heart of a neutralised Europe.

Khruschev did not stop there, deciding to use East Germany, the German Democratic Republic, to put pressure upon the Western powers. On the night of 12/13 August 1961 a wall was built dividing the West sector of Berlin from East Berlin, thus effectively sealing the border, making it impossible for East Germans to enter the West sector and from there to escape to West Germany. The building of the wall had a serious impact on German opinion on both sides. In particular it meant that East Germany became far more solid and dictatorial than previously. Its population could no longer leak across the border and, as a result, productive efficiency grew rapidly. The division of East and West Germany became apparently permanent, and the possibility of a unified and neutralised Germany ceased to be discussed, even though Adenauer paid an official visit to Moscow.

Adenauer eventually retired as Chancellor (but not as the CDU's chairman until 1966) shortly after Strauss's resignation, following a scandal when Strauss tried to prosecute the publishers of *Der Spiegel*, which had published secret documents on NATO manoeuvres in West Germany. Adenauer's resignation thus led inevitably to the succession of Ludwig Erhard, his Finance Minister.

Erhard's record was remarkable. During the rehabilitation of the economy, twelve million refugees were resettled in Germany. At the same time the per capita national income rose by five times in real terms. By the mid 1950s Germany was the leading creditor nation in Europe, to which most other European nations were in debt. By the late 1950s the Mark was, after the Swiss franc, the strongest currency in Europe, and by 1963 Germany was the largest trading country in the world after the United States.

Erhard's initial political prestige arose from the stabilisation of the Mark, Germany's swift recovery from the war, and also from his strong initial support of Adenauer. But the issue that undermined him was Germany's relationship with Eastern Europe. By his attempt to develop closer links with East Germany – indirectly through better relationships with the other satellite countries of Eastern Europe – he became less close to France, and was therefore bitterly criticised by Adenauer.

Erhard, '*der Vater des Wirtschaftswunders*', was, however, extremely popular. He won the 1965 general election with a large vote, but it soon became apparent that his pro-American and pro-détente policies, which were criticised in his own party by Adenauer and Strauss, were a handicap. The era of Christian Democrat supremacy was over. Adenauer had been virtually a President on the American scale, but with his departure there was no longer a clear choice between men; the choice was now between policies. And the priority seemed to be to strengthen the centre in Germany, to preserve its economic and constitutional success, while trying to develop an *Ostpolitik* – a softening of relations with East Germany – and to prevent the Social Democratic party, the SPD, from drifting to the left because it was never allowed to hold office.

A slight fall in the rate of economic growth in 1966 and early 1967 led the FDP, the small Liberal party, to switch its support from the CDU to the SPD. Erhard resigned and a new coalition was formed which brought the SPD into a Federal Republic government for the first time; indeed it had not held office since the Weimar Republic, though it had governed several *Länder*, notably Hamburg and Berlin.

The interim Chancellor was Kurt Kiesinger, a member of the CDU, who had been Minister President of Baden-Württemberg. Kiesinger continued Erhard's policies, which included an agreement with de Gaulle once more to accept the French veto to Britain's second application to join the Common Market, and an attempt to develop relationships with the East. But this latter policy was brought to an end by the Soviet invasion of Czechoslovakia in October 1968. The year 1968, as in other Western nations, was marked by violent student revolts, organised by Marxists, who were determined to regard the Federal Government as the product of the 'generation of Auschwitz'. Violent revolts and demonstrations against the Vietnam War, the atom bomb and the West German constitution were held all over Germany, and the universities were in uproar. In the 1969 elections the CDU lost a few seats, while the SPD gained substantially. Willy Brandt, the Mayor of Berlin and head of the SPD, offered the FDP a coalition, which was formed on 27 September 1969 with Brandt as the new Chancellor. Brandt was the first German politician to become leader or Chancellor who had spent the war in exile from Nazi Germany, and indeed fought against it; he formed a major coalition with the FDP, which carried on in every respect the tradition of the great CDU coalitions.

Brandt fought the election in 1972 on the strength of *Ostpolitik*, which had been begun by Gerhard Schroeder, the CDU Foreign Minister, and entailed the abandonment of the doctrine that the German Federal Republic was the only legitimate spokesman for

Germany, and the recognition of East Germany as a possible negotiating partner. Between 1970 and 1972 Brandt renounced all claims to the German territories which had been lost to the Soviet Union and Poland, and at the same time recognised the GDR in the basic treaty of November 1972. On the basis of this achievement of some form of détente in foreign policy and the continuation by the SPD of the social market economy policies, Brandt won the 1972 election, although Franz Josef Strauss, leader of the CSU – the Bavarian ally of CDU – and former Minister of Defence, who was bitterly opposed to the *Ostpolitik*, made significant gains in Bavaria. But the CDU lost seats in North Germany. This emphasised the extent to which the conservative policies of Strauss were attractive to the Bavarians. In the North the way in which the SPD had captured the traditional Catholic working-class vote both in urban and rural areas showed that a conservative policy there would not have been so successful.

Germany faced the OPEC crisis comparatively well. The German national income was stationary in 1974 and fell by 3 per cent in 1975, but rose by 5½ per cent in 1976. Willy Brandt, however, had resigned in May 1974, when it was found that one of his close assistants, Günter Guillaume, had been an East German spy. He was succeeded by Helmut Schmidt; his former FDP colleague, Walter Scheel, was elected President; and Genscher of the FDP became Foreign Minister. The Schmidt–Genscher government pushed through the new co-determination law, which gave workers a share in the control of enterprises, and developed several other progressive reforms.

West Germany, a prosperous, stable and powerful country, allied to all the countries of the West, was divided by a wall from the rest of Germany. Yet in some respects its self-confidence seemed to have been sapped. Nothing was more obvious than the disparity between a prosperous and liberal West Germany and the oppressive dictatorship of East Germany, nonetheless there seemed to be a profound uneasiness of spirit abroad in the German Federal Republic.

It was in Greece that a real 'Fascist' coup took place and led to an orchestrated left-wing outcry, suggesting that the coup might be the harbinger of many others.

Greece emerged from a pre-war dictatorship, a severe occupation by the Nazis and a savage civil war, during which nearly one hundred thousand Greeks died and seven hundred thousand became refugees, to become an ordinary, modest, prosperous, constitutional democracy. Then it suddenly became a dictatorship.

Though economic recovery was swift, political instability was endemic. The monarchy maintained parliamentary institutions but the regime was perpetually unstable, mainly because of proportional representation which led to the frequent collapse of coalitions. The Americans put great pressure on the Greek government, by reducing aid and seeking to end the political instability by changing the proportional representation system to one of a simple majority. The cries against foreign interference were loud; but the system was altered and in November 1952 elections were held and Field Marshal Papagos won five sixths of the seats in Parliament and just under half the popular vote. This victory led to eleven years of steady administration during which the economy was completely reconstructed following the German free social market system, beginning with devaluation and stabilisation of the currency and the ending of inflation. A major economic boom took place; democracy and prosperity were linked.

Greece joined NATO and its relationship with Yugoslavia dramatically improved as a result of Tito's changes in policies. A defence treaty was also signed between Greece, Turkey and Yugoslavia. In foreign affairs the major difficulty was the demand of the Greek Cypriots, led by Makarios, Archbishop of Cyprus from March 1950, to join Greece. He was supported by Colonel George Grivas, who organised armed resistance, through his EOKA guerrillas, against the British presence in Cyprus. (Cyprus was at that time a British colony and an apparently essential NATO base.) This led to violent reaction by the Turks on the island, as well as riots in Istanbul against the Greeks who still lived in Turkey. Papagos had to appear strongly to support *enosis* (union with Greece) whilst seeking at the same time to discourage the creation of underground armies. This entailed Greek hostility to the British policy in Cyprus, which in turn threatened the stability of NATO.

Papagos died in October 1955 and King Paul and the Greek right and centre parties asked Konstantine Karamanlis to form a government. He was a most admirable Prime Minister, efficient and tough, who continued to win the next two elections. Meanwhile in March 1956 Makarios was deported to the Seychelles. The level of violence in Cyprus considerably increased, and in April 1957 his deportation was ended and he returned to live in Athens. The British attempted to repress the violence by appointing Field Marshal (later Lord) Harding as Governor, but his attempt at more severe repression led to further violence, so he was replaced by Sir Hugh Foot, later Lord Caradon, a Liberal, who sought to end the difficulties in Cyprus by retreating from them.

In February 1959 Karamanlis met the Turkish Prime Minister in Zurich to negotiate an independent Cyprus, and in August 1960 Cyprus became an independent Republic in the Commonwealth, with Archbishop Makarios as President, and the Turkish leader, Dr Kutchuk, as Vice-President, while Britain maintained some military bases on the island. Negotiations had succeeded in achieving what the illegal armies had not.

Between 1951 and 1956 per capita national income in Greece increased by two and a half times, and it doubled again by 1964. This was strongly helped by the restoration of agriculture, the development of industry, the enormous growth of tourism and by the large numbers of Greeks who worked overseas.

Throughout this period the left argued that Karamanlis was unpopular and undemocratic, despite his electoral victories, and that he was the tool of King Paul and of King Paul's authoritarian German wife, Queen Frederika. The left alleged intimidation and corruption by the militia and police in the rural areas in the 1961 elections. This agitation coupled with the extreme right wing's disillusion with the Cyprus policies of Karamanlis, fostered the view that the government which had survived the civil war in essence was no longer adequate to Greek needs. Prosperity led not to moderation but to extremism.

In 1963 Karamanlis resigned and moved to Paris, to be succeeded, after some interim governments, by Papandreou, leading a left-wing coalition, which won a substantial majority in 1964.

Violence broke out in Cyprus between the Greeks and the Turks. First the British intervened, followed by a United Nations peace-keeping force, which separated the two sides. Makarios became increasingly disillusioned with his Greek allies. Meanwhile Papandreou, helped by his son, Andreas Papandreou, sought to introduce a series of progressive reforms, including raising the school leaving age, cutting civil service salaries and introducing some elements of a welfare state. He also released almost all those who were still imprisoned as a result of the civil war. There was also the apparent discovery in that year of a plot to overthrow the government by a left-wing conspiracy, though the person who revealed it, Colonel George Papadopoulos, was in fact himself a conspirator for the right wing.

In March 1964 King Paul died and was succeeded by his son, Constantine, who was twenty-five, and whose sister was married to the future King of Spain. Constantine manoeuvred Papandreou to resign, and a massive political crisis broke out, followed by an election which Papandreou marginally lost. As Papandreou became increasingly radicalised through his son's influence, and

Andreas Papandreou was continually suspected of left-wing radical plotting, he was at one stage arrested. This led to further troubles, and it was revealed that the King was making plans for the leaders of the army to intervene if disorder broke out as a result of the election.

Before the election, however, on 21 April 1967, a group of colonels, acting in ignorance of the plotting between the King and the generals, organised a coup and formed a civilian government under Constantine Kollias, putting an end to the parliamentary regime. The real leader was Colonel George Papadopoulos, supported by Colonel Makarezos and Brigadier Pattakos. This ushered in an intensely reactionary regime which sought to organise Greece on quasi-authoritarian lines under martial law.

The King declined to support them at first, but subsequently found that he was obliged to accept their wishes. Eight months later he organised a counter-coup, which failed, and he was forced to flee into exile. General Zoitakis now became Regent with Papadopoulos as Prime Minister, eventually assuming most offices as Minister of Foreign Affairs, Minister of Defence, Minister of Education, Minister of Government Policy and then, in 1972, Regent.

The Colonels immediately persecuted all known radicals and organised the state on authoritarian lines, using the security and military police to enforce long terms of imprisonment and torture throughout Greece, while prominent Greek liberals were exiled or fled. A tremendous body of protest built up against the behaviour of the Colonels, who were denounced by the European Commission of Human Rights; Greece also withdrew from the Council of Europe, before being expelled, though it remained in NATO; nor was its Treaty of Association with the EEC abrogated.

It was alleged that the Colonels' coup had been organised by the CIA to prevent the arrival of Andreas Papandreou as a major figure on the international stage; they feared he might well have led Greece into a neutral anti-NATO stance. From the United States point of view Greece was an important staging post to Israel, on which most of its Middle Eastern policy was at that time based, and therefore the American government was careful not only not to offend Greece but to support it. President Nixon declared that no military aid could be cut off from Greece, which in turn offered permanent port facilities for the US Sixth Fleet.

The Colonels actively encouraged Greek unification with Cyprus. The Greek Cypriots refused to agree to this, and communal talks continued for a long time after the Greeks had withdrawn. In Greece itself high inflation helped to fuel continual unrest. A student sit-in at the law faculty of Athens University in March 1973 led to further disturbances, followed by a naval mutiny in May. Later in the year a student revolt in Athens Polytechnic and in the universities of Salonika and Patras led to the use of troops and tanks by the authorities. At the Polytechnic alone thirty-four students were killed, several hundred wounded, and arrests were widespread.

On 25 November 1973 the army, supported by the navy and the air force, overthrew Papadopoulos and a new 'civilian' government was installed, dominated by Brigadier Dimitrios Ioannidis, who was the commander of the military police. The regime's economic policies, however, went from bad to worse, particularly with the oil crisis which followed the Yom Kippur War. Some oil was discovered off the island of Thasos, which led to a dispute between Turkey and Greece about rights in the Aegean. Meanwhile relationships with Makarios in Cyprus deteriorated, and in a coup Makarios escaped from Cyprus, leaving Nikos Sampson as President. A Turkish landing in the Kyrenia region of northern Cyprus led to a threat of war between the two countries; though this was averted the division of Cyprus led to great political strain.

On 23 July 1974, with the position deteriorating, Karamanlis returned from exile, and the Colonels' regime was overthrown, to universal joy. This led to the restoration of democracy and, incidentally, to the formal end of the monarchy, just as Constantine's brother-in-law Juan Carlos was enthroned in Spain. The accepted version of the Colonels' seven years of rule was that European reaction, backed by the CIA, had conspired against democracy. This was false. The Colonels' coup was an integral part of modern Greek history, which had been marked by civil war and coups d'état. The surprise lay not in the coup, but in the restoration of constitutional democracy.

The nations of Europe thus escaped authoritarian rule – or 'Fascism' – with governments that mainly ruled in a liberal and constitutional way. How far this political success was due to the prosperity of Western Europe which endured for so long it is hard to say, but the coincidence of the two was notable. The liberal market economic system – what the Germans called the social market economy – was certainly responsible for the economic prosperity, and it could only fully function in a non-authoritarian political system, though it should be noted that high rates of economic growth were also achieved in Spain and Yugoslavia which were one-party states. Nevertheless the engine room of the prosperity was West Germany, Northern France and Northern Italy, with the rest of the Continent (as it were) geared to that high level of activity.

The prosperity coincided with liberal democratic regimes, and also with the European Economic Community. This organisation provided the framework in which France and Germany collaborated politically and to some degree economically, but it would be an error to suppose that it caused the prosperity. The lowering of tariff barriers throughout the world greatly increased trade, and the virtual elimination of barriers to trade within Continental Europe made a powerful contribution. That the EEC did not have the secret of success, however, was shown by the United Kingdom's experiences when it joined the Common Market in 1973 and immediately became labelled the 'Sick Man of Europe', a dramatic change from its image in the previous decade as 'Swinging London'. The British economy continued to deteriorate, the number of unemployed rose and by October 1976 the pound sterling was worth only $1.57 compared with $2.80 ten years before. Whatever else the EEC offered Britain, it was not an immediate cure for economic ills. Nor indeed is there any reason to suppose that France, Germany and Italy would not have prospered in the 1950s and 1960s without the EEC.

By the end of the 1970s Europe was once more rich and powerful, and while the United States was in the doldrums politically, because of Vietnam, Europe had shed itself of empire, and to a great degree was conducting a selfish foreign policy, independent of the United States, typified by Germany's *Ostpolitik*. The fear of Soviet aggression had almost vanished, despite the occupation of Czechoslovakia in 1968, and Europe rested under the American nuclear umbrella, increasingly critical of American policies, and sanguine about the future.

Chapter 30

The United Kingdom

Britain ended the war in apparent triumph; the only free and victorious power in Europe, it had an unequalled position. Moreover it was able to transform its vast empire into a Commonwealth of independent states with remarkable ease. But as other nations settled down to spectacular bursts of prosperity, Britain lagged far behind. As Dean Acheson said, Britain had lost an empire and not found a role.

The Labour government under Attlee initiated the welfare state and encouraged socially democratic policies but these did not create economic prosperity. Wartime controls were clung on to for far too long and in addition, the United Kingdom had continual problems with its balance of payments. Diagnoses and cures were offered in profusion: the pound was overvalued; Britain needed to export (its 'export drive' was successful, but as the 1950s proceeded, less so than other countries'); its reserve currency status handicapped it (yet the Bretton Woods agreement clearly envisaged an international reserve currency); all these explanations failed to account for Britain's relatively lacklustre economic performance.

At first the coronation of the new Queen in June 1953 seemed to symbolise the beginning of a new and more prosperous period compounded of Elizabethan nostalgia and hope. But the presence of the ageing Churchill as Prime Minister seemed to continue to foster the illusion of great power status. The Conservative government encouraged every link with the United States, encouraged the Commonwealth and encouraged European unity but all the time Britain stood on the sidelines. The Geneva conference, which temporarily solved the Indochina problem and allowed the French to quit was perhaps Britain's, and Anthony Eden's, most important achievement at this time; that and the London Agreement which created the Western European Union.

But then disillusion and disaster soon struck under the leadership of Anthony Eden. He had been Churchill's heir apparent for many, many years and at first seemed controlled, capable and in command. But in 1956 the economy seemed to turn sour, and in retrospect this was the moment when Britain began demonstrably to fall behind its competitors. Problems arose which clearly Eden was neither interested in nor competent to deal with; moreover, he was almost entirely preoccupied with the Middle Eastern situation. He became paranoid about Nasser, arguing that here was a dictator no different in kind and as great a threat as Hitler. It was not just because he had attacked British oil interest, but Eden had formed the view that opposition to a dictator in the early stages was essential if there was to be sufficient opposition to the dictator later on. The secret agreement which he reached with the French and the Israelis but not with the Americans flew in the face of all experience in the Churchill administration that a close alliance with the United States was necessary and inevitable. Eden's tantrums and the neglect of his duties, his increasingly authoritarian, indeed impetuous approach, were furthered by the continuous stress and strain involved in facing an opposition outraged by Suez in the House of Commons, led by Hugh Gaitskell.

Harold Macmillan, the Chancellor of the Exchequer, was following the expansionary policies which he had advocated in the inter-war period. He supported the Suez campaign, until serious losses on the balance of payments caused a world flight from the pound, when he rapidly reversed his position and became the architect of the Cabinet's decision to withdraw from Suez. This crisis, which accompanied or led to Eden's breakdown in health, precipitated Eden's resignation. Macmillan thereupon became Leader of the Conservative party and Prime Minister in January 1957, a role many expected would go to R. A. Butler, who had been the principal architect of the government's domestic policy.

Hugh Gaitskell had now succeeded Attlee as Leader of the Labour party, which marked the culmination of two trends: the alienation of the left wing, a recurrent theme of Labour party history, from the time of the Popular Front in the late 1930s to the attack on Bevin's policy in the Cold War and his handling of the Palestine issue; and it also gave a coherent intellectual leadership to what had been called the Social Democrat wing of the Labour party. Gaitskell defined his theme as equality in a mixed economy.

As Attlee's successor, Gaitskell was a bitter opponent of the left and of Communism; his Winchester and Oxford education and his middle-class origins were, to a considerable degree, resented by the more radical members of the Labour party. He took a strong stand against the Conservative government over the Suez affair, which earned him the distrust of the political and the civil service establishments, while at the same time the rise in the popularity of the nuclear disarmament movement among radical left-wingers forced him into bitter opposition to the unilateral disarmament of Britain. The arguments about Suez and about nuclear disarmament gave him, however, a reputation, almost wholly deserved, for principle and integrity, and his transparently open personality and sincerity made him an eloquent advocate of the Social Democratic position in European affairs. He was an English Adlai Stevenson.

After Labour's savage electoral defeat in 1959 – its third in nine years – Gaitskell concluded that the party's problem was its vestigial commitment to a version of a Socialist society which was wholly incompatible with the realities of the mixed economy, and he therefore sought to amend the Labour party constitution. This caused bitter divisions within the Labour party and, in particular, the hostility of the working-class and left-wing leader, Aneurin Bevan, who had earned a reputation as a superb administrator while being responsible for introducing the National Health Service.

Following Gaitskell's defeat, however, on this issue of fundamentalist doctrine, an issue which he had raised partly because the Social Democratic party in Germany had succeeded in radically changing its constitution to make itself a moderate reformist party rather than a fundamental Socialist one, Gaitskell and Bevan were reconciled. It seemed as though Gaitskell might become Prime Minister in a government which would radically restructure the British economy and lead Europe forward into a moderate Social Democratic system. He was, however, opposed to the Common Market, which in turn separated him from some of his own leading supporters such as Roy Jenkins, who resigned from his Shadow Cabinet on this issue. In January 1963, however, Gaitskell died. The sense of loss was profound, and in its suddenness shattered the Social Democratic wing of the Labour party, which was left leaderless and rudderless. His death was regarded, indeed, as one of the most significant political events in mid-twentieth-century British history. Yet, paradoxically, Gaitskell's opponent, Macmillan, stole most of his clothes while Gaitskell was bathing in the shallow pools of Socialist dogma. Though he never embraced the doctrine of equality, Macmillan embraced affluence, which would eventually lead to greater equality.

Equality was a theme to be developed, not only in Britain, for it was a criticism of the 'affluent society' that it apparently left the poor behind. Though the process of economic growth had advantages in consumption for many people, it had dual disadvantages – affluence seemed to damage the environment, and there was a relative (and occasionally absolute) decline in standards of public service compared with private living standards. Thus Democratic Socialism was an attack on the consumer society which was the product of the great economic boom. In the election of 1959 Harold Macmillan was misquoted as saying to the British, 'You've never had it so good', yet it was true and was to become even more true, but it was used as an attack on him. In fact, Britain steadily slipped behind other nations in its economic achievements. Balance of payments difficulties loomed large and, from 1959 onwards, inflation became a serious problem.

Harold Macmillan dominated the Conservative party for eight years, becoming a major political figure. In his early years he had been a supporter of the new Keynesian prescriptions for the revival of the economy and in his book *The Middle Way*, he sought to reconcile state intervention with belief in freedom. He had been a tremendously successful Minister of Housing and he now set about pursuing prosperity with zealous enthusiasm. At first he was strikingly successful. Thereupon, he found that his belief in the affluent society began to play him false. Inflation grew, possibly through the generous monetary policy which he adopted and over which his Chancellor, Peter Thorneycroft, resigned. Thus in 1961 Macmillan had to impose the first of the wages policies which successive governments followed for the next twenty years, the so-called wages pause. He then devoted himself to achieving some form of détente with the Soviet Union and with establishing a close relationship with President Kennedy.

Britain's loss of prestige and self-confidence stemmed, in part, from foreign affairs. The rapid disengagement from empire was generally welcomed. But the Suez engagement of 1956 was a fiasco and a diplomatic blunder of the first magnitude. The decision not to join the newly-established European Economic Community in 1957 was seen five years later to be a mistake. But Britain's application to join was vetoed by Macmillan's old comrade, President de Gaulle. Nothing so clearly indicated Britain's loss of international prestige as this veto by a Frenchman who had been honourably received as a refugee only twenty years before.

The political changes in the Conservative governments of what came to be called by Harold Wilson 'the thirteen wasted years' are of no great significance in themselves. What happened was a growth of affluence coupled with a sense of political decline. When Macmillan retired from the Prime Ministership in 1963, he left a deeply divided Conservative party with the obvious candidates for the Prime Ministership – R. A. Butler, Quintin Hogg and Reginald Maudling – passed over in favour of a Tory peer from the Scottish lowlands, Lord Home. The Labour party, too, having suffered a tremendous blow in the death of Gaitskell, replaced him by the arch-pragmatist – though then thought to be very left-wing – Harold Wilson. The choice of Home caused major difficulties in the Conservative party, since the alternative leader, R. A. Butler, was once more rejected, and the bitterness was acute.

All four Conservative governments during this period encouraged a continuation of the basic themes of the Attlee government. Only iron and steel were denationalised; the welfare state was maintained and expanded; economic development continued, albeit at a lower rate than in many other countries, but higher hitherto than for many years in Britain; and the disengagement from Empire continued, although with occasional hesitations.

Of Britain's four Conservative Prime Ministers between 1951 and 1964 three – Churchill, Eden and Home – were almost exclusively interested in foreign affairs. But after R. A. Butler's successful budgets, building on the restoration by Attlee, economic policy lost its way. There was no sustained programme for the modernisation of British industry. What few plans there were seemed constantly to be reversed by elections. The adversarial style of British parliamentary democracy, without proportional representation, led both parties to kowtow to their extremists so that the Labour party was constantly asserting its Socialist credentials.

Harold Wilson was elected as a left-wing leader of the Labour party. He had opposed Gaitskell over nuclear disarmament and over the debate on the future of the Labour party's fundamentalist philosophy which made him distrusted by a substantial element of the party, indeed, he was regarded by some as a crypto-Communist. The whole of Wilson's rise to power was dominated by issues of Socialist dogma, whilst the Germans and the French Socialists during these years were united with the Christian Democrats in creating powerful and affluent economies in their countries. In Britain the Labour party barely approached this question, and its paymaster, the trade union movement, was almost defiantly obscurantist and troglodyte.

Paradoxically, Wilson swiftly revealed himself as a master political tactician. During his Prime Ministership he established a reputation for brilliant political compromises which was unsurpassed. He substantially and immediately betrayed the left-wing causes which had been largely responsible for his election, without, at the same time, gathering the support of the Social Democratic wing of the Labour party around a programme which had political and moral attractions.

The election held in October 1964 gave the Labour party a majority of only three. The government was soon overwhelmed by a series of economic difficulties – a balance of payments crisis, mounting inflation and stagnant output. The government was run with a degree of secrecy, intrigue and incompetence that was disguised by continual activity.

Wilson's pragmatism and expediency earned him a reputation as a political trimmer which substantially diminished the attraction of moderate Social Democracy as an alternative either to Marxism for the extreme left wing or to the social market economy which was being developed by the Germans and French. In this sense, therefore, Wilson was responsible for a substantial degree of disillusion with Social Democracy. But he was amazingly successful electorally, since his personality appealed to wide sections of the working class, and his political pragmatism was such that he managed to engender the support of disparate groups. At the same time, he balanced his Cabinet in such a way that no faction in the Labour party ever established dominance. It became clear immediately, too, that his own reputation for left-wing opinions was false and that he was, in fact, a conventional pragmatic British politician. The government that he formed was balanced between the two economic ministers, James Callaghan at the Treasury, and George Brown at the newly-created Ministry of Economic Affairs. The Treasury was to be analogous to a Ministry of Finance, while the Department of Economic Affairs was to concern itself with the long-term economic reconstruction of the United Kingdom. In the event, the plan proved unworkable, the traditional British government machine could not be reconstructed so drastically, and, anyway, the Treasury's dominance soon made itself felt. Wilson was not helped by the personality clashes between Callaghan and Brown. The government's refusal to devalue sterling immediately it came into office meant that its entire term was dominated in shoring up the pound at $2.80, which strained its capacity for dealing with internal questions.

In the spring of 1966, in a fresh general election, the Wilson government was returned once more but with a substantial majority. Its economic problems mounted, however. An incomes and prices freeze was imposed, followed by the adoption of a permanent policy supervised by the Prices and Incomes Board. In the summer, in an attempt to save the pound, a severe budget was introduced with taxation increases, public expenditure reductions, and substantial rises in interest rates. Nevertheless, in late 1967 the pound was devalued from $2.80 to $2.40. Callaghan resigned as Chancellor of the Exchequer and was replaced by Roy Jenkins, who greatly intensified the fiscal and monetary measures adopted by the government, so that by 1970 the balance of payments was in surplus and inflation was under control.

But of the long-term reconstruction of the economy, much talked about, little was seen. Iron and steel were nationalised once more and a number of state bodies were established to reorganise industry, but the level of investment remained obstinately low, and the level of productivity increase correspondingly low too.

Wilson's Foreign Secretaries aligned the country closely with the United States. The main objective of the Conservative government, to join the European Economic Community and to share in Continental European prosperity, was adopted by the Labour government and in 1967, after renewed negotiations, the British application for membership was once more vetoed by de Gaulle. This therefore left the central foreign policy of the government seriously in question. Two further matters arose to distract it: the unilateral declaration of independence by Rhodesia in 1965, which resulted in the imposition of sanctions by the United Nations, and the preoccupation with the special relationship with the United States, which led the government to support Lyndon Johnson's Vietnam policy, but not to send British troops. While Rhodesia as a part of the decolonisation of Africa was badly handled, and occupied a great deal of the government's energies, Labour's support for the United States in Vietnam outraged the radical left wing of the party, and caused much the same damaging divisions as had occurred twenty years earlier when the Cold War had begun in Bevin and Truman's time.

Domestically, the Wilson government was noted chiefly for reforms, hence the 'Swinging Sixties' developed into the 'permissive society'. Relaxation of the laws against homosexuality and abortion, the abolition of the death penalty, the easing of the criminal law, all took place against a background of radical change in social behaviour, particularly amongst the young. These sets of measures illustrated the rise of 'permissiveness' throughout the Western world, and Britain, as the centre of the popular music industry, with the enormous popularity of the Beatles and of youth fashions in London's Carnaby Street, was a centre of this trend. It was obviously a different ethos entirely from the strong puritan morality which had informed wartime and immediate post-war Britain.

The hangover of empire and a feeling of guilt about the Third World informed the atmosphere in which legislation to reduce the inflow of coloured immigrants was introduced. The immigrants, mainly from the Caribbean and the Indian sub-continent, had been a feature of the economic boom under the Conservatives. They had British passports, and the reduction in the costs, and greater ease of travel, together with acute labour shortages in Britain, led to an influx of well over a million, perhaps two million, coloured immigrants, mainly to menial jobs. Inevitably considerable social unrest followed as first the Conservative and then the Labour government imposed increasingly severe limitations on immi-

gration, against a chorus of well-meaning liberal opposition, drawing analogies with the racial situation in the United States.

Ireland provided a further hangover of imperialism which sent
the British through spasms of guilt. The end of the Labour government's period of office saw the outbreak of a rebellion in Northern
Ireland, organised by the Irish Republican Army in 1968, under
the cover of a claim for 'civil rights' for the Roman Catholic
population. The IRA had links with other terrorist organisations
and began a campaign of bombing and shooting which obliged the
government to call in troops. The charge of colonialism, freely
made, was wholly false. The prevalent view of the immensely
complex history of Ireland is derived from the Irish nationalists.

The gaining of independence by Eire in 1921 was the first
successful example of a rising by a Nationalist minority against one
of the major European powers, and formed a model for the people
of India, and also for such diverse groups as the Hungarians in the
Austro–Hungarian Empire and, eventually, for the Arabs
throughout the Middle East. Thus the apparent success of the Irish
Nationalists in defeating the British on their own doorstep was a
model which was much admired and followed. It was also important, because in the period when nationalism became overwhelmingly fashionable, during and after the Second World War, the
story of Ireland was enveloped in a more general theory of the
oppression of racial minorities by the imperialist powers.

In the late 1960s the rhetoric of the American Civil Rights
movement and the anti-imperialist arguments sweeping Europe,
partly as a consequence of the Vietnam War and the successful
prosecution of the Algerian War against the French, coalesced in a
revival of the Irish Republican Army in Northern Ireland. This
group was, in turn, split between the official IRA, which adopted a
Marxist programme but was in essence non-violent, and a more
atavistic Nationalist group, Fascist in orientation, which became
known as the Provisional IRA, rather like the division between the
Mensheviks and the Bolsheviks in Russia sixty years before.

The Provisional IRA first manifested its militancy through an
apparently innocuous group of students who demanded civil rights
for Catholics. Its claim was in itself tendentious, since the Catholics
had exactly equal civil rights to the Protestants in Northern Ireland, with votes for the Parliament of the United Kingdom, and for
the Parliament of Northern Ireland, known as Stormont. Nor was
there any evidence of discrimination in the United Kingdom
services such as the social services or access to the courts. It was
believed, however, that the Catholics were discriminated against,
to some extent, by Protestant employers and also in municipal

housing by the predominantly Protestant local authorities in Northern Ireland. It was also alleged that local government elections were jerrymandered. Most of these allegations were false, since they rested upon an incorrect correlation of Protestantism and Catholicism being the difference between the well-to-do and the poor. Many of the differences were in fact perfectly explicable in normal sociological terms between urban and rural dwellers. Nevertheless, undoubtedly some small discrimination did exist.

The Northern Ireland government, led by Captain Terence O'Neill, instituted a programme of reforms which were supported by the Labour government of the United Kingdom. O'Neill argued that 'In every aspect of our life justice must not only be done, but be seen to be done to all sections of the community.' Meanwhile Catholic and Protestant feeling grew stronger, and the Civil Rights movement was penetrated by the Provisional IRA. O'Neill lost political support because of his package of reforms, was replaced by Major James Chichester-Clark, who presided over a government which saw severe riots in 1969 in Londonderry, followed by riots in the Falls Road and the Ardoyne in the Roman Catholic districts of Belfast. In August 1969 British troops were called in to protect the Roman Catholics from Protestant violence. In initially searching Protestant houses for arms, the army caused bitter resentment. The local police were forbidden to carry arms and were put under United Kingdom rather than Northern Irish control. The Provisional IRA was strongly helped with support from the South. Charles Haughey was subsequently acquitted of smuggling arms into the Republic, but was never charged with smuggling arms into Northern Ireland. Mr Haughey was then the Republic's Minister for Finance. The riots and shooting worsened in 1970, and gradually the United Kingdom troops in the North of Ireland were viewed by the Catholic population less as their defenders against Protestant attacks, but more as defenders of the existing regime against Catholic attacks. This shift, in which there was no truth, became an important element in anti-British propaganda. By 1971 a full-scale civil war was raging in the North.

When Labour fell, in May 1970, therefore, in the opinion of many of its more articulate supporters it had 'betrayed' Socialism; it had compounded Britain's economic failure; it had racial unrest at home and a 'colonial' civil war raging in Ireland.

The new Conservative Prime Minister was Edward Heath, a former chief whip of drive and ability. Heath was a somewhat rigid and distant man, an amateur musician of some stature, a yachtsman with a compulsion to win, clearly driven by inner forces that marked perhaps a bitter, certainly a tortuous character. He now

successfully negotiated the British accession to the Treaty of
Rome, railroading all opposition so that Britain at long last joined
the European Economic Community on 1 January 1973. This gave
a common external tariff, tariffs for the first time on foodstuffs, and
relatively free trade within the nine EEC countries. The Common
Market was to be a panacea. A European federation would restore
morale. But the immediate impact was a rapid rise in food prices
and in indirect taxation.

The Conservatives now set about tackling the problems of
Northern Ireland by abolishing their Parliament at Stormont and
putting the whole province under direct rule by the central government of the United Kingdom. An attempt was made to agree with
the Republic of Ireland at a conference at Sunningdale on a
settlement of the Northern Irish issue by establishing a power-
sharing executive in the North, representative both of the Protestants and the Roman Catholics, and acknowledging the existence
of the so-called Irish dimension. The Protestant working class
refused to accept these agreements in election after election, and
eventually a general strike brought the power-sharing executive to
an end. The civil war continued.

The Heath government adopted policies of rapid economic
growth, by unbalancing the budget, orthodox Keynesian remedies.
This led, inevitably, to an adverse balance of payments and
the beginning of a rapid inflation. In 1972, having decided in 1970
to adopt a laissez-faire attitude over incomes and prices, the
government about-turned and adopted a statutory incomes and
prices policy. The occasion was a damaging miners' strike, which
led to a severe energy shortage. This was followed by the Yom
Kippur War in 1973 which led to oil scarcity and price rises in the
winter of 1973–4.

Behind the economic difficulties of the Heath government lay a
substantial history of damaging strikes and industrial unrest, with
which Wilson had attempted to deal by appealing to trade union
loyalty to the Labour party; by attempting to bribe the leaders with
jobs and the members with social security benefits; and, eventually, in 1969, by legislation, prepared as a White Paper called 'In
Place of Strife' by Barbara Castle, the Secretary of State for
Employment, and defeated by James Callaghan. Heath's government decided to adopt a mild form of the United States legislation
(the Taft-Hartley Act), in the Industrial Relations Act, 1971. This
led to massive protests, organised by the extreme left, which
soured the relations between the government and the unions to
such a degree that the massive disruptions of the winter of 1973–4
seemed inescapable.

The government which Heath led was composed of men and women of talent and ability, but in almost every respect, domestically and abroad, it was unsuccessful. The Industrial Relations Act led to a series of sustained strikes and demonstrations against the government which brought about its downfall in the confrontation with the miners in February 1974. The Conservatives also reorganised local government, introduced decimal currency and railroaded through Parliament membership of the European Economic Community, all of which proved exceptionally unpopular. Consequently when Heath went to the country at the end of February 1974, he was narrowly defeated by the Labour party, still headed by Harold Wilson. Once more the British system of extremes in electoral politics, and its irresponsible trade union movement, had brought the nation to its knees.

When Wilson took office after the February election he removed the wages and price controls imposed by Heath, and inflation immediately mounted to over 20 per cent, while at the same time he attempted a 'renegotiation' of the Treaty of Accession to the European Economic Community. The terms of the renegotiation were eventually approved in a referendum in the summer of 1975.

A further election in October gave Labour more seats, but still no substantial majority in the House of Commons. Wilson had now won four elections out of five, a feat unprecedented in British history. On his resignation, still unexplained, in March 1976, on his sixtieth birthday, he had been Prime Minister for longer than any other in the twentieth century. Opposing him now was Margaret Thatcher who had succeeded Heath as leader of the Conservatives in February 1975.

Britain had come a long way since the victory of 1945, mostly downhill. Its empire had gone. Its place in Europe, which had been powerful, was now peripheral. It was poorer than Germany and France. It was no longer one of the world's three major powers. On the other hand, its political and social stability had survived the great strain of the post-war readjustment and though less prosperous than its Continental neighbours, it was astonishingly more prosperous than ever before. But it had lost, relatively, to its former enemies, and it had lost its nerve, though its armed forces had been strengthened and tested.

Perhaps its true weakness lay in foreign policy, in its indecision as to its role (beyond decolonisation) in world affairs. Britain had played a major role in creating the Atlantic alliance in the late 1940s. There was no nation prepared, twenty and thirty years later, to continue to play that part.

Chapter 31

America in the doghouse: Nixon and Watergate

The position of the United States in the mid 1970s was central to the collapse of Western morale and ideology. Internationally the United States had organised opposition to what was seen as Soviet aggression and expansionism; domestically America had prospered, and as it generated half the non-Soviet world's national product, its prosperity spread. But the involvement in Vietnam, which brought down Johnson, also shattered the Democratic party and became the issue which dominated Nixon's Presidency. More fundamental, possibly, was the retreat of America from a positive, crusading spirit of free enterprise and free institutions, to a morally defensive attitude to Communism, with which strategically it was necessary to co-exist, and towards the nationalism of the Third World, where liberal institutions were rare.

Nixon was potentially a strong President with substantial electoral support. Yet he was a failure. Truman had said that he felt the sun, the moon and the stars had fallen on him when Roosevelt died and he became President. That, it seemed, was exactly what had happened to Richard Nixon. His long-sought Presidency ended in personal failure – the only President to resign in 200 years – and his bold attempt to restore American foreign policy came to naught.

Nixon was a tortured, withdrawn man, driven by ambition, with a few very close friends of no great intellectual pretensions. In some way his personality was projected to middle America through the media, while at the same time his gift for upsetting the intellectuals was dramatic.

Richard Nixon was born of a Quaker family in California in 1913, and after serving in the war was first elected to Congress in 1946. Dominated by his mother, and poorly educated, he was a classic loner. He first leapt to prominence in his pursuit, with Senator Joseph McCarthy, of the Communists who had penetrated the United States government. It was here he first earned the undying enmity of United States liberals, even though his attacks on Alger Hiss were, in the light of subsequent trials, justified. After his success in the House, he became a United States Senator for California, and in 1952 President Eisenhower chose him as his Vice-Presidential nominee. The campaign was marked by allegations from the Democratic press that Nixon had accepted substantial bribes which, though never proved, gave him the reputation of not only being a ruthless and dirty political fighter, but also of someone who totally lacked conviction and was corrupt as well. He appeared on television with his dog, Checkers, allegedly a gift to his daughters, protesting his innocence in a performance of nauseating sentimentality; thereafter no person of aesthetic sensibility could bear him.

His eight years as Vice-President, with Eisenhower's warm support, were successful; he gained much experience in international affairs and became a leading figure in the Republican party who adopted him as Presidential candidate in 1960. Defeated by John F. Kennedy by a narrow margin, he also subsequently lost the 1962 Senatorial election in California. He used the years following his defeats to tour the country while practising as a Wall Street lawyer, and built up support in Republican groups. In consequence, after the dramatic defeat of Senator Goldwater, the Republican nominee in 1964, by Lyndon B. Johnson, Nixon became the obvious candidate for the 1968 Republican nomination, an election which the Republicans were almost certain to win, following Johnson's extreme unpopularity and the association of Vice-President Humphrey, the Democratic candidate, with his Vietnam policies. America was clearly swinging to the right domestically. Nor was it true to say that America wanted peace at any price. The radicals were convinced that the Vietcong had right on their side, but the majority of Americans still wanted to win the war. In the primary election, it was clear that in the Republican party the right-wing view was uppermost. Nixon defeated Nelson Rockefeller, the liberal Governor of New York, as the Republican nominee. The Democratic party candidate was Vice-President Hubert Humphrey, who had the double disadvantage of having to defend President Johnson's record in Vietnam while also seeking to dissociate himself from it. The subsequent campaign was fought with great bitterness: America was still in the throes of the campus revolt. Senator Robert Kennedy was assassinated in California, Martin Luther King was murdered in Atlanta, and Eugene McCarthy, the students' candidate, was humiliatingly defeated early on in the Democratic primaries.

Nixon won handsomely, and immediately attracted attacks from the United States liberals. Certainly, Nixon made no serious effort to gain the support of the intellectuals in America. It was quite clear from his choice of friends that he admired and respected business people and had a certain affinity with small-time crooks, but no interest of any serious kind in ideas. It was clear, however, that he was a consummately brilliant politician. His Cabinet, as was not untypical of Republican Cabinets, was undistinguished, his domestic programme unadventurous, being concerned chiefly with seeking to end the internal bitterness arising from the Vietnam War. An enormously popular politician in middle America, he was loathed by the liberal intelligentsia and by large sections of the press and television, particularly the *Washington Post* and the *New York Times*, which were the newspapers catering for the official and intellectual classes. He had no vision of restoring and revitalising the capitalist system, though he made one bold move which collapsed the Bretton Woods system of international monetary settlements and precipitated the capitalist crisis of the 1970s: he dissociated the dollar from gold.

Nixon inherited a Presidency which was deeply embattled and a nation which had suffered considerably in its pride. In particular he inherited internal racial difficulties, as well as the deep opposition by articulate young people to the Vietnam War and the draft. Internationally, too, the non-Communist world was in disarray and the long post-war boom was coming to an end.

Nixon's Presidency was affected by his personality and his choice of advisers. His Cabinet was reduced to a purely advisory role, with individual Cabinet officers given executive responsibility, but subject to particular specialists on the President's own staff in the White House, who were superior. Thus, for example, William Rogers, the Secretary of State, was subordinated to Henry Kissinger, the national security adviser and the White House staff man responsible for foreign policy. Similarly, access to Nixon himself was entirely through two adjutants, H. R. Haldeman and John Ehrlichman who, through holding positions in the White House, were effectively more influential and important than any member of the Cabinet; in the Cabinet, too, the traditional highest officers – Secretary of State and Secretary of the Treasury – were subordinated to Patrick Moynihan, the Head of the Urban Affairs Council, which he described in his memoirs as the 'domestic policy equivalent of the National Security Council on Foreign Affairs'; and John Mitchell, the Attorney General, was a most influential crony.

Nixon's foreign policy was increasingly identified as Kissinger's, whose flamboyance contrasted with the President's introverted personality. The crucial factors in Nixon's foreign policy were his decision to bring China into the world community, to end the Vietnam War, and to strengthen the position of the United States with respect to the USSR while at the same time securing some measure of détente.

Nixon chose as his foreign policy expert someone who had been born in Germany, had not become an American citizen until he was twenty in 1943, and who spoke with a thick German accent. In 1947 Henry Kissinger went to Harvard where his Ph.D. thesis was on the Congress of Vienna and its settlements. At Harvard he was considered arrogant, boorish and ambitious. He then tried to serve in Kennedy's administration but was not acceptable.

When Nixon took office the Vietnam War was at its height, with a major Communist offensive taking place into South Vietnam. Bombing began inside Cambodia in March 1968 in order to attack what were known as the 'sanctuaries' of the North Vietnamese troops. Meanwhile, endless and pointless negotiations continued in Paris between the Americans and the North Vietnamese. The view was taken that the North Vietnamese were strongly influenced by the Soviet Union, more, probably, than by the Chinese, so the United States therefore secretly approached the Soviet Union for peace talks behind the more formal negotiations. In the meantime, Nixon decided to 'Vietnamise' the war by withdrawing American troops from South Vietnam and increasing the bombing, thus stepping up the war rather than de-escalating it, in order to strengthen his negotiating position.

In the United States the campus riots continued, a mixture of demonstrations against Vietnam and of black uprisings, particularly at Berkeley, Duke and Cornell universities, where the students' union was occupied by blacks armed with rifles and shotguns. The propaganda was clear. The Vietnamese War was an imperialist crusade to support a corrupt government in South Vietnam, itself a creature of the CIA, and that Ho Chi-minh represented a genuine Nationalist movement which was only incidentally Communist. To this was allied the doctrine that the repression of blacks, or other minorities, and possibly of women, was a domestic counterpart to imperialism abroad. This view was eagerly copied in other countries, notably France and West Germany, and almost certainly had its origins in Moscow or Peking. The growing violence on the campuses spread to a so-called Vietnam moratorium held on 15 October 1969 in Washington, which succeeded a week of violent demonstrations; this so encouraged the North Vietnamese and put such pressure on Nixon that it made it difficult for him to negotiate in secret to end the war. The violence may therefore have been deliberately counter-productive in its overt purpose.

The remarkable period of world economic growth which began

Diversity: the 1970s

after 1945 and continued for twenty years now began to slow down with rising rates of inflation. The rate of growth of output until that time had been accompanied by high investment in the industrialised countries and by substantial growth in productivity, particularly where capital accumulation was highest, as in Italy, France and West Germany. Consumption patterns changed, so that manufacturing, whilst still growing, diminished as a proportion of output; in all economies there was a switch to the service sector.

Exports became a larger part of each economy. Wider international markets, in conditions of growing free trade, enabled country after country to develop by export-led growth. And by technological change these enlarged markets in turn produced substantial changes in methods of production, accelerated by heavy investment. How different from the recent past. Now trade liberalisation and regional unification of markets reversed pre-war trends to self-sufficiency.

The decline in the rate of growth of the world's economy was really marked in 1969, when the United States, which produced two fifths of the output of the Western economies, found itself in a recession with, for only the second time in thirty years, a real decline in the Gross National Product.

This was accompanied by balance of payments difficulties and a rise in prices. The dollar, having been for years a 'hard' currency, became a 'soft' one, and the public began to shift into gold and foreign currencies.

In 1971 Nixon broke the link with gold, in a dramatic move tantamount to a devaluation of the dollar. The long-term effects were catastrophic. A new currency regime replaced Bretton Woods which had more or less fixed exchange rates for long periods; in the later 1960s substantial revaluations and devaluations took place and exchange rates began to fluctuate widely. The new arrangements were known as the Smithsonian Accord, in which the permissible limits of exchange fluctuations began to vary. This regime of 'free floating', precipitated by the 1967 devaluation of the pound, led to substantial variations in the relative rates of exchange of different economies. Some of the European countries joined what was called the European Joint Float, also known as the 'Snake'.

The Smithsonian Accord broke down in 1973, when the regime of freely floating exchange rates became almost universal in the Western economies. At repeated meetings of the IMF attempts were made to put together a new system, but during this period the United States experienced a rapid decline in the value of the dollar, both internally and externally.

One response to this international economic turbulence was a growing sense of desperation in the Third World in which many countries found their own prosperity adversely affected by the difficulties of the industrialised countries, which provided their markets, investment and aid. As a result they began to organise cartels of their own. OPEC, which had begun as an alliance of oil states to try to prevent falling prices, was turned into an aggressive price-raising cartel, to which the United States, Europe and Japan had no effective diplomatic, political or economic response. The rise in oil prices as the result of OPEC's decision following the Middle East War of 1973 put all major countries into deficit. It also precipitated almost universal inflation. The United States GNP declined in 1974 and 1975, as did that in the European Community. At the same time, the levels of unemployment began to rise, masked in the case of Central Europe by the repatriation of guest workers, and in the case of the United States by the relatively low rates of reporting of unemployment.

Nixon was therefore responsible for the upset of the regime initiated under Roosevelt and Truman which had been accompanied by so much prosperity. He failed – as did the Europeans – to devise any international monetary mechanism to replace that which had collapsed. This was probably his most serious action in weakening the West.

Throughout his administration he had great difficulty with Congress, as the Republicans were in a minority in both Houses. He even had two nominations to the Supreme Court rejected, which was unprecedented. Abe Fortas, who had been nominated as Chief Justice by Johnson, had, it turned out, been involved in shady deals on behalf of the former President, and his nomination was therefore withdrawn, while Warren Burger, an undistinguished right-winger, was nominated by Nixon as Chief Justice and accepted by the Senate. Nixon's subsequent Supreme Court nominations were denounced as racist, and twice rejected, but nevertheless in the first term of his Presidency three other Justices were nominated by Nixon and were confirmed by the Senate, which gave the Supreme Court an overwhelmingly conservative majority.

The space programme, which Nixon inherited, added to his reputation quite fortuitously. On 20 July 1969 Neil Armstrong became the first man to walk on the Moon. Thus Nixon had a considerable American achievement to boost his Presidency early on in his first term.

The war in Vietnam spread, however, rather than diminished. On 18 March 1970 Prince Sihanouk, the head of state of Cambodia, uneasily divided, was overthrown by General Lon Nol, and the impression was gained – incorrectly as it happened – that it was the CIA who had organised the coup. Lon Nol immediately proceeded unsuccessfully against the Khmer Rouge, the Communist forces in Cambodia. The Khmer Rouge were allied to the North Vietnamese and supplied by them; so the war spread into Cambodia. The Communists now advanced on the capital of Cambodia, Phnom Penh, which in a knock-on effect led to a decision by Nixon that American and South Vietnamese troops should enter Southern Cambodia and that the so-called Communist 'sanctuaries' in Cambodia should be bombed. This began on 29 April 1970.

The effect of the bombing on the progress of the war was less important than its domestic consequences for it was followed by massive campus demonstrations, including the burning of part of the library of the Yale Law School and of the Center for Behavioral Studies at Stanford. President Nixon denounced the students as 'campus bums', while the other 'kids, who were just doing their duty', stood tall and proud in Vietnam. He was never forgiven by liberal opinion for what might be called a legitimate statement of the obvious. The 'campus bums' speech caused further riots, in particular one at Kent State University in Ohio, where the National Guard intervened, opened fire, and killed four students. This created the impression that Nixon was even tougher and more reactionary than had hitherto been assumed by the liberal press and was prepared not only to shoot yellow men in Asia, but Americans at home. He had, of course, no knowledge of the Kent State shootings and no authority over the National Guard, but by early May 450 colleges and universities had been closed by student demonstrations. On 9 May a massive march in Washington reminded people of the student insurrection in Paris in 1968 which eventually and indirectly drove de Gaulle from office. It was essentially counter-productive, however, in electoral terms since the older people – and probably a majority of the students – supported the President. Its impact on world opinion, however, was grave.

The Cambodian operation, as it was called, was militarily successful in that it deprived the North Vietnamese of large quantities of equipment and also virtually cleared Cambodia of Communist troops, which in turn allowed the Americans to withdraw. In the long run, however, the Cambodian operation had devastating consequences. It spread the war way beyond Vietnamese frontiers into the rest of Indochina.

A far-reaching decision was taken on 18 January 1971 by the President and his senior advisers, Laird, the Secretary of State for

Defense; Rogers, the Secretary of State; Helms, the Head of the CIA; Kissinger, and his deputy, former General Alexander Haig; and the Chairman of the Joint Chiefs of Staff, Admiral Thomas Moorer, to undertake the invasion of neighbouring Laos to cut the Ho Chi-minh trail by which the North Vietnamese supplied the Vietcong in the South. The operation was at first thought militarily to be successful. But when the Americans withdrew, the North Vietnamese returned, which gave the impression to the South Vietnamese after their initial euphoria that the future was dark. Despite this pessimism, during 1971 there was no major Communist offensive. The Laos invasion appeared to have achieved its military purpose. In the short run, moreover, these moves may have led, in US minds, to the possibility of a truce, since the North Vietnamese position in the negotiations seemed to moderate.

Then, behind the scenes, and secretly, Nixon's genius for self-destruction began to manifest itself. In February 1971 a tape-recording system was installed throughout the White House to record automatically all Presidential conversations and all phone calls. This replaced a manually-operated system which President Johnson had inherited from Kennedy and Eisenhower. Nixon was later to allege that as far back as Franklin Roosevelt a microphone was placed in a lamp in his office secretly to record important conversations. Truman, however, appears to have had no use for such devices. Nixon may have wished merely to use the system – as his predecessors had done for immediately political purposes – to record views in private that were later denied publicly; but it is more likely that, as he said subsequently, he wished to keep a record to help in writing his memoirs which were to be the central feature of the deposit of the Nixon Memorial Library.

The taping system became the key to Nixon's downfall. But it was also connected with another event, the publication of secret government papers, 7000 pages long, studying the American involvement in Vietnam from 1945 to 1968. The papers purported to show a consistent pattern of secret CIA and military involvement, almost wholly at variance with the official reasons for American policy. Vietnam, it alleged, was an American and not a Communist plot. The documents, in breach of official secrecy, were published in 1971 in the *New York Times*, America's leading newspaper of record. They had been leaked by a member of the Pentagon staff, Daniel Ellsberg, who had come to have a deep conviction that the war was wrong. It was characteristic of the attitudes of the time that Ellsberg was treated by many as a public hero for his profound breach of trust. In consequence, the confidentiality of public affairs dramatically decreased, thereby making

government difficult, especially for a man as secretive and introverted as Nixon. (It was not paralleled by a similar lack of
confidentiality in Communist countries, especially North Vietnam.) Nixon and his staff were understandably concerned and
furious at what they saw as part of a widespread conspiracy to
undermine his foreign policy and, indeed, his whole Presidency,
though the documents were, if anything, more damning of Kennedy and Johnson than of Nixon who was, after all, trying to end
the war rather than win it.

The White House conducted a major investigation against
Ellsberg to discover whether he was part of an anti-war conspiracy.
His psychiatrist's office was broken into to find evidence that might
discredit his motives and diminish the value of his evidence. This
break-in was one of the first actions of a group known as 'the
Plumbers', that is to say, those who plug leaks. Recruited from the
CIA, they later gained notoriety working for the Committee for
the Re-election of the President, the initiators of what became
known as the Watergate affair. The Ellsberg issue, however, was
important at the time, because the Nixon administration became
increasingly convinced of a conspiracy to overthrow the government in order to bring the Vietnam War to an end; and it seemed
possible to them that such a conspiracy might lead back further to
the Russians.

The Ellsberg revelations preceded the 1972 election in which
Nixon's opponent was thought likely to be Senator Edmund
Muskie. Meanwhile the Kennedy family had no runner, because of
yet another tragedy, in which Edward Kennedy, the surviving
Kennedy brother, and Senator for Massachusetts, drove a car
off a bridge at Chappaquidick in Massachusetts in July 1969, in
which his girl companion, Mary Jo Kopechne, was drowned in
bizarre circumstances. This removed Kennedy from the race for
the Democratic nomination to oppose Nixon and left Muskie and
Senator McGovern, who both ran on a strong anti-war ticket.
During the primaries Muskie had a public breakdown and withdrew, which left McGovern as the Democratic nominee by default.

McGovern was naïve, radical and sincere; Nixon was experienced, tough and abrasive. In particular he distracted attention
from the anti-war campaign by foreign policy accomplishments of a
spectacular nature. The President who had sent a man to the Moon
sent himself to China, up till then hermetically sealed. Through the
diplomatic office of Pakistan and Romania, Kissinger arranged that
the United States would recognise China. On a secret trip to
China, in which he spent over seventeen hours in meetings with
Chou En-lai, he arranged Nixon's visit, and the necessary diplo-

matic steps whereby the United States reversed twenty-four years of voting at the United Nations to admit the People's Republic of China and to expel Taiwan, the surviving remnant of Chiang Kai-shek's Nationalist regime. As a result in February 1972 Nixon flew to Peking and talked with Mao Tse-tung.

This visit began the American alliance with China, which gave rise to much anxiety and even fear in the Soviet Union, who felt surrounded by a new Chinese–American alignment. The Nixon visit also led ultimately to a break between the Chinese and the North Vietnamese (though this was only to emerge later), which was part of Kissinger's strategy to end the war.

Rapprochement with China represented a major contribution to Nixon's re-election. At this moment he appeared a most successful American President internationally and clearly he stood a chance of ending the war.

Nixon was gradually withdrawing troops from Vietnam, as his relationship with China improved, but in the meantime the North Vietnamese started a major new offensive. The Americans retaliated by intensifying the bombing of North Vietnam's capital, Hanoi, and Haiphong, its port, while all the time reducing its number of troops. The North Vietnamese, however, were still apparently unprepared to negotiate seriously with Kissinger. Nixon decided, therefore, in May 1972, to go on the offensive, by mining the North Vietnamese ports and using his air power to destroy all communications between North Vietnam and the outside world. This was an attempt to force the Russians, North Vietnam's chief supporters, to come to the negotiating table, and it succeeded.

On 21 May Brezhnev, Kosygin, Podgorny, Gromyko and Dobrinin met Nixon and Kissinger in Moscow in a major initiative, first to bring the Vietnam War to an end, and also to advance SALT, the Strategic Arms Limitation Treaty, which had been deadlocked at Vienna for over three years. Agreement was reached on an Anti-Ballistic Missile Treaty that banned future development of anti-ballistic missiles beyond what had already been achieved. The Soviet Union also agreed to use its influence to bring the North Vietnamese to negotiate.

These superb foreign policy achievements were masked, however, by the calamitous end of his administration. Nixon was re-elected in November 1972 by the largest majority that any President had hitherto seen, against the ultra-liberal, politically defective Senator McGovern. But this election itself sowed the immediate seeds of his resignation a year and a half later.

During the election an allegation was made by Jack Anderson, a newspaper columnist, that ITT – International Telephone and Telegraph, one of the major American corporations – had made a large contribution towards the Republican Convention in San Diego, in return for anti-trust proceedings against it being dropped. Although it subsequently transpired that the documents published were forgeries, the allegation fed Nixon's insecurity about the campaign being waged against him, and the possibility of dirty tricks in the election. He therefore sought to defend himself by using secret (and often illegal) methods of espionage and so to drift more and more into the hands of the 'Plumbers', through the agency of a man called E. Howard Hunt, who was hired by Chuck Colson, a White House aide.

The political atmosphere was poisonous, full of charges and countercharges. It was suspected that Nixon, like other Presidents before him, notably President Kennedy, was using the FBI and the CIA in order to gain information on his political opponents.

Nixon's Presidency was destroyed by what became known as the Watergate affair. Campaigning between McGovern and Nixon began towards the end of 1971, a year before the actual election. Under the relatively strict United States law, it was important to differentiate the expenditure of President Nixon as President, and the expenditure by his supporters who were seeking his re-election for a second term of office, from 1972 to 1976. A committee to re-elect the President, CREEP, was established, headed by John Mitchell, the Attorney General, with the assistance of Maurice Stans, the Secretary for Commerce, who sought support from businessmen and others to finance the Presidential campaign. This was perfectly normal and acceptable. The opposition, the Democratic National Committee, established McGovern's headquarters in the Watergate Building, a complex of hotel, offices and flats, on the Potomac River near the Kennedy Center in Washington, D.C.

On 17 June 1972 the office of the Democratic National Committee in the Watergate Building was broken into and the burglars caught. The case seemed at the time petty and inexplicable when the burglars appeared in court next morning, but a *Washington Post* journalist, and a collaborator, decided that there was more in the case than met the eye. The *Washington Post*, under the ownership of Mrs Kay Graham, was fanatically anti-Nixon, and Ben Bradlee, the editor, was an addict of 'investigative journalism'. The journalists, Bob Woodward and Carl Bernstein ('Woodstein' as they became known) continued their investigation and eventually established that a number of the men involved in the burglary were CIA personnel connected indirectly with John Mitchell, the Attorney General.

After Nixon's re-election it was found that substantial campaign donations, in excess of the amounts permitted by law, had been received by CREEP, having first been 'laundered' in Mexico and then brought back to the United States through various illegal accounts. The President maintained a dignified aloofness and ignorance of these proceedings, but it became the conviction of Bernstein and Woodward, in almost daily articles in the *Washington Post* that there had been a conspiracy leading directly into the White House, to use a whole series of 'dirty tricks' to discredit the Democrats in order to secure Nixon's re-election. Such a conspiracy was in fact highly unnecessary, since Nixon would have defeated almost any candidate, let alone one as ineffectual as McGovern. Nixon received forty-seven million votes to McGovern's twenty-nine million.

In the year after the election, quite independently of the investigation of the Watergate affair, Vice-President Agnew, who had been a notably corrupt Governor of Maryland, was forced to resign his office and was subsequently convicted of corrupt practices while acting as Vice-President. This inevitably led to the general view, certainly in liberal circles, that President Nixon's whole entourage was crooked. A Federal case was mounted before Judge John J. Sirica alleging a conspiracy among persons unknown to burgle Watergate at the same time as a Congressional Committee began hearings on the Watergate affair. At these hearings it was accidentally revealed that throughout his period of office President Nixon had secretly tape-recorded everything. The issue then became whether or not there were in existence tape-recordings proving the complicity in the affair itself and of the cover-up of his own personal officers H. R. (Bob) Haldeman and John T. Ehrlichman. If Haldeman and Ehrlichman had had prior knowledge of the affair, and of the subsequent cover-up, and had shared this knowledge with Nixon, then Nixon was a co-conspirator to defeat justice – a serious criminal offence by Haldeman, Ehrlichman and Nixon. After an immense amount of complex legal negotiations and in a blaze of publicity both Haldeman and Ehrlichman were dismissed by the President on the ground that they had had knowledge of the conspiracy to burgle the Watergate offices, though he denied a cover-up. This was followed by the conviction of Maurice Stans, the Commerce Secretary, and the arraignment of John Mitchell, the Attorney General, for their parts in the conspiracy.

The tapes were finally heard by Judge Sirica, and the transcripts released to the Congressional Committee, but the crucial interview in which John Dean, a counsel to the President, alleged that he had discussed Watergate with the President, demonstrating that he had knowledge of the affair, was missing. The explanation from the President's secretary, that she had accidentally erased it, seemed implausible.

In the meantime, as the nation was engrossed by Watergate, Kissinger was seeking peace in Vietnam. A cease-fire was negotiated with the North Vietnamese in Paris, to be followed by an exchange of prisoners and a possible National Council of Reconciliation and Concord, representing the South Vietnam government, the Vietcong and neutral members. On the way back from North Vietnam, Kissinger saw President Thieu, who tried to hold up the agreement. The North Vietnamese broke off the negotiations and on 18 December 1972 American bombing of the North was renewed with great intensity. This was in order to force the North Vietnamese to negotiate and once more caused enormous outcry from the opponents of the war, from the *Washington Post* and the *New York Times*, and throughout the campuses. The bombing was suspended on 20 December, and in the New Year negotiations were resumed. Agreement was once again reached with the North Vietnamese, but Thieu still refused to accept it. Nevertheless a cease-fire came into operation on 27 January 1973. Throughout the negotiations the Watergate affair had been rumbling. By mid-January, with the appointment of the Ervin Committee of the Senate to investigate the matter with full power and authority, it came to dominate all political life. The replacement of Haldeman and Ehrlichman by the much-respected General Haig was an important step in restoring the Presidency, but the Watergate slide for Nixon continued.

In the summer of 1973 Brezhnev and Kosygin visited the United States to further the cause of détente. The negotiations for SALT II developed and the end of the Vietnam War approached. A resolution of the United States Congress cut off funds for further bombing of Cambodia. On 1 August 1973 Vice-President Agnew was accused of conspiracy, extortion, bribery and tax fraud. On 10 October 1973 – less than a year after the election – Agnew resigned as Vice-President and was later convicted. This raised the problem of a successor Vice-President, and an innocuous member of the House of Representatives, Gerald Ford, was chosen by Nixon – his fourth choice. The favoured candidates, Connally, Rockefeller and Reagan, were not proposed as Nixon feared that they would not be confirmed by the Senate, as required by the Constitution, so great was his loss of authority.

The Vice-President's resignation took place during the Yom Kippur War, considerably handicapping the part that Nixon himself could play in that settlement, but allowing Kissinger a greater free rein. Kissinger began a series of journeys which became known as shuttle diplomacy.

The Yom Kippur War was so serious that the United States forces were put on a nuclear alert. This led to the agreements between the Soviet Union and the United States that they would intervene to mitigate the Middle East crisis. Yet Nixon, with his great experience of world affairs and of diplomacy, and with major diplomatic achievements to his credit, could hardly concentrate on these vital matters.

Watergate came completely to dominate the American political scene. Eventually the President's position became untenable. On 8 August 1974 the President announced on television his intention to resign the following day. On 9 August Gerald Ford was therefore sworn in as President of the United States for the remainder of what had been Nixon's term of office.

The decision to drive Nixon out of office for breaking the law by conspiring in burglaries and by taking part in electoral malpractices had been taken early on by leading Democratic publicists, in particular the owners of large television chains and of the *Washington Post*. It represented the triumph of a certain sanctimonious line of thought in America which held that people in elected office were almost inescapably corrupt, but should in fact be Simon Pure.

Ford's first act as President was to pardon Nixon retrospectively, so that no further prosecution could be brought against him, and in this flurry of dishonour and disharmony the Nixon Presidency came to an end. Kissinger, who kept aloof from the undercover operations, continued in office. The fact that Nixon had himself been far less personally corrupt and far less brutal to his opponents than the Kennedy family or Lyndon Johnson seemed of little account in this mood of hypocrisy, but it effectively left Kissinger in charge of the foreign policy of the United States, since Gerald Ford was totally inexperienced in international affairs. In 1975 South Vietnam collapsed and a complete Communist military and political victory was achieved.

The consequences of the Nixon Presidency were depressing. There had been a major collapse of the Western world monetary system as a result of the oil price rises and the new balance of world economic power. Nixon's decisions were foolish and hasty. In Vietnam his strategy was neither straightforward nor successful. He left Vietnam prepared to fall and it fell. The consequences for United States prestige were serious. The American armed forces were demoralised and ineffective. On the other hand, Nixon successfully brought about the realignment of American relations with China that might, in the longer run, be of great significance.

Kissinger played a game of high strategy. He wanted to achieve détente on the basis of American strength. He achieved it on the basis of defeat and weakness.

Chapter 32

Détente

The aim of the West was peace, prosperity and freedom. The
Soviet Union desired peace. Was this a basis for compromise? The
supreme effort made by Nixon to achieve a settlement between the
Soviet Union and the United States marked a shift away from the
doctrine of containment of the Soviet aggressor. It meant that the
Soviet Union was no longer seen as mainly an expansionary power;
it possibly meant acceptance of the relativist doctrine that one
system was perhaps as good as the other; and it certainly meant
that realistically the Soviet system was at least as enduring, stable
and permanent as liberal democracy. None of these views had been
shared by Kennedy, who had confronted the Soviet Union over
Cuba; and the domino theory – that one state after another would
fall to Communism – became the basis of United States involvement in Vietnam. Nixon's policy reversal was therefore fundamental. To some degree it rested upon an assumption that the
world was divided into two power blocs and that a supreme and
lasting settlement could be achieved between them. This had been
the Soviet assumption at Yalta, or something like it. But this was
simplistic. There were now many independent powers in the Third
World and Europe; the OPEC alliance especially was a law unto
itself. There were many and diverse causes of unrest and distress in
the world not directly linked to the conflict between the two
superpowers. Even if some accommodation between the Soviet
Union and the United States had been arrived at, therefore, many
diverse sources of fundamental disturbance of the equilibrium
would have remained. Nevertheless no relationship was as critical
as the United States and Soviet confrontation, if only because it
rested upon the possibility of a major nuclear exchange.

For the first decade after the war, the principal cause of the
instability was perceived as Soviet aggression. Yet even then two
major conflicts – the civil war in China and the Suez affair – broke
out which were only indirectly connected with Soviet strategy. As
different sources of instability appeared – the Israeli–Arab conflicts and the disputes between India and Pakistan – the American
doctrine of containment, aimed specifically at the Soviet Union
and articulated most fully by Dulles, began to seem inapplicable.

Despite or even because of Hungary in 1956, Soviet expansion seemed to find a natural limit. Its sphere as defined at Yalta was kept, and no Soviet foot crossed that often arbitrary boundary, even into Yugoslavia. The death of Stalin and Khruschev's 'secret' denunciation of him seemed to herald a coming together of the world's major economic systems, around a moderate reformist programme induced by affluence. One of the theorists behind America's Vietnam policy, Walt Whitman Rostow, argued this thesis most persuasively. In the late 1950s it seemed that if the Soviet Union were a threat, it was principally because the USSR had put its strength behind nuclear missiles, of which Sputnik, launched in 1957, was the most dramatic sign. This enabled the American homeland itself to be attacked. The Soviet Union was not necessarily an aggressor. It might over-react, however. Kennedy was elected on a platform of overcoming the 'missile gap', yet this subsequently proved fictitious.

A basis for stability through stalemate was now sought, both by those who thought the nature of the Soviet beast had changed (the doves) and by those who thought it had not changed (the hawks); but both camps agreed that Soviet ambitions had to be contained by agreement between the superpowers, not by threats and defeat.

The Kennedy administration formed the view that as Soviet conventional forces were not as strong as they had seemed, the strengthening of NATO conventional forces would be sufficient to contain them, especially as Russia was no longer trigger-happy. In America it was thought unlikely that the Soviet Union would risk nuclear war; the hair-raising events of 1962 and the Soviet retreat from the Cuban missile sites seemed to confirm this view. A basis for a cynical but realistic settlement therefore probably existed. It became United States policy to build up NATO's conventional forces in Europe, particularly the land and air forces of the Western Europeans. The purpose was to create a stalemate in conventional forces as well as a balance of nuclear terror; in this way what came to be called détente might be achieved. The acceptance of this view meant abandoning the idea that the Soviet empire might be rolled back. But there was a note of optimism. It might be that Poland and Czechoslovakia could not be rescued. But it was argued in America that increasing affluence would of itself soften and moderate Soviet tyranny and so make the iron curtain a more plastic divide.

The US policy of détente conflicted, however, with the Soviet concept of peaceful coexistence: to create a buffer zone between the Soviet Union and the United States by the neutralisation of Germany and large parts of Europe, in order to reduce the conventional forces in Europe, including those stationed in the

Warsaw Pact zone. After this was achieved – and it had been a possible Soviet aim since 1945 – the eventual reduction of nuclear weapons would begin. By depriving the United States of some of its most powerful allies and bases this neutralisation policy would in fact have weakened the Western alliance disproportionately. 'Peaceful coexistence' looked like a Soviet victory. Yet to the Soviet Union, the American policy of détente, which meant strengthening West Germany, seemed provocative. But to the United States and its allies the demilitarisation of Europe seemed an obvious strategy for a Soviet takeover by internal 'Finland-isation' – creating a Western Europe that though 'free' was externally controlled by the Soviet Union and was freely available for invasion whenever the Soviet Union felt like it.

In the absence of some kind of neutralisation, there seemed no possibility of agreement on the elimination of nuclear weapons. Frightened by Sputnik and Soviet missile capacity, the Kennedy administration developed Polaris nuclear submarines and Minute-man missile warning programmes to provide both an offensive and defensive capability beyond the capacity at that time of the Soviet Union to destroy them. Thus the United States gained an apparent overwhelming capacity for a trenchant blow to Soviet forces, if it were prepared to risk large parts of America being destroyed by Soviet missiles launched before American missiles destroyed their launching pads. In such a nuclear exchange America would 'win' because, though its major cities might lie in ruins, it would still have its nuclear arsenal, while the Soviet Union would have lost its entire nuclear capacity. This was an appalling prospect. Was the alternative to virtual annihilation some kind of neutralisation?

McNamara, who was Secretary of Defense in Kennedy's and Johnson's administration and co-author of the Vietnam strategy, thought not. He argued that the correct strategic doctrine for America should be one of controlled response, that is to say, to each level of provocation the United States would respond with slightly more than the same degree of force. If a Soviet bomb destroyed New York, then Moscow and Leningrad would go; for the whole of the East Coast, the whole of Siberia; and so on – just more than tit for tat. But it was also clear that in any conceivable war the process of escalation would make such precise measures of counter-destruction impossible to achieve. It required a cool nerve on the part of everybody while millions of people were incinerated. Controlled response was therefore abandoned. But the dilemma remained. A new doctrine, adopted in 1963, emerged. It was Assured Destruction. At this point the ultimately unthinkable had to be considered: that any nuclear exchange between the Soviet

Union and the United States would result in a hundred million deaths in both countries. McNamara calculated that if the Soviet Union launched any kind of nuclear attack the United States would be instantly ready to destroy between 20 and 25 per cent of the Soviet population and 50 per cent of its industrial capacity, and accept a similar level of destruction itself.

This meant that at any stage of conflict the United States would accept a mutual or catastrophic level of destruction. But, it was argued, the advantage of an unthinkable doctrine was, precisely, to make such conflict impossible. It might seem, therefore, that Assured Destruction would limit the American attempt to stock-pile weapons in an ever-growing arms race with the Soviet Union, by making such a contest absurd; the US would also risk being overtaken by the Soviet Union. In other words, it was perhaps a step towards self-imposed nuclear arms limitation. Détente was to be achieved by default.

The optimistic theory led in turn to the idea of non-nuclear strength being the prime deterrent to Soviet attack. The Soviet strategists would possibly have come to the same conclusions as American strategists and would not, therefore, start a nuclear war. So the next war would be a conventional one. Thus McNamara's ultimate strategy was based on conventional forces. If the Soviet Union advanced in Europe for any reason it would use infantry and tanks, which would be stopped by infantry and tanks. World War Three would be like the two earlier world wars. This at least saved Europe, America and Russia from incineration. But the war might still be lost. As Vietnam proved, American conventional forces were not good enough, which would mean that the United States would lose World War Three. For destruction, defeat had been substituted.

In fact, nuclear stockpiling did not stop. All this theorising proved empty. Following Nixon's election, the United States doctrine changed yet again to one which recognised the diversity of threats to world order. In this theory of strategic sufficiency strategic forces would be strong enough to inflict damage on those – wherever they might be found – who threatened to attack the United States in any way; the forces would also be strong enough to prevent the United States' allies being coerced. For each level of attack by whatever level of force of any kind by whatever nation, an appropriate response was prepared. In no single future crisis was this doctrine effective in practice. But it formed a notional limit to the level of military preparedness, with the critical exception of the nuclear arms race itself, which carried on as before.

From this doctrine of strategic sufficiency the conclusion was drawn that should any international crisis develop, there was no point, no incentive to the Soviet Union to strike first with nuclear weapons, because the retaliation was automatic; consequently it was vitally important to have enough US missiles to ensure that they had as much power to inflict damage on the Soviet Union's towns and industries as the Soviet Union had to inflict damage on the United States; and both sides had to know this was so and fully to believe it. But at the same time it was also necessary to be able to defend the United States and its overseas bases and allies against small attacks or even against accidental launches of devastating missiles. The concept of a nuclear accident, the accidental firing of a weapon, now became relevant, because any misinterpretation, or a smaller attack – say on a third party – could lead to the ultimate response.

The doctrine of strategic sufficiency meant having a second strike capability adequate to deter an all-out surprise attack on the United States forces; that is to say, the moment the Soviet Union attacked, missiles would automatically be on their way to the Soviet Union; or, less apocalyptically, the moment an American embassy was burned or occupied a helicopter squadron would intervene.

It became essential, therefore, for the United States and the Soviet Union to be sure they were on the same wavelength, that they knew exactly what each was intending. It was this which gave real impetus to détente. As an idea, détente began soon after Stalin's death and first surfaced in the 1954 Geneva Conference which settled differences in Indochina, manifesting itself again in the Austrian State Treaty in 1955. It could have led to a neutralised Germany, a neutralised Vietnam and perhaps to a more general European settlement had it been interpreted as peaceful coexistence. There was a move from the almost total mutual hostility between Stalin and Truman to normal, though scarcely friendly, relations between two great superpowers.

This early stage of the process of détente was already strained by Suez and Hungary in 1956, and it broke up with the collapse of the Summit in Paris between President Eisenhower, Macmillan, de Gaulle and Khruschev in 1960 and the subsequent confrontation between Kennedy and Khruschev over Berlin and the Cuban missile crisis in 1962. A dialogue was, however, maintained even during the crisis years of the Kennedy Presidency. During the uneasy period of stalemate while Khruschev remained in power the full realisation of a final nuclear conflict became more apparent as a result of the horrors of the Vietnam War. Both détente and peaceful coexistence changed their meaning: the aim was to avoid nuclear war and not much more.

In the later 1960s President Johnson announced a policy of 'bridge-building', and began serious negotiations on arms control. This second process of détente was interrupted, however, by the Soviet invasion of Czechoslovakia in 1968. Despite this President Nixon, elected in 1968, laid the foundation for a peace agreement between the two blocs, which culminated in 1972 in ten formal agreements between the United States and the Soviet Union and five declarations of co-operative intent. This was the process of détente for which Kissinger claimed credit. Shocking though the Soviet invasion of Czechoslovakia was, there seemed to be no permanent interruption of the process of détente.

Out of the Strategic Arms Limitation Talks came the first SALT Agreement in 1971, and this in turn led to a coexistence declaration in May 1972 and an accord on avoiding war signed in June 1973. Nixon and Kissinger attempted to secure a stable and long-lasting peaceful relationship with the Soviet Union on the one hand, and with China on the other, partly for immediate domestic reasons in limiting the arms bill, and in guaranteeing the security of the United States at a lower than anticipated cost, but also partly for foreign policy reasons: to extricate themselves from Vietnam and to secure a final end to the period of international conflict which the United States had experienced under Kennedy and Johnson.

Kissinger drew the conclusion that Brezhnev was more likely to secure an international system of peaceful coexistence than any other Soviet leader since the revolution; and that such peaceful coexistence did not mean a *de facto* Soviet victory. Brezhnev was both strong and realistic and he had no serious rivals. He appeared to be uninterested in expansion, and pragmatic about Communist peace policy. The principle of détente was, therefore, one to which both Kissinger and Brezhnev attached importance, since it could institutionalise peace, without any great showdown or 'final' settlement, or ideological compromise between Communism and capitalism.

The particular solutions reached by Nixon and Brezhnev were based on the Soviet Union and the United States having reached nuclear strategic parity. Each, indeed, could destroy the other effortlessly. It was seen, however, and mutually recognised by Nixon and Brezhnev, that the Sino–Soviet conflict made the Soviet Union anxious to avoid confrontation on two fronts, Asia and Europe. The Soviet leaders appeared to be more interested in building a peaceful world than in acts of aggression, but at the same time they were not slow to seek to extend the sphere of Soviet influence way beyond the original zones agreed at Yalta, when the opportunity arose, as in Cuba and, later, Africa.

The age of the superpowers was over. The consequent rigidity of postures, and of calculating everything in terms of military bipolarity – how strong was America compared with Russia? – was something that had passed. Instability arose from adventitious acts by smaller and often not especially aligned countries, such as Rhodesia, or Chile, or Ethiopia, or, above all, Israel and its neighbours. There was a growing view that the two competing systems of American capitalism and Soviet Communism were now stable and equally balanced. Each had to accept that the other was here to stay. Many Americans comforted themselves with the thought that the Soviet Union was moving towards a more liberal society, partly through the rising standard of living of the working people which made them keen to limit arms spending and partly through the lassitude of affluence and the satiety of power. This led American thinkers to the view that the Soviet Union would persevere with strategic arms limitations regardless. It was thought to have a compelling domestic need to avoid major military conflicts which might escalate into nuclear war, or which might upset its own consumers by imposing too great an arms bill on them. The development of trade based on credits and access to American technology was seen as a vital Soviet interest in satisfying rising Soviet consumer demand. The American view was that the struggle had moved from arms towards ideology – a struggle for Third World minds, and in this context the Communism with a Human Face, which was the hallmark both of the Prague Spring and of Euro-Communism, as expressed by the Italian Communist party, was perhaps the key to one of the ways the USSR would in future conduct its foreign policy. It was a happy doctrine: almost the coca-cola-isation of Communism.

After 1973, however, the negotiations between the superpowers cooled, and the war in the Middle East showed that while high-level military conflict between the United States and the Soviet Union could be avoided at a period of high tension, nevertheless the Soviet Union continued to be hostile to the United States and capable of exercising its military strength in a threatening way if it suited.

Within Europe, détente did not mean a settlement of such issues as a united Germany, still less the divisions of Yalta and Potsdam; it was marked by the growth of such policies as *Ostpolitik* by the Federal Republic and its recognition of East Germany. This accepted the division between East and West, but made the division apparently softer. This process continued with West Germany establishing diplomatic relations with Romania and Yugoslavia in 1967, followed by an agreement on the inviolability of all European frontiers between Egon Bahr, the West German Foreign Minister, and his Russian opposite number, Gromyko, in Moscow in August 1970. This led in turn to the Four Power Treaty on Berlin in 1971, which guaranteed access routes to Berlin and, furthermore, a traffic agreement between West and East Germany in May 1972, and then the basic treaty signed in December 1972 and ratified in June 1973, which established permanent diplomatic relations between Bonn and East Berlin, and involved the recognition of East Germany by the West. The unification of Germany was not brought about, but gradually the division was formalised, recognised and accepted. In 1975 a State Treaty was signed by West Germany with Poland which confirmed the Oder–Neisse border and allowed the emigration of 125,000 Polish citizens of German origin in exchange for substantial German economic aid to Poland. This was a further step to normality. In December 1973 a treaty had been signed with Czechoslovakia which formally ended the Munich Agreement of 1938. All this effectively settled 'the German question' until and if the pressures for German reunification became irresistible in the future. The major cause of two world wars was in some sense settled.

In July 1975 a positive step to peace was taken – almost the first since Yalta – towards settling 'the European question': the Conference on Security and Co-operation in Europe, the Final Act, was signed on 1 August 1975 in Helsinki. The original Russian plan had been a new European security system in which the Continent would be neutralised or 'Finlandised', as the word had it. As a step towards that end – acceptable if Russia had indeed abandoned aggression – all states on the European land mass would guarantee each other's frontiers and security. And in Basket 3, which was the third part of the Treaty, involving co-operation in humanitarian and other fields, there was a commitment by the Soviet Union and the East European states, at the prompting of Yugoslavia, Romania, Finland and Sweden, for non-intervention in internal affairs, and also some degree of individual personal rights in all countries. The experience of Czechoslovakia in 1968 remained vividly in the mind. If the Soviet Union took its plan seriously, then 1968 could not be repeated, and the Eastern zone could be gradually liberalised, though not of course liberated.

Helsinki offered the liberal face of 'Finlandisation', in a detailed treaty modest in its aims, but a major step away from the Cold War. Under Basket 1, the signatories pledged to respect each other's sovereign equality and right to freedom and political independence and to refrain from the threat or use of force.

This Helsinki agreement led to Human Rights groups developing in the East, notably the Czech Charter 77 group, which argued most strongly against the repression of human rights. Groups were formed elsewhere, as repression remained severe in the Eastern European states. The East Germans exiled many of their leading intellectuals, and the Soviet Union and Czechoslovakia not only exiled their dissenting intellectuals, but sent many to prison and some to psychiatric treatment. The gulag, though not as full as it had been, was by no means empty.

In other words, the fundamental aims and practices of the Soviet system had not really changed. The Helsinki agreements, and all that part of détente that rested upon an optimistic interpretation of the convergence of industrialised countries into a kind of open, market-oriented liberal society, was false. Nevertheless the American defeat in Vietnam, and the demoralisation of American public policy-makers and of the American armed forces drove Washington to hold exactly the opposite conclusion. Détente meant acceptance of totalitarianism in the East. But the peace established in 1945 endured; the freedom of Western Europe was safeguarded – as was its prosperity; and there was a hope – admittedly slight – that there might be a shift of opinion and policy in Soviet-occupied Europe.

Chapter 33

Conclusions

Human life is a continuum. Events have lasting consequences. The consequences of the Second World War will endure for generations, just as in Europe contemporary thoroughfares follow the line of Roman roads built 2000 years ago, and English county boundaries were often determined by the pattern of Saxon settlement. Israel was brought into existence by the holocaust; it will take a second holocaust to bring it to an end. The division of Germany, the division of Europe itself, the end of imperialism – all these came about as a result of the Second World War, but by 1975 the immediate consequences had worked themselves out. Nixon had reversed Truman and Eisenhower's policies. The Europeans had repudiated American leadership. The newly-independent nations were well established. The prosperity of the post-war boom was finished. The optimism of 1945, the pessimism of 1948, the hopes and the fears of the post-war world changed to an acceptance of the normality of the abnormal.

The world after 1975 was no longer working out the consequences of the settlement of 1945. That was now part of history. It was living out the consequences of the events of the 1960s and the early 1970s. Had the peace not been squandered, had it been otherwise, then there might have been greater grounds for optimism.

The illusion of victory by the forces of light over the forces of evil was soon lost in 1945. The cattle trucks taking the 'liberated' displaced persons to the Russian border to be shot or sent to Siberia; the systematic persecution of all independent-minded people throughout Eastern Europe; the French campaign against Ho Chi-minh and the Dutch campaign against Sukarno – all these proved beyond doubt that many of the hopes aroused before the victory had been an illusion. Chiefly the cause was one man: Joseph Stalin. But outside the range of his power, oppression and savagery often triumphed, usually in the name of 'freedom'. But since freedom and prosperity and happiness are desirable and since they are attainable (within the limits set by man's fallen nature), why has so much of the world chosen tyranny, sacrifice and misery as their lot?

Such a lot has not been chosen, of course, by the masses, or even (consciously) by their leaders, but imposed by revolution and conquest. Yet despite the risings in Portugal, Hungary, Poland, East Germany and Czechoslovakia – all parts of historic Europe – there is singularly little sign of an overwhelming and successful mass movement towards the ends that (according to revolutionaries everywhere) humanity is striving for. Indeed it is those countries that have most nearly approximated to the revolutionary ideal – America, West Germany, Britain – that have been most consistently attacked as the oppressors. Mainly, of course, this is because of Marxist casuistry; normal pluralist society is interpreted as 'oppressive', whereas the uniformity enforced by brutality in Marxist states is interpreted as the manifestation of the (unconscious) proletarian will.

But, clearly, there is something even deeper at work. The powerful classes, the political zealots, the intellectuals, the half-educated – however those who run the oppressive systems may be described – are far too solidly behind the intolerant ideologies and practices to be merely the victims of casuistry. Oppression must be willed.

Why, then, has the world shifted towards oppression?

Partly because of the unexpected strength of Marxist states. Russia did not collapse when Hitler attacked. Stalin's terror was renewed and still Russia survived – and not merely survived, but spread the terror to the occupied states. Its sympathisers overtly and covertly came close to capturing Italy and France. Even as the truth about Stalin's Russia became widely known and irrefutable the attraction of the idea of the Soviet Union (and even more of a purged and purified Socialism) scarcely slackened. It is not as if the political and social oppression, the tawdry police state culture, the pervasive militarism, remained a secret. The myth was (and is) powerful.

Yet, at another level, the reality of America was attractive. Immigration had to be restrained. Coca-cola, jeans, films, soap operas, pop music, all of what was castigated as the consumer society was irresistible, especially to the young, to whom it represented a scarcely-to-be-dreamed-of standard of living, high not only materially but high because of its obvious personal freedom.

Perhaps the most interesting and saddest question is why the United States, which represented the economic, social and political system that most people in the world would have wished to have for themselves had they been free to choose, lost so much of the post-war struggle against aggressive Marxism and nationalism.

The answer is not easy to find. The most obvious response is that the United States never sought to win. As a pluralist society, dedicated to pluralist values, it was virtually impossible for the United States to run a campaign, backed by armed threats of external intervention or internal insurrection, to establish liberal regimes on its own pattern everywhere – though that was the logic of Roosevelt's anti-colonialism. Where the United States and its allies had absolute power, as in Japan and West Germany, such regimes were most successfully established; other countries freed by the Americans and their allies almost all became liberal democracies. The exceptions were South Korea and South Vietnam, despite vigorous attempts to establish liberal democracies. And, of course, in Latin America the succession of dictatorships supported by the United States offered clear evidence to its detractors and critics that its apologies for democracy were humbug. In a sense the critics were right. The United States preferred a 'safe' government; it made often ineffectual attempts to support the growth of democratic institutions; it opposed movements that were labelled democratic but were in fact Marxist, as in the case of Allende in Chile. But its greatest defeat was that it never imposed constitutional democracy on the Continent as a whole; it never used its might to impose what was right.

Two desirable ends clashed: the right of one nation not to be dominated by another, and the need to establish constitutional rule. America chose the first and wished for the second.

On a high philosophic plane, therefore, America's philosophy had to sell itself rather than be enforced or propagated. Where it was enforced, as in Germany, or propagated, as in Israel, it was strikingly successful in creating powerful states. Would that more had been done in other parts of the world.

But at another level there was an even more acute dilemma. It arose from the conflict between America's national interest, including its role as leader of the West, and the embodiment of the idea of constitutional liberalism. When it sought to give a lead other countries saw its obvious self-interest rather than its idealism. As a result the West was perennially at sixes and sevens. A supreme example was the Suez affair where the interests of the American oil companies tended to dominate American views of world interests, while the British, the French and the Israelis saw the scene completely differently. Personalities, especially of Dulles and Eden, played their part, but they did so largely because the United States was unable to express itself as a world leader but was perceived rather (and correctly so perceived) as acting purely as a national power.

Indeed, despite so much that can be said to the contrary, the persistent failure of the Americans to act as leaders of the West was perhaps the major cause of the squandering of the opportunities that the victory in the war gave. The reasons for this failure repay examination. Each episode shows a characteristic pattern; a sacrifice of long-term objectives for short-term advantages (usually for electoral reasons), which jeopardise the policy or even make it fail. Lend-lease, a device whereby America's productive capacity could be used to support its wartime allies, was terminated so precipitately and abruptly that it partly caused the monetary crisis that required the creation of the Marshall Plan. Far from withdrawing money from Europe, America had to put more in. The decision to monopolise the secrets of the manufacture of the atom bomb led directly to the British decision to make one for themselves and so indirectly to nuclear proliferation, exactly the opposite of what the Americans wanted. The Soviet Union quickly made their own bombs. Thereafter the West was without any serious atomic strategy; the United States acted in its own narrow defence interest, not appearing to note the urgency of adopting a coherent Western defence strategy or a strategy for the peaceful use of atomic energy. To take another example, the headlong rush into massive energy-using patterns of behaviour which made the United States so dependent on oil, and soon on imported oil – a fantastic paradox for so oil-rich a nation – may be seen as the supreme example of the continual temptation towards taking an immediate advantage without thought for the long-term strategic considerations that were at stake.

This confusion between America's own short-term interests or satisfactions and its obligations as leader of the West was never made explicit. This was especially so at Yalta. There Roosevelt treated with Churchill and Stalin as two equals – neither was to be favoured over the other, Churchill not to be treated as the intimate and ally any more than Stalin. This fundamental miscalculation was not only a mistake about Stalinist Russia's character and intentions. Roosevelt was thinking of an American-led world coalition, including the Soviet Union. But countries dedicated to constitutional liberalism were bound to be divided – though not necessarily bitterly and actively so – from the Marxist-dominated countries. Roosevelt asked the wrong question and got the wrong answer.

When it was belatedly realised that this was so, notably because of the actual and apparent military threats from the Soviet Union, the West responded. Initially the response was military. Fundamentally it was, however, an ideological struggle.

Stalin obviously toyed from time to time with the idea of a neutral Europe. Austria became independent within ten years of

its division by the occupying powers. Finland was never com-
munised. The idea of a neutral and disarmed but united Germany
was frequently raised. A grand settlement of Europe might have
been possible. What would it have meant? No US or Soviet troops
in Europe, for a start. Who would then have policed the Balkans,
since each nation had a border dispute? The Czechs would have
been a liberal democracy, but no other state had liberal traditions,
except Hungary (to some degree). Even so, authoritarian regimes
would have been greatly preferable to what actually happened in
Eastern Europe. And would people have been prepared to trust an
undivided Germany?

These immediate and practical questions are at once raised
by the fundamental idea that some agreed détente between America and Stalin might have left a Europe which, in some respects,
was 'free', even if not all countries were as liberal and constitutional as – say – Belgium or Norway. The fundamental idea is
that the Cold War was either unnecessary or equally the fault of
both sides. The revisionist historians seem to be wrong. The
evidence of Stalin's terror in Russia, of his terror in Eastern
Europe before the end of the war and long before the open
breaches of 1946 and 1947, suggest that only a change in Russia of
an astonishing degree would have made such an accommodation
possible. In such an accommodation two major European
powers – Britain and France – would have been *de facto* the
policemen. And they were allies of America in ideas as well as
in economic and military interest. America's struggle was their
struggle.

This struggle was the Cold War. The struggle was perceived as
war by other means. The Marshall Plan, into which America
stumbled through overwhelming difficulties in supporting its zone
in Germany, saved (or helped to save) Western Europe for liberal
democracy and reconstituted the Western economic order which
had been disrupted since 1914. But it had not been America's
original intention to do so, as the Bretton Woods negotiations
vividly demonstrated. And once the Plan had successfully revived
the Western economy, the Americans became jealous economic
and political rivals of the Western European powers, France and
Britain. Yet it was Western unity and strength which was bound to
be a fundamental part of any major attempt to save the rest of the
world from the fate of bankruptcy and totalitarianism to which
Europeans had so nearly succumbed at the end of the Second
World War. It may seem hard, perhaps even a counsel of perfec-
tion, to reproach America for its short-sightedness when the
courage and generosity of its statesmen, notably Truman and

Marshall, had preserved the peace and guaranteed European prosperity, but the facts clearly show that the ruling groups in America had no idea of the power of constitutional liberalism to defeat Marxism and to create prosperity. Consequently they would neither prepare a consistent long-term strategy to do just this nor would they sacrifice America's apparent short-term interests in deference to its allies.

American statesmen were fallible as the evidence abundantly shows. In particular, after Stalin's death, and while Mao was still consolidating his power in China, just before Sputnik (in 1957) and after the Macmillan initiative a year later, some sort of American–Soviet deal might have been struck. Perhaps even at the Paris summit, apparently aborted by the U2 incident, a settlement could have been achieved. But that would have required Russia to trust America, and not only not to seek to impose Communism, but to withdraw from the occupied states. Poland, Hungary, Prague, show how reluctant such a withdrawal would have been.

America's interests, despite their statesmen, have on the whole been the interests of free people. Perhaps it is unwise to entrust 'freedom' to the national interest of any power, even if such a power is a great and wealthy constitutional democracy.

A nation can know its own interests and, if it has the will, defend them. There is strength in the argument that all else is ideological speculation, dangerous because woolly-minded liberals on the march create havoc wherever they go. Roosevelt was one such and the result of his meddling at Teheran and Yalta gave millions of people unnecessarily into Stalin's grip – particularly the Czechs, the Hungarians and (perhaps) the Poles. Dulles was another muddled thinker. After his combination of American self-interest and woolly internationalism at Suez, he delivered the Middle East into the hands of Muslim nationalists who, less than twenty years later, were to bring the Western economy to near-disaster by the oil boycott, having risked nuclear war twice on the way. And by his 'agonising reappraisals' Dulles condemned France, and many influential people elsewhere, to a permanent anti-American posture that effectively killed off the hope of a coherent Western policy based on an idea. The great question is whether an *idea*, an organised set of values, can be as compelling as the nation–state in demanding the allegiance of men and women prepared to risk all – literally all – to serve it.

The Marxists, with just such a grand strategy, have achieved so many of their ends. And these ends are not a narrow Russian pan-Slavism. They are far wider – a vision of a Socialist world. Had liberalism proceeded as remorselessly and implacably as

Marxism, led by the Kremlin, but not uniquely inspired by it, to
establish the conditions in which it could flourish, then its achievement could have realised what the people of the world wanted in
1945. The prosperity which came to Western Europe after 1948
and to Southeast Asia in the late 1950s might have spread more
rapidly and far more widely; it would have been uninhibited by
nationalism and 'planning'. More than prosperity, freedom could
have come. Civil liberties would certainly have been respected in
more countries, and (above all) liberalism would not have been
ideologically forced on the defensive. It could have triumphed.
The marches and demonstrations against South Africa and Vietnam, no doubt frequently orchestrated, were matched by none
against the countless acts of tyranny in Marxist states. The world
could have marched against totalitarianism and authoritarianism
wherever it was to be found.

I blame America. Only America had the vision, the energy, the
power and the wealth to bring it off.

The central weakness of the West was for its biggest and most
liberal state to fail to give a lead. Although it is impossible for a
second in command to fill the gap, there is a second culprit. Britain
tried (and France did not) to fill the gap. It failed. Britain's failure
to face up to its responsibilities was even more sad than America's.
Its failure was not surprising. After all, Britain's war effort had
been marked by feeble efforts on many fronts – over Britain itself,
in Southern and Western Europe, in the Middle East, in Burma
and the Far East, all extravagantly wide of its base and all equally
unsuccessfully prosecuted until other allies took the pressure off
the British forces directly or by diversionary tactics. There was a
fatal ambiguity. Britain had been a bulwark of constitutional
liberalism, but it offered the face of a colonial power to the world,
especially to the Americans, who were naïvely anti-colonialist. In
Ireland, where Britain's case is overwhelmingly correct and just,
its actions are perceived as colonialism. The major change in
British attitudes and policies is marked by the hasty evacuation of
India in 1947. But this did not become a celebration of a new
post-imperial age; it was instead the beginning of a sad retreat.
After 1947 it was merely a matter of time for the rest of the British
Empire to be granted independence. This basic shift after three
centuries was not trumpeted abroad as a triumph of idealism over
opportunism, of generosity over exploitation. But the change was
only slowly observed by the outside world, because it seemed to
take so long (mainly just one decade, the 1950s), and it was marked
by colonial conflicts, as in Malaya and Cyprus, in which it often
looked as though the British had been pushed out rather than

taken positive steps to grant independence on the basis of liberal constitutional doctrine and capitalist prosperity. An Englishman must acknowledge that disastrous British bossiness which insisted on time to 'prepare' the natives for self-government. This preparation obviously failed, since in almost every instance the result was a one-man or one-party dictatorship, riddled with corruption and mouthing the slogans of Socialism and neutralism. The idea that a nation goes through prep school and a public school education is obviously preposterous. They are, after all, as grown up as us. This idea of 'preparation' had a most unfortunate effect on British official and political opinion: delusions of continued power and influence in places they were in effect abandoning led them to overestimate their contribution to the world – above all to the American debate about the future of Western defence. The British contributed too much (spread far too thin) to the Western defence effort. They assumed a series of burdens which helped to diminish the power of the British economy to rise to a sufficiently high rate of growth to maintain even its position in Europe. In other words, ambition and guilt led to the very failure that above all the British had struggled to avoid.

The uncertainty over Britain's role arose from its imperial past, with trade and political relationships of great importance, its role in liberating wartime Europe and occupying Northwest Germany, which gave the British, for over twenty years, a superiority complex. Above all its 'special relationship' with the United States, in which it regarded itself as the eastern end of a triumphal Anglo–Saxon arch erected across the Atlantic, was a fantasy. We loved them. They did not love us. In attempting to balance these mutually incompatible roles, Britain repeatedly fell over, and lost sight of its own true interests.

Those who support a *Realpolitik* view of the way that states should conduct themselves see the British case as proof of a nation that did not seek to serve its own interest and so ended up by serving nobody's. Had the British, they argue, concentrated on economic recovery, severely limited their overseas commitments to what they could afford, and sought international economic arrangements that served their own interests, then they would have ended up as a more powerful and more secure pillar of the West. This is undoubtedly true, but ignores the continuous pressures of the real world – from the guarantee to Poland which precipitated the Second World War, to the need to defend India, to help to reconstruct Europe, to occupy Germany, to come to the aid of America in Korea, to be a bulwark against Russia, to safeguard its oil supplies in the Middle East – a simple policy of cutting and

running, attractive as it might have been, and correct as it undoubtedly would have been, was not politically or even morally
feasible. The Third World was completely cynical about British
assurances, unrealistically so, since the British usually meant what
they said and were not self-interested. A great power cannot cut
and run. Especially if what it is defending is Liberty itself. Yet
nevertheless had it been possible to cut and run, then the squandering of the peace might not have been so profligate. Britain's
economic failure, its preference for an illusory Commonwealth
rather than a European Defence Community and, subsequently, a
European Economic Community, made it impossible to build up a
European identity that was based on constitutional liberal principles, using the social market philosophy so successfully adopted
by the West Germans as the basis for their economic recovery. All
the running in the ideological stakes in the Cold War was therefore
left to the Americans.

It seemed at one time that France and West Germany would
form the European centre of an acceptable ideological movement
in a massive contest for the hearts and minds of the world. French
civilisation, indeed, was in many respects the basis for such a
movement. In 1789 the Revolution (and its successor in 1871)
provided France with an impeccable revolutionary image; its
culture had spread throughout its empire on an apparently non-
racialist basis; its recovery from the war was rapid and successful;
its rapprochement with Germany, after an initial period when it
sought ruthlessly to grab all it could, and so precipitated the
American response which eventually created the Marshall Plan,
led to a growth of self-confidence; and, above all, its sustained
attempt to make a warm and close treaty relationship with Germany. As a successful and old European culture France could have
established itself as the moral leader of the West. But it behaved
with consummate folly in Indochina and Algeria, countries where
the indigenous cultures were sophisticated and sympathetic and a
compromise was eminently possible. But dreadful wars developed
which led France into imperialist aggression and its inevitable
defeat. And the intense parochialism of the French frequently
meant (especially under de Gaulle) courses of action which were
intensely counter-productive – for example over British membership of the European Community – not only from the point of
view of the West as a whole but from the narrow French interest as
well.

France, Britain and the United States – the three countries,
then, adopted different policies and attitudes to the Marxist and
nationalist threats to a liberal world order. They were themselves

pulling in separate directions. And though at a deep level their ultimate values were so similar as to be identical, their immediate actions were in conflict. The French resistance to American domination, their hostility to their liberators that was greater than to their conquerors, was symptomatic of the nationalism that had had such corrosive effects in Europe and which spread like an infection through the rest of the world.

Nationalism appeared most dangerously in the Middle East where the confrontations between the Egyptians on the one hand and the British and the French on the other, between the French and the Algerians, between the Jews and the Arabs, and between the Muslims themselves remained the continual source of disruption and danger. The inability to settle the Middle East conflicts sprang from an inability to control nationalism; all forms of a grand settlement sank on this rock. The Middle East played its part in creating the tensions among the Western nations, whose growing dependence on its main product, oil, made them directly vulnerable. To regard the instability of the Middle East as a cause of much of the weakness of the West is to mistake cause and effect, since it was the weakness of the West that allowed the unrest to develop and, in the case of Algeria and Suez, fomented it. There was no coherent policy towards the Middle East, but a multiplicity of policies, several of them adopted simultaneously by the United States – favouring Israel, yet depending on the Muslim states through ever-growing imports of oil.

The Middle East was the test of the strength of the Western liberal democracies and repeatedly they failed it, never taking steps to secure their control over the oil or to avoid their dependence on it, never separating the combatants, nor taking a consistent view of the future of Israel. Yet the Soviet Union scarcely intervened at all in the Middle East, nor did Marxism (to be differentiated from Marxist rhetoric) play any significant part in the continuing problem. It might be thought that the Muslim culture has shown itself peculiarly resistant to liberal constitutional political arrangements; Pakistan, for example, lapsed into dictatorship long before India, and nowhere in the Arab world was there any semblance of choice of regime; either traditional leaders were reinforced in their power or military dictators evicted them.

But this sad story was true of the greater part of the post-colonial world. In few places was a liberal constitutional order to be found, with a few notable exceptions, including India, some Southeast Asian countries, and Chile and Venezuela. Everywhere else – and sometimes in those few exceptional cases – dictatorships ruled. And not only dictatorships, familiar from Bolivar onwards in Latin

America, and in the Balkans, in which a group in the dominant and invariably corrupt and indolent oligarchy sought to conserve its power, by fair means and usually foul, but dictatorships clothed in nationalist and Socialist rhetoric.

The cant of the age is Socialist and nationalist. From Nehru's India to Nasser's Egypt, from Cuba to Pakistan, inefficient and authoritarian governments have disguised their lack of achievement by appealing to patriotism, equality, production for use and the other tired slogans with which Stalin filled the gulag and Hitler filled the concentration camps.

The manifest success of those societies which adopted market economies as the basis for their economic policy belied at every turn the analytical and factual basis of the Socialist and nationalist rhetoric. Ironically, much of the aid that went to Third World countries from America and Europe went to prop up elaborate economic planning systems full of grandiose projects in so-called 'basic' industries which Stalin had popularised in his Five-Year Plans.

The United States in particular found itself supporting economic systems which most of the time literally failed to supply the goods, and political systems dominated by élites, frequently military in origin, which gloried in their 'neutralist' stance, which (in the case of India) often meant a positive preference for Soviet aims and ideals.

Yet capitalism on the march was the last thing they had to fear. Those who sought to show its advantages were smeared and dismissed as 'Fascists', and Fascism was regarded as a deformation of capitalism, not of Communism.

It is this power of ideology and the weakness of demonstrable actuality that is perhaps most puzzling.

It is evident that the desire to avoid liberal and constitutional rule sprang basically from the desire not to lose office and the profits that spring from it, a natural and human response. The terms for not losing office included the adoption of the rhetoric of Socialism. This was necessary not only because of open cynicism, as being the only way to get the support of the mob and of the students, always a potent source of disruption, but because the dictators and their henchmen were themselves brought up in this tradition of rhetoric and were unable to express themselves, or indeed to think, in any other way. The debates at the United Nations were not hypocritical so much as revealing how delegates thought they thought.

Indeed, so powerful has this movement been that one of the major reasons for the failure of Marxism to spread faster and further has been the division of the Communist world, first by the defection of Tito from the Stalinist camp and then, twelve years later, the split between Russia and China. These major developments in what had been designed with care as a monolithic system were indicative of the possible future fissures that might open up because of nationalism. The reaction of the Soviet leadership was to fear the recrudescence of capitalism.

What was happening, however, was different. All empires, all global systems, come to their natural term. A monolithic Communist system is vulnerable to every heresy, especially nationalism. But a liberal world order, predicated upon pluralism, is the very opposite of monolithic. If the world survives – and it looks increasingly possible that it will *not* survive – it will be because people have the strength to choose freedom.

Selective Bibliography

As the introduction explains, many books and articles have contributed to this book. A full bibliography would be impossibly expensive to print and even so would remain hopelessly incomplete. In what follows there are listed books which will prove interesting, even though sometimes controversial and biased, and superseded by later works.

ALLON, Yigal, *The Making of Israel's Army*, Valentine, Mitchell, London, 1970

ALPEROVITZ, Gar, *Atomic Diplomacy: Hiroshima and Potsdam*, Vintage, New York, 1967; Secker & Warburg, London, 1965

AMME, Carl H., Jr, *NATO without France: A Strategic Appraisal*, The Hoover Institution on War, Revolution and Peace, Stanford University, Stanford, California, 1967

ARKES, Hadley, *Bureaucracy, the Marshall Plan and the National Interest*, Princeton University Press, Princeton, New Jersey, 1972

ARMYTAGE, W. H. G., *A Social History of Engineering*, 4th edn, Faber, London, 1976

ARON, Raymond, *De Gaulle, Israel and the Jews*, André Deutsch, London, 1969

ARON, Raymond, *Immuable et Changeante: de la IVe à la Ve République*, Calmann-Lévy, Paris, 1956

ARON, Raymond and LERNER, Daniel (eds), *La Querelle de la C.E.D.*: (Essais d'analyse sociologique), Librairie Armand Colin, Paris, 1956

AUTY, Phyllis, *Tito: a Biography*, Longman, London, 1970

BAILEY, Kenneth, *Science and Invention*, Collins, Glasgow, 1974

BAKER, David, *The Rocket...*, New Cavendish Books, London, 1978

BOLITHO, Andrea, *Japan: An Economic Survey 1953–1973*, Oxford University Press, Oxford, 1975

BORISOV, O. B. and KOLOSKOV, B. T., *Soviet–Chinese Relations 1945–1970*, Indiana University Press, Bloomington and London, 1975

BRANDT, Conrad, *Stalin's Failure in China 1924–1927*, Harvard University Press, Cambridge, Massachusetts, 1958

BRANDT, Willy, *A Peace Policy for Europe*, Weidenfeld & Nicolson, London, 1969

BROWN, A. and KASER, M. (eds), *The Soviet Union since the Fall of Khrushchev*, Macmillan, London, 1975

BROWN, John, *Who's Next?: The Lesson of Czechoslovakia*, Hutchinson, London, 1951

BUCHAN, Alastair, *The End of the Postwar Era (A new balance of world power)*, Weidenfeld & Nicolson, London, 1974

BURNS, E. Bradford, *A History of Brazil*, Columbia University Press, New York and London, 1970

BUTLER, J. A. V., *Modern Biology and its Human Implications*, Hodder & Stoughton, London, 1976

CALVOCORESSI, Peter, *World Politics since 1945*, 2nd edn, Longman, London, 1971

CARR, Raymond and FUSI, Juan Pablo, *Spain: Dictatorship to Democracy*, Allen & Unwin, London, 1979

CERNY, Karl H. and BRIEFS, Henry W., *Nato in Quest of Cohesion: A Confrontation of Viewpoints at the Center for Strategic Studies, Georgetown University*, A. Praeger, New York and London, 1965

CHRISTMAN, Henry M. (ed.), *The Essential Tito*, David & Charles, Newton Abbot, 1971

CHURCHILL, Winston S., *The Second World War*, Cassell, London, 1954

CIRIA, Alberto, *Parties and Power in Modern Argentina (1930–1946)*, State University of New York Press, Albany, 1974

CLARK, Ronald W., *The Scientific Breakthrough, The Impact of Modern Invention*, Nelson, London, 1974

CLEMENS, Diane Shaver, *Yalta*, Oxford University Press, New York, 1970

CLIVE, Howard F., *Mexico – Revolution to Evolution 1940–1960*, Oxford University Press, London, 1962

CLOGG, Richard, *A Short History of Modern Greece*, Cambridge University Press, Cambridge, 1979

COCHRAN, Bert, *Harry Truman and the Crisis Presidency*, Funk & Wagnalls, New York, 1973

COLLINS, Larry and LAPIERRE, Dominique, *Freedom at Midnight: How Britain gave away an Empire*, Collins, London, 1975

CONANT, James Bryant, *Germany and Freedom*, Harvard University Press, Cambridge, Massachusetts, 1958

CONQUEST, Robert, *Russia after Khrushchev*, Pall Mall Press, London, 1965

CONQUEST, R., *Power and Policy in the U.S.S.R.: The Struggle for Stalin's Succession, 1945–1960*, Harper & Row, New York, 1967 (Harper Torchbooks); originally published by Macmillan, London, and St Martin's Press, New York

CRAWLEY, Aidan, *De Gaulle*, Collins, London, 1969

CROZIER, Brian, *Franco: A Biographical History*, Eyre & Spottiswoode, London, 1967

CUMBERLAND, Charles C., *Mexico; The Struggle for Modernity*, New York Oxford University Press, New York, 1968

CZERWINSKI, E. J. and PIEKALKIEWICZ, Jaroslav (eds), *The Soviet Invasion of Czechoslovakia: Its Effects on Eastern Europe*, Praeger Publishers, New York and London, 1972

DAHRENDORF, Ralf, *Society and Democracy in Germany*, Weidenfeld & Nicolson, London, 1968

DAVENPORT, T. R. H., *South Africa: A Modern History*, 2nd edn, Macmillan, London, 1978

DE GAULLE, Charles, *War Memoirs: Salvation 1944–46* (3rd of 3 vols), trans. J. Griffin, Weidenfeld, 1960.

DEUTSCHER, I., *Stalin: A Political Biography*, 2nd edn, Oxford University Press, London, 1967

DOBYNS, Henry E. and DOUGHTY, Paul L., *Peru: A Cultural History*, Oxford University Press, New York, 1976

DORNBERG, John, *Brezhnev: The Masks of Power*, André Deutsch, London, 1974

EDEN, Anthony, *The Reckoning; The Eden Memoirs*, vol. 3, Cassell, London, 1960–5

EISENHOWER, Dwight D., *The White House Years*: vol. I, *Mandate for Change 1953–56*, Heinemann, London, 1963–5

EISENHOWER, Dwight D., *The White House Years*: vol. II, *Waging Peace 1956–61*, Heinemann, London, 1966

FEIS, Herbert, *Between War and Peace: The Potsdam Conference*, Oxford University Press, London; Princeton University Press, New Jersey, 1960

FEIS, Herbert, *Churchill, Roosevelt and Stalin*, Princeton University Press, New Jersey, 1957

FITZGERALD, C. P., *China and South-East Asia since 1945*, Longman, London, 1973

FITZGERALD, C. P., *A Concise History of East Asia*, Heinemann, Hong Kong, 1966

FITZGERALD, C. P., *Mao Tse-Tung and China*, Hodder & Stoughton, London, 1976

FLEMING, D. F., *The Cold War and its Origins; 1917–1960*, Allen & Unwin, London, 1961

FLOYD, David, *Mao against Khrushchev, A Short History of the Sino–Soviet Conflict*, Pall Mall Press, London, 1964

FRANCO, Victor, *The Morning After: A French Journalist's Impressions of Cuba under Castro*, Pall Mall Press, London & Dunmow, 1963

FREYRE, Gilberto, *The Mansions and the Shanties: The Making of Modern Brazil*, Alfred A. Knopf (Borzoi Books), New York, 1968

GARDNER, John W., *Science Today*, A. R. Mowbray & Co. Ltd, London, 1970

GIMBELL, John, *The Origins of the Marshall Plan*, Stanford University Press, Stanford, 1976

GINZBURG, Evgenia Semyonovna, *Into the Whirlwind*, Collins/Harvill, London, 1967

GITTINGS, John, *Survey of the Sino–Soviet Dispute 1963–1967*, Oxford University Press, London, 1968

GOLDMAN, Eric F., *The Tragedy of Lyndon Johnson*, Macdonald, London, 1969

GOLDSMITH, Maurice, *Science and Social Responsibility*, Macmillan, London, 1975

GROSSER, Alfred, *Germany in Our Time; A Political History of the Postwar Years*, Pall Mall Press, London, 1971

GYORGY, Andrew and GIBBS, Hubert S., with JORDAN, Robert S.

(eds), *Problems in International Relations*; 3rd edn, Prentice-Hall Inc., Englewood Cliffs, New Jersey, 1970

HALBERSTAM, David, *The Best and the Brightest*, Barrie & Jenkins, London, 1972

HALECKI, O., *A History of Poland*, Routledge & Kegan Paul, London, 1978

HALES, E. E. Y., *Pope John and his Revolution*, Eyre & Spottiswoode, London, 1965

HALLE, Louis J., *The Cold War as History*, Chatto & Windus, London, 1970

HALPERIN, Maurice, *The Rise and Decline of Fidel Castro*, University of California Press, Berkeley, 1972

HALPERIN-DONGHI, Tulio, *Politics, Economics and Society in Argentina in the Revolutionary Period*, Cambridge University Press, Cambridge, 1975

HAMBY, Alonso L., *Beyond the New Deal – Harry S. Truman and American Liberalism*, Columbia University Press, New York and London, 1973

HANRIEDER, Wolfram F., *West German Foreign Policy, 1949–1963: International Pressure and Domestic Response*, Stanford University Press, Stanford, California, 1967

HARRISON, Harry, *Mechanism*, Reed Books, Los Angeles, 1978

HATCH, John, *A History of Post-War Africa*, University Paperbacks, Methuen, London, 1967

HEIDELMAYER, Wolfgang and HINDRICHS, Guenter, *Documents on Berlin 1943–1963*, R. Oldenbourg Verlag, Munich, 1963

HISCOCKS, Richard, *Democracy in Western Germany*, Oxford University Press, London, 1957

HOOPES, Townsend, *The Devil and John Foster Dulles*, André Deutsch, London, 1974

HORNE, Alistair, *A Savage War of Peace; Algeria 1954–1962*, Macmillan, London, 1977

HUDSON, G. F., LOWENTHAL, Richard and MacFARQUHAR, Roderick, 'The Sino–Soviet Dispute', *The China Quarterly*, London, 1961

HUDSON, Michael C., *Arab Politics: The Search for Legitimacy*, Yale University Press, 1977

HUGHES-EVANS, David, *Environmental Education: key issues of the future*, Pergamon, Oxford, 1977

IRVING, R. E. M., *The Christian Democratic Parties of Western Europe*, Allen & Unwin, London, 1979

JOHNSON, Lyndon Baines, *The Vantage Point: Perspectives of the Presidency 1963–1969*, Weidenfeld & Nicolson, London, 1972

JONES, Joseph Marion, *The Fifteen Weeks (February 21–June 5, 1947)*, Harcourt, Brace & World, Inc., New York, 1955

KAROL, K. S., *Guerrillas in Power*, Cape, London, 1971

KAROL, K. S., *The Second Chinese Revolution*, Cape, London, 1974

KEARNS, Doris, *Lyndon Johnson and the American Dream*, André Deutsch, London, 1976

KECSKEMETI, Paul, *The Unexpected Revolution: Social Forces in the Hungarian Uprising*, Stanford University Press, Stanford, California, 1969

KIDWELL, Claudia B., *Suiting Everyone: The Democratisation of Clothing in America*, Smithsonian Institute Press, Washington, 1974

KILLIAN, James R., *Sputnik, Scientists and Eisenhower*, M.I.T. Press, Cambridge/London, 1977

KIMCHE, Jon and David, *Both Sides of the Hill: Britain and the Palestine War*, Secker & Warburg, London, 1960

KIMCHE, Jon, *The Second Arab Awakening*, Thames & Hudson, London, 1970

KOJIMA, Kiyoshi, *Japan and a New World Economic Order*, Croom Helm, London, 1977

KOLAKOWSKI, Leszek, *Main Currents of Marxism*, Clarendon Press, Oxford, 1978

KOLKO, Gabriel, *The Politics of War*, Random House, New York, 1968

KOSTELANETZ, Richard, *Social Speculations: Visions for our Time*, Morrow, New York, 1971

KRIVITSKY, W. G., *I Was Stalin's Agent*, Hamish Hamilton, London, 1939

KUSIN, Vladimir V., *Political Grouping in the Czechoslovak Reform Movement*, Macmillan, London, 1972

KUZNETS, Simon, *Postwar Economic Growth: Four Lectures*, The Belknap Press of Harvard University Press, Cambridge, Massachusetts, 1964

LACQUEUR, Walter, *Europe since Hitler*, Penguin Books, London, 1972

LACQUEUR, Walter, *The Road to War 1967: The Origins of the Arab–Israeli Conflict*, 2nd edn, Weidenfeld & Nicolson, London, 1969

LARSON, Arthur, *Eisenhower, The President Nobody Knew*, Leslie Frewin, London, 1969

LAWLESS, Edward W., *Technology and Social Shock*, Rutgers University Press, New Brunswick, 1977

LAYTON, Edwin T., *Technology and Social Change in America*, Harper & Row, London, 1973

LEFEBVRE, Georges, *The French Revolution* (2 vols), *From its Origins to 1793*, translated from the French by Elizabeth Moss Evanson, Routledge & Kegan Paul, London, 1965

LEONHARD, Wolfgang, *Child of the Revolution*, Collins, 1957

LEONHARD, Wolfgang, *The Kremlin since Stalin*, Oxford University Press, London, 1962

LLOYD, Selwyn, *Suez 1956, A Personal Account*, Jonathan Cape, London, 1978

LOMAX, Bill, *Hungary 1956*, Allison & Busby, London, 1976

MacARTHUR, Douglas, *Reminiscences*, Heinemann, London, 1964

MacGREGOR-HASTIE, Roy, *Pope Paul VI*, Muller, London, 1964

MACMILLAN, Harold, *The Blast of War 1939–1945*, Macmillan, London, 1966

MACRIDIS, Roy C., *French Politics in Transition; the Years after De Gaulle*, Winthrop, Cambridge, Massachusetts, 1975

MAMMARELLA, Giuseppe, *Italy after Fascism: A Political History, 1943–1965*, University of Notre Dame Press, Notre Dame, Indiana, 1966

MANCHESTER, William, *American Caesar: Douglas MacArthur 1880–1964*, Little, Brown, New York, 1978

MARTIN, James, *The Wired Society*, Prentice-Hall, Englewood Cliffs, New Jersey, 1978

MATTHEWS, Herbert L., *Castro: A Political Biography*, Allen Lane, The Penguin Press, London, 1969

MAY, Brian, *The Indonesian Tragedy*, Routledge & Kegan Paul, London, 1978

MEE, Charles L., Jr, *Meeting at Potsdam*, André Deutsch, London, 1975

MENSCH, Gerhard, *Statement in Technology: Innovations Overcome the Depression*, Ballinger, Cambridge, Massachusetts, 1979

MERKLS, Peter H., *Germany Yesterday and Tomorrow*, Oxford University Press, New York, 1965

MIKOLAJCZYK, Stanislaw, *The Pattern of Soviet Domination*, Sampson Low, Marston & Co. Ltd, London, 1948

MONROE, Elizabeth, *Britain's Moment in the Middle East, 1914–1956*, Chatto & Windus, London, 1963

MORAN, Lord, *Churchill: Taken from the Diaries of Lord Moran*, Constable, London, 1966

MORGAN, Dan, *Merchants of Grain: Power and Profits of the Five Giants at the Centre of the World's Food Supply*, Weidenfeld & Nicolson, London, 1979

MORTON, H. W. and TOKÉS, R. L. (eds), *Soviet Politics and Society in the 1970's*, Collier Macmillan, London, 1974

MOSS, Robert, *Chile's Marxist Experiment*, David & Charles, Newton Abbot, 1973

MURRAY-BROWN, Jeremy, *Kenyatta*, Allen & Unwin, London, 1972

NIEDERGANG, Marcel, *The Twenty Latin Americas* (trans. Rosemary Sheed), Penguin Books Ltd, Harmondsworth, 1971

NOLUTSHUNGU, Sam C., *South Africa in Africa: A Study of Ideology and Foreign Policy*, Manchester University Press, Manchester, 1975

O'BALLANCE, Edgar, *The Algerian Insurrection 1954–62*, Faber & Faber, London, 1967

O'BALLANCE, Edgar, *The Electronic War in the Middle East 1968–70*, Faber & Faber, London, 1974

O'BALLANCE, Edgar, *The Greek Civil War, 1944–49*, Faber & Faber, London, 1966

O'BALLANCE, Edgar, *The Indo-China War, 1945–54*, Faber & Faber, London, 1964

O'BALLANCE, Edgar, *Korea 1950–53*, Faber & Faber, London, 1969

O'BALLANCE, Edgar, *Malaya: The Communist Insurgent War, 1948–60*, Faber & Faber, London, 1966

OSGOOD, Robert Endicott, *NATO: The Entangling Alliance*, The University of Chicago Press, Chicago and London, 1962

OXLEY, Andrew, PRAVDA, Alex and RITCHIE, Andrew, *Czechoslovakia: The Party and the People*, Allen Lane, The Penguin Press, London, 1973

OZAWA, Terutomo, *Japan's Technological Challenge to the West, 1950–1974*, M.I.T. Press, Cambridge, Massachusetts, 1974

PAVLOWITCH, Stevan K., *Yugoslavia*, Ernest Benn Ltd, London, 1971

PAYNE, Stanley G., *Falange*, Oxford University Press; Stanford University Press, Stanford, California, 1962

PAYNE, Stanley G., *Politics and the Military in Modern Spain*, Stanford University Press, Stanford, California, 1967; Oxford University Press, London, 1967

PETHYBRIDGE, R. W., *A History of Postwar Russia*, George Allen & Unwin, London, 1966

PHILIPS, C. H. and WAINWRIGHT, M. D. (eds), *The Partition of India: Policies and Perspectives, 1935–1947*, Allen & Unwin, London, 1970

PLUVIER, J. M., *South-East Asia from Colonialism to Independence*, Oxford University Press, London, 1977

PODBIELSKI, Gisèle, *Italy: Development and Crisis in the Post-war Economy*, Oxford University Press, Clarendon Press, Oxford, 1974

POLONSKY, Antony (ed.), *The Great Powers and the Polish Question, 1941–1945: A Documentary Study in Cold War Origins*, Orbis Books (London) Ltd, for L.S.E., London, 1976

POPOVIC, Nenad D., *Yugoslavia: The New Class in Crisis*, Syracuse University Press, Syracuse, 1968

PRESTON, Paul (ed.), *Spain in Crisis*, Harvester Press, Hassocks, 1974

PRITTIE, Terence, *The Velvet Chancellors*, Frederick Muller, London, 1979

RANGEL, Carlos, *The Latin Americans*, Harcourt Brace Jovanovich, New York, 1976

REISER, Stanley J., *Medicine and the Reign of Technology*, Cambridge University Press, Cambridge, 1978

REMINGTON, Robin Alison, *The Warsaw Pact: Case Studies in Communist Conflict Resolution*, The M.I.T. Press, Cambridge, Massachusetts; London, 1971

RIDLEY, Jasper, *Napoleon III and Eugénie*, Constable, London, 1979

ROBERTS, Geoffrey K., *West German Politics*, Macmillan, London, 1972

ROUHANI, Fuad, *A History of O.P.E.C.*, Praeger, New York, 1971

RUSHBROOK WILLIAMS, L. F., *The State of Pakistan*, Faber & Faber, London, 1966 (revised edn.)

RUSINOW, D., *The Yugoslav Experiment 1946–1974*, R.I.I.A., London. 1977

RUSSELL, C. A. and GOODMAN, D. C., *Science and the Rise of Technology since 1800*, Wright, Bristol, 1972

RYBCZYNSKI, T. M. (ed.), *The Economics of the Oil Crisis*, Macmillan Press Ltd, Basingstoke and London, 1976

SACHAR, Howard M., *Europe Leaves the Middle East, 1936–1954*, Allen Lane, London, 1974

SACHAR, Howard M., *A History of Israel*, Basil Blackwell, Oxford, 1977

SAFRAN, Nadav, *Israel the Embattled Ally: The Shaping of American–Israeli Relations and the Creation and Transformation of Israel through Three Decades of Middle East Crises and Wars*, The Belknap Press of Harvard University Press, Cambridge, Massachusetts; London, 1978

SALISBURY, Harrison E., *The Coming War between Russia and China*, Secker & Warburg, London, 1969

SCHICK, Jack M., *The Berlin Crisis 1958–1962*, University of Pennsylvania Press, Philadelphia, 1971

SCHNEIDER, Eberhard, *The G.D.R.: The History, Politics, Economy and Society of East Germany*, C. Hurst & Co., London, 1978

SCHNEIDER, Ronald M., *The Political System of Brazil: Emergence of a 'Modernizing' Authoritarian regime; 1964–1970*, Columbia University Press, New York and London, 1971

SCHUURMAN, Egbert, *Reflections in the Technological Society*, Wedge Pub. Foundation, Toronto, 1977

SCHWARTZ, Harry, *Prague's 200 Days: The Struggle for Democracy in Czechoslovakia*, Pall Mall Press, London, 1969

SEBALD, Ambassador Wm, with BRINES, Russell, *With MacArthur in Japan: A Personal History of the Occupation*, The Cresset Press, London, 1967

SETON-WATSON, Hugh, *The East European Revolution*, Methuen & Co. Ltd, London, 1956 (3rd edn)

SHAMOS, Morris A. and MURPHY, George M. (eds), *Recent Advance in Science, Physics and Applied Mathematics*, New York University Press, New York, 1956

SIGMUND, Paul E., *The Overthrow of Allende and the Politics of Chile, 1964–1976*, University of Pittsburgh Press, Pittsburgh, Pa., 1977

SIMPSON, George Gaylord, *Biology and Man*, Harcourt, Brace & World Inc., New York, 1969

SKIDMORE, Thomas E., *Politics in Brazil, 1930–1964: An Experiment in Democracy*, Oxford University Press, New York, 1967

SLOAN, Stephen, *A Study in Political Violence: The Indonesian Experience*, Rand McNally & Co., Chicago, 1971

SLUSSER, Robert M., *The Berlin Crisis of 1961 – Soviet American Relations and the Struggle for Power in the Kremlin*, Johns Hopkins University Press, Baltimore and London, 1973

SNELL, John, *The Meaning of Yalta*, Louisiana State University Press, Baton Rouge, 1966

SNOW, Edgar, *Red Star over China*, Gollancz, London, 1937

SORENSEN, Theodore C., *Kennedy*, Hodder & Stoughton, London, 1965

SPEAR, Percival, *India, Pakistan and the West*, Oxford University Press, 1967

STAAR, Richard F., *Communist Regimes in Eastern Europe*, 3rd edn, Hoover Institution Press, Stanford, California, 1977

STOCKING, George W., *Middle East Oil*, Allen Lane, London, 1971

SULZBERGER, C. L., *The Coldest War*, Harcourt Brace Jovanovich, New York, 1974

SYKES, Christopher, *Crossroads to Israel 1917–1948*, Indiana University Press, Bloomington/London, 1973 (First Midland Book Edition)

THOMAS, Hugh, *Cuba or The Pursuit of Freedom*, Eyre & Spottiswoode, London, 1971

TOLSTOY, (Count) Nikolai, *Victims of Yalta*, Hodder & Stoughton, London, 1977

TRUMAN, Harry S., *Memoirs (Autobiography*, 2 Vols), Doubleday, Garden City, New York, 1955–6

ULČ, Otto, *Politics in Czechoslovakia*, W. H. Freeman, San Francisco, 1974

URQUHART, Brian, *Hammarskjöld*, Knopf, New York, 1972; The Bodley Head, London, 1972

U.S. DEPT. OF STATE, *Conference of Berlin (The Potsdam Conference) 1945*, Foreign Relations of the United States, Diplomatic Papers (2 Vols), U.S. Govt. Printing Office, Washington, 1960

VÁLI, Ferenc A., *Rift and Revolt in Hungary: Nationalism versus Communism*, Harvard University Press, Cambridge, Massachusetts, 1961

VANDENBERG, Arthur H., Jr (ed.), *The Private Papers of Senator Vandenberg*, Victor Gollancz, London, 1953

WASSERSTEIN, Bernard, *Britain and the Jews of Europe*, Oxford University Press, Oxford, 1979

WEBSTER, Richard A., *The Cross and the Fasces; Christian Democracy and Fascism in Italy* (Vols 5 and 6), Stanford University Press, Stanford, California, 1960

WEIZMANN, Chaim, *Trial and Error: Autobiography*, Hamish Hamilton, London, 1949

WHITNEY, Thomas P., *Russia in My Life*, Harrap, London, 1963.

WILLIAMS, Philip M., *Hugh Gaitskell*, Jonathan Cape, London, 1979

WILLIAMS, Trevor I. (ed.), *A History of Technology* (Vols 6 and 7, Parts 1 and 2), Clarendon Press, Oxford, 1978

WILMOT, Chester, *The Struggle for Europe*, Collins, London, 1952

WILSON, Duncan, *Tito's Yugoslavia*, Cambridge University Press, 1980

WILSON, Monica and THOMPSON, Leonard (eds), *The Oxford History of South Africa: Vol. II, South Africa 1870–1966*, Clarendon Press, Oxford, 1971

WISKEMANN, Elizabeth, *Italy since 1945*, Macmillan, St Martin's Press, London, 1971

WOODWARD, Ralph Lee, Jr, *Central America: A Nation Divided*, Oxford University Press, New York, 1976

YERGIN, Daniel, *Shattered Peace*, André Deutsch, London, 1976

Index

Compiled by Robert Urwin